Women, War, and Violence

Topography, Resistance, and Hope

Volume 1

MARIAM M. KURTZ AND LESTER R. KURTZ, EDITORS

Praeger Security International

PRAEGER™

An Imprint of ABC-CLIO, LLC
Santa Barbara, California • Denver, Colorado

32| 2924

AUG 1 7 2016

Library of Congress Cataloging-in-Publication Data

Women, war, and violence : topography, resistance, and hope / Mariam M. Kurtz and Lester R. Kurtz, editors.
        volumes ; cm. — (Praeger security international)
    Includes bibliographical references.
    ISBN 978-1-4408-2880-5 (hardback : alk. paper) — ISBN 978-1-4408-2881-2 (epub)   1. Women and war.   2. Rape as a weapon of war.   3. Women—Violence against.   4. Abused women.   I. Kurtz, Mariam M., editor. II. Kurtz, Lester R., editor.
    HQ1233.W664 2015
    362.82'92—dc23   2014047406

ISBN: 978-1-4408-2880-5
EISBN: 978-1-4408-2881-2

19 18 17 16 15   1 2 3 4 5

This book is also available on the World Wide Web as an eBook.
Visit www.abc-clio.com for details.

Praeger
An Imprint of ABC-CLIO, LLC

ABC-CLIO, LLC
130 Cremona Drive, P.O. Box 1911
Santa Barbara, California 93116-1911

This book is printed on acid-free paper ∞
Manufactured in the United States of America

To Amina, Amani, and Brian

Contents

Acknowledgments

Women, War, and Violence, like all book projects, was a collective endeavor rather than simply the product of the people whose names are on the cover. It is risky to single people out for thanks, because we will miss someone crucial, but we do want to mention some of the many who played key roles in the process.

Many friends and colleagues, along with many of the contributors to this project, shaped the process of finding the right topics and recruiting the best authors. We turned first to Sandra Cheldelin at the Center for Gender and Conflict at George Mason University's School for Conflict Analysis and Resolution, along with other key scholars, including Richard Rubenstein, Nancy Hanrahan, Leslie Dwyer, and Yukiko Furuya (who helped to map out the literature).

One of the joys of working on this project was interacting with pioneers in this crucial interdisciplinary field, like Betty Reardon, Dorota Giercyz, and Mary Elizabeth King, and getting a sense of a community of scholars and activists around the world who have been struggling to understand and mitigate violence against women.

Behind the scenes was a remarkable team of people who know how to turn ideas into books, from Alice Merritt, who first got us involved, through Steve Catalano, who shepherded the project through many hurdles, and many others including Peter Feely and Nicole Azze.

Finally, we are grateful to our patient children—Amina, Amani, and Brian—who supported us with their energy and time. This project is for them in hopes it makes a small contribution to making their world a better place with more empowered women who face much less violence.

CHAPTER 1

Introduction: Women, War, and Violence

Mariam M. Kurtz and Lester R. Kurtz

A brief look at the facts can drive you to despair: there are many cases of sexual assaults, rape, discrimination, femicide, wife battering, and maternal mortality occurring today. Women are being driven from their homes by civil war and ethnic strife. The list goes on. The violence is ubiquitous and brutal. Although the circumstances vary widely in frequency and intensity, no society is completely free from the scourge of humanity known as violence against women (VAW).

That is not the only narrative of this two-volume project, however; there is also an emphasis on the resistance and hope emerging as women and their allies mobilize against the violence. The collected wisdom of the authors expands our knowledge and understanding of the problem in frank terms, to map out the topography of this violence, and this collection also looks at ways in which VAW is being resisted and mitigated in many ways around the world. A wide range of remedies are explored, from international law to the inclusion of women in politics and diplomacy, to the mobilization of social movements dedicated to a broader definition of peace that addresses what Turpin and Kurtz (1997) call the "web of violence" at all levels and in all of its forms.

THE TOPOGRAPHY

More than one out of three women worldwide have experienced physical and/or sexual violence inflicted by their partners or others according to a report by the World Health Organization (WHO) and its collaborators (2013). Of those women with partners, an estimated 30 percent have

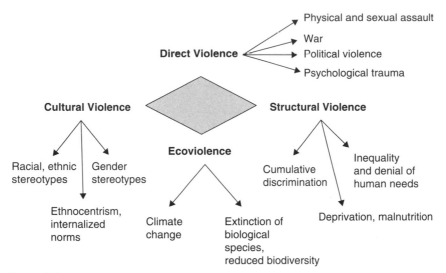

Figure 1.1

Web of Violence

been recipients of sexual or physical violence, or both, by those partners. This dire situation, as reviewed by Danielle Dirks and Emily Troshynski in Chapter 6, views violence against women as a public health problem because it is treated by health professionals.

To get the lay of the land, however, we begin not with the statistics but with the broader theoretical view: to what kinds of violence are women subjected, and what violence do they participate in or tacitly support? What is the broader relationship between gender and conflict, and what is the role of cultural themes such as patriarchy and masculinity?

Much of the literature in the field is shaped by the health professions because they address the consequences of violence in a pragmatic way on a daily basis around the world. Public health professionals—at local, national, and transnational levels—have often led the way in defining violence as a health issue. Governmental and United Nations (UN) organizations have pioneered much of the research in this area, and WHO has created a typology that informs many of the resulting efforts to map out types of violence against women. The nature of violence—physical, sexual, psychological, and that based on deprivation or neglect—is cross-checked with micro to macro levels of violence, from the self-directed to the interpersonal (family/partner and community) to the collective (social, political, and economic).

Our backgrounds in conflict analysis, sociology, and journalism lead us toward a broader definition of violence than the one used by the health professions, as helpful as it is, so these volumes are intended to complement the extensive research on gender violence in the public health fields. We organized our search for topics and contributors along the lines of Johan Galtung's (1990) landmark violence triangle of structural, cultural, and direct violence. To these we have added a fourth kind of violence—what we call ecoviolence, which is the harm done to the environment—so that Galtung's triangle is expanded to a diamond. Not only has ecoviolence become a major issue in recent years, but it has serious impacts, especially on women, because global climate change disproportionately affects women, children, and the poor. Addressing this issue in these volumes is a chapter written by a group of women scientists, Leeanne E. Alonso et al., organized to fight against ecoviolence.

Galtung's sociological approach recognizes that not all violence is the kind of direct violence treated by medical personnel in the emergency room or on the battlefield. Structural violence, such as the inequality of resource distribution and cumulative discrimination, is harm caused by social structures and is just as real as gunshot or rape. This kind of violence is discussed in depth by Kathleen Maas Weigert in Chapter 5 and by Johan Galtung himself in Chapter 4. Weigert defines it as "preventable harm or damage to persons (and by extension to things) where there is no actor committing the violence or where it is not practical to search for the actor(s); such violence emerges from the unequal distribution of power and resources or, in other words, is said to be built into the structure(s)." Cultural violence refers to cultural themes such as patriarchy and demeaning stereotypes that shape internalized norms and behavior and are used to justify both direct and structural violence based on what Galtung calls "absurd theories about women." His idea is that the three types of violence are interconnected and can lead to one another or come together in nefarious ways: "The female half of humanity has been exposed to two vicious combinations of direct and structural violence: patriarchy in marriage and society, and patriotism in war and the world."

The violence women experience—and sometimes foster—is best seen as a particular way of carrying out conflict, as Sandra I. Cheldelin explores in Chapter 2 by looking at the themes of power, performance, and privilege as they are carried out in conflicts. Because gender is socially constructed with psychological, cultural, and structural consequences, she observes that violence against women is portrayed in a particular way in the media, the marketplace, and the arts. Both violent behaviors (rape, torture, etc.) and peacemaking activities are consequently gendered, that is, seen through the lens of gender.

A key to understanding the relationship between women and violence, then, is to analyze how being male or female is defined in terms of social and cultural categories rather than biological ones and the intersectionality of gender and conflict that Cheldelin explores. She reminds us of Simone de Beauvoir's (1989) famous quip "One is not born, but rather becomes, a woman." These constructions of gender are significant in conflicts because they are assigned different levels of prestige and status, which in turns affects all aspects of one's life, including the degree to which one is vulnerable, making women more likely victims and men more likely to feel entitled to use violence. This process of making one gender more susceptible to violence and the other more likely to use it is what Mariam M. Kurtz takes up in Chapter 3. Rituals of privilege such as systematic discrimination and demeaning everyday talk, backed up by direct violence or its threat, increase the chances that women will be physically or psychologically harmed or deprived of human needs.

At the core of that vulnerability is, of course, patriarchy, that is, a system of cultural and social structures that legitimate and enforce male dominance, distributing power and resources unequally between the genders, privileging men and discriminating against women on the basis of an ideology that posits male superiority as inherent in the nature of the world.

Betty Reardon was a pioneer in research focusing on what she calls a "reciprocal relationship" between patriarchy and the institution of war in her 1985 book *Sexism and the War System*. Because weaponry "is the main determinant of power in the present international state system," it legitimates violence in other spheres. Moreover, she argues in Chapter 7, "It is in the interest of patriarchy not so much to reject the legitimation of state violence as to avoid gender equality." The same system establishes social and economic systems of dominance and undermines equality and democracy. Militarism, Diana Francis argues in Chapter 8, is the crude manifestation of a "dominatory approach to relationships," which in turn "stems from the 'eat-or-be-eaten' worldview" that promotes life as a daily struggle and gives way to many kinds of violence. Consequently, she argues, a fundamental element of that culture of domination is gender, which "positions men as dominant and characterizes them as aggressive and heroic." War is an expression of that culture.

Lynne Woehrle raises questions, however, in Chapter 9 about creating a false bifurcation between women as peacemakers and men as war makers, ironically shoring up "systems of thinking and cultural practices that have contributed to the oppression of women for thousands of years. . . . by embracing an archetypal division between the genders." She argues for a more nuanced view of gender and its implications for creating structures such as those within the United Nations that seek to reduce gender-based violence. The fundamental problem, she argues, is that "cultural expectations for power, habits around gender norms, and our failure to embrace both the differences and similarities between the needs of men and those of women set up a failure of the community as a whole to flourish."

That kind of power is not all we have as humans, however. Francis notes (Chapter 8), for example, the Naga women of northeast India, believe it is their job to intervene when violence breaks out between men: "Their power, which requires great courage, takes the form of talking, listening, challenging, pleading and mediating, as well as physically interposing themselves between the warring parties." It is this power for and with others, rather than over them, that Francis claims can shift us away from violence.

Chapter 6 is an overview entitled "International Violence against Women" by Dirks and Troshynski that draws upon a 2013 WHO report and other broad surveys of the phenomenon worldwide. Here is where the bleak picture comes in. The statistics are numbing if you read them as a story about individuals experiencing physical and psychological trauma, often suffered in silence and with lifelong consequences. More than a third of women in the 79 countries included in the WHO study had experienced gendered violence, with an incidence of 45.6 percent in Africa, which is also where the largest number of violent conflicts occur.

After this overview, we burrow into specific types of violence in various parts of the world. In Chapter 12 Mariam M. Kurtz and Mwamini Thambwe Diggs look at rape as a weapon of war in the Democratic Republic of the Congo, where wartime rape is used as a deliberate strategy to destroy the enemy's society, starting with the family. They also discuss how rape does not end at the personal level of suffering but affects the family and surrounding community; it is a threat even to the general public health.

Other chapters explore the violence experienced by women who move from their home society to another—either as immigrants, as in Pilar Rodríguez Martínez's review of violence against women immigrants (Chapter 10), or especially as refugees forced to leave their homeland, as outlined by the United Nations High Commission on Refugees (2011) report on women as refugees.

Although refugees experience high levels of violence, as one might expect because they are vulnerable in so many ways, women immigrants are, for the most part, surprisingly no more subject to gender violence than their indigenous counterparts. This finding is significant because gender violence against immigrant women is often explained—and even justified—as the consequence of cultural norms brought from their home countries. Violence against immigrant women is complex, Rodríguez Martínez contends, because it becomes racist and classist; moreover, these women "suffer an extra, symbolic violence" because they confront the problem of hypervisibility on the one hand and invisibility on the other.

Maryann Bylander gives us a global overview of sex trafficking in Chapter 11, arguing, "What we *think we know* about trafficking is far greater than what we *actually know*." Moreover, what we do know reveals a very complex and highly politicized terrain, with disconnects in terms of definitions, the scope of the problem, patterns, and actions being taken. In each area, she argues, the dominant antitrafficking approach being used conflicts with the best evidence.

Most of us who write and read about violence are distant from the everyday lived experience of those who suffer it most. Four of our chapters provide a glimpse into the lives of women immersed in the phenomenon we study in different parts of the world: ubiquitous direct violence in Latin American and Mexican contexts. There are women living under the cultural violence of restrictive versions of sharia law in specific Muslim countries, discrimination against women even prior to their birth in India, and the ambiguous case of women in the U.S. military who are trained to use violence under strict circumstances but then also fall victim to it in a complex way. Meredith Kleykamp and Molly Clever note, in Chapter 21, that although women are officially excluded from combat, because of the changing nature of war, they are exposed to combat and are injured and killed. Moreover, they note, the problem of gender inequality in the U.S. military is "manifested in an ongoing sexual assault crisis," which is also the subject of Chapter 35, by Ashley M. Belyea. Ironically, although the nature of military culture may increase the probability of sexual assaults, the culture and structures of military institutions also make it easier to demand positive changes, similar to the case of racial discrimination.

Each of these chapters presents significant theoretical issues about the nature of gendered violence and how to resist it. Manuel Llorens, Verónica Zubillaga, and John Souto, who wrote Chapter 13, work as community psychologists and researchers in what they say may be the most dangerous city in the world, Caracas. It is characterized by lethal weapons and chains of revenge carried out by disempowered armed young men. They explore the roles women play in the dynamics of their Caracas barrio, and they relate how they resisted the violence and helped broker negotiated agreements, but also inadvertently contributed to the reproduction of violence in their neighborhoods.

In Chapter 15 Miriam Gutiérrez-Otero describes the psychological defenses put up by citizens in another city declared the most violent in the world, Ciudad Juarez, Chihuahua, on the Mexican border just across the river from El Paso, Texas. She provides an important psychological angle on gender violence that is covered inadequately elsewhere in these volumes.

With more killings than occur in countries at war, such as Iraq, the citizens of Juarez are caught up in drug wars and suffer from kidnappings, disappearances, extortions, and armed robberies, as well as femicides and female assassinations. The question she asks is, how do people live in such a context? "How does a mother calm herself and her child?" Indeed, perhaps we should offer an editorial warning to those about to join in the journey into the heart of darkness this moving chapter provides: the reader may need to employ the "banalization of violence" strategy that the women of Juarez use to survive, a covert self-protection of the psyche that the women need to tell their stories differently and to heal their wounds.

Just as the neighborhoods of Juarez have been hijacked by drug lords, the tradition of Islam has been taken in an unintended direction by patriarchal forces in some places, with the institutions of the faith used to subject women to harsh rule. Muslim scholar Reza Aslan, in fact, charges that some aspects of the tradition as it developed after the death of the Prophet Mohammad was a kind of backlash against the liberation of women that he had initiated. Aslan traces much of the subsequent efforts to oppress women within the Muslim community to Umar, one of the most powerful successors to the Prophet. He initiated many of the practices that Saira Yamin condemns in her important and critical presentation in Chapter 16, "Sharia Law and Its Implications for Women's Status and Rights." Umar attempted unsuccessfully to confine women to their homes and prevent them from praying in the mosque. He restricted the Prophet's widows "and instituted a series of several penal ordinances aimed primarily at women," such as stoning adulterers, "a punishment which has absolutely no foundation whatsoever in the Quran" (Aslan, 2011, p. 71).

In India, Madhu Kishwar argues in Chapter 14, cultural violence begins in the womb. The rapid spread of amniocentesis and ultrasound technologies has resulted, she notes, "in sex-selective abortions of hundreds of thousands of female fetuses," as reflected in an imbalance in favor of males in the Indian population for at least the past century. Although several states banned the practice after women's rights groups mounted campaigns against it, the laws have not been enforced and the practice has continued.

The ambivalence toward violence and our response to it has been particularly acute in the Middle East, where the Arab uprising of 2011 in Tunisia and Egypt mobilized women and brought them into public life in an unprecedented way. Chapters 17–20, on women in Egypt, Syria, and Lebanon, look at models of how women have resisted the systemic violence of their societies and also suffered from a backlash for their actions. In the end, however, the role of women in the region has been changed forever. Mariam M. Kurtz observes in Chapter 20 that Egyptian women found their voice through the revolution. Their fear is gone and they have broken the taboos. The struggle is not over, however, as Althea M. Middleton-Detzner, Jillian M. Slutzker, Samuel F. Chapple-Sokol, and Sana A. Mahmood note in Chapter 19. Perhaps, they conclude, "with unity, planning, and nonviolent discipline, Egyptian women will be able to escape the cycle of post-revolution marginalization and carve out a new space for women in a new Egypt."

It may come as a surprise to some that Syrian women have also engaged in well-organized nonviolent struggle, as Rajaa Altalli and Anne-Marie Codur found in their study reported in Chapter 18. Despite the fact that the uprising against the Assad regime eventually devolved into violence, Syrian women were "able to seize the opportunity" of the 2011 uprising across the Arab world "to open a political and social space that had been closed to them previously."

According to Rita Stephan and Nicole Khoury in Chapter 17, women in Lebanon have been involved in nonviolent struggle since the 19th century, drawing on both maternalist and egalitarian frames to mobilize for change. Their reaction against the trauma of Lebanon's 15-year civil war and subsequent Syrian occupation made them even more committed to nonviolence. Unlike traditional nonviolent actions such as street demonstrations and strikes, the Lebanese women focused on insider actors and strategies, using shared cultural and symbolic values to promote gender equality, peace building, and civil egalitarianism.

RESISTANCE AND HOPE

What is surprising is not that women are the victims or even the perpetrators of violence, but that so much resistance is emerging to specific kinds of violence and to violence against women as a general principle. Most of the chapters in these two volumes address this global uprising.

We begin with Riane Eisler, one of the grand thinkers in this area, who in Chapter 23 suggests four broad types of resistance:

1. **The Human Rights/Social Justice Case:** Recognizing and changing traditions that violate women's human rights in both the public and private spheres;
2. **The Social and Economic Case:** Demonstrating that ending traditions of violence against women is foundational to building a more peaceful and equitable world for all;
3. **The Moral Case:** Bringing together spiritual leaders to raise their voices against gender violence, especially since it has often been justified on "moral" grounds;
4. **The Legal Case:** Using international law to hold governments accountable when they fail to protect the female half of humanity from egregious and widespread violence.

Perhaps the most helpful aspect of her analysis is that she presents the arguments against each case and then rebuts them, creating the sort of internal dialogue with the opposing forces that sharpens our thinking and facilitates the development of smarter strategies in the fight against violence.

In Chapter 31 Lester R. Kurtz offers a conceptual toolkit for thinking about the resistance, including a paradigm designed to guide strategic analysis across the dimensions and causes of violence against women to help readers understand what supports the current system and how people can be mobilized to transform it.

In Chapter 24 Anne-Marie Codur and Mary Elizabeth King highlight the historically significant roles of women in civil resistance from ancient Egypt through contemporary struggles against tyranny and nonviolent noncooperation with systems of injustice. The crucial participation and leadership of women brought to light by their overview is too often missed by historians. King then addresses the role of women in the American civil rights movement more specifically in Chapter 25. Active in the Student Nonviolent Coordinating Committee (SNCC) during the 1960s, she talks about how the movement was launched by a group of women in Montgomery, Alabama, that shook the foundations of American political life. She was personally involved in controversies over women's role in the movement and sets the record straight, explaining how despite some limitations, their group constituted the major popular grassroots force for civil rights in the United States.

As with the civil rights movement, much of the movement against gender violence is aimed at changing laws, from local to transnational levels. Much of the leadership in this area has originated in and around the UN; these efforts are outlined by Dorota Gierycz in Chapter 27 and by Susan F. Hirsch and Caroline Sarkis in Chapter 28. International rights lawyer Gierycz, who worked for many years with the UN, takes us through the historical development of a legal framework as leverage to address gender violence and to shift cultural attitudes worldwide. In the end, she argues,

Only the elaboration of a comprehensive treaty, addressing prohibition, prevention, and punishment of all forms of violence against women, in all circumstances (armed conflict and peace) can create proper conditions for ending the impunity for crimes against women, strengthening accountability of perpetrators and responsibilities of political leaders as well as elaboration of more focused and effective laws at national and international levels.

The effort to establish universal jurisdiction for rape and sexual violence cases and thereby delegitimize violence against women is not always well received, however, and this is the dilemma taken up by Hirsch and Sarkis in studying the complicated case of South Africa's investigation of crimes in Zimbabwe. The development strengthened the trend toward condemning sexual violence but also created a backlash and unleashed hidden agendas, exposing the fact that "laws and legal processes tend to reinforce established hierarchies and that these can favor masculinist values." Gierycz extends this analysis of efforts to use transnational legal frameworks that incorporate human rights and gender perspectives in Chapter 32, addressing the important issue of trafficking in human beings.

At the transnational level the fight against gender violence has been undergirded by a structural change at the UN with the creation of UN Women, reviewed by Erin M. Stephens in Chapter 26. This new entity brings together fragmented and under-resourced units within the UN to create a strong front advocating gender equality. UN Women is building on a series of landmark developments in this area, from the creation of the Commission on the Status of Women in 1946 to the historic Convention on the Elimination of All Forms of Discrimination against Women (CEDAW) in 1979, the Beijing Declaration and Platform for Action in 1995, and the Millennium Development goals of 2000. The UN Security Council Resolution 1325, passed in 2000, picked up the call for "gender mainstreaming" from the Beijing Declaration and urged the participation of women in all aspects of security and decision making.

The cause of gender equality is often promoted at the diplomatic level simply by bringing women to the table. Chapter 30, by Deborah Cavin and Ambassador Swanee Hunt, provides evidence for a sea change at the negotiating table when it does not gather only males to create an agreement. One woman whom the ambassador interviewed expressed her experience in this way:

We have different ways of looking at things, and we need both—the women and the men—at the table. The men were "positioning"—Who's going to be the president, vice president? But the women asked—When will my children get food? When will my relatives get water? Water, food, feeding the community are not "women's issues," they're community issues. So whenever people talk about women's issues, we need to challenge them; we need to change the mindset. (Hunt, 2010)

Changing mindsets is the goal of another major strategy in the fight against gender violence, education. In Chapter 34 Anamika Gupta notes that because India signed and ratified CEDAW, there is an entrée for educating people in that country about aspects of gender violence that are now illegal. The Indian government now says officially that prohibited gender violence includes conduct ranging from "lewd comments, leering, groping, to more aggressive assaults such as rape and gang rape, emotional and physical torture, and murder, and spans both public and private spaces." Simply declaring something illegal is not enough, however; Gupta proposes that a human rights curriculum be integrated into the Indian educational system, as well as other institutions in civil society, to bring up a new generation with different attitudes about gender violence and other violations of human rights.

The issue of sexual assaults in India was thrust to the top of the policy agenda with the brutal gang rape of a 23-year-old student; the mobilization around this issue is taken up by Madhu Purnima Kishwar in Chapter 29. Kishwar observes that while there is a widespread demand for more "stringent" laws (including calls for castration and even the death penalty), the crucial problem is the "gap between what the law prescribes and what actually happens in practice," an issue compounded by a lawless police force. In short, she argues, more stringent laws would simply widen the potential for abuse by the police; far-reaching police and judicial reforms are necessary, and the legal reform should be guided by a "surgeon's precision" rather than a "butcher's hatchet." Moreover, she proposes, nonlegal measures are important as well, such as safe footpaths, citizen-friendly public spaces, adequate and safe public transport equipped with cameras, and a national debate on all of these issues.

Public institutions are usually the locus of debate regarding violence against women, but they are not always responsible to the most crucial issues. In Chapter 22 Jonathan Edmunds takes up the hidden side of post-traumatic stress disorder (PTSD) that the government and military usually fail to address: the PTSD suffered by spouses and families of those in combat, especially the women married to servicemen in combat. Speaking from his own personal experience and interviews with the spouses of combat veterans, Edmunds explains how spouses and family members of combatants are in a constant state of fear, connected to the war through the media and facing their own trauma. They are then confronted with the servicemen returning. "Not only do they suffer while the absent loved one is at war," Edmunds claims, "they are sometimes subjected further to violence once their absent ones return home." Although the military has finally started to address the dilemmas of the veterans themselves, there is little support for their suffering spouses.

Finally, in Chapter 36 we shift attention from the micro-level violence of the family to the largest scale of violence, that against the ecosphere that all of us share. This topic is addressed by an international team of scientists from five continents: Leeanne E. Alonso, Shivani Bhalla, Alexis Bermudez, Mary K. Cline, Christina M. E. Ellis, Ana Liz Flores, Renée González Montagut, Martha M. Hurley, Rebecca Kormos, Patricia Moreno-Casasola, and Annette L. Tjon Sie Fat. Just as women have taken the lead in civil resistance against authoritarian structures, they are also behind much of the action against environmental degradation. Because of significant differences in their rights and roles in many societies, women are more vulnerable than men to changes in the ecosystem:

Given the socio-cultural barriers often faced by women, their lack of equal rights, access to resources and decision-making power, as well as their heavy reliance on natural resources, women are on the front lines of social-economic, environmental and climate risks.

Because women interact directly with the natural environment daily, collecting food and water and providing a healthy environment for their communities, they often feel the effects of environment degradation first and they are often the first to act in reducing the damage, especially in areas where adult female literacy rates are high. Unfortunately, however, women's specific knowledge of ecosystems is not always taken into account because their voices are not sought or heard during stakeholder consultations. Alonso et al. take us on a whirlwind tour of women taking action, such as the Green Belt Movement, founded by Nobel laureate Dr. Wangari Maathai in Kenya; and the Piñonal nursery in Mexico, a cooperative that manages an important wetland area. Yevgeniya Chirikova and her colleagues campaigned to save the Khimki Forest outside of Moscow, and the Guyana Mangrove Restoration Project (www.mangrovesgy.org) teaches people in villages about the benefits of mangroves for humans, animals, and fishes.

PRESENTING A KALEIDOSCOPE

To fully represent the broad scope of research being done across the disciplines on women, war, and violence, we would need a multivolume encyclopedia and probably a series of well-funded conferences bringing first-rate scholars from around the world to meet face-to-face and work out the intricacies of this topic. These two volumes are more of a kaleidoscope than a comprehensive summary of all that we know about this high-priority area of inquiry.

We did not have access to Pentagon-level resources for this work, but we have built upon the thousands of large and small research projects by scholars in the field around the world, whose numbers have grown over recent decades. We benefited especially from the generosity of our authors, who have shared their knowledge and insights into best practices as to how to address the problem of violence and war as it relates not just to women, but to the human community itself.

This field is ripe with research questions, from the need for both breadth and depth on the issues addressed in these two volumes, so that we will learn more about violence against and even by women around the world and a deeper understanding of the facts we already know. In reflecting on the collection here as we go to publication, two significant areas emerge that have received insufficient attention: violence against lesbians, gays, bisexuals, and transsexuals (LGBT) because of their sexual orientation, on the one hand, and the issue of the intersectionality of race, class, and gender on the other. Both of these areas of important research in recent years go to the heart of the relationship between gender and violence more broadly framed.

In the midst of a cultural revolution in many places regarding LGBT rights and same-sex marriage, as well as pushback against it, is the subject of news headlines and deserves more scholarly reflection and empirical analysis. Research on violence and gender has focused traditionally on VAW, but the movement for LGBT rights and hate crimes legislation has stimulated questions about binary understandings of gender and the emergence of "queer theory" as a robust area of research (see Gamson and Moon, 2004) emphasizes the constructionist nature of gender.

The concept of the intersectionality of gender, race, and class (Collins, 2000) has become a central theoretical paradigm in women's and gender studies (and a major contribution of that field to the social sciences at large—see McCall, 2014; Dhamoon, 2011). It has also shaped our understanding of VAW in recent decades as has the organized transnational struggle against VAW. More than 20 years ago, Kimberle Crenshaw observed that the politicization of VAW "has transformed the way we understand violence against women." For example, battering and rape, once seen as private (family matters) and aberrational (errant sexual aggression), are now largely recognized as part of a broad-scale system of domination that affects women as a class (Crenshaw, 1991, p. 1241). Moreover, the tension between identity politics that highlights differences between groups (gender, racial, and class) also sometimes ignores variation within them. This is most salient with the issue of violence, Crenshaw notes, because "the violence that many women experience is often shaped by other dimensions of their identities such as race and class" (Crenshaw, 1991, p. 1242). This intersectionality is an important dimension of our topic that requires more empirical study of VAW worldwide and theoretical rethinking that includes the voices and perspectives of survivors of violence who do not have the privilege of scholarly investigation and reflection but struggle daily to survive.

We offer the sample of insights in these volumes in hopes that it will stimulate further research projects, term papers, theses, dissertations, books, and, yes, action projects that address these issues on the ground. We hope it will facilitate the global movement that advocates in the halls of corporations and in parliaments, households, and schools for the mitigation of violence against women and the empowerment of those who struggle against it.

BIBLIOGRAPHY

Ackerman, Peter, and Jack DuVall. 2001. *A Force More Powerful: A Century of Non-Violent Conflict*. New York: Palgrave Macmillan.

Aslan, Reza. 2011. *No God but God: The Origins and Evolution of Islam*. Toronto: Random House of Canada.

Brah, Avtar, and Ann Phoenix. 2004. Ain't I a Woman? Revisiting Intersectionality. *Journal of International Women's Studies*, 5 (3): 75–86.

Crenshaw, Kimberle. 1991. Mapping the Margins: Intersectionality, Identity Politics, and Violence against Women of Color. *Stanford Law Review*, 1241–1299.

De Beauvoir, Simone. 1989 [1952]. *The Second Sex*. Trans. H. M. Parshley. New York: Vintage Books.

Dhamoon, Rita Kaur. 2011. Considerations on Mainstreaming Intersectionality. *Political Research Quarterly* 64 (1): 230–243.

Galtung, Johan. 1990. Cultural Violence. *Journal of Peace Research* 27 (3): 291–305.

Hunt, Swanee. 2010. Interview with Mobina Jaffer. Institute for Inclusive Security Policy Forum, uploaded November 17, 2010, http://www.youtube.com/watch?v=755YwYpzEmU

Krug, Etienne G., Linda L. Dahlberg, James A. Mercy, Anthony B. Zwi, and Rafael Lozano, eds. 2002. *World Report on Violence and Health*. Geneva: World Health Organization, http://www.who.int/violence_injury_prevention/violence/world_report/chapters/en/

McCall, Leslie. 2014. The Complexity of Intersectionality. *Signs* 40 (1): 1771–1800.

Reardon, Betty. 1985. *Sexism and the War System*. New York: Teachers College Press.

Turpin, Jennifer E., and Lester R. Kurtz. 1997. *The Web of Violence: From Interpersonal to Global*. Urbana: University of Illinois Press.

United Nations High Commissioner on Refugees. 2011. *Survivors, Protectors, Providers: Refugee Women Speak Out*. United Nations High Commissioner on Refugees. http://www.unhcr.org/cgi-bin/texis/vtx/home/opendocPDFViewer.html?docid=4ec5337d9&query=women%20as%20refugees%20report.

Watts, Charlotte, and Cathy Zimmerman. 2002. Violence against Women: Global Scope and Magnitude. *Lancet* 359 (9313): 1232–37.

World Health Organization, London School of Hygiene and Tropical Medicine, and South African Medical Research Council. 2013. *Global and Regional Estimates of Violence against Women*. Geneva: World Health Organization, p. 15, http://www.who.int/reproductivehealth/publications/violence/9789241564625/en/

CHAPTER 2

Gender and Conflict: What Do We Know?

Sandra I. Cheldelin

INTRODUCTION

What do we know about gender and conflict? The good news is that we know a lot. As a practitioner having worked domestically and abroad with more than 150 organizations and communities on issues of conflict and violence, I have witnessed firsthand the gendered components in conflict, and I appreciate the ways in which they both escalate and resist intervention. Issues related to gender and conflict present themselves at all levels—interpersonally and in families, in communities, in organizations and workplaces, and especially where people navigate large systems and structures such as health care, law, education, politics, and the like. I have had the privilege to explore more than 100 topics related to gender and conflict over a decade-long series of graduate research seminars on the subject, with access to a transnational (though disconnected) network of organizations, agencies, scholars, and practitioners working with gender and conflict, and it is my hope this chapter will give the reader a broad as well as deep understanding of what we do know about gender and conflict.*

Themes of power, performance, and privilege are woven throughout the chapter in three broad topics: the social construction of gender—the ways we understand and make meaning of gender-based conflicts, especially the psychological, cultural, and structural impacts, and ways such violence is portrayed in the media, the marketplace, and the arts; gendered violent behaviors, including rape, torture, domestic and cultural violence,

---

*The author acknowledges and appreciates the many graduate students over the years who researched topics and contributed papers to inform our gender and conflict database.

sex trafficking, combat, and terrorism; and gendered peacemaking and intervention strategies.

WHAT IS GENDER?

I remember how astonished I was when reading Phyllis Chesler's exchange with her male colleague. Chesler asked him what came to his mind when she said the phrase "woman's inhumanity to woman." He replied, "Nothing much. Jealousy, maybe." She then asked him, "And what do you think of when I say 'man's inhumanity to man'?" "Oh," he responded, "That's a big one. War. Fracticide. Slavery. Greed. Evil" (Chesler, 2001, p. 9). Although Chesler was making a different point with this exchange, I was surprised at the extraordinary disparity in terms of her colleague's perceptions of how men and women are *inhumane* toward their respective sexes. Subsequently, I have asked this question in many of my classes with quite similar responses: generally men are tagged as responsible for far greater violence and hostility toward men while women are said to use much more indirect and subtle tactics.

I also ask my students how their lives would be different if they woke up the next morning and found they were of the opposite sex. The responses are immediately engaging and broad in topics and domains. Female students speak of freedom from housework and child care; they imagine walking alone and at night with little fear, and traveling whenever and wherever they might want to go. They imagine what they would do with the twenty-five-cents-on-the-dollar pay raise—a significant annual increase. They speak of new freedoms around their sexuality and dating behaviors, and how they would be likely to act on their fantasies concerning others (even if married). Males, too, get it. They are intrigued by how they would be obsessed with their weight and their clothes and how they would compare themselves with other women. They are not sure what they would do to replace their time watching or engaging in sports, or how they would make friends if not working. They would stop fretting about the amount of money they had to make to support their families. Some don't like the double standard of responsibility for pregnancy and child rearing. They were sure, though, they would nag more now that they were women.

It would be interesting to ask this question systematically to a sample from a number of other cultures to identify differences in cultural constructs and discourse around the meaning of gender. Although the activity is always entertaining, these responses are representations of what we know about our conceptions of gender. Broadly defined, gender is the "state of being male or female" (*Merriam-Webster*, n.d.) and typically refers to the social, cultural, and psychological differences rather than biological ones. Women imagine, for example, new sources of freedom in the public domain, and men imagine constraints on their appearance and increased responsibility for the family—firmly centered in the private domain. It seems clear that gender is a powerful construct that shapes the way we see others (and others see us). Moreover, social and cultural constructed conceptions of gender—at home and around the world— have led to significant disparities in economic status; access to education, health care, and legal representation; and other cultural indices of suc- cess. They have been used to justify such violence as sexual and physi- cal abuse, rape, mutilation, torture, imprisonment, and killing. There are profound implications to our social constructions of gender, including the ways language and stories—our narratives—shape and reflect gendered attitudes, expectations, and norms. So while we think of men as being more violent with men than women are with women, and we understand how rights and privileges are differently available to men and women, there is much more we know about the intersectionality of gender and conflict.

Our initial understanding of gender focused on the concept of "differ- ence" and how it is constructed within a society. In the United States we have such conceptions of difference—often referred to as the "master statuses"—as race, sex, social class, sexual orientation, and disability statuses (most of which are protected by laws). Each of these has assigned levels of prestige and refers to positions in a social structure. The *Oxford Diction- ary of Sociology* defines these master statuses as "those in most or all social situations [that] will overpower or dominate all other statuses. . . . Master status influences every other aspect of life, including personal identity" (Marshall, 1994, p. 315).

Framing gender as difference has produced volumes of empirical research that has accentuated the oppositional nature of these categories and often located the cause of social problems in women. Much of the cur- rent research, however, has moved from studying gender as categories of difference to a social constructionist frame. It is well captured in Simone de Beauvoir's (1949) famous line "One is not born, but rather becomes, a woman" and has been thoroughly explained by sociologists Berger and Luckmann (1966) in *The Social Construction of Reality*, intended "as a sys- tematic, theoretical treatise in the sociology of knowledge." Crawford (1995) notes that, from a constructionist perspective, gender is "not an attribute of individuals but a way of making sense of transactions between and among individuals. Gender exists not in persons but in transactions; it is conceptualized as a verb, not a noun" (p. 12). Thus, our sources of mean- ing and our behavior—the presentation of our values in human action— are informed by and captured in the relational connections we have with one another.

When gender is understood as a system of meanings or meaning making (not as attributes), then differences in power and influence, for example, can be considered within the larger influences of society—its culture, traditions, and structures—and we can see how those differences impact interpersonal and intergroup dynamics in families, organizations, and communities. While all societies recognize biological differentiation—labeled male and female—gender is "what culture makes out of the 'raw material' of (already socially constructed) biological sex" (Crawford, 1995, p. 13). When the boy or girl is born into the world and immediately decked in blue or pink, respectively, gender presents itself and our discourses of masculinity and femininity begin to shape that child's own meaning-making system of identity.

To add conflict to this understanding of gender, it is useful to map it using a framework such as the one offered in Figure 2.1 (Cheldelin and Lucas, 2004, p. 14). It helps "locate" gender in a conflict. While there are many frameworks in the field of conflict analysis and resolution, this one makes explicit the impact of the multitude of forces attributed to gendered behavior. To explain the framework briefly, three nested concentric spheres reflect three levels of analysis of a conflict. At the inner sphere are the social and psychological aspects of a conflict, including the type of conflict, its sources, and its dynamics. The middle sphere reflects the contextual issues—the identities of the parties in conflict and any particular or unique situation that impacts their conflict. The outer circle represents the macro or structural aspects of the conflict, including the culture and traditions of the society.

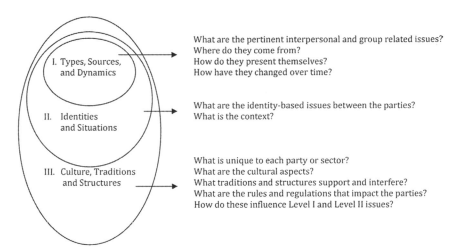

Figure 2.1

A Framework for Conflict Analysis (Cheldelin, Sandra I. and Ann F. Lucas, *The Jossey-Bass Academic Administrator's Guide to Conflict Resolution*, San Francisco: Jossey-Bass, 2004, p. 14. © 2004 by John Wiley & Sons, Ltd. Used by permission.)

In this framework the primary location of gender presents itself at level II, Identities and Situations, yet it is influenced by levels I and III. That is, how the parties make sense of the transactions that occur according to the *type* of conflict (the parties' motivations, behaviors, issues, and hopes), the *sources* of the conflict (their relationships, needs, interests, values, and ideologies) and the *dynamics* of the conflict (the interaction of the perceived differences and injustices)—all at level I—influence the *identity* of the parties and the *situational* nature of their conflict (level II). Similarly, the *culture* and *traditions* of society and the social *structures*—organizational, political, economic, and legal—are witnessed in level III. When significant differences in interests, power, and basic needs occur, or perceived needs are not met, or when the struggle is embedded in a traditional culture that privileges one group over another—usually men over women—the *situation* is ripe for a gender-based conflict to erupt. Embedded in social *structures* are power relations, and typically the public domain provides men greater access to, and therefore control over, people's lives, influenced by government, laws, decision making, and public discourse. Their voices are privileged; women's voices are more likely muted.

Our language and discourse become a set of strategies for negotiating and navigating areas where we are (and are not) privileged. Our narratives become powerful resources, and, as Crawford notes, we use them in a variety of ways: to influence others, enlist help, protect ourselves, save face, justify our behavior, establish important relationships, and present ourselves as having the qualities that we most admire (Crawford, 1995). Why is this important? When gender and language are considered from a constructionist perspective, different questions can be asked and different agendas become important. We can challenge those master statuses in terms of the ways those constructs justify privilege and power. We can also probe the ways such constructs can be deconstructed. We can change the social processes of the political, legal, economic, and religious institutions that create differences and assign meanings. Early in the women's movement in the United States, for example, when it was gaining momentum and strength, women demanded: "Don't call me 'lady'—it's a four-letter word! Call me 'woman'!" Women demanded that they no longer be positioned by the dominant group (men) to be "lady-like," with all the corresponding social expectations of femininity.

Jean Kilbourne has produced a long-standing chronicle of gender representation in U.S. advertising (beginning in the 1970s), and her award-winning series *Killing Us Softly* presents evidence of the extraordinary power and influence commercial advertising has on our constructions of gender. Similarly, Jackson Katz, in *Tough Guise: Violence, Media and the Crisis in Masculinity*, illustrates that the images of ruggedly individualistic and violent masculinity can and must be challenged as it does not work for boys (or girls). Unfortunately, the U.S. culture, like most others, still strongly subscribes to core stereotypes about gender. When we studied Hillary Clinton's historic candidacy for the U.S. presidency, we found that the gender stereotypes consistently portrayed agentic behaviors of independence, assertiveness, self-reliance, and power as masculine—witness the strong anti-Hillary campaign from men—while females continued to own the expectations and responsibilities of communality, caring, and helpfulness (Tinsley et al., 2009). Moreover, when women do demonstrate success, assertiveness, self-reliance, and similar qualities, their behaviors are interpreted as counterstereotypical and in violation of injunctive-based gender norms (Tinsley et al., 2009). These stereotypes make women vulnerable to the very powerful, dichotomous "likability versus competence" trap: when women are seen as competent they are not very likable (a common charge by commentators against Hillary), and when women are perceived as likable, they are seen as not competent (a common charge by comedians, for example, on *Saturday Night Live*, against Sarah Palin) (Schneider et al., 2010). Sources of media powerfully shape our conceptions of gender and serve as sources of gendered violence.

GENDER AND VIOLENCE

The dominant narrative about gender and violence is that overwhelmingly men are the perpetrators and women are over-represented as victims. This supports the stereotype that men are more abusive than women, in general. There is evidence that gender-based violence (GBV) has received increased attention and traction since the United Nations (UN) Convention on Rights of Children. Unfortunately, the data are suspect as GBV is under-reported for many reasons: fear of social stigma and dishonor to the family and community, lack of psychosocial support to navigate social systems, over-representation of men in the official processes, lack of access to education and the breadth of illiteracy among women, and difficulties encountered in challenging traditional cultural values of women as "property" and men as determining women's destinies.

What follows chronicles what we know about several types of gender-based violence. While full chapters in these two volumes explore many of these topics more deeply, our broad sweep here includes domestic violence, honor-based violence and forced marriage, sex trafficking, combatants and child soldiers, and rape and war.

GENDER AND DOMESTIC VIOLENCE

There is little question that domestic violence is a serious and persistent global problem. Advocates for human rights declare the problem to be of epidemic proportions (Stop Violence Against Women, 2013a). Women in significantly greater numbers are becoming victims of such violence. The

World Health Organization (WHO, 2013) reports, "overall, 35% of women worldwide have experienced either physical and/or sexual intimate partner violence or non-partner sexual violence" and notes that, in addition, there are many other forms of violence women are exposed to (p. 2). WHO also reports that of women who are murdered, 38 percent were killed by intimate partners, and 42 percent of women raped by their partners are physically injured (though these data are likely underestimated) (Stop Violence Against Women, 2013a, para. 2).

In the United States, four in five victims are women (Stop Violence Against Women, 2013a, para. 1); however, the rate of decline during the period 1993–2010 was an impressive 64 percent —from 9.9 to 3.6 victims per 1,000 (age 12 or older) (Catalano, 2012). This still represents 907,000 intimate partner victims in 2010, and a four-fifths predominance means that 724,000 were female victims. The category includes "rape, sexual assault, robbery, aggravated assault, and simple assault committed by an offender who was the victim's current or former spouse, boyfriend, or girl-friend" (Catalano, 2012, para. 2), and the database sources are police and crime survey statistics. What these data do not reflect are the unreported or untreated cases of abuse. Again, the numbers are likely to be higher for both women and men as victims of domestic violence, because accurate data are difficult to obtain.

We know there are differences in motivation and tactics between men and women who engage in domestic violence (Stop Violence Against Women, 2013a, para. 1–4). Hart and Brassard (1990) developed five categories of psychological abuse used predominantly by men: spurning, terrorizing, denying emotional responsiveness, isolating, and exploiting. Schecter (1982) chronicles the battered women's movement. Women surely have the capacity to act with aggression, yet they tend to act out nonviolently or with milder forms of abuse—slapping, shoving, kicking, biting—shaped by internalized gender roles. When they inflict injury the results are usually visible—scratches and bite marks. Women also act aggressively in self-defense or on the basis of a history of severe violence from their partners. The Stop Violence Against Women project advocates for human rights and captures the complexity of this kind of violence (as well as the difficulty of obtaining accurate data):

She may use preemptive force—if she believes that an assault may be imminent, she may initiate the violence in an attempt to gain control over the place and time of the assault, either to increase her safety or to minimize the embarrassment and disruption the assault will cause. . . . [She] may retaliate for a history of abuse. (Stop Violence Against Women, 2013a, para. 2)

Men's sense of entitlement to violence is also shaped by internalized gender roles regarding control and power. Hines, Brown, and Dunning

(2007) note that societal power structures permit men to misuse and control women, even if violence is necessary. With the use of force, men's abuse may have different physical manifestations—choking, hitting, and punching—because they know women are uncomfortable revealing evidence of bruising to law enforcement or the public (Stop Violence Against Women, 2013a, para. 4).

Research also informs our theories about domestic violence. We have evolved from the 1970s thinking that domestic violence was caused by psychopathology on the part of both parties: men were mentally ill and could be cured through medication and treatment; women were similarly categorized and often institutionalized because of their hysteria, with the physical and psychological long-term effects of such abuse not fully taken into account. Today advocates for eliminating domestic violence realize:

A logical outcome of relationships of dominance and inequality—relationships shaped not simply by the personal choices or desires of some men to [dominate] their wives but by how we, as a society, construct social and economic relationships between men and women and within marriage (or intimate domestic relationships) and families. . . . [forces us to] understand how our response to violence creates a climate of intolerance or acceptance to the force used in intimate relationships. (Stop Violence Against Women, 2013b, para. 21)

At the international level, the UN Women section of the UN Entity for Gender Equality and the Empowerment of Women has taken on issues of violence, first by successfully navigating the General Assembly to adopt the Declaration on the Elimination of Violence Against Women (A/RES/48/104, December 19, 1993) and, years later, on December 22, 2003, resolution 58/147 was adopted by the General Assembly: the Elimination of Domestic Violence Against Women (see Chapter 27 in Volume 2). It lays out the previous agreed-upon resolutions and specifically states that domestic violence is a human rights issue, a societal problem that reflects "a manifestation of unequal power relations between women and men," and that such violence has long-term health implications. It recognizes that while domestic violence occurs in the private sphere, it is a public concern requiring governments to take serious action to protect victims and prevent violence.

HONOR-BASED VIOLENCE AND FORCED MARRIAGE

One of the most perplexing issues facing women is the practice of forced marriage and honor-based violence (HBV). Aisha Gill (2012), at the UN Division for the Advancement of Women, captures the difficulty in understanding the notion of "honor" in forced marriages:

At its most basic level, [forced marriage] refers to a person's righteousness in the eyes of their community. It is often employed to ensure that people act morally. In this respect, if people follow what is considered socially good, they are honoured. If not, they are shamed. (para. 3)

These families also believe that if their women engage in any number of misbehaviors—the most common including refusal to enter into an arranged marriage, seeking divorce (even from an abusive husband), committing adultery or having sex with an unmarried partner, flirting or chatting with boys on social media such as Facebook and Twitter, or texting—or are victims of sexual assault or rape, they must rectify the dishonorable act. Too often, however, these dishonorable behaviors result in murder.

According to the UN Population Fund database (2000), 5,000 women and girls each year are victims of honor killings. This violence occurs around the world—from the poorest countries, such as Bangladesh, to some of the richest or progressive countries in Northern Europe—and the cases are similar. A 16-year-old was killed by her 24-year-old brother in Israel. She had moved out of the family home to live with her partner in the city. Though she returned upon her family's demand, her brother slashed her throat. He reported the crime to the police willingly, knowing it was a crime, but more important, he brought "honor" back to the family. An 18-year-old was killed by her father in Turkey. He, too, called the police to say he knew it was against the law but he did it willingly to clean his "honor." A Swedish court sentenced a 17-year-old to eight years prison for having stabbed his 19-year-old sister 107 times. She had fled from Iraq, where she was married against her will to an older man who beat and raped her.

Turkey has the greatest incidence of honor killing among its Kurdish population. The Kurds are the largest stateless minority in the world; 15 to 20 million live primarily in Iran, Iraq, Syria, and Turkey. Between 2000 and 2005, 1,091 Kurdish women were victims of HBV. Too often fathers, brothers, and uncles order the girls to kill themselves "to clean our shame or we will kill you first" (Bilefsky, 2006, para. 1). Because Turkey, like confirmed members of the European Union, has implemented harsh punishments for attacks on women and girls—including life imprisonment—parents are pressing their daughters to commit suicide. Girls are locked in their rooms with poison, guns, or ropes and left alone until they take their own lives. Sadly, at the same time the Turkish government is seeking membership in the European Union, the incidence of honor suicides is increasing.

HBV stands as an international human rights violation. It encompasses emotional, physical, and sexual abuse and financial control, and when women resist, they are murdered or forced into suicide. Members of the family and community collude in perpetuating the practice. Though

HBV is often ignored or dismissed as a cultural tradition, the UN General Assembly in 2002 adopted Resolution 57/179 to "[work] towards the elimination of crimes against women committed in the name of honour" and "raise awareness of the need to prevent and eliminate crimes against women committed in the name of honour, with the aim of changing the attitudes and behaviors that allow such crimes to be committed." (In 2004 the language was updated to include "girls.") Further, UN Secretary-General Kofi Annan demanded prompt, impartial, and full-scale investigations of "violence against women committed in the name of honour." He challenged that in "countries with immigrant communities, protection should be given to victims and potential victims in connection with asylum and immigration procedures" (UN News Centre, 2002, para. 10).

GENDER-BASED VIOLENCE IN EGYPT AND THE ARAB SPRING

The Arab Spring is the name given to the series of violent and non-violent protests that began in December 2010 and involved—directly or indirectly—the sweep of Arab nations from the northern Atlantic Ocean across North Africa along the Mediterranean and Red seas to the Arabian Sea. In particular, Tunis, Egypt, Libya, and Yemen anchored the revolution as citizens within these countries fought against the structural corruption embedded in their governments as well as demanding alternatives to dictatorship, unemployment, poverty, and human and women's rights. The presidents of the four countries were ousted. Though the trigger event occurred in Tunis in response to a young man's setting himself on fire after the police confiscated his fruit and vegetable cart for lack of a permit (NPR, 2012), mass protests spread quickly in many of the other Arab countries.

There was a call to protest in Egypt on January 25, 2011, using a Facebook page, "We are all Khalid Said," in response to Said's death from beating by the Egyptian security forces after his arrest in June 2010. Large numbers of Egyptians—Muslims, Christians, men, and women of all ages—protested against political corruption and demanded that President Mubarak step down. Women were prominent figures and leaders in the revolution, challenging corruption, poverty, unemployment, and restrictions on freedom of speech. In response, prior to Mubarak's resignation on February 11, 2011, the Mubarak regime used sexualized violence to try to prevent women from protesting: sexual harassment, and gang rape was common in Tahrir Square as well as other places in Egypt (Chiao , 2011; Kingsley, 2013) Women were arrested and subjected to "virginity tests." This violence continued under the Mohamed Morsi regime (February 2011 to July 2013).

Human Rights Watch (2013) reported the sexual violence epidemic in Egypt, challenging Egyptian officials and political leaders to condemn and stop the "horrific levels of sexual violence against women in Tahrir

Square" (para. 1). They posted a videotaped interview of several sexual assault survivors willing to speak publicly about their abuse. Each woman described the horror and intentionality of the rape and harassment in the Tahrir Square demonstrations (including their own). One woman said she was knocked to the ground, and for 90 minutes men ripped her clothes and nearly 100 men assaulted and raped her:

> At the height of the attack, I looked up and saw 30 individuals on a fence. All of them had smiling faces, and they were recording me with their cellphones. They saw a naked woman, covered in sewage, who was being assaulted and beaten, and I don't know what was funny about that. This is a question that I'm still thinking about, I can't stop my mind from thinking about it. (Human Rights Watch, 2013, para. 14)

Heba Morayef, the Egyptian director of Human Rights Watch, speculated that "impunity has led to a situation where the perpetrator feels that he won't be held accountable and also [has] led to a rise in these types of attacks" (Human Rights Watch, 2013, para. 18). Today sexual harassment is part of women's daily life on the Egyptian streets. When women and men in Cairo were interviewed about this claim, the women's consistent story was about the extreme level and number of harassments they individually encounter every day, and the men acknowledged that while it is probably not good, they believe the women made them do it: "From the way they dress, from the way they walk, everything; they push Egyptian men to do this!"

Human Rights Watch has documented the problem of assault on the streets, but the government's response has been negligent or worse, has exacerbated the situation. General Adel Afifi, a member of Egypt's legislative body, said this about the mob assaults in Tahrir: "Women contribute 100% in their rape because they put themselves in such circumstances" (Human Rights Watch, 2013).

SEX TOURISM AND HUMAN TRAFFICKING

Engaging in domestic and international travel to participate in nonreproductive sexual activity is the common definition of sex tourism. It is one of the most profitable sectors of the economy for developing nations and is particularly active in Southeast Asia and Latin America. In Asia it is the second largest source of foreign exchange (following crude oil), providing jobs for 50 million people (United Nations Office on Drugs and Crime, 2009a). The most common form of human trafficking is sexual exploitation (79 percent), followed by forced labor (18 percent), and women and girls make up the largest proportion of victims. Worldwide nearly 20 percent are children, but in some African countries and the Mekong region of southern Vietnam, nearly 100 percent are children (United Nations Office on Drugs and Crime, 2009a). The UN claims that sex tourism and human trafficking represent the third most prevalent criminal activity (following drug and arms sales), impacting 2 million victims globally and resulting in more than $30 billion in earnings annually (Laws.com).

The UN Office on Drugs and Crime (UNODC) submitted its latest Global Report on Trafficking in Persons in February 2009 and identified several important issues. The executive summary, titled *A Knowledge Crisis about a Crime That Shames Us All*, claims that *trafficking*—that is, the transaction of the crime—is too misleading a term and the practice should instead be labeled *enslavement* (United Nations Office on Drugs and Crime, 2009b, p. 1). Naming it modern-day slavery—clearly an international human rights violation—creates a different narrative from the current one of commodification of women as partners in the sex market exchange. Since UNODC's previous report, in April 2006, more people—including civilians and government leaders—are willing to mobilize forces against this crime but are unaware of its breadth and scope. More than 155 countries (double the previous number) are taking steps to implement the UN Protocol Against Trafficking in Persons, and the number of convictions is also increasing (United Nations Office on Drugs and Crime, 2009b, para. 6–7). It is perhaps not surprising, yet still disturbing, that the new data identify women as among the traffickers—many of them former victims. "Female offenders have a more prominent role in present-day slavery than in most other forms of crime" (United Nations Office on Drugs and Crime, 2009b, p. 1). The report chronicles the problems of gathering accurate data. For example, there are no multidimensional databases with logical categories established to differentiate the exploitation of child begging from the sex trade at a brothel or a father selling his underage daughter to those operating illegal immigrant sweat shops (p. 3).

In her research on the global nature of sex tourism, Tioseco (2008) claims that the gendered issues involve complex layers of social, economic, and legal asymmetries. The unevenness of access to education, health care, and alternative employment opportunities for women is especially persistent in poor countries. Further, the unique laws, policies, and economic histories of the host tourist countries exacerbate the problem. During the Vietnam War years (especially the 1960s), governments encouraged tourism by providing U.S. soldiers "rest and recreation services." These sexual service hubs evolved throughout the Philippines, Vietnam, and Thailand, and the buyers of such services included international citizens as well as those within the country or region.

Today the lack of serious enforcement within police codes of laws to monitor, regulate, and prosecute public and private establishments permits trafficking and tourism to thrive, and the globalization processes reinforce gender ideologies of women's participation in the workforce.

This is exacerbated by global access to social media, resulting in increased traffic by both veteran and first-time tourists. Links to such sites as the World Sex Guide (www.worldsexguide.com) allow tourists to share information, search for sex tourism, and market "package deals" allowing low-cost travel and access to brothels. Vitit Muntarbhorn, special rapporteur for the UN Secretary General on Child Prostitution and Trafficking, has stated, "We've focused a lot on supply issues. It's time we placed as much focus on demand" (Renton, 2005, para. 38). This is extraordinarily difficult when we are confronted with reports such as this one by an Englishman in Thailand:

They [Asian women] know how to make a man feel looked after. Squeezing the toothpaste on the brush so it's waiting for you when you go into the bathroom in the morning, that's what I call caring. How many women in England would do that? (Augustin, 2007, p. 83)

Renton acknowledges that

Thailand appears to have accepted its role as provider of sexual services to the rest of the planet. All that can be realistically asked is that it sets about doing it as cleanly and kindly as possible and that means tackling poverty in the rural north and corruption in the police force, as well as properly addressing the problem of the trafficked and the underage. (Renton, 2005, para. 39)

Around the world the lack of equitable exchange between the tourist and the sex worker contributes to this asymmetrical conflict. The continued demand for sex tourism reflects gender ideologies and embedded conceptions of gender roles, including male fantasies and idealization of women as submissive.

COMBATANTS AND CHILD SOLDIERS

The book *Women Waging War and Peace* (Cheldelin and Eliatamby, 2011) chronicles many ways in which gender is obvious (and not) during protracted violent conflict, especially in wartime. The dominant narrative is the story of women as victims of war—as mothers grieving for their missing or dead sons, as heads of households with lost husbands struggling to navigate traditional gendered roles within their cultures, and at the same time coping with other atrocities, including rape, torture, displacement, impairment, shame, humiliation, and even death. Men, of course, are responsible for much of this. Yet women have played key roles as combatants in very protracted wars, too.

In their research on wars in Eritrea, Nepal, Sri Lanka, and Chechnya, Eliatamby (2011) and Eliatamby and Romanova (2011) uncovered gendered differences specific to combatants. The popular notion that females become terrorists because of their psychological vulnerability or that they are coerced into suicide seems inadequate to explain the large number of willing female perpetrators. Eliatamby and Romanova (2011) conclude that the Sri Lankan Black Tigresses of Death and the Chechnyan Black Widows provide sufficient evidence to demonstrate that female terrorists are "victims and perpetrators trapped in the calculated logic of men's wars. . . . The structural violence embedded in the structure of terrorists groups, as well as society in general[,] positions women in subordinate roles" (pp. 62–63). They found that beyond the explanation of psychological vulnerabilities, women are willing to engage in suicide terrorism for other reasons. Some believe they will gain the elite, privileged status offered to families of suicide cadres. Others hold radical Islamic religious beliefs that allow them to offer their lives, or believe they need to fight against the presence of unwanted and unwelcome foreign forces. Persistent across cases are extreme socioeconomic challenges: life in poverty, lack of basic human needs, and lost husbands and families.

Graca Machel, former First Lady of Mozambique and South Africa, captures the horror of war for children: "War violates every right of a child— the right to life, the right to be with family and community, the right to health, the right to the development of the personality and the right to be nurtured ad protected" (United Nations Peacekeeping Issues, n.d., para. 2). For two decades war raged in northern Uganda, and tens of thousands were killed and 1.7 million uprooted and placed in internally displaced persons (IDP) camps. The documentary *Invisible Children* depicts many of the atrocities children were exposed to during their time in the Lord's Resistance Army (LRA). Children were kidnapped from their homes or IDP camps: boys abducted into rebel forces and girls as sex slaves or spies. Immediately after abduction, children were forced to kill or engage in other acts of atrocity, often against family members, to desensitize them to extreme violence. To gain respect from older members of the LRA they were forced to kill bystanders.

In her study of children in the protracted wars of Liberia and Sierra Leone, Maulden (2011) found that international agencies believe that 300,000 children serve in irregular military forces around the world as child soldiers (under 18), with an average age of 12. Child soldiering is significantly linked to life disadvantages, including "physical injury, sexual abuse, illness, infection, loss of education, trauma, feelings of guilt, fear of retribution, shame, stigmatization, and ostracism by family and community." However, child soldiering activities also provide children with "a sense of purpose, mission, or importance, gaining protection, inclusion, validation, respect, identity, skills and access to resources" (Maulden, 2011, p. 67).

Save the Children found that girls were more likely to be abducted into warfare activities as they walked down roads or worked in the fields.

Nearly half of all children engaged with arms are girls; an estimated 120,000 girls (as young as 8) were front-line fighters or supported armed groups (Save the Children, 2005, pp. iv–1). Girl soldiers are also referred to as the "shadow army" in their roles as cooks, sexual possessions, cleaners, and other less visible roles. Children—boys and girls—in all civil wars witness the tragedies of death, loss, and disruption in their families and their fractured communities. They learn early on that adults cannot protect them.

Credit must be given to UN Peacekeeping efforts in the establishment and implementation over the past 20 years of disarmament, demobilization, and reintegration (DDR) programs for child soldiers. Disarmament personnel collect, document, and dispose of guns, ammunition, and explosives from civilians. Demobilization services discharge all active combatants and provide short-term psychosocial assistance. Reintegration provides reentry support of children to civilian status to acquire sustainable income (United Nations Peacekeeping, *Disarmament*, n.d.).

At the end of many protracted wars, boy soldiers are offered DDR programs to disband their units and reintegrate them into their respective communities. Unfortunately, DDR programs are must less accessible to girl soldiers for a number of reasons. Most believe girls are not as violent or dangerous as former boy soldiers. There is also the dishonor girls have brought to their families, which makes them unwelcome in their communities. Two powerful books that chronicle the intricacies of daily life as a child soldier and the difficulties of reintegration are A *Long Way Gone: Memoirs of a Boy Soldier* (Beah, 2007), and *I, Nadia, Wife of a Terrorist* (Gacemi, 2006).

Although Save the Children demonstrates that "family and community are vital in ensuring children get the necessary help to reintegrate after conflict," the organization also acknowledges that when girls return to their homes after war they encounter ostracism and receive little psychosocial support. Girls remain isolated, emotionally and developmentally (United Nations Peacekeeping, *Disarmament*, n.d., p. 2). Girls need mediation efforts within their families and communities to help them reunify. They need access to education and training, medical care with special attention to reproductive health, as well as economic opportunities. These collective services for girls are absent in current DDR programs (United Nations Peacekeeping, *Disarmament*, n.d.).

RAPE AND WAR

The greatest threat to civilian women during conflict is rape and sexual violence by armed, uniformed state and nonstate forces and by civilians (Tesanovic, 2003). This is nothing new; the induction of Helen of Troy and the rape of the Sabine women are archetypal. "Victims of Rape and

Gendercide: All Wars" (Cheldelin, 2011) chronicles horrific stories around the world of the brutality—torture and mutilation—of gang rapes and intentional impregnation, and presents evidence that rape is now a strategic and tactical method of war. War rape is a mass rape that is a deliberate, state-sanctioned strategy of war to exterminate a race of people and is also known as genocide; the deliberate extermination of a particular sex or gender is known as gendercide (Cheldelin, 2011).

The data on rape from the UN Office for the Coordination of Humanitarian Affairs (OCHA) seem unbelievable. The overall number of rapes in Vietnam is unknown. In South Africa in the 1980s, 25,000 women were raped. During the Bosnia-Herzegovina war of 1992–1993, 20,000 to 70,000 were raped. In 1994, 250,000 women were raped in Rwanda (resulting in 2,500 to 10,000 pregnancies). In the first six months of the war in the Eastern Congo, 12,000 women were raped. Gendercide Watch Case Studies summarize 22 current and historical gendercide cases, including Armenia (1915–1917), the Jewish Holocaust (1933–1945), Nanjing (1937–1938), Stalin's many purges, Bangladesh (1971), the Kashmir/Punjab/Delhi massacre (1984), Bosnia-Herzegovina (1992–1995), Rwanda (1994), Srebrenica (1995), Kosovo (1998–1999), East Timor (1999), and Colombia (since 1948) (Gendercide Watch Case Studies , n.d.).

The most significant development in the rape disaster is the determination of rape to be a crime of war by the international community. To provide some history, on May 25, 1993, the United Nations approved the creation of the first International Criminal Tribunal for the Former Yugoslavia (ICTY). The only precedents for this course of action were the post–World War II international war crimes tribunals at Nuremberg and in the Far East, and these tribunals did not consider rape. In March 2000 the ICTY convened, and in July the Foca trial began, in which three Bosnian Serb paramilitary fighters were accused of rape of Muslim women and girls. (The trial took place in Foca, the town in Bosnia that was victim to the Serbs' mission to rid the district of its Muslims.) This was the first time prosecutors in The Hague attempted to place rape in the same category and punishable as an international war crime. A year later, in November 1994, the International Criminal Tribunal for Rwanda (ICTR) was convened to respond to those responsible for the Rwandan genocide in 1994. Scheffer notes that these two ad hoc criminal tribunals changed the course of history and war: rape and sexual violence are now categorized as tactics of genocide and individual crimes against humanity (Scheffer, 1999).

GENDER, ROLES, AND PEACE EFFORTS

The greatest change toward ending wars and brokering and sustaining peace efforts is reflected in the work of women (see Chapter 31 in Volume 2). For more than a decade now the agenda of gender empowerment and equality have been critical variables in local, regional, and international post-conflict reconstruction and peace building efforts. In fact, we know that without such an agenda the sustainability of peace is less likely. In 2000 the United Nations gave powerful credence to this agenda by issuing the now famous Security Council Resolution 1325, calling for the inclusion of women in all aspects of peace building—from grassroots initiatives to national decision making authority. Evidence of women's efforts is global, and ways women embrace various roles permit them a wide range of influence. What follows are a few examples of ways women have used roles as mothers and wives to stop or intervene in violence, and as mainstreamed decision makers to engage in sustainable peace efforts.

"Mothers" are rarely perceived as a threat to military or governmental leaders or to dictators; mothers take care of families in the community. During the late 1970s Argentina was led by a brutal military dictatorship, with extreme internal turmoil ultimately leading to the Dirty War, which continued for seven years (1976–1983). Fourteen mothers joined together to find their missing children, believing the government had abducted them. In 1977 these women formed the Madres de la Plaza de Mayo (Mothers of the Plaza) and demonstrated in the main square of Buenos Aires, in front of the presidential palace. Hundreds of women joined the Madres for weekly demonstrations. The same year an offshoot of this group created a human rights organization—the Asociacion Civil Abuelas de Plaza de Mayo, or Grandmothers of the Plaza—and this was the beginning of a national human rights movement to find abducted grandchildren (along with their parents) as well as grandchildren abducted or born in captivity. The Madres and Abuelas were key agents in stopping the war and since then in seeking resolutions to the injustices and human rights violations that occurred during the war. An excellent account of this movement is available online by Lester Kurtz (2010).

Fifteen years into the quarter-century long war in Sri Lanka, Visaka Dharmadasa initiated a grassroots effort that ultimately played a key role in brokering dialogue and building peace between the Sri Lankan government and the Liberation Tigers of Tamil Eelam (LTTE). Her leadership is chronicled by Eliatamby (2011). Her son had joined the Sri Lankan Army (SLA) only three months before the deadly attack by the LTTE in the Northern Province at Kilonochchi in 1998. He had not yet received his identification tag, and he was unaccounted for after the attack. Ultimately the SLA could not determine if he was dead. Dharmadasa organized a group of mothers with missing sons and created the Association of Parents of Servicemen Missing in Action (PSMIA), with three goals: "1) take all necessary steps to find out the fate of those MIA; 2) secure the release of all detainees; and 3) prevent such problems by bringing peace to the country" (Eliatamby, 2011, p. 86). There were profound bureaucratic challenges and roadblocks associated with each initiative, yet their persistent and creative grassroots tactics toward brokering peace proved successful and demonstrated the critical role of community-driven efforts. By 2007 two organizations—PSMIA and later the Association for War-Affected Women (AWAW)—were 12,000 women strong, representing both Sinhalese and Tamil women who had lost children or other family as result of the war.

In Liberia, by the end of the two civil wars (1989—1996 and 1999—2003) between the government and rebel fighters, women had witnessed or been victims to rape, loss of children and other family, displacement, and other atrocities brought on by the protracted violence. Women seized the opportunity to stop the war and became catalysts in the reconstruction of their broken country. They created a loose global network of peacemakers, Women of Liberia Mass Action for Peace (WIPNET), and engaged a number of initiatives, including the Women of Liberia Mass Action for Peace Campaign. The documentary *Pray the Devil Back to Hell* chronicles some of the women's activities. By means of word-of-mouth and radio, they invited urban and rural women, dressed in all white, to the fish market to pray, sing, and demand peace. With national and international news coverage they forced the government to meet with rebel groups, and to continue meeting when the peace efforts broke down (threatening to undress in front of international news cameras) until an agreement was signed. Later they were instrumental in the selection of Ellen Johnson Sirleaf as a presidential candidate and actively engaged in her successful election campaign. WIPNET has been instrumental in changing the roles of women in Liberia—and since then has expanded its efforts to Sierra Leone and Nigeria—with the "broad goal to elevate women from their state of obscurity to the fore to enable them to play roles alongside men in building peace" (Global Network of Women Peacebuilders, n.d., para. 1).

Since the end of the violence in 2003 in Liberia, the UN has established one of the largest peacekeeping operations, including DDR programming for former child soldiers, supporting democratic elections, and providing on-the-ground security forces. Women's empowerment has been a primary agenda for President Ellen Johnson Sirleaf (the first woman Liberian president and first woman African president). She created the Ministry of Gender as a new unit of her cabinet and uses her bully pulpit to advocate for women involved in civil society initiatives. In 2005 her national government established the Truth and Reconciliation Commission (TRC) to investigate crimes during the war. Liberia's Truth Commission "Opens" involved UN-trained interviewers around the country to investigate alleged human rights violations. The TRC Final Report stated in its Mandate (II, Section 4) that TRC would "investigate gross human rights violations and violations of international humanitarian law as well as abuses that occurred, including massacres, sexual violations, murder, [and] extrajudicial killings" (Republic of Liberia Truth and Reconciliation Commission, 2008, p. 18). The report found that nearly 30 percent of reported violations were against women (26,000) and that women "disproportion-ately suffered from sexual violence including gang rape, sexual slavery, outrages upon personal dignity, and torture, among others" (Republic of Liberia Truth and Reconciliation Commission, 2008, pp. 44–45). These vio-lations against women were documented with "thousands of heart break-ing narratives about how they were brutalized during armed conflict" (Republic of Liberia Truth and Reconciliation Commission, 2008, p. 44).

Women have created, participated in, and led many nongovernmental organizations (NGOs) such as WIPNET and the West Africa Network for Peacebuilding (WANEP) to promote peaceful and sustainable commu-nities. WANEP, the largest regional peace building network in western Africa, states its vision to be "where the dignity of the human person is paramount and where the people can meet their basic human needs and decide their own direction" (WANEP, n.d., para. 1).

GENDER EMPOWERMENT

Some of the most current research related to the outcomes of recent poli-cies on gender and empowerment will be available soon in *Deconstruct-ing Women, Peace and Security: A Critical Review of Approaches to Gender and Empowerment* (Cheldelin and Mutisi, 2015 forthcoming). It is clear that while gender and women's empowerment efforts have been at the policy-making forefront during the past two decades, implementation practices, on the ground, remain uneven.

Natukunda-Togboa studied mainstreaming practices in Burundi, South Sudan and Uganda, where governments have openly ratified mechanisms to ensure critical masses of women's representation in pre- and post-conflict decision making settings. She makes a case that in African tradi-tional societies women are assigned the role of "educator" of their children and that peace building is part of children's upbringing through stories, songs, and proverbs, handed down through generations and directed by the mother (or mother figure in her absence). Moreover, indigenous approaches to peacemaking reflect core African values—patience, toler-ance, honesty, respect for elders, community, mutuality, and compassion, to list just a few (Natukunda-Togboa, 2015 forthcoming). Unfortunately, these same traditions have not always promoted gender equality in the largely patriarchal African societies. She identifies the tension as a "public versus private" domain of authority:

[C]onflict and peace are located in the public space with [a] high degree of mas-culinization. This explains the glaring disparity between the woman's critical role as the pillar which binds the family together during the conflict and in the com-munity's post-conflict survival and her marginalization as the traditional agent of peace when it comes to peace processes. (Natukunda-Togboa, 2015 forthcoming)

While it is important that policies combine the best traditions with progressive modern standards to protect women's rights, Natukunda-Togboa thinks this combination has yet to be realized.

Mutisi researched the outcomes of quota policies currently practiced in eight countries: Kenya, Rwanda, Somalia, South Sudan, Uganda, South Africa, Mozambique, and Zimbabwe. The principle of quota policies and current practices are impressive on paper, but Mutisi found that the intended quota policy goals are undermined by lack of attention to other structural barriers to women's empowerment. Women must navigate patriarchal attitudes, competitive (sometimes violent) political environments, and unsupportive electoral systems. For quotas to be successful there must be parallel capacity-building activities and a strong movement to mobilize changes in attitudes and behaviors in the political arena. Regional organizations responsible for quota setting, monitoring, and evaluation need to engage in concerted efforts toward legal reforms for gender empowerment to be successful (Mutisi, 2015 forthcoming).

Eliatamby found that postwar programs such as the popular UN-sanctioned DDR processes are fraught with challenges in Sri Lanka and Nepal. As discussed previously in this chapter, the lack of DDR resources for girls and women exacerbates the already troubling reintegration problems girls face as they return to their communities in these countries (Eliatambi, 2015 forthcoming).

DISCUSSION

This chapter has identified three broad topics related to what we know about gender: the tenacity of our social construction of gendered roles, the complexity and breadth of gender-based violence (GBV), and the gendered aspects of peacemaking and intervention activities. The dominant narrative, that women have one paramount role in the story of war—overwhelmingly as the victim, must be changed. Without doubt, women and children are adversely affected by war and its aftermath, but this narrative has limitations and misconceptions, chief among them being the idea that men are spared victimhood and it is limited to women. Men, especially civilians, are overwhelmingly the casualties of mass genocides. Take, for example, the systematic ways the Pakistani Army, in response to the Bengali bid for independence, rid the country of boys and men who could, one day, become freedom fighters. The prevailing narrative also ignores how women's lives change as a result of war and other traumatic experiences, and how women have forged creative strategies to survive those situations. It dismisses the evidence we have of women's capacity of agency, of adopting new roles that transform gender dynamics in the societies from which they come.

Thousands of women join armed groups as combatants, for many reasons. In Eritrea, women and men fought shoulder-to-shoulder against the Ethiopian occupation of their country. Women believed they could (and did) prove their worth on the battlefield to achieve some semblance of equality following the war. By the end of the 30-year war, women constituted 30 percent of the army. The quality of women's lives after the war did change; so did their society. Women became legal owners of property, large tracts of land were redistributed to the landless and poor peasants, and women were given land in equal share to that of men. Polygamy was officially abolished and compulsory marriage was deemed illegal. Women could divorce and the laws would protect them. Women are changed when they become combatants. Some give their lives for the great cause (e.g., Black Widows and Tigresses). Some produce munitions or otherwise support war efforts. Some choose to be catalysts for societal changes.

Rape during war is a crime against humanity. Profound legal decisions, especially from the UN, have made a difference. UN Resolution 1325 reaffirms the important role of women in the prevention and resolution of conflicts, and stresses equal participation in all efforts to promote peace and security. It gives international political recognition that women and gender are relevant to international peace and security efforts and sustainability. It is the first directive to call for women's direct engagement in conflict resolution, peace building processes, and legislative decision making. To change the dominant narrative, legal structures are essential. The key is to have international laws with international consequences. While laws are now in place to convict perpetrators, women must testify, sign indictments, and deal with the family and community fallout. If they admit they have been victim to rape, they may not be able to protect their children from rape or suffering social stigmas.

It is unreasonable to believe that all member states will take it up as a priority just because the UN declares that we must put an end to gender and human rights violations. GBV and sustainable peacekeeping efforts need vigilant attention by academics, practitioners, NGOs, and the like to place pressure on leaders and policy makers, charging them with the responsibility for and accountability of supporting local and national agendas to prevent violence.

Research on gender and conflict has identified a number of lessons to be learned and corrective actions implemented. Yamin (2011) provides an extensive list of what to do. Among the measures, local, national, and international communities must promote education for girls and women from primary school through higher education. After all, if you teach women to read, more than 98 percent will teach their own children to read. Such an effort will stop illiteracy in a generation or two. It is also likely to result in greater economic independence for women and increase their participation in public life. Education of boys and men about mitigating violence is essential, too. Mechanisms and legislation for women's involvement should be promoted in the public domain—governmental decision making, access to employment opportunities in all professions, equal pay, and access to public support networks and systems. Development agendas must be changed to reach out to women where violence exists, including rural areas, to provide economic opportunities and promote mechanisms that give women a voice in politics and governance. During the Occupy Wall Street movement in the United States, people joined because they were aligned by consciousness, not by nation-state, religion, or local boundaries. Perhaps the lesson for change is to build on women's (and men's) demands for a peaceful life, a sustainable future, economic justice, and basic democracy. There is much we do know about gender and conflict. There is still much to do.

BIBLIOGRAPHY

Augustin, Laura Maria. 2007. *Sex at the Margins: Migration, Labour Markets and the Rescue Industry*. London: Zed Books.

Beah, Ishmael. 2007. *A Long Way Gone: Memoirs of a Boy Soldier*. New York: Sarah Crichton Books.

Berger, Peter, and Thomas Luckmann. 1966. *The Social Construction of Reality*. Garden City, NY: Doubleday.

Bilefsky, Dan. 2006. How to Avoid Honor Killing in Turkey? Honor Suicide. *New York Times Europe*, http://www.nytimes.com/2006/07/16/world/europe/16turkey.html?pagewanted=all&_r=0 (accessed January 25, 2014).

Catalano, Shannan. 2012, November. U.S. Department of Justice, Office of Justice Programs, Bureau of Justice Statistics Special Report, "Intimate Partner Violence, 1993–2010." NCJ239203, http://www.bjs.gov/content/pub/pdf/ipv9310.pdf (accessed January 21, 2014).

Cheldelin, Sandra. 2011. Victims of Rape and Gendercide: All Wars. In *Women Waging War and Peace: International Perspectives on Women's Roles in Conflict and Post-Conflict Reconstruction*, edited by Sandra Cheldelin and Maneshka Eliatamby. New York: Continuum International Publishing, pp. 12–34.

Cheldelin, Sandra I., and Ann F. Lucas. 2004. *An Academic Administrator's Guide to Conflict Resolution*. San Francisco: Jossey-Bass.

Cheldelin, Sandra I., and Maneshka Eliatamby, eds. 2011. *Women Waging War and Peace: International Perspectives on Women's Roles in Conflict and Post-Conflict Reconstruction*. New York: Continuum International Publishing.

Cheldelin, Sandra I., and Martha Mutisi, eds. 2015 Forthcoming. *Deconstructing Women, Peace and Security: A Critical Review of Approaches to Gender and Empowerment*. Pretoria, South Africa: HSRC.

Chesler, Phyllis. 2001. *Woman's Inhumanity to Woman*. Hudson, NY: Plume.

Chiao, Rebecca. 2011, February 28. Calling Out the Catcallers. *Johns Hopkins Magazine*, http://archive.magazine.jhu.edu/2011/02/calling-out-the-catcallers/ (accessed March 26, 2014).

Crawford, Mary. 1995. *Talking Difference: On Gender and Language*. Thousand Oaks, CA: Sage.

De Beauvoir, Simone. 1989 [1949]. *The Second Sex*. Trans. H. M. Parshley. New York: Vintage Books.

Eliatamby, Maneshka. 2011. Challenging Warfare: Sri Lanka. In *Women Waging War and Peace: International Perspectives on Women's Roles in Conflict and Post-Conflict Reconstruction*, edited by Sandra Cheldelin and Maneshka Eliatamby. New York: Continuum, pp. 85–98.

Eliatamby, Maneshka. 2015 forthcoming. Women's Lives after Warfare: Disarmament, Mobilization, Rehabilitation and Reintegration of Female Combatants in Nepal and Sri Lanka. In *Deconstructing Women, Peace and Security: A Critical Review of Approaches to Gender and Empowerment*, edited by Sandra I. Cheldelin and Martha Mutisi. Pretoria: HRSC.

Eliatamby, Maneshka, and Ekaterina Romanova. 2011. Dying for Identity: Chechnya and Sri Lanka. In *Women Waging War and Peace: International Perspectives on Women's Roles in Conflict and Post-Conflict Reconstruction*, edited by Sandra Cheldelin and Maneshka Eliatamby. New York: Continuum, pp. 52–65.

Gacemi, Baya. 2006. *I, Nadia, Wife of a Terrorist*. Lincoln: University of Nebraska Press.

Gendercide Watch Case Studies. n.d. http://www.gendercide.org/case.html (accessed February 28, 2014).

Gill, Aisha. 2012, February 1. "Honour"-Based Violence Runs Deep and Wide. *Guardian*, http://www.theguardian.com/commentisfree/2012/feb/01/honour-based-violence-deep-wide (accessed January 25, 2014).

Global Network of Women Peacebuilders (GNWP). n.d. http://www.gnwp.org/members/wipnet, para. 1 (accessed February 28, 2014).

Hart, S. N., and M. R. Brassard. 1990. A Psychological Maltreatment of Children. In *Treatment of Family Violence: A Sourcebook*, edited by R. T. Ammerman and M. Hersen. Somerset, NJ: John Wiley and Sons.

Hines, Denise, Jan Brown, and Edward Dunning. 2007. *Characteristics of Callers to the Domestic Abuse Helpline for Men*. Springer Science, Business Media (published online).

Human Rights Watch. 2013, July 3. Egypt: Epidemic of Sexual Violence: At Least 91 Attacks in 4 Days; Government Neglect Means Impunity Rules. http://www.hrw.org/news/2013/07/03/egypt-epidemic-sexual-violence (videotaped interview, accessed January 22, 2014).

Kingsley, Patrick. 2013, July 5. 80 Sexual Assaults in One Day—the Other Story of Tahrir Square. http://www.theguardian.com/world/2013/jul/05/egypt-women-rape-sexual-assault-tahrir-square (accessed March 26, 2014).

Kurtz, Lester. 2010. The Mothers of the Disappeared: Challenging the Junta in Argentina (1977–1983). International Center on Nonviolent Conflict, http://nonviolent-conflict.org/index.php/movements-and-campaigns/movements-and-campaigns-summaries?sobi2Task=sobi2Details&sobi2Id=28 (accessed March 26, 2014).

Laws.com. n.d. 4 Facts That You Need to Know about Sex Tourism. http://sex-crimes.laws.com/prostitution/4-facts-that-you-need-to-know-about-sex-tourism (accessed February 22, 2014).

Marshall, Gordon. 1994. *The Concise Oxford Dictionary of Sociology*. Oxford: Oxford University Press.

Maulden, Patricia. 2011. Fighting Young: Liberia and Sierra Leone. In *Women Waging War and Peace: International Perspectives on Women's Roles in Conflict and Post-Conflict Reconstruction*, edited by Sandra Cheldelin and Maneshka Eliatamby. New York: Continuum, pp. 66–79.

McCandless, Erin, and Necla Tschirgi. 2010. Strategic Frameworks That Embrace Mutual Accountability for Peacebuilding: Emerging Lessons in PBC and Non-PBC Countries. *Journal of Peacebuilding and Development* 5 (2): 20–46.

Merriam-Webster dictionary. n.d. http://www.merriam-webster.com/dictionary/gender (accessed January 17, 2014).

Murithi, T. 2006. African Approaches to Building Peace and Social Solidarity. *African Journal on Conflict Resolution* (ACCORD publication) 6 (2).

Mutisi, Martha. 2015 forthcoming. Add Women and Stir: Implications of Gender Quotas. In *Deconstructing Women, Peace and Security: A Critical Review of Approaches to Gender and Empowerment*, edited by Sandra I. Cheldelin and Martha Mutisi. Pretoria, South Africa: HSRC.

Natukunda-Togboa, Edith Ruth. 2015 forthcoming. Regional, National and NGO Discourse Bringing Women into Peace Processes: Lessons from Burundi, South Sudan and Uganda. In *Deconstructing Women, Peace and Security: A Critical Review of Approaches to Gender and Empowerment*, edited by Sandra I. Cheldelin and Martha Mutisi. Pretoria, South Africa: HSRC.

NPR. 2012. Timeline: The Major Events of the Arab Spring, http://www.npr.org/2012/01/02/144489844/timeline-the-major-events-of-the-arab-spring (accessed January 22, 2014).

Renton, Alex. 2005, May 21. *Learning the Thai Sex Trade*, http://www.prospect magazine.co.uk/magazine/learningthethaisextrade/#.UwzNN3kvMTs (accessed February 24, 2014).

Republic of Liberia Truth and Reconciliation Commission. 2008. Volume 1: Preliminary Findings and Determinations, http://trcofliberia.org/resources/reports/final/volume-one_layout-1.pdf, p. 18 (accessed February 25, 2014).

Save the Children. 2005. Forgotten Casualties of War, http://reliefweb.int/sites/reliefweb.int/files/resources/F15963BA5348938DC1256FEE003EC2B1-SCF_apr_2005.pdf (accessed February 25, 2014).

Schechter, S. 1982. *Women and Male Violence: The Visions and Struggle of the Battered Women's Movement*. Boston: Southbend Press.

Scheffer, David J. 1999, October 29. Rape as a War Crime: Ambassador-at-Large for War Crimes Issues Remarks at Fordham University, New York, http://www.converge.org.nz/pma/arape.htm (accessed February 25, 2014).

Schneider, Andrea Kupfer, Catherine H. Tinsley, Sandra I. Cheldelin, and Emily T. Amanatullah. 2010. Likeability v. Competence: The Impossible Choice Faced by Female Politicians, Attenuated by Lawyers. *Duke Journal of Gender Law and Policy* 17 (2) (Marquette University Law School Legal Studies Research Paper Series, Research Paper No. 42).

Stop Violence Against Women: A Project of the Advocates for Human Rights. 2013a, August. Prevalence of Domestic Violence, http://www.stopvaw.org/prevalence_of_domestic_violence (accessed January 21, 2014).

Stop Violence Against Women: A Project of the Advocates for Human Rights. 2013b, August. Evolution of Theories of Violence, http://www.stopvaw.org/Evolution_of_Theories_of_Violence (accessed January 22, 2014).

Tesanovic, Jasmine. 2003. Women and Conflict: A Serbian Perspective. In *Women on War: An International Anthology of Writings from Antiquity to the Present*, edited by Daniela Gloseffi. New York: Feminist Press at the City University of New York.

Tinsley, Catherine H., Sandra I. Cheldelin, Andrea Kupfer Schneider, and Emily T. Amanatullah. 2009. Negotiating Your Public Identity: Women's Path to Power. In *Rethinking Negotiation Teaching: Innovations for Context and Culture*, edited by C. Honeyman, J. Coben, and G. DePalo. St. Paul, MN: Dispute Resolution Press, Hamline University School of Law.

Tioseco, Stephanie. 2008, November 18. Sex Tourism: A Gendered Perspective on the Global Economy. Unpublished research paper (available by contacting Sandra Cheldelin).

United Nations News Centre. 2002, August 7. Violence against Women in the Name of Honour Should Be Criminalized—UN Report, http://www.un.org/apps/news/story.asp?NewsID=4391 (accessed January 25, 2014).

United Nations Office on Drugs and Crime (UNODC). n.d. Trafficking in Persons, http://www.unodc.org/documents/data-and-analysis/tocta/2.Trafficking_in_persons.pdf (accessed March 31, 2014).

United Nations Office of Drugs and Crime (UNODC). 2009a, February. Report on Human Trafficking Exposes Modern Form of Slavery, https://www.unodc.org/unodc/en/human-trafficking/global-report-on-trafficking-in-persons.html (accessed February 23, 2013).

United Nations Office of Drugs and Crime (UNODC). 2009b, February. Global Report on Trafficking in Persons Executive Summary, https://www.unodc.org/documents/human-trafficking/Executive_summary_english.pdf (accessed February 23, 2013).

United Nations Peacekeeping. n.d. Children in Conflict: UN Peacekeeping Issues, http://www.un.org/en/peacekeeping/issues/children/index.shtml (accessed February 28, 2014).

United Nations Peacekeeping. n.d. Disarmament, Demobilization and Reintegration, http://www.un.org/en/peacekeeping/issues/ddr.shtml (accessed February 28, 2014).

United Nations Population Fund. 2000. *The State of World Population 2000: Lives Together, Worlds Apart, Men and Women in a Time of Change,* Chapter 3, "Ending Violence Against Women and Girls: A Human Rights and Health Priority," p. 29, http://www.unfpa.org/sites/default/files/pub-pdf/swp2000_eng.pdf (accessed February 17, 2015).

West African Network for Peacebuilding (WANEP). n.d. Mission and Vision, http://www.wanep.org/wanep/index.php?option=com_content&view=category&layout=blog&id=2&Itemid=14 (accessed February 28, 2014).

World Health Organization. 2013. Global and Regional Estimates of Violence against Women: Prevalence and Health Effects of Intimate Partner Violence and Non-Partner Sexual Violence: Executive Summary, apps.who.int/iris/

bitstream/10665/85239/1/9789241564625_eng.pdf (accessed February 21, 2014).

Yamin, Saira. 2011. Challenging Patriarchy: Pakistan, Egypt, and Turkey. In *Women Waging War and Peace: International Perspectives on Women's Roles in Conflict and Post-Conflict Reconstruction,* edited by Sandra Cheldelin and Maneshka Eliatamby. New York: Continuum, pp. 235–258.

CHAPTER 3

Gendering Vulnerability: Are Women Victims of Systemic Violence?

Mariam M. Kurtz

Vulnerability is gendered. That is, women are more vulnerable to all kinds of violence and tragedies around the world than are men. This phenomenon is primarily a result of the patriarchal systems of social organization that empower men and make women subject to direct, cultural, and structural violence. This chapter focuses on the causes and consequences of that gendering process. As Mary Crawford argues, "gender" is a social construct, that is, "a system of meaning that organizes interaction and governs access to power and resources." Consequently, "gender is not attribute of individuals but a way of making sense of transaction. Gender exists not in person but in transaction; it is conceptualized as a verb not a noun" (Crawford, 1995, p. 12). To "gender" something is a complex social process, and to understand violence against women, it is helpful to explore how vulnerability to violence becomes gendered and institutionalized.

Johan Galtung (1969) calls the harm that is done to people because of the nature of social structures "structural violence." This type of violence interacts with and helps to create both the cultural violence that harms people by demeaning the value of certain social groups, societies, and even civilizations, and the direct violence that we usually associate with the term. Women are generally more subject to all three types of violence than are men. The structure of patriarchal culture leads women to become victims more often than men even though women themselves sometimes perpetuate the violence (see Chapter 27 in Volume 2). It makes women more vulnerable by giving power to the men in a society while devaluing its women, making them a disadvantaged group. Patriarchy, according to Sylvia Walby (1990, p. 20), is "a system of social structures and practices in which men dominate, oppress, and exploit women." It is, Walby contends, "composed of six structures: the patriarchal mode of production," male violence, and patriarchal relations in paid work, the state, sexuality and cultural institutions (ibid.).

"In patriarchy," Taylor and Miller (1994, p. 13) contend, "women are disadvantaged because they are less valued and/or less powerful than men." Social structures in a patriarchal society are shaped by this cultural norm demeaning women and are characterized by the marginalization of women within their kinship collectives, as well as the marginalization of the men of those collectives over which dominance has been established. As Crawford (1995) argues, gendering processes influence behavior, thought, and feeling in individuals; they affect interactions among individuals; and they help to determine the structure of social institutions.

GENDERING VULNERABILITY TO STRUCTURAL AND CULTURAL VIOLENCE

The Global Gender Gap Report (Schwab et al., 2013), which measures gender-based disparities in countries around the world, demonstrates that the gap between women and men is narrow in some nations and much broader in others. We can say that the extent to which vulnerability to structural violence is gendered varies from culture to culture, nation to nation, and situation to situation (Schwab et al., 2013). North America and Europe have narrowed the gap by about 70 percent. In Latin America and Eastern Europe it has been reduced by 67 percent, in sub-Sahara Africa by 64 percent, and by 58 percent in the Middle East and North Africa using four parameters to measure the magnitude of the gap: economic participation, education attainment, political empowerment, and health and survival (cf. Leatherman, 2011, p. 68). Where the gender gap is larger, women's vulnerability is even more pronounced and we can say the culture is more thoroughly gendered.

For more effective comparison across regional and income groups over time, the Global Gender Gap Index benchmarks national gender gaps in terms of economic, political, education and health variables:

There are three basic concepts underlying the Global Gender Gap Index. First, it focuses on measuring gaps rather than levels. Second, it captures gaps in outcome variables rather than gaps in means or input variables. Third, it ranks countries according to gender equality rather than women's empowerment.

Gaps versus levels. Because each country is different, the index is designed to measure gender-based gaps based on people's access to resources and opportunities and not the actual levels of the available resources and opportunities found in those countries. The index is constructed to rank countries on their gender gaps, not on their development levels. Second, the index ranks countries according to their proximity to gender equality rather than to women's empowerment. For example, several decades ago Nordic countries reached 99–100 percent literacy and demonstrated gender equality in their primary and secondary levels of education. They are also among the top 25 countries in economic participation and opportunity subindex. They have the highest rate of women participation in the labor force, and salary gaps between women and men are among the lowest in the world. The opportunities available to women from these countries support their rise to leadership positions (Schwab et al., 2013).

Judith Butler, in *Gender Trouble* (2008, p.12), notes that viewing the notion of patriarchy as a universal concept can be a problem, however, because it could override or limit significant articulations of gender asymmetry in different cultural contexts. Universalizing the patriarch would lead to failure to identify other gender oppressions in particular contexts. That approach, Butler (2008, p. 5) argues, has been criticized as an effort

to colonize and appropriate non-Western cultures to support highly Western notions of oppression, but . . . they tend as well to construct a "Third World" or even an "Orient" in which gender oppression is subtly explained as symptomatic of an essential, non-Western barbarism.

Nonetheless, patriarchal culture is widespread and is very pronounced in some countries and more subtle in others. Sometimes the culture of the more patriarchal societies encourages women to engage in violence themselves, justifying their acts as important to their liberation from being victims but ironically increasing the levels of violence in their social environment and thus increasing their own vulnerability. For example, the lack of education among women makes them more vulnerable to terrorist recruitment. The Black Widows in Chechnya and the Black Tigresses in Sri Lanka (see Jacques and Taylor, 2012; Pape, 2005) are claimed by some to demonstrate women's ignorance and susceptibility to "brainwashing." Inadequate education for women also increases their unemployment, producing economic hardship that would force some of these women to make a living through terrorism, which could also be perceived as a way to restore their identities (see Jacques and Taylor, 2012; Atran, 2003) Thus, women sometimes become perpetrators as well as victims of violence, thinking that they are somehow more powerful and placing themselves more directly in harm's way. For example, the 2000 Protocol to Prevent, Suppress and Punish Trafficking in Persons confirms that women and children are the most vulnerable to trafficking in human beings (THB). In the "global industry" the more than US$32 billion annual gain is generated mainly by men and the majority of offenders are men, but nonetheless women constitute a high proportion of the traffickers in women and girls for sexual exploitation (see Chapter 33 in Volume 2).

These structural conditions often lead to what Richard Rubenstein (1999, p. 173) calls a "structural conflict," the product of a patterned social relationship that fails to satisfy the basic needs or secure the vital interests of one or both parties. When women are denied their basic needs more frequently than men, their vulnerability is gendered. Their suffering and victimization are gendered as well.

A similar source of gendered vulnerability is what Leatherman (2011) calls "hegemonic masculinity," that is, a male-centered order that gives men, instead of women, primary access to power and privilege. It also organizes power relations between women and men and creates a political agenda that is sustained in a hierarchy defined by a successful claim of authority based on the use of direct violence. "Allied masculinities are empowered, while subordinates and marginalized masculinities are ostracized or exploited along with womanhood and femininity" (Leatherman, 2011, p. 18). For Foucault (1987, p. 26), "the power exercised on the body is conceived not as a property but as strategy, [and] its effect[s] of domination are attributed not to 'appropriation,' but to dispositions, manoeuvres, tactics, techniques, functioning." Power is not simply a " 'privilege,' acquired or preserved, of the dominant class" (Foucault, p. 26), which in a patriarchal system means the men. Of course, as Patricia Hill Collins (2000) and others have shown, the gender aspect of stratified systems intersects with race and class, so that women of color who do not have a privileged socioeconomic status are the most vulnerable.

Women's vulnerability is sustained by rituals of privilege—from systematic discrimination to demeaning everyday talk—and backed up by direct violence when women fail to comply. When power is exercised to the detriment of women, it results in various kinds of systemic violence. Galtung (1990) argues, for example, that even threats such as unsatisfied human needs for a certain group could also be violence. The denial of basic human needs, for example, could lead to both *direct* and *structural violence*. Galtung categorizes basic human needs as *survival needs* (negation, misery, morbidity), *identity, meaning needs* (negation, alienation), and *freedom needs* (negation, repression). He draws a distinction between direct violence and structural violence by highlighting consequences of the failure to satisfy basic human needs as a way of killing, maiming, siege, sanctions, misery, decolonization, resocialization, repression, detention, and expulsion. Exploitation treats others as secondary citizens; penetration, segmentation, marginalization, and fragmentation thus create structural violence. Again and again, women suffer from these types of violence more than men because of their exclusion from power in public life and their systematic denial of opportunity and resources.

In his 1969 essay Galtung (p. 171) observes, "If people are starving when this is objectively avoidable, then violence is committed. . . . Thus, when one husband beats his wife there is a clear case of personal violence, but when one million husbands keep one million wives in ignorance there is structural violence."

Galtung describes the absence of both structural and direct violence as positive peace, where there is a "pattern of cooperation and integration between major human groups." Positive peace is thus a characteristic of social justice, which is defined as a condition where there is an egalitarian distribution of power and resources. Structural violence does not prevent social change but makes it difficult to accomplish (Galtung, 1969). Systemic violence is a broad umbrella concept referring to all three types of violence identified by Galtung as they are generated by a social system; it occurs whenever people are marginalized in obtaining political, legal, and economic systems or cultural traditions (see Rubenstein 1999). When these structures of inequities have been long-standing in a society, they come to be viewed as ordinary or even natural; this is the way things are and always have been. Women's vulnerability is a result of a process by which it is gendered, given meaning by a way of viewing the world and the place of women in it that privileges men and demeans women. It is caused by the systemic violence that exists in many patriarchal societies in which structures are constructed to marginalize women and cultures legitimate the inequality by presenting it as somehow natural. Crawford (1995, p. 13) contends that gender is "a system of power relations." Consequently, men have more public power in most societies, controlling government, law, public discourse, and academics." In those cultures, and even many others where patriarchy is formally gone but exists beneath the surface, women are assigned to the private sphere while men are associated with the public sphere where decisions are made about the distribution of resources. The process I call "gendering vulnerability" thus results in the unequal distribution of vulnerability to all kinds of systemic violence (see Chapter 4 in this volume).

According to Galtung (1990), social differentiation emerges and brings or increases inequality; those in power will then be looking for ways to maintain the system that benefits them, and cultural violence will be used to justify acts of structural and direct violence against women. Structural violence often leads to direct violence and vice versa (Winter and Leighton, 2001).

It is the structural problem of the hierarchical system in patriarchy that gives men power to dominate women while at the same time devaluing the feminine—female and female-identified values, behaviors, or objects (Taylor and Miller, 1994, p. 13). A patriarchal system gives men control through male dominance or male-identified dominators, which is backed by force (direct violence) when needed. Cheldelin (2011, p. 29) notes that in a patriarchal system women are valued "most for their reproductive identity and virginity." Therefore, "rape in wartime is a consequence of the social definitions of men's honor and purity of women in their community." Moreover women are required to follow socially established codes of behavior because it brings honor to the men (Zabeida, 2010, p. 24).

The reward of a male martyr is the pleasure of marrying 72 virgins (*houris*) in paradise. So what is the reward for a female martyr? According to the Hamas website on January 18, 2002,

> The female martyr gains the same reward as does the male, with exception of this one aspect [the *houris*], so that the female martyr will be with the same husband with whom she dies. "And those who have believed and their progeny, followed them in belief, we shall join their progeny to them. We shall not deprive them of any of their work; every man shall be bound by what he has earned" (52:21). The one who is martyred and has no husband will be married to one of the people of paradise. (Cook, 2005, p. 381)

Cultural violence against women is quite complex and often hidden. Anthropologists Marilyn Strathern and Carol MacCormack note that nature/culture discourse, for example, regularly figures nature as female and in need of subordination by a culture that is invariably figured as male, active, and abstract (MacCormack and Strathern, 1980). For Butler this demonstrates the existence of misogyny where "reason and mind are associated with masculinity and agency while body and nature are considered to be mute facticity of the feminine, awaiting signification from an apposing masculine subject" (Butler, 2008, p. 50).

A recent quantitative transnational study of sexual violence rates by Yodanis (2004, p. 670) found that gender inequality is one of the measures of structural violence and that the structure of gender inequality is in turn associated with a culture of violence against women. For example, structural theory places an emphasis on structural factors that position women as being at greater risk of sexual violence in wartime and highlights factors such as economic and other gender forms of oppression and marginalization, injustice, and structural violence. Gierycz (Chapter 27 in Volume 2) claims that national laws are among the factors that perpetuate discrimination against women from the family level and cause inequality in decision making on such matters as the dissolution of marriage, the spacing of childbirths, the choice of family name, and ownership of family possessions. Oppressive gender relations in patriarchal societies lead women to be vulnerable during natural disasters as well as in wartime. Women are unarmed, are unprotected, and lack mobility, especially when traditional forms of moral community and institutional safeguards are falling apart.

Weapons proliferation puts women at risk to all kinds of violation, such as rape as an organized form of warfare in an effort to humiliate and demoralize an enemy population unable to "protect" its women (Bouta et al., 2005, p. 33). The amount of human trafficking and sexual exploitation, for example, tends to increase in wartime. Economic and social discrimination against women uses sex as a means of bargaining power, and as a result, many women become victims of gender bias and sexual violence as well as transmitting and acquiring sexually transmitted diseases, including HIV/AIDS.

The HIV/AIDS pandemic has left 58 percent of women living with HIV/AIDS in sub-Saharan Africa (Gierycz, Chapter 32 in Volume 2). In Sierra Leone 94 percent of displaced households have experienced sexual assaults, including rape, torture, and sexual slavery (Bouta et al., 2005). More women than men become victims of natural disasters as well. According to an OXFAM survey in the Besar Aceh district of Indonesia, "189 out of 676 survivors were female. Male survivors outnumbered female survivors . . . almost 3:1. . . . In the worst affected village, Kuala Cangkoy, for every male who died, four females died—or in other words 80 percent of deaths were female." In human trafficking women and girls make up 76 percent of trafficked people worldwide (Gierycz, Chapter 32 in Volume 2).

The Culture of Violence and Gender Repression

Rebecca Blank's (2005) concept of "cumulative discrimination" and cumulative disadvantage shows how the significant impact of women's marginalization of power and resources through religious interpretations and cultural norms can affect a person's lifetime. As she describes it, "Cumulative disadvantage measures changes in outcome gaps between a disadvantaged and an advantaged group over time. It may reflect the impact of explicit discrimination but it is likely also to reflect other social and economic factors." Discrimination against women in the patriarchal cultures made them become the disadvantaged group in terms of lacking equal legal justice, economic, social, and political opportunities.

A violent structure leaves marks not only on the human body but also on the mind and the spirit. The next four terms can be seen as parts of exploitation or as reinforcing components in the structure. They function by impeding consciousness formation and mobilization, two conditions for effective struggle against exploitation. *Penetration*, implanting the top dog inside the underdog so to speak, combined with *segmentation*, giving the underdog only a very partial view of what goes on, will do the first job. And *marginalization*, keeping the underdogs on the outside, combined with *fragmentation*, keeping the underdogs away from each other, will do the second job. However, these four should also be seen as structural violence in their own right. And more particularly as variations on the general theme of structurally built-in repression. (Galtung, 1990, p. 294)

Cultural violence legitimizes direct and structural violence or institutionalized violence, which is usually invisible. Structural violence is embedded in ubiquitous social structures and normalized by stable institutions. It appears and feels normal and acceptable. Logic or mathematics can be used to justify or legitimize structural violence as well as direct violence (Galtung, 1990). "One way cultural violence works is by changing the moral color of an act from red/wrong to green/right or at least yellow/acceptable" (p. 292).

Butler (2008, p. 3) contends, "Juridical notions of power appear to regulate political life in purely negative terms—that is through limitation, prohibition, regulation, control, and even 'protection' of individuals related in political structure." This is misleading, however, because the "subjects regulated by such structures are, by virtue of being subjected to them, formed, defined, and reproduced in accordance with requirement of those structures" (p. 3). The institutions that should provide protection become sources of further systemic violence.

Human societies have a broad range of systems regarding the degree to which vulnerability is gendered, however. Riane Eisler (1987), in her analysis of archaeological evidence regarding the history of violence and human rights, distinguishes between the *dominator model* and the *partnership model* of human relations. In terms of gender relations, violence, and social structure, these two models demonstrate stark differences. On the one hand, the partnership model has an egalitarian social structure with low degrees of violence and a sexually egalitarian society in which masculinity and femininity are equally valued.

The dominator model, on the other hand, is associated with inferiority and superiority where the superior dominate the inferior. The dominator model characteristically values male over female as well as indicating a higher value for traits and social values stereotypically associated with "masculinity" rather than "femininity." It is associated with a higher degree of institutionalized social violence and abuse ranging from wife and child beating to warfare and psychological abuse by superiors in the family, the workplace, and society at large. A predominantly hierarchical and authoritarian social organization with a high degree of male dominance is characteristic. Societies falling into this category have violence prevailing from the private to the public spheres, with women more often the victims.

When freedom, democracy, equality, rationalism, and women's rights are suppressed in a patriarchal culture; in these contexts women become subjects of men unconsciously as well as consciously. They are distrusted, despised, and dominated by men. In Egyptian, Pakistani, and Turkish subcultures, where violence against women is high, women are discouraged from seeking legal justice within the tribal, religious, and secular parallel judicial systems, notable for their high cost of litigation, lack of access to legal aid, sexual harassment by law enforcement agents, and gender bias and unfair judicial structure (Yamin, 2011, p. 236). Judith Butler in *Gender Trouble* claims that the law excludes certain groups, such as women, who are subject to it. "In other words," she contends (2008, p. 3),

The political construction of the subject proceeds with certain legitimating and exclusionary aims, and these political operations are selectively concealed and naturalized by a political system that takes juridical structures as their foundation. . . . In effect, the law produced and then conceals the notion of "a subject before the law."

Yamin (2011) introduces the term "culture of femicide" as a culture that promotes violence against women and that leads to killing. She claims that in patriarchal cultures women are perceived as symbols of honor; in many cultures around the world, a woman is a personification of "honor" while a man is its custodian. "Honor must never be violated. A woman who shames her community must not live" (Yamin, 2011, p. 235). Women became vulnerable to death just because they are involved in a forbidden relationship, such as marrying outside the clan, or even interacting with the opposite sex.

Patriarchal culture, moreover, misrepresents religious traditions to the detriment of men. As Yamin (Chapter 16 in this volume) points out (cf. Alasti, 2007), although it is widely thought that the Koran prescribes the stoning of women for adultery, there is no mention of it in the Koran, whereas there is in the Torah and the Old Testament as well as in some of the Muslim Hadith, although that contention itself is controversial (see Chapter 16). According to the Koran itself, both unmarried women and men engaging in illicit sexual intercourse are to be punished by 100 lashes (Yamin, Chapter 16 in this volume; Noor and Ghazali, 2008), so countries that justify the stoning of women on the basis of Koranic teachings are following not the prescriptions of the Koran but the norms of patriarchy.

The gendering of vulnerability also intersects with class, status, and other sources of hierarchy in a society, however. Whereas Butler rightly describes women as subjects with limited access to justice, she fails to note that women from privileged groups are not victims of social justice in the same way. The educational and occupational status of women has a correlation with the prevalence of sexual violence in patriarchal countries, for example. Women with high status have a lower chance of becoming victims of sexual violence. Women of higher social economic status also have access to justice; for example, women in a privileged community are more likely to access justice through the legal system compared to women who live in unprivileged communities (Butler, 2008). In Egypt, Pakistan, and Turkey, for example, high illiteracy among women is caused by patriarchal religious interpretations, gender inequality, and uneven patterns of development as well as cultural practices that subvert women's growth, development, and welfare. Women in those countries live with poor social economic status both in rural and urban areas (Yamin, 2011).

Inger Egger (2004), in *Blue Room*, raises the issue of the violence committed against "dangerous women," suggesting that the most reviling form of sexual violence is against women political prisoners under the guise of social and political discipline of prisoners, but impacted by gender. She provides the example of Eva Forest and the experience of women prisoners in Spain in 1885, which highlights the structural aspect of violence against women. The oppression of women is carried out by the existing sexual- political power structure.

How does that power structure work? For Weber (1978), the major sources for the distribution of power in society are status groups, parties, and class (see Breen, 2005). The unequal distribution of power from all three sources has an impact on people's life chances, affecting their opportunities and shaping the course of their lives. Foucault (1987, p. 27) warns us that power is "not exercised simply as obligation or a prohibition on those who do not have it."

As useful as their theories are for understanding the dynamics of power, however, both Foucault and Weber fail to identify gender as one of the aspects of power distribution, especially in the context of a patriarchal system in which women are marginalized and oppressed, therefore having fewer life chances. Weber describes the market as distributing life chances according to the resources an individual brings to it. He recognizes that resources could vary by property ownership or its lack, and by skill and other assets (Breen, 2005). These dynamics are sometimes hidden, however, within the narratives of a culture. As Susan Nan (2011, p. 239) notes,

Foucault's work is based on the understanding that dominant narratives, or deep structures reflected in these dominant discourses, are usually invisible to those operating within them. These invisible forces privilege voices that fit the prevailing consciousness, and marginalize those that do not fit. Conflict resolution approaches seek to empower those whose voices are not privileged.

WOMEN AS AGENTS OF CHANGE: STRUCTURAL TRANSFORMATION

Society meets a threat, according to Marcuse (1974, Kindle locations 946–947), "chiefly in a strengthening of controls not so much over the instincts as over consciousness, which, if left free might recognize the work of repression in bigger and better satisfaction of needs." Women should take the lead in confronting the systems of repression, and in some cases have done so. Rwandese women and the president of Liberia are great examples of the role of women as agents of change. Ellen Johnson-Sirleaf was elected president of Liberia after the civil war ended, in large part because of the power of the woman's movement, which forced the men to stop fighting and replaced Liberia's dictator with a democratically elected president. One of her agenda items was to speak out against gender-based violence (GBV) and the ministries of Labour, Justice, and Education were mobilized to recognize rape as an intolerable offense (Chandler et al., 2010).

Marcuse notes that

According to Freud's conception the equation of freedom and happiness tabooed by the conscious is upheld by the unconscious. Its truth, although repelled by consciousness, continues to haunt the mind; it preserves the memory of past stages of individual development at which integral gratification is obtained. And the past continues to claim the future: it generates the wish that the paradise be recreated on the basis of the achievements of civilization. (Marcuse, Kindle Locations 289–292)

Rwandese women suffered gendercide and genocide, but then they became the catalysts for peace building. They are now involved in making structural changes and advances in policy and decision making (Uwineza and Brown, 2013, p. 139).

According to the Inter-Parliamentary Union, in sub-Saharan Africa there has been no significant change, even though in worldwide statistics there has been a significant but slow improvement of women entering the parliaments. According to a 2010 United Nations Department of Economic and Social Affairs report on world women's trends and statistics, the number of women in national parliaments in 2010 was still low. In 2015, the number of women in parliaments worldwide had doubled since the 1995 Beijing Conference on Women, but was still at only 22 percent (UN Women, 2015). In January 2015, 10 women served as Head of State and 14 served as Head of Government.[1] Moreover, UN Women (2015) reports that as of January 2015, in the Nordic countries, women were 41.5 percent of the parliaments; in the Americas, they were 26.3 percent. In Europe, excluding Nordic countries, women constituted 23.8 percent of the parliaments and in sub-Saharan Africa, 22.2 percent; in Asia they were 18.5 percent; and in the Middle East and North Africa, 16.1 percent.

In the ministry positions worldwide, women tend to hold ministries related to nurturing roles, such as social affairs, family, children, youth, elderly, disabled, gender, and the environment (UN Women, 2014). Men predominate in such decision-making ministries as parliamentary affairs and media and information that shape the national narratives.

Similar findings apply to the private sector: women are underrepresented in most boards of directors of large companies. Furthermore, the glass ceiling has hindered women's access to leadership positions in private companies. This is especially notable in the largest corporations, which remain male dominated. Of the 500 largest corporations in the world, only 13 have a female chief executive officer (United Nations, 2010).

Some countries. such as Tanzania, Ethiopia, and Madagascar, have shown improvements even though they still facing obstacles reinforced by the patriarchal system. The Inter-Parliamentary Union highlights common barriers for women's participation in parliament as cultural and social variables as well as women's ability to access financial resources. According to a survey of daily election news stories women candidates during the 2010 general election in Tanzania did not get as much media coverage as their male counterparts. Male politicians dominated the news as both the subjects and sources of election stories. In Sudan there were reports that women lost elections because they lacked media coverage. At the same time women campaign workers in Bosnia and Herzegovina claimed that female candidates' photographs were common in the media but not their opinions. Another example involves Julia Gilard, Australia's first woman prime minister. When she met with the media the focus was on her hair color and choice of clothes.

The United States–based nongovernmental organizations (NGOs) Women's Media Center and She Should Run conducted research for a project called "Name It. Change It. Sexism and equality don't mix" to look at the impact of sexist media coverage of female candidates. An online survey of 1,500 likely voters nationwide, with an over sample[2] of 100 young women voters, examined how a woman's appearance affected her performance as a candidate. It found that when the coverage focuses on a women's appearance, it negatively affects her favorability, the likelihood she is seen as possessing positive traits, and how likely voters are to vote for her.

- This experimental survey shows that when media coverage focuses on a woman's appearance, she pays a price in the race: her favorability, her likelihood to be seen as possessing positive traits, and how likely voters are to vote for her.
- Neutral, positive, and negative descriptions of the woman candidate's appearance all had a detrimental impact on her candidacy. Importantly, the adverse reactions are not isolated to critiques of a woman's appearance; even appearance coverage that purports to be neutral or complimentary damages the woman's chances.
- While this appearance coverage is very damaging to women candidates, the male opponents paid no price for this type of coverage.
- Acknowledging and responding to the sexist appearance coverage helps the woman regain some of the ground she lost.

The Guardian reports that Rwandese women took positions in some of the most important government ministries and make up 56 percent of the country's parliamentarians, including the speaker. As decision makers they succeeded in changing the constitution, and there was a reduction in the number of rape cases, wife beating, and male domination of women in the country. More girls attended schools, and women attained rights to land and property ownership as well as inheritance. Married women also gained the right to choose to pool their assets with those of their husbands or to keep them separate. As a consequence of these changes, divorce rates have increased. In post-conflict Rwanda, women have learned to say yes to a positive morality, which Nietzsche refers to as the "noble morality," and they have freed themselves from a "slave morality says 'no' on principle to everything that is 'outside,' 'other,' 'non-self': and this 'no' is its creative deed" (Nietsche, 2007, Kindle Locations 611–612). As with the 19th-century rejection of the law and other regulations that Foucault discusses (1987, p. 272), women resisting patriarchy in the 21st century are struggling "against those who set them up in their own interests" and even "against all the agents of injustice" as well as "against the law itself and the justice whose task it was to apply it."

In the West, change in the democratic states is the consequence of pressure built up by the civil societies, including activists and lobbyists, as well as a realization of the power of the vote, pressuring those in power to consider the needs of those who put them in power (Uwineza and Brown, 2013). In the United States the 2012 elections led to the 113th Congress having 20 female senator seats, and during the election campaign women were key to Democrats' wins. Moreover, women shaped the rhetoric of the campaign; so-called women's issues such as equal pay, reproductive rights, and women's health care influenced women's choice for president. In the 2012 election, 55 percent of women voters chose President Obama because he appealed to women as the better candidate for handle women's issues. The first bill Obama signed into law was the Lilly Ledbetter Fair Pay Act, signed within nine days after he was sworn into office, as a response to a May 2007 Supreme Court ruling that made it difficult for employees to file pay discrimination claims.

While rates of women exposed to violence vary from one region to another, statistics indicate that violence against women is a universal phenomenon and that women are subjected to different forms of violence—physical, sexual, psychological, and economic—both within and outside their homes. The United Nations Office for Disaster Risk Reduction paper on the issue of vulnerability with specific reference to gender in the Asia Pacific post-2015 framework for disaster risk reduction consultation highlights social vulnerability as a consequence of social relations, institutions, and systems of cultural values. The level of "vulnerability" differs from country to country, and even though the region has seen significant progress in reducing vulnerability as part of its historic battle against poverty, patriarchy is still a significant source of vulnerability for girls and women.

CONCLUSION

Systemic violence in patriarchal cultures and structures has inhibited women's growth and development. A patriarchal system marginalizes women and separates them from power and natural resources, and that is where the process of gendering vulnerability begins. As Mary Crawford argues, gender is a verb rather than a noun. In her book *Talking Difference in Gender Language*, Crawford describes the conceptualization process by providing an example from Western society, where baby blanket colors are gendered. Blue and pink blankets serve as cues for the social treatment of baby boys and girls, respectively. Since gender ideology is created around narratives and scripts and concerns how people interpret and identify with the concept or meaning, and "because western cultures have long evaluated masculinity as inherently superior to femininity, claims of women's difference are likely to be assimilated into that framework" (Crawford, 1995, p. 11).

Given the fact that the discrimination and marginalization of women begins at the family level and progresses to the global level, women become subject to cumulative discrimination and inferior opportunity structures; consequently they are more vulnerable than men. In many societies, the voice of women does not count in family decision making. Girls, for example, are sometimes forced to interrupt their education to help their mothers take care of their siblings and sick members of the family (see Gierycz, Chapter 32 in Volume 2). Their opportunities are limited from early childhood because of their gender. Worldwide, there are few women in corporate board rooms and parliaments; only a handful of women are heads of state. Cultural and structural violence within patriarchal systems produces "cumulative discrimination" and cumulative disadvantages (Blank, 2005) that lead women to become victims of cultural, direct, and indirect violence during times of peace, war, or disaster. Vulnerability itself is gendered.

ACKNOWLEDGMENTS

Thanks to Sandra Cheldelin and Richard Rubenstein for their inspiration, comments, and suggestions.

NOTES

1. The difference between a Head of State and a Head of Government varies according to the type of political system in each country. See more at: http://www.unwomen.org/en/what-we-do/leadership-and-political-participation/facts-and-figures#notes.

2. More young women voters were included in the sample than other likely voters in order to get a better picture of what young women were thinking.

BIBLIOGRAPHY

Alasti, Sanaz. 2007. Comparative Study of Stoning Punishment in the Religions of Islam and Judaism. *Justice Policy Journal* 4 (1), http://www.academia.edu/download/30849363/comparative_study_0.pdf

Atran, Scott. 2003. Genesis of Suicide Terrorism. *Science* 299 (5612): 1534–39.

Background Paper: Issues of Vulnerability with Specific Reference to Gender in the Asia Pacific. In Post-2015 Framework for Disaster Risk Reduction Consultations. n.d. http://www.preventionweb.net/files/34051_background paperonissuesofvulnerabil.pdf

Blank, Rebecca M. 2005. Tracing the Economic Impact of Cumulative Discrimination. *American Economic Review*, 99–103.

Boseley, Sarah. 2010. Rwanda: A Revolution in Rights for Women. *The Guardian*, May 28. http://www.theguardian.com/world/2010/may/28/womens-rights-rwanda

Bouta, Tsjeard, Georg Frerks, and Ian Bannon. 2005. *Gender, Conflict, and Development*. Washington, DC: World Bank Publications. https://openknowledge.worldbank.org/bitstream/handle/10986/14873/30494.pdf?sequence=1

Breen, Richard. 2005. Foundations of a Neo-Weberian Class Analysis. *Approaches to Class Analysis*, 31–50.

Butler, Judith. 2008. *Gender Trouble*. New York: Routledge.

Chandler, Robin M., Linda K. Fuller, and Lihua Wang. 2010. *Women, War, and Violence: Personal Perspectives and Global Activism*. New York: Palgrave Macmillan.

Cheldelin, Sandra I. 2011. Victims of Rape and Gendercide: All Wars. In *Women Waging War and Peace: International Perspectives of Women's Roles in Conflict and Post-Conflict Reconstruction*, edited by Sandra I. Cheldelin and Maneshka Eliatamby. New York: Continuum, pp. 12–34.

Collins, Patricia Hill. 2000. *Black Feminist Thought: Knowledge, Consciousness, and the Politics of Empowerment*. 2nd ed. New York: Routledge.

Cook, David. 2005. Women Fighting in *Jihad*? *Studies in Conflict & Terrorism* 28: 375–384.

Crawford, Mary. 1995. *Talking Difference: On Gender and Language*. Thousand Oaks, CA: SAGE.

Eisler, Riane. 1987. *The Chalice and the Blade: Our History, Our Future*. New York: Harper & Row.

Foucault, Michel. 1987. *The Body of the Condemned*. New York: Arbor House, http://pittfemtheoryf11.wordpress.com/blog/page/25/

Galtung, Johan. 1969. Violence, Peace, and Peace Research. *Journal of Peace Research* 6 (3): 167–191.

Galtung, Johan. 1990. Cultural Violence. *Journal of Peace Research* 27 (3): 291–305.

Jacques, Karen, and Paul J. Taylor. 2009. Female Terrorism: A Review. *Terrorism and Political Violence* 21 (3): 499–515.

Leatherman, J. L. 2011. *Sexual Violence and Armed Conflict*. Cambridge: Polity Press.

MacCormack, Carol P., and Marilyn Strathern. 1980. *Nature, Culture and Gender*. Cambridge: Cambridge University Press.

Marcuse, Herbert. 1974 [1955]. *Eros and Civilization: A Philosophical Inquiry into Freud*. Boston: Beacon Press. Kindle edition.

Marcuse, Herbert. 1991 [1964]. *One-Dimensional Man: Studies in the Ideology of Advanced Industrial Society.* With an Introduction by Douglas Kellner. Kindle edition. London: Routledge.

Name It. Change It. Sexism and Equality Don't Mix. 1991. http://www.nameitchangeit.org/pages/4824

Nan, Susan Allen. 2011. Consciousness in Culture-Based Conflict and Conflict Resolution. *Conflict Resolution Quarterly* 28 (3): 239–262.

Nietzsche, Friedrich. 2007 [1887]. Nietzsche: "On the Genealogy of Morality" and Other Writings Student Edition (Cambridge Texts in the History of Political Thought), edited by Keith Ansell-Pearson, translated by Carol Diethe. Cambridge: Cambridge University Press, Kindle edition.

Noor, Azman Mohd, and Mohd Al-Ikhsan Ghazali. 2008. Interpreting and Understanding the Command of God: Authority of the Sunnah as a Source of Law in the Case of Stoning to Death of a Convicted Adulterer. *Journal Syariah* 16: 429–442.

Oxfam Briefing Note. n.d. The Tsunami's Impact on Women, http://www.preventionweb.net/files/1502_bn050326tsunamiwomen.pdf

Pape, Robert Anthony. 2005. *Dying to Win: The Strategic Logic of Suicide Terrorism.* 1st ed. New York: Random House.

Rubenstein, Richard E. 1999. Conflict Resolution and the Structural Sources of Conflict. In *Conflict Resolution: Dynamics, Process and Structure.* Aldershot, UK: Ashgate.

Schwab, Klaus, Börge Brende, Saadia Zahidi, Yasmina Bekhouche, Annabel Guinault, Amey Soo, Ricardo Hausmann, and Laura D. Tyson. Global Gender Gap Report, 2013, http://www3.weforum.org/docs/WEF_Gender Gap_Report_2013.pdf

Taylor, Anita, and Jude Bernstein Miller. 1994. Introduction. In *The Necessity of Seeing Gender and Conflict.* New York: Hampton Press, pp. 1–17.

United Nations. 2010. The World's Women 2010: Executive Summary. New York: United Nations. http://unstats.un.org/unsd/demographic/products/Worldswomen/Executive%20summary.htm

UN Women. 2015. Facts and Figures: Leadership and Political Participation. New York: United Nations. http://www.unwomen.org/en/what-we-do/leadership-and-political-participation/facts-and-figures#notes

UN Women and Inter-Parliamentary Union. 2014. Women in Politics 2014. http://ipu.org/pdf/publications/wmnmap14_en.pdf

Uwineza, Peace, and Vanessa Noel Brown. 2013. Engendering Recovery: Rwanda. In *Women Waging War and Peace: International Perspectives of Women's Roles in Conflict and Post-Conflict Reconstruction,* edited by Sandra I. Cheldelin and Maneshka Eliatamby. New York: Continuum, pp. 139–161.

Weber, Max. 1978. *Economy and Society: An Outline of Interpretive Sociology.* Univ of California Press.

Winter, Deborah DuNann, and Dana C. Leighton. 2001. Structural Violence. In *Peace, Conflict, and Violence: Peace Psychology in the 21st Century*, edited by D. J. Christie, R. V. Wagner, and D. D. Winter. New York: Prentice-Hall.

Woman Stats Blog. 2011. Increasing Mobile Phone Ownership for Women in Developing Countries, https://womanstats.wordpress.com/?s=%22Increasing+Mobile+Phone+Ownership+for+Women+in+Developing+Countries%22.

Women & Mobile: A Global Opportunity: A Study on the Mobile Phone Gender Gap in Low- and Middle-Income Countries. 2013. http://www.gsma.com/mobilefordevelopment/wp-content/uploads/2013/01/GSMA_Women_and_Mobile-A_Global_Opportunity.pdf

Women in Parliament. 2010. The Year in Perspective, http://www.ipu.org/pdf/publications/wmnpersp10-e.pdf

Yamin, Saira. 2011. Challenging Patriarchy: Pakistan, Egypt and Turkey. In *Women Waging War and Peace: International Perspectives of Women's Roles in Conflict and Post-Conflict Reconstruction*, edited by Sandra Cheldelin and Maneshka Eliatamby. The Continuum International Publishing Group, pp. 235–58.

Yodanis, Carrie L. 2004. Gender Inequality, Violence Against Women, and Fear A Cross-National Test of the Feminist Theory of Violence Against Women. *Journal of Interpersonal Violence* 19: 655–75.

Zabeida, Natalja. 2010. Not Making Excuses: Functions of Rape as a Tool in Ethno-Nationalist Wars. In *Women, War, and Violence: Personal Perspectives and Global Activism*, edited by Robin M. Chandler, Lihua Wang, and Linda K. Fuller. New York: Palgrave, pp. 17–30.

CHAPTER 4

Women, War, and Violence: Some Holistic Points

Johan Galtung

The female half of humanity has been exposed to two vicious combinations of direct and structural violence: *patriarchy* in marriage and society, and *patriotism* in war and the world. One origin in the West is in the Roman law concept of *patria podestas*, the rights and duties—neither transferable, nor renounceable, nor prescribable—of the father over all biological and adopted children, in or outside marriage. Only as recently as 1975 was this changed in Italy—as an example—from father to parents. The extension to patriotism is embedded in such concepts as the Fatherland, the Father of the nation, and the state as a family writ large, governed by the same structure.

Half of humanity has been suppressed by the structural violence of patriarchy in the family and been victims of violence in general, sexual violence in particular, selective abortion, infanticide, and the scourge of war brought upon the world almost exclusively by males; attempted justified by the cultural violence of absurd theories about women.

This half of humanity, mothers of all of humanity, is now rising, in consciousness, organization, confrontation, and nonviolent struggle, under the unifying slogan of *parity* between genders, in marriage, in society, and in the world. Partly as a result of this, patriarchy as a family system, and the state system as a way of organizing war and the world, are waning in significance. The alternatives emerging may be less clear: they include sharing rights and duties in the family but also dissolution of the nuclear family in favor of extended families living together, or in anarchy, and dissolution of the state system in favor of globalism, regionalism/localism, or anarchy. Or all of the above.

United Nations Security Council (UNSC) Resolution 1325 both denounces the victimization of women in war and calls for their active participation for peace—a watershed in politics and a brilliant coupling between the domestic and global levels. But what can we realistically expect?

Emancipation of women comes with the emancipation of lower classes, colored races, suppressed nations, and colonized-imperialized peoples and countries—canonized by the Covenants of Human Rights. UNSC 1325 covers not only the right not to be victimized but also the double duty of opening for women the opportunity to work for peace. Why not also develop a resolution empowering other victims, such as children and the aged, thus mobilizing all generations, and not only the two genders, for peace?

UNSC 1325 is against a system run by men, upper class and white, from dominant nations (e.g., Anglo-American-French, Christian-secular) from colonial-imperial countries clinging to the past. But women differ from all of them. Similar only to the young and the aged that are also in the families, some of those families are upper class in upper-class countries. This is good in the sense having direct access to power, and bad in the sense of possibly being co-opted structurally and culturally. They may have direct power or indirect power through spouses, but little to offer in the way of visions, and power without visions is no better than visions without power. This is not the case for lower classes, colored races, and suppressed nations or peoples, which are generally kept away from ruling families and is a reason why we have to look at not only domestic and global systems but also at the family. It is also a reason why there is so much violence against women—if they are to be suppressed, abused, and victimized— also has to be in the family, so that women know their place in the world and do not start talking and acting on behalf of others that are suppressed, like slaves, colonized peoples, possible victims of nuclear war.

Peace skills, such as empathy, nonviolence, creative multitasking, conflict resolution, *socially rooted* in women's marital roles, carry the stigma of deeds of necessity by the suppressed, unlike *biologically rooted* attributes of women. Monoamino oxidase blocks the release of adrenalin, which stimulates the body for "flight or fight" responses, and the corpus callosum, the nerve band connecting emotions and speech between the two halves of the brain, are more prominent in women, predisposing them to less physical— but possibly more verbal—violence but also to verbal peace.

RANK EQUILIBRIUM, CONCORDANCE; RANK DISEQUILIBRIUM, DISCORDANCE

The classical world system has been run by men, upper class, white, from dominant nations in the colonial-imperial center—*MeUpWhDoCe*— as opposed to women, lower class, colored, from suppressed nations in the colonial-imperial periphery—*WoLoCoSuPe*. These extreme profiles are equilibrated only with top dog or underdog status out of the 32 possible profiles we get with five dichotomies in this holistic approach. Gender is not the only variable carrying rank in the world. With the five attributes we get 1 profile with five top dog ranks, or score 5; 5 with score 4; 10 with score 3; 10 with score 2; 5 with score 1; and 1 with score 0.

Imagine that the two profiles with scores 5 and 0 were the only ones found. The world would be rank concordant, with a small group lording over the rest. But how about sex and procreation? Don't worry, Jefferson had a child by one of his black female slaves. But the offspring would not carry the top profile, so we had better admit women into the family, bringing rank disequilibrium, people with a mix of top dog and underdog statuses, into society. Add to this rank discordance—for example, between upper-class women and lower-class men—and we have a recipe for conflict and violence.

But the system described—a world run by upper-class white men with only two languages, only two worldviews, from only two countries running colonialism in Africa and Asia, and one running imperialism in South America, and racism at home—was the reality until the 1960s. There was no space for an alternative to class-producing capitalism, or for the newcomers to the state system—Germany, Italy, Japan—with revolutions and world wars, two hot and one cold, among the consequences.

Today colonialism is officially over, imperialism is declining and falling, and nations—defined by language and worldview—are all equal in rights, as are races, peoples, and countries. In principle. Class is more multidimensional, and gender is declared irrelevant. The inner qualities of humans are what matters. So, what happens?

WOMEN AS A SOURCE OF DISEQUILIBRIUM AND AS A SOURCE OF PEACE?

Most equilibrated top dog men with score 5 live with wives with score 4. The rank distance, 1, is manageable; distances of 5 and 4 are highly problematic, and so are distances of even 3 and 2—except for sex only.

The wife with score 4 is our first focus in terms of potential for peace. She has four resources, top-dog statuses, to draw upon, and one grievance motivating her for change: the inferior status attributed to her gender. But she may live with her husband's profile as her own, the two being one and indivisible, until death sets them apart. In principle.

However, imagine she wants nothing of underdog status in her profile. One strategy would be to prove gender irrelevance by achieving a major top-dog position in the class system, individually; another strategy is to act with many other score 4 women collectively, for example, for the right to vote.

But UNSC 1325 still applies: women with four out of four ranks—gender declared irrelevant—will still disproportionately be victims of war and not empowered for peace. Will these gender attributes also be among her grievances, old or newly acquired?

Not automatically. Her score 5 (or 4) context makes her a party to a major conflict: score 5 against the others, seen as us against the rest, "us" becoming US becoming West and "rest" becoming Rest. Law, order, and stability mean 5–4 being on top; security means the absence of violence against them, with the enormous amount of direct and structural violence at levels 3, 2, 1, and 0 made invisible. Chances are that a score 4 woman will share much of that. Her peace policy will be for security more than for equity, against direct rather than structural violence, for negative more than positive peace. Her socially and biologically rooted skills will serve her well but stop short of bringing any real change that might threaten her homeland, her family, or herself. Add to that the erosion of those skills through change in female roles in the household at the score 4 and 5 levels, and feminist denial of any biological differences.

At the other end of the rank spectrum, down to scores 0 and 1 with five or four grievances, the motivation for basic change may be high but the resources are minimal. So-called social stability is based exactly on this inverse distribution of grievances and resources.

The general conclusion would be to opt for the middle range, the scores 2 and 3, as a second focus for the female potential for peace. There are resources and there are grievances, about equal in number. One senses women, not upper but middle-lower class, not necessarily white, not necessarily from dominant nations and center countries. One senses the English middle-lower class women, close to trade unions and sectarian Christianity such as Quakerism, so instrumental in the fight against slavery and colonialism, and recently against patriarchy and patriotism and belligerence and arms in general.

This is where the realistic chances for change in the direction of peace are located. As opposed to score 4 women, scores 3 and 2 women have short rank distances and hence ease of communication in both directions, up and down, and can work both with nonviolence and for social change. They can have dialogues over a wide range to get a grip on the goals and aspirations at the different score levels and use that to arrive at constructive, concrete, and creative new visions.

But this is a different struggle. No longer is a woman concerned only with making gender irrelevant and *maybe*, in addition, with war and peace, finding UNSC 1325 or its many equivalents in writing and speech convincing, doing her best as very many do. Now it is gender + or ++: the gender aspect and one of four others—class, race, nation, state—for score 2, and any two of them for score 3. She may struggle for *full gender equality including war/peace correlates* and/or for *alternative economies, full racial equality, federalism for national equality,* and *equality for all states* (in the UN against the veto system).

The formula *Resources × Grievances = Power for Change* applies.

THE STRUGGLE AGAINST WAR AND FOR PEACE

Five dimensions, and a five-point political agenda, cover much of the world political struggle right now. With that agenda we may agree or not, but it is by no means a monopoly for women; men are also fully engaged, many with score 5, and even more often against, in their own interest (or so they think). But the focus is on women's struggle, the second focus above, women with scores 3 and 2, and also for women with scores 1 and 0. That broadens the agenda from the first focus, adjusting to the realities of the world.

How is that struggle fought? There has been much direct violence *against* class exploitation, racism, dominant nations, and the centers of colonialism-imperialism; and for all four there is also a tradition of nonviolent struggle. But in the physical sense women's struggle for equality has been overwhelmingly nonviolent, including the *Lysistrata* approach of denying sex—probably very widespread in its nondeclared form ("I am so tired tonight"). Reinforced by increasing parity, the assumption would be that women would use nonviolence also for the other four issues, including all forms of civil disobedience, and above all "being the future you want to see": practicing peace alternatives.

And there has been much direct violence *in favor of* the five structural violences in favor of the score 5 upper crust, including—as noted in the opening statement of this essay—against women, at all levels.

A more subtle *MeUpWhDoCe* strategy is to advocate democracy as the mechanism for social change: start a party, and aim at the majority. However, some of the issues are not carried by majorities but by human rights, which are not subject to votes in a national assembly. Thus, it took U.S. democracy a century from the official abolition of slavery in 1863 for the political system to make basic steps toward racial equality for the black minority; it took UK democracy much more than that to extend some equality to "their" colonies. Majority rule favors equals at the top.

And even so, majoritarian democracy is easily manipulated through media as carriers of opinion, and opinion changes, shaping votes, and also through money, financing candidates in return for political favors. The idea is good for I-culture societies not too ridden by the five inequities, but easily perverted, by nonviolent means, as a counter-strategy to social change struggle by civil disobedience from below. And it tends not to be used when the majority cannot be controlled, as witnessed in the difficulties in organizing UN General Assembly votes against the will of veto powers.

However, in spite of this the path into the future is paved with advances toward an increasingly equitable world. The stepping stones will, to a large extent, and disproportionately so, be laid by women not upper class, white, or from dominant nations and center states. What this means is that a peace strategy based on women is succeeding by spreading to new layers of the still very inequitable world society.

Above a short mantra has been given summarizing what it takes to mediate conflicts: *empathy, nonviolence, creativity*. Women are at present clearly superior in empathy and nonviolence, one mechanism probably being solidarity with mothers on the other sides, knowing very well their predicaments, with flights and fight excluded.

The problem may be creativity, envisioning a new reality that might accommodate the legitimate goals of all parties, by legitimate means. More than a question of identifying a "common ground," it may be a question of identifying and constructing an "embracing reality" accommodating all, beyond the aspirations of the conflict parties.

The problem, encountered by this author in real mediation and in workshops, is that women often have very creative ideas but not the courage and self-confidence to articulate them. On the other hand, when it comes forth, then they respond by proposing only as befits a good mediator, not imposing, as do many men.

CONCLUSION

We are heading for a more peaceful future in which women all over, eventually also at the U.S.-UK top, play a major role.

CHAPTER 5

Structural Violence against Women

Kathleen Maas Weigert

THE CONCEPT OF STRUCTURAL VIOLENCE

Introduced by Johan Galtung in 1969, the concept of structural violence (also called indirect violence and institutionalized violence) refers to "preventable harm or damage to persons (and by extension to things) where there is no actor committing the violence or where it is not practical to search for the actor(s); such violence emerges from the unequal distribution of power and resources or, in other words, is said to be built into the structure(s)" (Maas Weigert, 2008). Galtung thought this concept might offer a new direction for peace research: "a critical analysis of structures and possibly to efforts to transform structures pregnant with violence into less violent ones" (1985, p. 146). He used two examples to illustrate the concept: hunger and the case of husband-wife patterns. In the latter, Galtung argued that one husband beating his wife is an example of personal violence (a point to which I return below), "but when one million husbands keep one million wives in ignorance there is structural violence" (Galtung, 1969, p. 171). In his 1990 essay, Galtung augmented the relationship between personal (direct) and structural violence with the introduction of "cultural violence," leading to his formulation of a "vicious violence triangle," suggesting that violence could start at any corner (1990, p. 302).

The 1980s and 1990s witnessed some use of the structural violence concept in a variety of fields, including conflict resolution (Burton, 1997), international relations (Tickner, 1992, 1995), health and medicine (Farmer, 1996; Gilligan, 1996), and peace education (Reardon, 1988). While some authors make reference to Galtung's pioneering work, others do not. It is scholars such as Brock-Utne (1985, 1989, 1997) who actually build on and develop his framework. In the early 21st century, there appears to be a growing usage of the concept. Brewer (2010, p. 13), for example, seeks to incorporate Galtung's structural violence concept into his "communal violence" concept. Confortini (2006) is the most explicit in analyzing Galtung's framework and its relationship to gender (to which I return below).

In discussing to what extent and how the idea of "structural violence against women"—although not necessarily the term itself—is or can be used, this chapter explores theorizing and research in four main but overlapping areas: conflict studies, human rights, medicine and public health, and the military and militarization. The final sections explore what "structural interventions" might look like and the usefulness of the term "structural violence against women."

CONFLICT STUDIES

Research on national and international violent conflict, from pre-conflict through the conflict to "post-conflict" situations (the last term is in quotation marks since some find the term too definitive for what is really an ongoing process), has drawn the attention of many scholars and practitioners, with some raising the issue of structural violence and others not. In examining economic distress before the onset of violence, Cockburn (2001, p. 17), for example, makes explicit reference to Galtung's structural violence ideas and notes that while gender was not his main point, the concept of structural violence "prompts us to look again at male-dominant gender relations," suggesting that women may experience structural violence in a marriage and/or in a community that gives the husband power over the wife, long before her husband uses direct violence against her. She affirms that there was "an intensification of structural violence, of inequality between nations and within them" in the 1980s in many of the societies that experienced political violence or armed conflict in the 1990s (Cockburn, 2001, p. 17). The shifts in the discourse in pre-conflict situations are important. Cockburn (2001, p. 19) points to a divisive discourse that "is often accompanied by a renewal of patriarchal familial ideology, deepening the differentiation of men and women, masculinity and femininity." She contends,

Any increase in inequality, any widening of the gap between nations and classes, between men and women, weakens the inhibitions against aggression. It legitimates violence toward people considered worthless. And those who are made to feel of scant value sometimes resort to violence to gain self-respect or power. This, I believe, is what Galtung (1996) means when he points to the violence that can be latent in unjust social and economic power structures. (Cockburn, 2004, pp. 43–44)

She draws attention to the importance of institutions that "generate religion and ideology, science and art," arguing they can contribute to cultural violence, which provides an easy segue into Galtung's conceptualization of cultural violence (Cockburn, 2007, p. 191).

Others have focused as well on early warning indicators of conflict. Bunch (1990, p. 491) states, "The physical territory of this political struggle over what constitutes women's human rights is women's bodies." Kiamba and Waris (2006) undertake an examination of the Intergovernmental Authority on Development (IGAD) in East Africa to explore ideas about definitions and threats to security that in effect are not taking into account the full range of women's experiences and roles related to peace and security. They conclude (Kiamba and Waris, 2006, p. 105) that "despite the illusion of the use of women to determine future conflict the failure by IGAD to at the most fundamental level define women and then how they will use the women in conflict prevention seems to shoot the mechanism in the foot." Anderlini (2007, p. 27) decries the neglect of paying attention to women and their experiences as "indicators and potential warning signs in the monitoring and analysis of conflict." Citing the example of Rwanda, Anderlini (2007, p. 30) claims that the indicators "were particularly blatant, and in retrospect, it is clear that the propaganda would very likely lead to sexual violence against women."

The issues of women's roles and realities during violent conflict are the subject of many recent studies. Bouta and Frerks (2002, as reported in Kuehnast et al., 2011, p. 3) suggest a framework with seven different roles that women may play in internal conflicts: "They may be victims of (sexual) violence, combatants, peace activists in the non-governmental sector, actors in formal peace politics, coping and surviving actors, household heads, and/or employed in the formal or informal economic sectors. Combinations of these roles may also occur." That kind of listing helps remove the idea of "women as victims" as the primary lens. Although not using the term "structural violence" (nor evidently "cultural violence"), Anderlini (2007, pp. 30–31) points to elements in various cultures that can contribute to the direct violence against women that happens in war:

As in Bosnia, Darfur, and elsewhere, the sexual nature of the attacks is a particularly cruel means of attempting to destroy family ties and the very notion of ethnicity through forced pregnancies. In societies where men's honor is bound by their ability to protect their family, sexual attacks on women are also a means of bringing shame and dishonor to men. In effect, men communicate with each other through attacks on women: thus women's bodies are literally the front lines and battlefields of many contemporary wars.

Cohn (2013b, p. 11), too, comments, "Because a core aspect of hegemonic masculinity in most societies is men's control over and protection of their wives and daughters, the rape of male opponents' women can be seen as an effective way of unmanning/disempowering these men." As for the issue of economic survival for women in violent conflict, attention is brought to the issue of prostitution (or, as some call it, "survival sex"; see Enloe, 2010, pp. 58–60) and the lack of financial resources that pushes women into commercial sex, a complicated decision that can bring resources to her family while potentially bringing both physical and identity-related risks to the woman herself. Cultural, structural, and direct violence all play a part in these situations.

There are several concerns about women in "post-conflict" situations. One is that the female-male relationships that existed prior to the conflict might be returned to (and strengthened) afterward, even if substantial changes occurred during the conflict to loosen some of the patterns. Kuehnast et al. (2011, p. 4) put it this way: "marginalization of gender as a 'soft' issue in conflict resolution and reconstruction can thus perpetuate or re-create social inequalities that encourage conflict." Some worry that lip-service will be paid to "gender mainstreaming," with no real changes emerging (see Anderlini, 2007, p. 220; see also the section "Human Rights" below). Others propose a post-conflict reconstruction framework that "addresses gender through a rights-based approach, identifying the kinds of rights that must be guaranteed to women in the post-conflict period. These include not only the right to participate in policymaking and resource allocation but also the right to benefit equally from those resources and services" (Kuehnast et al., 2011, p. 4).

One concept that seems to be a natural linkage with Galtung's structural concept (and in fact with his work on direct and cultural violence as well), but doesn't appear to have been made with any frequency, is that of conflict transformation: "a complex process of changing the relationships, attitudes, interests, discourses and underlying structures that encourage and condition violent political conflict" (Austin, 2011, pp. 9–10). The idea of conflict transformation entered the lexicon at least as early as the 1980s (see Lederach, 2003). It has an "explicit grounding in social justice" (Parlevliet, 2011, p. 379) and deals with levels of processes, actors, and structures. The linking to social justice fits with Galtung's structural violence idea, since he states, "In order not to overwork the word violence we shall sometimes refer to the condition of structural violence as *social injustice*" (1969, p. 171, italics in original).

HUMAN RIGHTS

To start, it is perhaps helpful to refer to two distinctions. The first is that between the private and public spheres. As Eisler (1997, p. 163) put it,

Logically speaking, in a world where human rights are truly valued, the distinction between private and public violence, cruelty, oppression, and discrimination would be seen as absurd. Yet many people continue to see private or family relations as separate and distinct, or at best as far less important than, political and economic relations in the public sphere. (See also Bunch, 1990)

The second is the distinction between "human needs" and "human rights." In 1977 Galtung and Wirak argued for drawing a contrast between the two: "Whereas human needs are seen as being something located inside individual human beings, human rights are seen as something located *between them*" (1977, p. 251, italics in original; see also Galtung, 1994). Much has been written about human needs and human rights. Amartya Sen (2004), a leading scholar in this arena, has developed the capability framework. Nussbaum's version of the capabilities approach puts it in the context of constructing a theory of basic social justice and employs a specific list of "central capabilities" (e.g., Nussbaum, 2011).

Histories of the concept of human rights provide a picture of the varied ways in which the concept has been defined and debated for decades. While the Charter of the United Nations speaks of "the equal rights of men and women," the pivotal document is the Universal Declaration of Human Rights, which affirms the universality of the rights of "all." The challenges that human rights present to the idea of national sovereignty and to that of "universal" rights have been both acknowledged and disputed (see Glendon, 2001). And while the Declaration, employing the language of the time, speaks of "man/he/him/his," it is clear that "all people" are included. From the opening sentence of the document ("the inherent dignity" and "the equal and inalienable rights of all members of the human family") throughout the preamble (e.g., "the equal rights of men and women") and in the individual articles (many begin with "Everyone has the right to . . ."), the Declaration holds that these rights apply to everyone. There are two instances where the language changes: Article 16 talks of "men and women of full age" having "the right to marry and found a family," and Article 25, section 2 states, "Motherhood and childhood are entitled to special care and assistance. All children, whether born in or out of wedlock, shall enjoy the same social protection."

The idea of women's human rights received explicit recognition in the phrase "Women's rights are human rights," a conceptualization that attacks the framework upholding a "private/public" split. GABRIELA, a Filipino nationwide alliance established in 1984 that now has over 200 women's groups, is credited with originating the phrase (Laville, 2012, p. 229; see also http://www.gabrielaph.com). While many support that framing,

The main problem with the concept of women's rights/human rights, one that tended to divide feminists in North and South, was the inherent individualism of a human rights approach based in Northern liberal philosophy. Feminists from the

South are more inclined to recognize collective rights or, at times, to take the side of "culture" in a clash between a woman's individual rights or freedoms and cultural traditions. (Porter, 2007, p. 56)

A related concern was expressed by Galtung in the 1969 (n. 18, p. 188) piece. He argued that human rights "often suffer from the deficiency that they are personal more than structural. They refer to what individuals can do or can have, not to who or what decides what they can do or have; they refer to distribution of resources, not to power over the distribution of resources." And the idea of power is central to a discussion of structural violence and likewise to a discussion of structural violence against women.

As noted, the idea of "universal" human rights is fraught with difficulty, yet it appears that those concerned with women's rights tend toward a position that Johanna Bond proposed: "qualified universalism actually promotes the concept of 'universal' human rights"(cited in Romero, 2013, p. 87). There are at least two related issues. The first is the concept of intersectionality. Their 1977 statement helped credit the Combahee River Collective with originating an intersectional way of thinking (Hulko, 2009, p. 46), and Crenshaw helped advance the idea (see Reilly, 2009, n. 5, p. 167; Cohn, 2013b, n. 3, p. 242), which refers to the different social locations any one individual has, and which must be taken into account in understanding such key issues as power and agency. As Romero (2013, p. 88) argues, "Bringing human rights and intersectionality together moves us forward in developing an adequate set of universal human rights principles, rights, practices, and methods." And the second issue is the relationship between the local context and the universal norm. Without abandoning the idea of "universal human rights," many contend it is essential to fully acknowledge and incorporate the experiences in the concrete, local situation. Some refer to this as the "glocal" approach (see Brewer, 2010, p. 73).

The rich and disputed histories of the international conferences organized by the Commission on the Status of Women point to increasing attention to issues affecting women around the world. There have been four world conferences on women: Mexico (1975), Copenhagen (1980), Nairobi (1985), and Beijing (1995), with support expressed for (see http://5wcw .org/) and against (Porter, 2007) having a fifth world conference. It was the Beijing Conference that "brought the impact of war on women's lives and the issue of women's agency in international and national security issues to the attention of world leaders" (Kuehnast et al., 2011, p. 1).

In 2002 the United Nations (UN) issued *Gender Mainstreaming: An Overview*, a document that claimed "gender equality as the goal—gender mainstreaming as the strategy" (Office of the Special Adviser on Gender Issues and Advancement of Women, 2002, p. 1), a strategy that was endorsed in the Beijing Platform for Action. An often-cited document in the global work is SCR 1325, the resolution unanimously adopted by United Nations Security Council in 2000 calling on member states and all actors involved in peace agreements to adopt a "gender perspective" and urging member states (inter alia) to increase the representation and participation of women in decision making at all levels. Puechguirbal (2010, p. 184) offers a discussion of gender and patriarchy as presented in SRC 1325 and other UN documents, and concludes about the UN, "Thus relations of inequality and the imbalance of power between women and men within the UN system remain uncontested, despite the existence of resolution 1325." The UN Development Fund for Women issued a document, *Overview. 1325+10: Women Count for Peace*, which points to the creation by the General Assembly in July 2010 of the UN Entity for Gender Equality and the Empowerment of Women (UN Women), which will bring together the four UN entities that had, up until that time, been responsible for advancing the mandate of SCR 1325, thus helping to "streamline UN efforts to advance gender equality" (Office of the Special Adviser on Gender Issues and Advancement of Women, 2002, p. 2).

Nevertheless, the international documents are not without their critics. Some argue, for example, that women are routinely defined as vulnerable individuals, often associated with children, leading to Enloe's suggestive term "womenandchildren" (Enloe, 1993, originally in 1990), and leaving the male monopoly of power "unchallenged" and gender mainstreaming presented as "a non-political activity" (Puechguirbal, 2010, p. 172). Puechguirbal (2010, p. 182) claims,

There is an obvious lack of political will and commitment within the UN hierarchy, which, permeated as it is with highly masculinized attitudes, exhibits a persistent resistance to change and power-sharing. Indeed, by projecting a definition of women as vulnerable victims and consistently associating their status with children, the UN system resists a redefinition of tasks and responsibilities that recognizes the experiences and competencies of women.

The "barometer" of "well-grounded masculinist norms" define "who is included and excluded from the corridors of power. In this context, SCR 1325 may appear to be an aberration; its adopting was hailed as a transformatory triumph, but in reality it has been used as a means of co-opting gender dynamics in order to preserve the existing gender status quo" (Puechguirbal, 2010, p. 184).

The area of health (discussed more below) is one in which a rights-based approach has developed. Farmer and his Partners in Health launched the Health Action AIDS campaign in 2001 with Physicians for Human Rights (Farmer, 2010a, pp. 546–547). The public health community was willing "to embrace and promote the right to health." Farmer (2010a, p. 548) argues that "if we believe in health and human rights, we will need to broaden, very considerably, our efforts to promote social and economic rights for the poor. This, I would argue, is the leading human rights issue now facing public health." (See further discussion of this point in the "Structural Interventions" section below.) Farmer has been a strong proponent of the importance of considering structural violence in his field of public health (see "Medicine and Public Health" below).

Finally, one who has explicitly taken Galtung's structural violence concept and extended it in the human rights arena is Kathleen Ho, who has suggested the idea of "Structural Violence as a Human Rights Violation" (2007). She explores various examples, including the case of HIV/AIDs and its disproportionate effects on African Americans as a group and women in particular; she is less concerned with the issue of women per se and more interested in how structural violence is, in fact, a human rights violation, where the issue is the unequal distribution of power that impacts the agency of individuals. While she states that sexism is an instance of structural violence that constrains agency, she does not elaborate. Her basic contention is that "when agency is constrained to the extent that fundamental human needs cannot be attained, structural violence becomes a violation of human rights and thus constitutes a structural violation of human rights" (Ho, 2007, p. 5).

MEDICINE AND PUBLIC HEALTH

What do we know about structural violence and medicine–public health in relation to women? The concept of structural violence seems to have increasing usage. Paul Farmer, the anthropologist-physician who cofounded Partners in Health, was an early adopter (see his 2001 Sidney W. Mintz Lecture in Anthropology in Farmer, 2004), specifically recognizing the work of Galtung, and has incorporated the concept into much of his writing about the work he and colleagues have been doing in Haiti and elsewhere. Farmer has suggested that the concept provides a needed tool in understanding the circumstances under which certain people are more likely to become infected with the HIV virus. He and his colleagues have tried to prompt the medical field to incorporate the concept, arguing that "as long as medical services are sold as commodities, they will remain available only to those who can purchase them" (Farmer et al., 2006, p. 1689). He considers this a failure in the obligation of medical practitioners to contribute to enhancing the life chances of the most vulnerable populations. Farmer (2010b, p. 338) has written about gender and medicine. It is important to note, however, that he cautions, "In most settings, . . . gender alone does not define risk for such assaults on dignity. It is poor women who are least well defended against these assaults. This is true not only of domestic violence and rape but also of AIDS and its distribution." Here the concept of intersectionality comes to the fore, although it does not appear to be used by Farmer. Others as well have urged the incorporation of the structural violence concept into medicine. Rhodes et al. (2012, p. 226), for example, discuss the "social structural production of risk" and state, "Bringing the concepts of structural violence, structural vulnerability and risk environment into the basic lexicon of social epidemiology would revitalize our subdiscipline's distinguished mid-nineteenth century historical roots."

Women's human rights have been raised in the health context, where the issue of private-public split becomes central. Nussbaum (2011, p. 146) suggests that the family is often seen as part of the private sphere which has been, in classical liberal tradition, "off-limits to social justice." In considering obstacles to realizing women's human rights that she encountered when she was the health minister in a province of Pakistan, Ali (2007, p. 316) argues, "Women's failure to access health facilities may be attributable to entrenched gender roles that transcend social class and permeate public policy, legislative enactments and implementation mechanisms." She notes (p. 318) that the "lack of access to a toilet had resulted in problems for women in the public sphere. In sexually segregated societies such as Pakistan, women's bodies are considered 'private,' 'invisible' repositories of male honour."

Several researchers in the health field have used the structural violence concept specifically in the context of gender. Argento et al. (2011, p. 73) use the term in their study of sex work in Mysore, India, and explore how a sex workers' organization that is "based on an occupational health approach to empowerment" is working at altering structural violence as experienced in the lives of sex workers. Rhodes et al. (2012, p. 224) do refer to Galtung in their study of HIV risk among injection drug users and sex workers in several countries, and they state, "Gender is particularly interesting because of the multiple and complex ways it articulates, with distinct material forces, cultural values, individual practices and political policies (including immigration and law enforcement), and it becomes a primary vector for structural violence." And Wadhwa (2012, p. 1203) talks about "gendered vulnerability to structural violence" in India, commenting on the "overarching patriarchal nature of Indian society" (2012, p. 1205). Using a "grief model" in her analysis, she develops the link between women and structural violence, focusing on the way in which health policy is formulated in India. She contends that such a model provides explanatory power, arguing that the "power-resource inequities in society and the political economy" point to "the commission of structural violence, particularly against women, and the resultant suffering" (2012, p. 105).

Yet not all in that field agree on the usefulness of the structural violence concept. Some oppose its usage, fearing that it might "generate more moral heat than analytical light" (response by Wacquant, p. 322 in Farmer, 2004), a point explored below.

THE MILITARY AND MILITARIZATION

The military is seen by many researchers as a (if not "the") central institution in which female-male differences in power, status, roles, and agency are most clearly constructed and developed. It is important, as Segal (2008) urges, that we be cautious in drawing links between gender and militarism. Nevertheless, Betty Reardon early on argued that sexism and the war system are not just "symbiotically related, but are twin manifestations of the same underlying cause" (1985, p. 2), and they are "two interdependent manifestations of a common problem: social violence" (1985, p. 5). While Reardon uses the term "structural violence," she does not cite Galtung's work for it, and she gives "structural design" a secondary role to that of "significant changes in human relations," arguing that the structural changes "should emerge from the changing relations rather than coming prior to them" (1985, p. 84). Thus, while Reardon argues for the rootedness of both sexism and the war system in social violence, she does not claim that either is a form of structural violence against women. She (1985, p. 6) urges that since both sexism and the war system are "culturally conditioned," they are "therefore subject to change."

The relationship between certain types of masculinities and direct violence is a long-standing subject of interest, one for which cross-cultural work has provided important insights. As noted above, one of the examples Galtung used in his piece on structural violence was the case of male-female relations. He chose to say that one husband beating his wife is an example of "personal violence" whereas "when one million husbands keep one million wives in ignorance there is structural violence" (1969, p. 171). The critique of that statement is not so much to disagree with the latter example as being an instance of structural violence as to find fault with Galtung for not having also labeled the former example as an instance of structural violence (see Bunch, 1990, p. 491). This is related to the social construction of a certain kind of masculinity, one that claims physical power to subdue as the male's prerogative (and obligation for some) in a male-female relationship. Such masculinity seems to be at the basis of some military training. Reardon contends, for example, that "indoctrination in misogyny is an essential part of basic training" (1985, p. 29) and that "Fear of feminine characteristics is essential to military socialization" (1985, p. 30).

The issue of male prerogative brings in the concepts of "masculinism" and patriarchy. Kiamba and Waris (2006, p. 90) state that masculinism "is defined as an ideology justifying male domination." While not all researchers agree on the definition of patriarchy, an oft-cited idea is attributed to Enloe, who states,

It is not men-on-top that makes something patriarchal. It's men who are recognized and claim a certain form of masculinity, for the sake of being more valued, more "serious," and "the protector of/and controllers of those people who are less masculine" that makes any organization, any community, any society patriarchal. (cited in Puechguirbal, 2010, p. 179)

In her exploration of the lives of four Iraqi and four U.S. women, Enloe (2010, p. 3) suggests that thinking of them together, in the same war, "might make starkly visible how wars and their prolonged aftermaths depend both on particular ideas about and practices of femininity and masculinity, and on women in warring states *not* discovering their connections with one another" (italics in original). In concluding her study, Enloe states (2010, p. 217), "Making feminist sense of any war—during each of its several distinctively gendered phases—requires taking women seriously: their calculations, their analyses, their actions, and, of course, their silences." Cohn (2013a) and her colleagues present important theorizing and research about a range of issues that relate to women and war.

And on the relationship between militarism and the field of conflict transformation, Francis (2011, p. 506) argues that to understand conflict writ large it is necessary to pay attention "to the global phenomenon of militarism and the model of power from which it arises." It is her contention that the structure and culture of global militarism "constitute the context for all violent conflict" (2011, p. 510).

STRUCTURAL INTERVENTIONS

As noted above, in offering the concept of structural violence, Galtung (1985, p. 146) thought it would contribute to new directions for peace research, and "possibly to efforts to transform structures pregnant with violence into less violent ones." Thinking about the relationships between the local and the global is key to such transformation, with stress on the importance of paying attention to the struggles in concrete situations without losing the concern with the universal elements involved. That leads back to the issue of generalizability. As Reilly (2009, p. 161) contends, in order to advance a non-oppressive global feminism, it is necessary to begin with "an acceptance that there are persistent structural forces at work worldwide that disadvantage women and girls in gender-specific ways." She states (2009, p. 161), "A core contention of this book is that decentered, bottom-up, critical engagement with human rights norms and mechanisms is integral to promoting and sustaining non-oppressive feminist dialogue, solidarity and action in the cosmopolitan tradition." Theorizing about gender as "a structural power relation" (Cohn, 2013b, p. 4) is essential.

So how do individuals, groups, and/or nations work to change structural violence? Clearly, resistance is one way. Some choose to do that violently: "*Structural violence* may refer to an oppression so life-threatening that outbreaks of physical resistance seem justified" (Cockburn, 2004, p. 30, italics in original). Galtung (1969, p. 184) himself raised this question in the original article on structural violence in discussing possible trade-offs between direct and structural violence: "Thus, if our choice of means in the fight against structural violence is so limited by the non-use of personal violence that we are left without anything to do in highly repressive societies, where the repression is latent or manifest, then how valuable is this recipe for peace?"

More nonviolent approaches draw attention from many. Galtung presented ideas on the importance of nonviolence in his 1996 book. Francis (2011, p. 510) argues for a focus on two things that have been neglected so far:

One is identifying and building the power of nonviolence, as a means to address oppressive power relations and actual or threatened violence. The other is exposing and transforming the global culture and systems of war and establishing those of peace. These two are interlinked, in that it is not possible to build the power of nonviolence without building belief in it. Habitual reliance on armed violence and trust in its efficacy discourage such belief.

Conceptual and practical work is being pursued. Kiamba and Waris (2006, p. 95) discuss "structural prevention," the type of prevention that

aims at perverting the manifestation of root causes of conflict. This means that the inequalities experienced in society are remedied and that there is promotion of human rights and human needs such as dignity, belonging, and identity. Structural prevention in brief encompasses the long term steps that reduce the potential for violence, addressing human rights, justice, good governance, development and human security.

And very practically yet profoundly, Ali (2007, pp. 331–332) observes, "Women's disadvantages are often based on structural injustices; rethinking human rights through innovative mechanisms, such as ensuring toilets for women in the public arena, may be some of the opportunities to address those injustices and make women's human rights a reality."

In the particular field of conflict research, Anderlini (2007, p. 33) urges that paying attention to men's and women's experiences

can enhance international efforts to prevent violence and ensure more effective and better-timed responses in political, humanitarian, and developmental terms. Consultations with men and women themselves are critical. First, they can show aid agencies which actions are acceptable. Second, those consulted may have alternative strategies and capacities that could be drawn upon and strengthened.

Kuehnast et al. (2011, p. 3) insist that projects focusing on women and war must take into account "both the underlying gendered power relations that affected women's roles before the conflict broke out, and the dynamics of social change that occur over the conflict cycle." Page et al. (2009) provide a number of recommendations from policies to empowerment to increase women's participation in peace. As noted above, the concept of conflict transformation is rooted in social justice, making it a normative approach with "constructive social change at its core," one that "acknowledges the need for addressing power imbalances and recognizes a role for advocacy and the importance of voices that challenge the status quo. Its concern with direct, structural and cultural violence is thus also highly relevant from a rights perspective" (Parlevliet, 2011, p. 379).

The issue of human rights and what is included in them comes to the fore again. One of the only authors to come close to using the actual term "structural violence against women" is Eisler (1997, pp. 170–171), who laments, "The sad fact is that economic discrimination (or to borrow Johan Galtung's term, 'structural violence' [1980]) against women is ubiquitous, varying only in degree." And in a more recent study, Farmer et al. (2006, p. 1689) claim that the lack of social and economic rights is "fundamental to the perpetuation of structural violence." Thus, they contend, interventions geared to increasing the agency of poor people will lessen, for example, their risk of HIV. Many have urged that the so-called second-generation rights, i.e., economic and social rights, be included among human rights (see Bunch, 1990, p. 488; Sen, 2004). Will the idea of the "indivisibility of human rights" gain traction (see Reilly, 2009, p. 165)?

Galtung stated that the opposite of structural violence is structural peace. And in this context Galtung (1996, p. 271) proposes,

Rather, let one thousand conferences blossom, use modern communication technology to generate a visible flow of peace ideas from everywhere in society. Proposals may be contradictory—but why should peace look the same at all places? Tap the insights all over, marginalizing nobody, making peace-making itself a model of structural peace.

And perhaps it is fitting to conclude with these two ideas from Galtung: "The therapy for pathological structures is a long-haul problem, not a single shot, quick fix" (Galtung, 1996, p. 94), and "And yet theory-building is not the goal: action to reduce violence and enhance peace is the goal" (Galtung, 1996, p. 265).

STRUCTURAL VIOLENCE AGAINST WOMEN: THE REALITY, THE CONCEPT, AND WHERE WE GO FROM HERE

While it is clear that the actual phrase "structural violence against women" is rarely employed in works from the fields examined here, it is also clear that elements of the idea are replete in those very works.

Researchers have worked hard to illuminate the factors that construct and constrain the lives of women around the globe, from conflict situations to ordinary daily living. As a result, the empirical reality of structural violence against women seems well documented in the research. Let me discuss four interrelated issues and questions that researchers and practitioners alike must continue to address.

First is the concept of intersectionality. Any "essentialist" argument about "women" versus "men" seems much weaker once this concept is brought into the picture. Some contend that we cannot speak of a generalizable category of "women": there are too many contextual factors that we need to address to fully understand an empirical reality, and only then can we undertake feasible interventions to address the constraints of the women in those various empirical situations. The question becomes, are there any constraints that "all" women, irrespective of their other identifiers, experience, or is "structural violence" itself different in different areas?

Second is the question of power and agency, which brings up the importance of unraveling the links among direct, cultural, and structural violence. If power typically resides in the male members of a family, a society, or a nation, what options are there for women and men? How is their agency to be considered? What is possible if the norms are stronger for considering an individual to be first and foremost a part of a larger collectivity, with rights and responsibilities residing in the collectivity, versus considering an individual to have rights and responsibilities apart from that collectivity? Are the cultural norms defining women as "weaker" and "emotional," for example, and men as "stronger," and "rational" so strong that an individual (male or female) may not "see" options to alter that reality? Many researchers have pointed to the military, with its emphasis on organization and tradition, as a prime example of the embeddedness of "male" and "female" norms, the legitimacy of direct violence, and the creation of structures that perpetuate violence. To resist and overcome such processes and structures is a formidable challenge, to say the least, and needs further analyses.

That leads to a third issue, namely the roles of violent and nonviolent action. If violence continues to be a sanctioned means of resolving conflicts, from the domestic to the global arenas, with the concomitant idea that "peace is weak," what kinds of theorizing and practices will move policy makers and publics alike to consider alternative views? Here the work being done on the "effectiveness" of nonviolent action from grassroots efforts to global movements needs greater attention from the policy arena and the media as well as from educational institutions.

Fourth, is the actual concept of "structural violence against women" a useful one after all? Or does it provide "more moral heat than analytical light," as suggested by Wacquant (in Farmer, 2004, p. 322)? The argument against his suggestion is partly lodged in the importance of the very term "structure," which helps move us away from the prevalent view that it is "individuals" who do or do not make change, who are "responsible" for their own lives, who can resist if they so "choose," and so on. Structure, then, provides for a larger framework, not ignoring individual-level analysis but suggesting that that level alone is insufficient to enable us to understand the complex realities of our increasingly globalized world. Does the concept advance our thinking and our practice when it comes to the "realities" of violence against women?

The challenges of our intricate, globalized world and the life experiences of women and men in it cry out for more research on and greater understanding of the psychological, cultural, and structural roots of violence and, even more important, of the structures and processes that build peace. All of us—researchers, practitioners, and citizens at large—have our work cut out for us.

BIBLIOGRAPHY

Ali, Shaheen S. 2007. Where Is the Toilet? Getting Down to Basics in Accessing Women's Rights. In *Human Rights, Plural Legalities and Gendered Realities: Paths Are Made by Walking*, edited by Anne Hellum, Julie Stewart, Shaheen Ali, and Amy Tsanga. Harare, Zimbabwe: Southern and Eastern African Regional Centre for Women's Law (SEARCWL), pp. 316–333.

Anderlini, Sanam N. 2007. *Women Building Peace: What They Do, Why It Matters*. Boulder, CO: Lynne Rienner.

Argento, Elena, Sushena Reza-Paul, Robert Lorway, Jinendra Jain, M. Bhagya, Mary Fathima, S. V. Sreeram, Rahman S. Hafeezur, and John O'Neil. 2011. Confronting Structural Violence in Sex Work: Lessons from a Community-Led HIV Prevention Project in Mysore, India. *AIDS Care* 23: 69–74.

Austin, Beatrix. 2011. Introduction. In *Advancing Conflict Transformation: The Berghof Handbook II*, edited by B. Austin, M. Fischer, and H. J. Giessmann. Opladen and Farmington Hills, MI: Barbara Budrich, pp. 9–21.

Brewer, John D. 2010. *Peace Process: A Sociological Approach*. Cambridge, UK: Polity Press.

Brock-Utne, Birgit. 1985. *Educating for Peace: A Feminist Perspective*. New York: Pergamon Press.

Brock-Utne, Birgit. 1989. *Feminist Perspectives on Peace and Peace Education*. New York: Pergamon Press.

Brock-Utne, Birgit. 1997. Linking the Micro and Macro in Peace and Development Studies. In *The Web of Violence: From Interpersonal to Global*, edited by Jennifer Turpin and Lester R. Kurtz. Urbana: University of Illinois Press, pp. 150–160.

Bunch, Charlotte. 1990. Women's Rights as Human Rights: Toward a Re-Vision of Human Rights. *Human Rights Quarterly* 12 (4): 486–496.

Burton, John. 1997. *Violence Explained*. Manchester: Manchester University Press.

Cockburn, Cynthia. 2001. The Gendered Dynamics of Armed Conflict and Political Violence. In *Victims, Perpetrators or Actors? Gender, Armed Conflict and Political Violence*, edited by C. O. N. Moser and F. C. Clark. London: Zed Books, pp. 13–29.

Cockburn, Cynthia. 2004. The Continuum of Violence: A Gender Perspective on War and Peace. In *Sites of Violence: Gender and Conflict Zones*, edited by Wenona Giles and Jennifer Hyndman. Berkeley: University of California Press, pp. 24–43.

Cockburn, Cynthia. 2007. *From Where We Stand: War, Women's Activism & Feminist Analysis*. London: Zed Books.

Cohn, Carol, ed. 2013a. *Women & Wars*. Cambridge, UK: Polity Press.

Cohn, Carol. 2013b. Women and Wars: Toward a Conceptual Framework. In *Women & Wars*, edited by C. Cohn. Cambridge, UK: Polity Press, pp. 1–35.

Confortini, Catia C. 2006. Galtung, Violence, and Gender: The Case for a Peace Studies/Feminism Alliance. *Peace & Change* 31: 333–367.

Eisler, Riane. 1997. Human Rights and Violence: Integrating the Private and Public Spheres. In *The Web of Violence: From Interpersonal to Global*, edited by Jennifer Turpin and Lester R. Kurtz. Urbana: University of Illinois Press, pp. 161–185.

Enloe, Cynthia. 1993. *The Morning After: Sexual Politics at the End of the Cold War*. Berkeley: University of California Press.

Enloe, Cynthia. 2010. *Nimo's War, Emma's War: Making Feminist Sense of the Iraq War*. Berkeley: University of California Press.

Farmer, Paul. 1996. On Suffering and Structural Violence: A View from Below. *Daedalus* 125: 261–283.

Farmer, Paul. 2004. An Anthropology of Structural Violence. *Current Anthropology* 45: 305–325.

Farmer, Paul. 2010a. Making Human Rights Substantial. In *Partner to the Poor: A Paul Farmer Reader*, edited by Haun Saussy. Berkeley: University of California Press, pp. 545–560.

Farmer, Paul. 2010b. On Suffering and Structural Violence: Social and Economic Rights in the Global Era. In *Partner to the Poor: A Paul Farmer Reader*, edited by Haun Saussy. Berkeley: University of California Press, pp. 328–349.

Farmer, Paul E., Bruce Nizeye, Sara Stulac, and Salmaan Keshavjee. 2006. Structural Violence and Clinical Medicine. *Plos Medicine* 3: 1686–1691.

Francis, Diana. 2011. New Thoughts on Power: Closing the Gaps between Theory and Action. In *Advancing Conflict Transformation: The Berghof Handbook II*, edited by B. Austin, M. Fischer, and H. J. Giessmann. Opladen and Farmington Hills, MI: Barbara Budrich, pp. 505–525.

Galtung, Johan. 1969. Violence, Peace, and Peace Research. *Journal of Peace Research* 6: 167–191.

Galtung, Johan. 1980. *The True Worlds: A Transnational Perspective*. New York: Free Press.

Galtung, Johan. 1985. Twenty-five Years of Peace Research: Ten Challenges and Some Responses. *Journal of Peace Research* 22: 141–158.

Galtung, Johan. 1990. Cultural Violence. *Journal of Peace Research* 27: 291–305.

Galtung, Johan. 1994. *Human Rights in Another Key*. Cambridge, UK: Polity Press.

Galtung, Johan. 1996. *Peace by Peaceful Means: Peace and Conflict, Development and Civilization.* Oslo: PRIO, International Peace Research Institute.

Galtung, Johan, and Anders Helge Wirak. 1977. Human Needs and Human Rights: A Theoretical Approach. *Security Dialogue* 8: 251–258.

Gilligan, J. 1996. *Violence: Our Deadly Epidemic and Its Causes.* New York: Putnam's.

Glendon, Mary A. 2001. *A World Made New: Eleanor Roosevelt and the Universal Declaration of Human Rights.* New York: Random House.

Ho, Kathleen. 2007. Structural Violence as a Human Rights Violation. *Essex Human Rights Review* 4: 1–17.

Hulko, Wendy. 2009. The Time- and Context-Contingent Nature of Intersectionality and Interlocking Oppressions. *Journal of Women and Social Work* 24: 44–55.

Kiamba, Anita, and Attiya Waris. 2006. An African Feminist Perspective on Security and Early Warning Mechanisms: IGAD. In *Rethinking Global Security: An African Perspective?*, edited by Makumi Mwagiru and Okello Oculli. Nairobi: Heinrich Boll Foundation, pp. 86–105.

Kuehnast, Kathleen, Chantal de Jonge Oudraat, and Helga Hernes. 2011. Introduction. In *Women & War: Power and Protection in the 21st Century*, edited by Kathleen Kuehnast, Chantal de Jonge Oudraat, and Helga Hernes. Washington, DC: United States Institute of Peace, pp. 1–18.

Laville, Helen. 2012. Stay Involved: Transnational Feminist Advocacy and Women's Human Rights. *Journal of Women's History* 24: 222–230.

Lederach, John P. 2003. *The Little Book of Conflict Transformation.* Intercourse, PA: Good Books.

Maas Weigert, Kathleen. 2008. Structural Violence. In *Encyclopedia of Violence, Peace, & Conflict*, vol. 3, edited by Lester Kurtz. Oxford: Elsevier, pp. 2004–2011.

Nussbaum, Martha C. 2011. *Creating Capabilities: The Human Development Approach.* Cambridge, MA: Belknap Press of Harvard University Press.

Office of the Special Adviser on Gender Issues and Advancement of Women. 2002. *Gender Mainstreaming: An Overview.* New York: United Nations.

Page, Michelle, Tobie Whitman, and Cecilia Anderson. 2009. *Strategies for Policymakers: Bringing Women into Peace Negotiations.* Washington, DC: Institute for Inclusive Security.

Parlevliet, Michelee. 2011. Human Rights and Conflict Transformation: Towards a More Integrated Approach. In *Advancing Conflict Transformation: The Berghof Handbook II*, edited by B. Austin, M. Fischer, and H. J. Giessmann. Opladen and Farmington Hills, MI: Barbara Budrich, pp. 377–404.

Porter, Marilyn. 2007. Transnational Feminisms in a Globalized World: Challenges, Analysis, and Resistance. *Feminist Studies* 33: 43–63.

Puechguirbal, Nadine. 2010. Discourses on Gender, Patriarchy and Resolution 1325: A Textual Analysis of UN Documents. *International Peacekeeping* 17: 172–187.

Reardon, Betty A. 1985. *Sexism and the War System.* New York: Teachers College Press.

Reardon, Betty A. 1988. *Comprehensive Peace Education: Educating for Global Responsibility.* New York: Teachers College Press.

Reilly, Niamh. 2009. *Women's Human Rights: Seeking Gender Justice in a Globalizing Age.* Cambridge, UK: Polity Press.

Rhodes, Tim, Karla Wagner, Steffanie A. Strathdee, Kate Shannon, Peter David-
    son, and Philippe Bourgois. 2012. Structural Violence and Structural Vul-
    nerability within the Risk Environment: Theoretical and Methodological
    Perspectives for a Social Epidemiology of HIV Risk among Injection Drug
    Users and Sex Workers. In *Rethinking Social Epidemiology: Towards a Sci-
    ence of Change*, edited by Patricia O'Campo and James R. Dunn. New York:
    Springer, pp. 205–230.
Romero, Mary. 2013. Race, Class, and Gender. In *The Handbook of Sociology and
    Human Rights*, edited by David L. Brunsma, Keri E. Iyall Smith, and Brian
    K. Gran. Boulder, CO: Paradigm, pp. 79–88.
Segal, Lynne. 2008. War and Militarism: Making and Questioning the Links. *Femi-
    nist Review* 88: 21–35.
Sen, Amartya. 2004. Elements of a Theory of Human Rights. *Philosophy & Public
    Affairs* 32 (4): 315–356.
Tickner, J. A. 1992. *Gender in International Relations: Feminist Perspectives on Achiev-
    ing Global Security*. New York: Columbia University Press.
Tickner, J. A. 1995. Introducing Feminist Perspectives into Peace and World Secu-
    rity Courses. *Women's Studies Quarterly* 23 (3 & 4): 48–57.
United Nations Development Fund for Women (UNIFEM). 2010. *Overview.
    1325+10: Women Count for Peace*. New York: United Nations.
Wadhwa, Vandana. 2012. Structural Violence and Women's Vulnerability to HIV/
    AIDS in India: Understanding through a "Grief Model" Framework. *Annals
    of the Association of American Geographers* 102: 1200–1208.

CHAPTER 6

International Violence against Women: Prevalence, Outcomes, and Prevention

Danielle Dirks and Emily Troshynski

INTRODUCTION

Violence against women and girls is a global epidemic, first identified by the United Nations as a serious international concern at the 1985 Nairobi World Conference. Since that time, a host of studies have demonstrated that the lives of girls and women are marked by violence, across all countries. This violence is rooted in a system of patriarchy that values and privileges men and boys over women and girls.

In this chapter, we describe the incidence and prevalence of violence against women globally; outline the immediate and long-term impacts of violence on physical, mental, sexual, and reproductive health; and describe international efforts in response to this epidemic using social service, criminal justice, public health, and preventive interventions.

GLOBAL VIOLENCE AGAINST WOMEN: PREVALENCE

Based on data from 79 countries and two territories, the 2013 World Health Organization (WHO) report on global and regional estimates of violence against women estimates that 30.3 percent of all ever-partnered women experience intimate partner violence during their lifetime (WHO, 2013). However, when data on women's experiences with nonpartner sexual violence is included, that figure increases to 35 percent. To rearticulate, well over one-third of all women worldwide have experienced physical and/or sexual intimate partner violence or nonpartner sexual violence (WHO, 2013).[1] The prevalence of global violence against women described below draws from the 2013 WHO report with supplemental data published in 2005.

Prevalence and Factors of Intimate Partner Violence

Worldwide, 30 percent of all ever-partnered women have experienced physical and/or sexual violence by their intimate partners. In some regions, however, this percentage increases to 38 percent (WHO, 2013; Devries et al., 2013; Stockl et al., 2013). For example, the prevalence of physical or sexual intimate partner violence was the highest for women in 6 countries of Southeast Asia (37.7%), 5 countries within the Eastern Mediterranean (37%), and another 17 countries within Africa (36.6%). Women living in 15 countries in the Americas constitute the fourth highest level of lifetime intimate partner violence (29.8%), followed by women living in 10 countries in Europe (25.4%) and 5 countries located in the western Pacific (24.6%). Finally, 23.3 percent of women living in 24 "high income" locations (WHO, 2013)[2] reported the lowest levels of lifetime intimate partner violence overall.

Beyond regional differences in rates of gendered violence, age is also an important factor (WHO, 2013).[3] Women ages 40 to 44 report the highest rates of lifetime intimate partner violence (37.8%), followed by women ages 35 to 39 (36.6%), 25 to 29 (32.3%) and 20 to 24 (31.2%). The prevalence of lifetime intimate partner violence for the youngest age group (15 to 19) was also high, with 29.4 percent of women reporting experiences with abuse. This figure means that almost a third of all young women ages 15 to 19 have already experienced violence at the hand of an intimate partner.

Lamentably, these figures do not decline with age: For women age 45 and older, rates of lifetime experiences with intimate partner violence are still remarkably high, at 29 percent of women ages 45 to 49 and 26 percent for women ages 50 to 54. Even though fewer data are available for women older than 49, global estimates demonstrate that 22 percent of all women ages 65 to 69 report lifetime physical and sexual abuse as well.

According to WHO's 2005 Multi-Country Study on Women's Health and Domestic Violence Against Women Survey (WHO, 2005),[4] partnership status is also associated with rates of violence. Women who are separated or divorced report higher levels of lifetime physical and/or sexual violence committed by an intimate partner than do women who are currently married and unmarried women living with their partners.

Levels of educational attainment are also associated with rates of violence. In Peru, Thailand, the United Republic of Tanzania, as well as cities in Brazil and Namibia, women with higher levels of education report experiencing lower rates of physical and sexual violence. Conversely, women with lower levels of educational attainment experience greater rates of physical and/or sexual violence. Higher levels of violence for this population of women could also be due to having a partner with lower levels of educational attainment, having fewer choices in partners, having less freedom to remain single for longer and not marry, as well as having less autonomy in accessing and controlling resources while married (WHO, 2005; Koenig et al., 2003; Koenig et al., 2006). Overall, it is unknown whether or not violence and education are confounded by age, marital status, or socioeconomic status.

There is a substantial overlap in the prevalence of physical and sexual violence in women's lives globally. Indeed, when experiences of physical and sexual violence are combined, 15 to 71 percent of women report an experience of victimization occurring over their lifetime; more than half of these women report either physical violence only or physical violence accompanied by sexual violence. For example, in most sites, 30 to 56 percent of women who had ever experienced any violence reported experiencing both physical and sexual violence. However, women cities in Japan, Brazil, Thailand, and Serbia report less than a 30 percent overlap of physical and sexual violence while women in other locations like Thailand have a larger proportion of women (44%) reporting that they experienced sexual abuse only. Overall, this 2005 study suggests that sexual violence occurs less frequently than physical violence but that sexual violence often accompanies experiences of physical violence as well.

Prevalence and Factors of Nonpartner Sexual Violence

Based on WHO adjusted data from 56 countries and two territories, the global prevalence of lifetime nonpartner sexual violence is 7.2 percent. In other words, 7 percent of women ages 15 years and older have experienced nonpartner sexual violence. Rates of nonpartner sexual violence vary by region, with 11.9 percent of women in the 16 African countries experiencing nonpartner sexual violence compared to 10.7 percent of women in 8 countries in the Americas. Rates of nonpartner sexual violence are lower in western Pacific countries (6.8%), 7 countries in Europe (5.2%), and six locations in Southeast Asia (4.9%) (WHO, 2005).[5] Lifetime sexual violence committed by intimate partners is three times more prevalent than nonpartner sexual violence, meaning that women's risk of sexual violence is much greater with the people closest to them than with nonintimates.

According to the 2005 WHO study, common offenders in nonpartner sexual violence include the respondent's father, other male family members, and other female family members. Nonfamily acquaintances also account for a large portion of physical violence committed by nonpartners. Between 15 and 30 percent of women acknowledged teachers as their physically violent perpetrators in Bangladesh, Namibia, and Samoa.

These findings suggest that experiencing physical violence by a nonpartner after the age of 15 includes multiple perpetrators and often involves family members.

Prevalence of Intimate Partner Violence and Nonpartner Sexual Violence

When rates of physical and sexual intimate partner violence and nonpartner sexual violence are combined, the realities of global violence against women prove dire. Countries with women age 15 and older reporting the highest rates of lifetime prevalence of gendered violence include Africa (45.6%), Southeast Asia (40.2%), and eastern Mediterranean regions (36.4%). Estimates suggest an average of 41 percent have experienced either physical or sexual intimate partner violence or nonpartner sexual violence in their lifetime in these three regions. This combined average compares with rates of overall victimization reported by women in the Americas (36.1%), "high income" (32.7%) designated countries, and the western Pacific (27.8%). Women in European countries report lower levels of combined violence (27.2%) (WHO, 2005).[6] Recent studies completed in the western Pacific region that were not included in the final WHO survey found even higher rates of physical or sexual intimate partner violence, ranging between 60 and 68 percent for the women in the study. If results from these three studies were also included, the comprehensive rate of violence against women would be even higher than that the one in three reported in the 2013 global survey (Secretariat of the Pacific Community, 2009, 2010; Vanuatu Women's Centre, 2011; WHO, 2013).

With the focus on the experiences of child sexual abuse, there is regional variance, with Bangladesh on the lower end (1%) and Peru (19%) and Namibia (21%) on the higher end. When asked to identify the perpetrator, roughly two-thirds of respondents from Bangladesh, Japan, and Thailand listed "stranger" as the most frequent response. A sizable but smaller number of women living in Serbia and Montenegro (39.3%) and Samoa (33.3%) also acknowledged a "stranger" as their violent offender. A majority of women in Brazil city (66.3%), Brazil province (54.1%), and Peru city (53.6%) listed a "family" member as the aggressor.

Moreover, in 10 of the 15 site locations, over 5 percent of women reported their first sexual experience under the age of 15 as forced. This figure was much higher in locations within Bangladesh, Ethiopia, Peru, and the United Republic of Tanzania, where more than 14 percent of women reported a forced first sexual encounter. Higher rates of forced first sex were reported by women living in regional provinces described as rural and less populated than in urban cityscapes. Comparatively, respondents within cities in Japan, and Serbia and Montenegro had less than 1 percent of women describing their first sexual experience as forced. In all sites except for Ethiopia province, the lower the woman's age of first sex, the greater the likelihood that it was forced. These findings are comparable to research completed on international rates of child abuse (see Barth et al., 2013) and document additional prevalence estimates of child sexual abuse ranging from 8 to 31 percent for women.

GLOBAL VIOLENCE AGAINST WOMEN: EFFECTS ON GIRLS AND WOMEN

Girls' and women's experiences of violence vary according to gender relations and inequality; poverty; access to legal, social, or health services; and local/regional/national practices and policies. While the form and nature of such violence may differ among women in low-, middle-, and "high-income" countries, the data are clear: the relationship between violence and negative health outcomes is significant and well documented. From this research we understand that the negative impacts of exposure to violence against women in less-developed or developing nations are s similar to or, at times, greater than those in developed countries. Below we describe the ways in which both intimate partner violence and sexual violence impact women's physical, mental, sexual, and reproductive health.

We should caveat these points with a methodological concern related to building causal (as opposed to correlational) associations between exposure to violence and poor health outcomes. While there is evidence that clearly documents that certain injuries are directly caused by physical or sexual violence, scholars have a much more difficult time establishing causality with cross-sectional or self-report research studies that examine violence data only at one point in time. This makes it much more difficult to establish causal relationships for less direct negative impacts of physical or sexual violence, such as more serious mental health, sexual, or reproductive problems. However, there is ample evidence to indicate that the directions of these associations demonstrate that poorer health is an outcome of violence rather than a precursor. Relatedly, unfavorable health outcomes do not appear to be explained by other variables, including age, education attainment, or marital status. Finally, as the 2013 WHO report indicates, exposure to violence operates both directly and indirectly on health outcomes.

Studies across the globe demonstrate that women's exposure to violence is linked to both acute and chronic physical, mental, sexual, and reproductive disorders and diseases (Ellsberg et al., 2008). A key factor in understanding the relationship between violence and outcomes is that physical, mental, sexual, and reproductive health impacts from exposure to violence can last for a lifetime, persisting long after the violence or threat of violence has ended. Below we discuss each of these impacts in turn.

Physical Health

One of the primary outcomes of violence is physical injury, which can involve both immediate and chronic consequences, including fatality. When men engage in physical violence toward women, they are significantly more likely to increase the severity of women's abuse, meaning that women are much more likely to sustain physical injuries from violence than are men. Research on intimate partner violence across the globe consistently shows that the most direct effects of violence include both nonfatal and fatal injuries and that men's intimate violence against women is a common cause of physical injury.

More acute physical injuries include bruises, cuts, burns, abrasions, bites, internal injuries, and broken or fractured bones and teeth. Men who engage in physically violent acts are most likely to target a woman's head, neck, and face. Some evidence suggests that men's intimate partner violence increases when women become pregnant and that men are more likely to target a woman's abdomen, breasts, genitals, or buttocks in those cases (Newberger et al., 1992).[7] In fact, in the United States, femicide has been a leading cause of death for pregnant women in at least one state (Horon and Cheng, 2001), and this pattern holds in India and Bangladesh (WHO, 2005). Physical injuries related specifically to sexual violence include gynecological trauma such as vaginal tearing or tearing in the areas between the vagina and rectum or bladder (or both), ulcerations, infections, or childbirth-related complications. Some of the longer-lasting physical effects of violence include chronic pain, persistent headaches, hemorrhages, irritable bowel syndrome, abdominal or gastrointestinal disorders, and gynecological problems. Women in abusive intimate relationships are likely to be physically injured by their partners and will sustain multiple types of these injuries. Severe physical injuries can prove fatal, amounting to homicide, a form of aggravated assault that ends in death. Globally, women are most likely to be killed by an intimate—someone close to them, typically a current or former male partner or a family member (e.g., in certain parts of the Middle East and south Asia, family members engage in "honor killings" of women for perceived "sexual transgressions") (Jaden and Thoennes, 2000). In the United States, killing by male intimates is a leading cause of death for young women, but particularly for women of color (Hewitt et al., 2011). This pattern of femicide—the killing of women related to gendered oppression—holds steady throughout studies on developed and developing nations.

Mental Health

In addition to physical injuries sustained from physical or sexual violence, women are significantly more likely to experience poor mental health outcomes as a result of being exposed to violence. However, some evidence suggests that women with severe, debilitating mental illnesses are much more likely to experience violent victimization than women without such difficulties (Friedman and Loue, 2008). Additionally, mental health problems such as depression and anxiety disorders can also be risk factors for victimization, including intimate partner or sexual violence. In this case, it is important to point out that pre-existing mental health concerns will be compounded by the experience of abuse or violent victimization, whether it involves intimates or strangers. There is a consistent pattern that demonstrates that women who were victimized as girls or adolescents are much more likely to be revictimized as adults, and the pathways and explanations for such revictimization patterns need further exploration. Finally, early traumas can play a key role in predicting poor mental health outcomes and also future violence—for perpetrators and for victims.

The data on the health outcomes for women who have been exposed to violence are clear: experiences of physical and sexual violence are linked to adverse mental health outcomes in women's lives. Most commonly, these include depression, suicide ideation, suicidal behavior, self-harm, post-traumatic stress disorder (PTSD), stress and anxiety disorders, sleeping disorders, disordered eating, and psychosomatic disorders. These disorders are accompanied by a constellation of emotional difficulties including feelings of intense shame, self-blame, fear, sadness, isolation, powerlessness, and helplessness.

Key to understanding the link between exposure to violence and depression, anxiety, and suicidal thoughts and behaviors is "traumatic stress"—the experience of fear, isolation, and stigma in the aftermath of a traumatic event. Traumatic stress can be compounded by the social consequences of revealing one's identity as a victim. Girls and women who share that they have been victimized risk ostracism, rejection by their loved ones and community, decline in social standing, and increased poverty. These social consequences ensure that the mental health effects of violent events can extend for years or even decades beyond the violent events and can encourage girls and women to suffer in silence rather than seek help.

One response to managing traumatic stress can be seen in girls' and women's suicide ideation and attempts in the aftermath of violent victimization. Here again, the pattern is clear: women who have experienced physical or sexual violence (or both) are significantly more likely to have considered ending their lives or have attempted to do so. When one's life is filled with trauma, depression, stress, dissociative symptoms, and anxiety, suicide appears as a means by which to end this suffering. It should be noted that attempting to end such deeply traumatic stress through suicide is a pattern that emerges globally.

Sexual and Reproductive Health

In addition to the immediate and long-term physical and mental health effects of exposure to violence, research consistently shows that violent victimization is significantly associated with women's sexual and reproductive health outcomes. Here, it is clear that patriarchy and gender inequality directly impact women's lives in their experiences as targets of gender-based violence but also in their ability (or lack thereof) to control their own bodies. Quite clearly, patriarchal societies that valorize masculinity place women in the greatest harm, and this equates to unfavorable sexual and reproductive health outcomes for women such as acquiring sexually transmitted infections (STIs) such as HIV, unwanted pregnancies, forced or unsafe abortions, miscarriages, stillbirths, hemorrhaging, and other gynecological problems. Below we outline the ways in which patriarchal ideas about sex, men's access to women's bodies, and sexual violence are linked to a host of sexual and reproductive health problems.

In patriarchal societies, men's risky, predatory, or violent behaviors toward women are not only celebrated but normalized. These are not only the foundations for "rape-prone societies" found throughout the developed and developing world, but serve as the means by which men's sense of entitlement to girls' and women's bodies originates (Sanday, 2007). This right to access the female body allows men to have multiple sexual partners and to set the tone and control the expectations for all sexual interactions. Across the world, men who engage in acts of physical or sexual abuse are more likely to engage in risky sexual behaviors, and in some parts of the world, men are significantly more likely to have HIV or other STIs. Additionally, women who report that they have been physically abused are significantly more likely to report that they know that their partners have had multiple sexual partners outside of their relationship.

It is within this pathway that men can expose women to STIs and HIV directly (through unwanted or forced sexual intercourse) but also indirectly given that women are often unable to control their sexual interactions. Women who lack the power to negotiate when, how, or with whom they have sexual intercourse are at an increased risk of being raped and sexually assaulted. Additionally, such women are much less likely to be able to negotiate condom usage and therefore use condoms much less frequently, increasing their likelihood of acquiring HIV or other STIs from male partners. Women who experience intimate partner violence and sexual violence perpetrated by intimate partners are repeatedly exposed to HIV and other STIs in the context of abusive longer-term relationships where men rape and sexually assault their partners.

In addition to having an increased likelihood of contracting HIV or other STI, women who experience intimate partner violence are significantly more likely to have unintended or unwanted pregnancies, abortions, miscarriages, and low-birthweight babies (WHO, 2013). Again, these negative health outcomes are related to both direct and indirect pathways. Unintended pregnancies may be a result of rape or related to men's contraceptive sabotage, or the impossibility of negotiating contraceptive use without the fear of violence (Moore et al., 2010).

Additionally, women who experience intimate physical or sexual violence are much more likely to have negative pregnancy-related health outcomes. Women with violent partners are less likely to receive prenatal and postnatal care and more likely to experience periods of extreme stress, anxiety, and depression during and after the baby is born—all factors linked to higher rates of miscarriages, abortions, low-birthweight babies, and maternal mortality (WHO, 2011).

GLOBAL VIOLENCE AGAINST WOMEN: INTERVENTIONS

Nations across the globe have intensified their efforts to combat intimate partner and sexual violence against women in recent decades in light of new research on the scope, severity, and cost of this epidemic. Starting in 1993 with the World Conference on Human Rights and the Declaration on the Elimination of Violence Against Women, governments have formally recognized violence against women as a human rights and public policy concern and have established international standards to document this epidemic. The United Nations Commission on the Status of Women classifies the prevention of violence against women as a top priority (United Nations Women, 2013b).

The vast majority of resources expended for violence prevention programs worldwide are allocated to support services for victims and to the arrest and incarceration of perpetrators (Dobash and Dobash, 2000). These interventions occur in the aftermath of violent victimization, but emerging research shows that preventing violence before it happens is the best long-term solution. This section describes the major approaches to preventing intimate partner and sexual violence against women: social service programs, criminal justice interventions, public health initiatives, and prevention programs.

The Social Service Approach

Countries across the globe now offer domestic violence shelters and rape crisis services to victims of intimate partner and sexual violence through government and nongovernmental organizations (NGOs). State and federally supported domestic violence shelters sprang up in Western industrialized nations in the 1960s in response to an emerging domestic violence movement, and now over 2,000 shelters exist in the United States, serving over 50,000 victims on a daily basis (National Network to End

Domestic Violence, 2008). Starting in the 1980s, the international women's movement promoted antiviolence awareness campaigns and programs on every continent. Antiviolence legislation is more likely to pass in wealthy democracies that have greater female political representation, but most countries provide at least some services to support victims of intimate partner and sexual violence through government programs and/or NGOs (Giridhar, 2012). Rape crisis centers materialized around the same time as domestic violence shelters in Western industrialized nations. These centers provide direct support services (e.g., health care, counseling), referrals, legal advice, and crisis hotlines for those who have experienced a sexual assault. Rape crisis centers exist in every country but are more prevalent in higher-income democracies. International coalitions that promote victim support services are growing in number and size, including the Women Against Violence Europe (WAVE), the United Nations Interagency Campaign on Women's Human Rights in Latin America and the Caribbean, and the Communities Against Violence Network.

The Criminal Justice Approach

Most countries have passed laws to criminalize intimate partner and sexual violence in recent decades, although implementation is uneven (Giridhar, 2012). Wealthy democratic countries are more likely than other countries to both pass and implement domestic violence and antirape legislation. In 2013, the European Union passed legislation to enforce restraining orders against perpetrators of domestic violence in all member countries (United Nations Women, 2013a). The main task of the criminal justice approach is to enforce these laws after violence has occurred, a task that involves properly identifying, adjudicating, and sentencing perpetrators (Aa, 2012). An effective criminal justice approach lowers the overall rate of violence against women through deterrence and perpetrator rehabilitation.

The Public Health Approach

WHO has classified violence against women as a "public health problem of epidemic proportions" that limits women's participation in society and puts their physical, reproductive, and mental health at risk (WHO, 2013, p. 2). Health responses to violence against women consist of both an immediate response to the violence (e.g., emergency room visits, postrape care, HIV testing) and a longer-term therapeutic response to reduce the harm of trauma and physical disabilities from the violence. While most countries are taking positive steps to expand services for survivors of sexual violence, comprehensive support services need to be more effective and accessible. Survivors of sexual assault and other forms of violence are often reluctant to come forward given the societal stigma attached to their victimization, and as a result, the vast majority of women who experience intimate partner and sexual violence do not seek needed services. Additionally, health care providers could be better trained in measures to serve the needs of traumatized victims, including providing privacy and confidentiality, ensuring that victims have access to referral services, and addressing both the mental and emotional damage from experiencing violence.

Beyond the service provision approach discussed above, the public health approach includes health care professionals playing an expanded role in identifying and addressing intimate partner and sexual violence against women. For example, when women seek needed medical services (e.g., family planning, postabortion care), health care providers can be trained to identify signs of violence and intervene with emergency and mental health services. The public health approach trains medical professionals to identify correlates of victimization so they can provide intervention and services for victims of violence. As discussed in the previous section, women who experience intimate partner or sexual violence present a host of deleterious health outcomes, including depression, anxiety, and self-injurious behaviors for coping. Additionally, women often have multiple injuries at one time or several injuries over time. Medical providers can be trained to look for these direct correlates of violence. Medical providers can also be on the lookout for indirect signs of violence against women, including unintended pregnancies from perpetrators disapproving of or sabotaging birth control, or disapproval of condom use.

Researchers consider the public health approach to be the most promising model for addressing violence against women, but it is resource intensive. The expanded role for health care professionals recommended by WHO requires better training for health care professionals in identifying issues of violence against women and responding effectively. Clinical training curricula would incorporate issues of violence, and every sector of the medical profession would need to be trained to identify health correlates of violence.

Preventive Approaches

The criminal, policy, and public health approaches are post hoc interventions for intimate partner and sexual violence against women, but surprisingly few efforts have been made to prevent violence from happening in the first place. Comprehensive service provisions will continue to be essential, but given the sheer magnitude and economic and public health costs of this violence, preventing violence before it occurs is the only viable long-term solution to this problem. Experts have identified a number of different proactive approaches to preventing violence against women, including the gender and human rights approaches, early childhood interventions, and a multisector approach.

The gender approach to preventing violence against women focuses on the root cause of violence: patriarchy and unequal power dynamics in the constructions of masculinity and femininity. This approach is premised on the finding that violence against women is deeply rooted in social norms of gender discrimination and gender stereotypes. Gender-approach interventions involve public education campaigns that make use of media and social media to shift community and societal norms. The United Nations Commission on the Status of Women concluded that prevention campaigns should aim to promote women's empowerment through ensuring their safety in private and public spaces, increase women's decision making power in the home and in politics, ensure women's economic security and autonomy, and include boys and men in programs that challenge deeply ingrained beliefs that men should have control over girls and women. The gender approach is a fundamental component of any effective effort to eliminate intimate partner and sexual violence against women.

The human rights approach is based on the assumption that states have an obligation to protect the rights of all citizens, so violence against women is classified as a violation of the rights to security, liberty, life, and equality. The 1979 United Nations Convention on the Elimination of All Forms of Discrimination Against Women, or CEDAW (Merry, 2003), and the 1994 Inter-American Convention on the Prevention, Punishment, and Eradication of Violence Against Women (Convention of Belem do Para) require that participating countries take necessary steps to end violence against women.

The life course approach takes into account that infant and early childhood experiences influence the likelihood of later perpetration of violence and establishes early interventions to address the problem. Unique intervention strategies (e.g., counseling, anger management, gender role education) are used at each stage of early life (infancy, 0–4 years of age), childhood (5–14 years of age), adolescence/young adulthood (15–25 years of age), and adulthood (26 years and older) and are tailored to violence intervention at each developmental stage.

Experts agree that a multisector approach is needed to effectively eliminate intimate partner and sexual violence against women. Since violence is the result of many factors, the more effective approach combines efforts from various sectors: health, social services, criminal justice, and education. A multisector approach is essential to reducing and eliminating the global epidemic of gendered violence, the harm of which can last a lifetime, span multiple generations, and affect the social, economic, and political well-being of individual, families, and communities.

CONCLUSION

For millions of girls and women, physical and sexual violence is commonplace. Global estimates suggest that over one-third (35.6%) of women have experienced either physical or sexual violence committed by intimate partners, sexual violence committed by nonpartners, or both. Intimate partner and sexual violence against girls and women is linked to both acute and chronic physical, mental, sexual, and reproductive disorders and diseases, and these effects can last a lifetime. Collectively, the costs of violence against women and the human suffering involved are huge. Despite the fact that violence against girls and women is a highly preventable phenomenon, states' approaches to ending this violence are still in their infancy. Most countries have responded to this crisis with criminal justice and social service responses, and recent research shows that the public health model—involving public health officials in identifying and addressing violence against women— shows promising results. Experts suggest that preventive and multisector approaches are needed in the long term to effectively eliminate intimate partner and sexual violence against girls and women.

NOTES

1. Data on intimate partner violence experienced by women older than age 49 came from high-income countries.

2. Calculated using the World Bank Atlas method, "high income" regions are based on gross national income per capita and include the following 23 countries: Australia, Canada, Croatia, Czech Republic, Denmark, Finland, France, Germany, Hong Kong, Iceland, Ireland, Israel, Japan, Netherlands, New Zealand, Norway, Poland, South Korea, Spain, Sweden, Switzerland, United Kingdom of Great Britain and Northern Ireland, and the United States.

3. The age groups analyzed here are each of length four years: 15–19, 20–24, 25–29, and so on to 65–69.

4. Site locations were chosen based on a combination of urban and rural locations: Bangladesh city (Dhaka), Bangladesh province (Matlab), Peru city (Lima), Peru province (Department of Cusco), Brazil city (Sao Paulo), Brazil province (Sona de Mata de Pernambuco), Thailand city (Bankok), Thailand province (Nakhonsawan), United Republic of Tanzania city (Dar es Salaam), United Republic of Tanzania province (Mbeya district), Ethiopia province (Butajira), Japan city (Yokohama), Namibia city (Windhoek), Serbia and Montenegro city (Belgrade), Samoa (entire country).

5. Information on the age of the women reporting nonpartner sexual violence was not included due to a lack of availability of age-specific data. Additionally, a lower rate of reporting for women living in conflict-affected countries is a relevant limitation not only to these data but for research on violence against women in general, while other noted regional differences in rates of nonpartner sexual victimization could also be based on under-reporting due to the stigma of disclosure.

6. WHO countries designated as "Europe" include low- and middle-income countries only (examples include Albania and the Ukraine). France, the United Kingdom of Great Britain and Northern Ireland, as well as Poland, Czech Republic, and Switzerland are classified under the aforementioned "high income" category.

7. However, some evidence suggests that pregnancy involves protection from violence in some settings given the reduction in violence that is reported during pregnancy (WHO, 2005).

BIBLIOGRAPHY

Aa, Suzan van der. 2012, June 1. Protection Orders in the European Member States: Where Do We Stand and Where Do We Go from Here? *European Journal on Criminal Policy and Research* 18 (2): 183–204. doi:10.1007/s10610-011-9167-6.

Barth, J., L. Bermetz, E. Heim, S. Trelle, and T. Tonia. 2013, June 1. The Current Prevalence of Child Sexual Abuse Worldwide: A Systematic Review and Meta-Analysis. *International Journal of Public Health* 58 (3): 469–483. doi:10.1007/s00038-012-0426-1.

Devries, K. M., J. Y. T. Mak, C. García-Moreno, M. Petzold, J. C. Child, G. Falder, S. Lim, et al. 2013, June 28. The Global Prevalence of Intimate Partner Violence Against Women. *Science* 340 (6140): 1527–1528. doi:10.1126/science.1240937.

Dobash, R. Emerson, and Russell P. Dobash. 2000, April 1. Evaluating Criminal Justice Interventions for Domestic Violence. *Crime & Delinquency* 46 (2): 252–270. doi:10.1177/0011128700046002007.

Ellsberg, Mary, Henrica A. F. M. Jansen, Lori Heise, Charlotte H. Watts, and Claudia Garcia-Moreno. 2008, April 5. Intimate Partner Violence and Women's Physical and Mental Health in the WHO Multi-Country Study on Women's Health and Domestic Violence: An Observational Study. *Lancet* 371 (9619): 1165–1172. doi:10.1016/S0140-6736(08)60522-X.

Friedman, Susan H., and Sana Loue. 2008, April 1. Intimate Partner Violence Among Women with Severe Mental Illness. *Psychiatric Times* 25 (4).

Giridhar, Nisha. 2012. The Global Spread of Domestic Violence Legislation: Causes and Effects. International Relations Honors Thesis, New York University, http://politics.as.nyu.edu/docs/IO/4600/Giridhar_Nisha.pdf

Hewitt, Lisa N., Premal Bhavsar, and Herb A. Phelan. 2011, February. The Secrets Women Keep: Intimate Partner Violence Screening in the Female Trauma Patient. *Journal of Trauma* 70 (2): 320–323. doi:10.1097/TA.0b013e31820958d3.

Horon, Isabelle L., and Diana Cheng. 2001, March 21. Enhanced Surveillance for Pregnancy-Associated Mortality—Maryland, 1993–1998. *Journal of the American Medical Association* 285 (11): 1455.

Jaden, Patricia, and Nancy Thoennes. 2000, February 1. Prevalence and Consequences of Male-to-Female and Female-to-Male Intimate Partner Violence as Measured by the National Violence Against Women Survey. *Violence Against Women* 6 (2): 142–161. doi:10.1177/10778010022181769.

Koenig, Michael A., Saifuddin Ahmed, Mian Bazle Hossain, and A. B. M. Khorshed Alam Mozumder. 2003, May 1. Women's Status and Domestic Violence in Rural Bangladesh: Individual- and Community-Level Effects. *Demography* 40 (2): 269–288. doi:10.1353/dem.2003.0014.

Koenig, Michael A., Rob Stephenson, Saifuddin Ahmed, Shireen J. Jejeebhoy, and Jacquelyn Campbell. 2006, January. Individual and Contextual Determinants of Domestic Violence in North India. *American Journal of Public Health* 96 (1): 132–138. doi:10.2105/AJPH.2004.050872.

Merry, Sally Engle. 2003, October 1. Constructing a Global Law—Violence Against Women and the Human Rights System. *Law & Social Inquiry* 28. (4): 941–977. doi:10.1111/j.1747-4469.2003.tb00828.x.

Moore, Ann M., Lori Frohwirth, and Elizabeth Miller. 2010, June. Male Reproductive Control of Women Who Have Experienced Intimate Partner Violence in the United States. *Social Science & Medicine (1982)* 7 (11): 1737–1744. doi:10.1016/j.socscimed.2010.02.009.

National Network to End Domestic Violence. 2008. *Domestic Violence Counts: 07: A 24-Hour Census of Domestic Violence Shelters and Services Across the United States*. National Network to End Domestic Violence.

Newberger, Eli H., Susan E. Barkan, Ellice S. Lieberman, Marie V. McCormick, Kersti Yllo, Lisa T. Gary, and Susan Schechter. 1992, November. Abuse of Pregnant Women and Adverse Birth Outcome: Current Knowledge and Implications for Practice. *Obstetrical & Gynecological Survey* 47 (11): 774–776.

Sanday, Peggy Reeves. 1981, October 1. The Socio-Cultural Context of Rape: A Cross-Cultural Study. *Journal of Social Issues* 37 (4): 5–27. doi:10.1111/j.1540-4560.1981.tb01068.x.

Sanday, Peggy Reeves. 2007. *Fraternity Gang Rape: Sex, Brotherhood, and Privilege on Campus*. 2nd ed. New York: NYU Press.

Secretariat of the Pacific Community. 2009. *Solomon Island Family Health and Safety Study: A Study on Violence Against Women and Children*. Honiara, Solomon Islands: Secretariat of the Pacific Community, http://www.spc.int/hdp/index2.php?option=com_docman&task=doc_view&gid=49&

Secretariat of the Pacific Community. 2010. *Kiribati Family Health and Safety Study: A Study on Violence against Women and Children*. Noumea, New Caledonia: Secretariat of the Pacific Community, https://www.spc.int/hdp/index2.php?option=com_docman&task=doc_view&gid=211&Itemid=44

Stockl H., K. Devries, C. Watts, A. Rotstein, N. Abrahams, J. Campbell, and C. G. Moreno. 2013. The Global Prevalence of Intimate Partner Homicide: A Systematic Review. *Lancet* 382 (9895): 859–865.

Stoltenborgh M., M. H. van Ijzendoorn, E. M. Euser, and M. J. Bakermans-Kranenburg. 2011. A Global Perspective on Child Sexual Abuse: Meta-Analysis of Prevalence Around the World. *Child Maltreatment* 16 (2): 79–101.

United Nations Women. 2013a, June 6. EU-Wide Protection for Victims of Domestic Violence Becomes Law, http://www.unwomen.org/en/news/stories/2013/6/eu-wide-protection-for-victims-of-domestic-violence-becomes-law

United Nations Women. 2013b. Focusing on Prevention to Stop the Violence, http://www.unwomen.org/en/what-we-do/ending-violence-against-women/prevention

Vanuatu Women's Centre. 2011. *The Vanuatu National Survey on Women's Lives and Family Relationships*. Port Vila, Vanuatu: Vanuatu Women's Centre, http://aid.dfat.gov.au/countries/pacific/vanuatu/Documents/womens-centre-survey-womens-lives.pdf

World Health Organization. 2005. *WHO Multi-Country Study on Women's Health and Domestic Violence Against Women*. Geneva: World Health Organization, http://www.who.int/gender/violence/who_multicountry_study/en/

World Health Organization. 2011. *Intimate Partner Violence During Pregnancy*. Geneva: World Health Organization, http://whqlibdoc.who.int/hq/2011/WHO_RHR_11.35_eng.pdf

World Health Organization, Department of Reproductive Health and Research, London School of Hygiene and Tropical Medicine, and South African Medical Research Council. 2013. *Global and Regional Estimates of Violence Against Women: Prevalence and Health Effects of Intimate Partner Violence and Non-Partner Sexual Violence*. Geneva: World Health Organization, http://www.who.int/reproductivehealth/publications/violence/9789241564625/en/

CHAPTER 7

Women or Weapons: The Militarist Sexist Symbiosis

Betty A. Reardon

INTRODUCTION

The start of the new millennium is a time of crucial choices for all human societies. The two most critical choices are between continuing the assertion of the legal right of states to use violence in the pursuit of social or political purposes or adopting new modes of protection of national interests; and between the recognition of universal human dignity or the continuation of doctrines and policies of authoritarian inequality. The role of women is central to both choices. Women are the largest group of human beings to be oppressed by doctrines and policies of inequality. In spite of voting rights, their exclusion from the center of political power has meant that they have had little or no part in decisions to prepare for or undertake the use of violence and force in the name of, or for the alleged benefit of, their societies. This exclusion has meant that women have been less able to mitigate violence in public affairs and have only in recent years been able to bring public attention to the "private" violence they suffer. It challenges us to consider the possibilities for overcoming violence that lie in the growing political empowerment of women. Women's political participation is the best hope and the most urgent need for the achievement of a culture of peace. The choice of nonviolence over militarism and of equality over sexism means choosing between a democratic peace culture or a weapons-dependent patriarchy.

THE STATE SYSTEM: AN ARMS-ADDICTED PATRIARCHY
VERSUS A HUMAN SECURITY PARTNERSHIP

Although more politically active than ever before, women are still a shockingly under-represented minority in the halls of power and affairs of state. The patriarchal state system has ensured that matters of peace and security remain "men's business" and has for all practical purposes rejected women's efforts toward a truly equal political partnership.

The present state system is a creature of patriarchy. It was devised and has functioned for nearly five centuries under the presumption of the inferiority of women to men, and the presumption that the security of the state requires it to be armed. It has never functioned to women's advantage, nor does it hold in its traditional form the promise to do so. Neither does it show serious consideration of any means of ensuring its security other than armed force. It continues to demonstrate a preference for weapons over women.

Given the reciprocal relationship feminists discern between patriarchy and the institution of war, and the growing focus by the peace movement on the urgency of disarmament, a deeper reflection on weapons as the tools and icons of the war system is sorely needed. We should consider the whole range of issues related to weaponry, the pragmatic rationale for the continued development of new forms of weaponry and the ongoing accumulation of armaments; the psycho-social, symbolic, and cultural functions of weapons; and their significance to a culture of violence.

Weaponry is the main determinant of power in the present international state system. Nations see the possession of "adequate" quantities of "advanced" weapons and "weapons systems" as what determines their respective positions in the world, how they are perceived and dealt with by other nations, and their capacity to defend their own interests. Vast amounts of resources are spent on weapons, perhaps more for purposes of status and a sense of national pride than for defense or "security". Only states may legally engage in the acquisition and possession of such weaponry and the maintenance of organized armed forces. They have the exclusive legal right to exercise organized violence, a right legitimized by the responsibility of the state to preserve social order and protect the national interest.

Preserving order and providing protection, however, have served to legitimate violence other than that carried out by the state. Indeed, the war system and the culture of violence legitimate and encourage violence by actors other than the state. It is, however, violence as a tool of the state that is the foundation for its continued legitimation as a tool for social or individual purposes other than those of the state. I would argue that were states to turn more toward nonviolent approaches to their policy goals, societies, too, would do so. The renunciation of war and weaponry would be the greatest possible single step toward the reduction of all forms of violence.

But such a shift would also require an authentic commitment to democracy and equality, to transcending all of the various forms of patriarchal power. States hold fast to their dependence on violence, in large part to maintain the present power arrangements. Armed force functions as a mechanism for perpetuating existing power structures as it purports to protect the state.

It is in the interest of patriarchy not so much to reject the legitimation of state violence as to avoid gender equality. Its exclusive claim to the lawful use of lethal force maintains the patriarchal state and limits the potential challenges to its power raised by rivals and dissidents, including the challenges of democracy and especially of women's equality.

The patriarchal structures perpetuated by the claim of the state to be the sole legitimate agent to possess and use organized armed force also holds in place social and economic systems of dominance that preclude the equitable and democratic relations essential to a culture of peace. Indeed, the factor responsible for the continuation of the legitimation of violence as exercised by public authority, and the general social acceptance of the primacy of dominance-subservience relationships that accounts for much of the violence against women, is the greater (though certainly not exclusive) access to superior force and to the use of a wide and sophisticated range of weaponry to exert that force. This factor has profound and pervasive effects on all human affairs and has produced the most destructive and agonizing experiences of human history. There is no greater evidence of the need for women's participation in the processes of determining if, when, and how weaponry is used than the frequency, ineffectiveness, and unbalanced (in all senses of the word) application of armed force. More than any other manifestation of patriarchy, the compulsive acquisition and excessive use of weaponry demonstrate the abuse of power by the male-dominated state system. Indeed, it seems a destructive addiction.

The culture of violence is perpetuated by this addiction, which has had a profound influence on all public policy and on the daily lives and well-being of most citizens. In the case of women, this influence has been decidedly negative. There has been extensive research indicating that the limitation on social expenditure imposed by arms spending has been a major factor in the inability of societies to meet human needs (Sivard, n.d.). When human needs are denied it is most frequently women who experience the greatest deprivation, and through their deprivation children, too, are deprived. It is thus widely recognized that policy makers have opted for weaponry over welfare, denying fundamental economic security to millions.

Other aspects of the way in which militarism and weapons expenditures erode fundamental human security and lower the quality of life through their effects on the environment, human rights, and the possibilities for nonviolent conflict resolution have also been documented. These effects can be said to constitute a net security deficit. In sum, war and preparation for war—most especially the design, development, deployment, and trafficking in weapons—make all societies less secure. These conditions have given rise to much of the recent activity in women's peace movements and have created much public discussion. Yet there has been little or no significant reduction in military expenditures, and even less consideration given to alternatives to weaponry for defense or to armed conflict for the resolution of serous disputes and contention for power. The reluctance to try to find alternatives to the obsessive continuation of destructive habits is addictive behavior. Even peacekeeping operations over recent years have become increasingly dependent on the use of armed force, and thereby made more costly.

Weapons are still the primary instruments of political power. Political leaders both of states and of state challengers remain wedded to the concept that the possession and use of weaponry are the most effective means to acquire and maintain power. Weapons are seen as the only reliable source of defense, which in turn is seen as the primary component of security in a world of intense power conflict. Even in the face of the dangers inherent in the accumulation of arms and growing recognition of the actual lack of security they impose, the dependency remains a veritable addiction among those who hold or seek power. The achievement of a culture of peace, therefore, requires a reconceptualization of security as the United Nations and many nongovernmental organizations (NGOs) and researchers have advocated. Even more significantly, it requires a reconceptualization of power, a transcendence of all that is symbolized and caused by weapons, and, most urgently, measures to confront the weapons addiction.

Women's movements have been a major influence on current trends toward the redefinition of security. Their mobilization against the arms race, military spending, and nuclear testing is among the evidence of their long-held view that military security is not synonymous with human security and is, in fact, detrimental to it. Women's peace groups were among the first to argue that real human security lies in the expectation of well-being that is found in protection against harm of all kinds, in the meeting of basic needs, in the experience of human dignity and the fulfillment of human rights, and in a healthy, natural environment capable of sustaining life (Reardon, 1993). As it can be demonstrated that all of these sources of human security are undermined by the fixation on military security and the dependency on weapons, many assert that women's participation in policy making or security matters would be conducive to the achievement of authentic human security. Women's experiences of providing for day-to-day human security and their more comprehensive and integrated perspective on what actually constitutes security are essential to the process of redefinition of both security and power.

Power within the patriarchal state system is conceived and applied as the ability to coerce or enforce. Many of the women now seeking political power see it in a very different light. Women are seeking a power partnership to transform the culture of war, by transforming power into a medium for the exercise of responsibility rather than privilege. It is this very notion of power as *responsibility* as well as *capacity* that lies at the heart of the drive to replace dominance with partnership. This notion of responsible partnership would apply to all elements of all the systems in which we participate: earth-human, governments-citizens, North-South, and women-men. Such responsibility cannot be exercised by agents who suffer from destructive addictions such as the weapons addiction of the present elites.

Like all addictions, the addiction to weaponry wreaks negative results on the systems in which it occurs. The most destructive effects, however, are suffered by the addicts themselves. For example, many people may be made uncomfortable by "second-hand smoke," and some may even suffer adverse effects from others' cigarettes, but it is the smokers themselves whose lives are most frequently ended by destroyed lungs and impaired hearts. They are the victims of these instruments of pleasure, which in the true sense of the word are, in fact, weapons. Weapons are frequently turned on those whose well-being they are supposed to protect.

Weapons are instruments used to incapacitate, injure, and, especially, kill. Any object used or intended to inflict harm is a weapon. A knife can be a kitchen implement or a murder weapon. The difference is determined by the mind, that is, the purposes and intentions of the user. Minds conditioned by a culture of war perceive weapons as essential instruments to mediate relations with others who are identified as threatening or different.

Addicts' minds perceive that they cannot function without that upon which they feel dependent for their sense of well-being, even though, as in the case of smoking and drugs, they know of the harmful effects of their addictions. Addicts are generally insecure persons who have severe problems confronting reality. Societies in our time "depend" upon weapons for their sense of security with a full understanding of the detrimental effects. The intersection between arms trafficking and drug trafficking makes this chillingly clear. So, too, the link between drug addiction and weapons-inflicted social violence deserves our attention as we consider the effects of weaponry.

Various citizens' groups, particularly women's peace groups, have struggled to bring these detrimental effects to the attention of policy makers and the general public. Conditioned by media that avoid all reflection upon the nature of the weapons culture and the policies that intensify its effects, most citizens fail to fully comprehend or at least to acknowledge these realities. In many ways, women peace activists and researchers play a role in society similar to that played by the spouses, families, and friends of addicts who seek to persuade them of the true effects of their behavior.

In the case of weapons addiction, these effects go beyond economic deprivation and the threat of armed conflict, which is always exacerbated by the possession of arms. Few nations today are free of violent crime, terrorist threats, attacks on individual citizens, and the police brutality that characterizes cultures of violence; these circumstances are often made possible by the types of weapons that governments have developed for purposes of "national security".

It is not, however, only this turning inward of lethal force that indicates the death-inducing nature of the weapons culture, but also the fact that weapons are seen as the necessary and effective tools of security. It would seem that many individual citizens, like their governments, do not feel secure without the capacity to threaten, injure, or kill others. Lethal weapons have become commonplace in many communities that are ostensibly at peace. Yet the reality is that a form of perpetual social warfare is destroying communities and undermining the essential security of daily life. The culture of war and weaponry is manifest at all levels of society. Women's peace organizations and movements have recognized this and responded with challenges to the cultural acceptance of the various manifestations of violence perpetrated at all these levels.

Little, however, has been said about the very concept of weaponry and the legitimacy of lethal tools for any social purpose, even among those who organize against "war toys" and violent computer and other games. The main critique of the anti–war toys movement is that they tend to socialize children to the acceptance of militarism and desensitize them to violence, closing their minds to the possibilities of nonviolent alternatives for defense and conflict resolution. Those who are critical of popular games and sports express concern about the way in which they emphasize competition against (rather than cooperation with) others outside one's team or cultural or social group. What has yet to be the subject of public discussion is the "weapons mentality", the way of thinking that makes weaponry a feature of much of human discourse as well as human affairs.

The weapons culture is apparent in our entertainment, art, and literature, and in our languages and metaphors. National holidays are often celebrated with parades displaying the largest, most fearful weapons to demonstrate the power and pride of the nation. Cannons, tanks, and the skeletons of old fighter planes appear in public places as monuments to national heroism. In my mother tongue, we constantly and unconsciously use the vocabulary and metaphors of weaponry. We "shoot down" ideas we disagree with or "go gunning" for those we intend to engage in argument. These are but a very few of the many ways in which our unreflective acceptance of weaponry holds us all in thrall to the weapons culture and indicates how deeply rooted in the human mind is the culture of war.

Of course, the most devastating consequence of the weapons addiction is war itself. It is all too clear that "armed conflict" is the inevitable result of serious conflict when weapons are at hand. Events have shown that the greater the availability of weapons, the more likely is the escalation of any conflict to a state of violence. Conflict may be inevitable, but armed conflict depends on arms. In the 1960s, students asked, "What if they had a war and nobody came?" I ask now, "What if there were a serious conflict, but there were no arms?" I submit that there would be great difficulties and problems, but human societies can overcome difficulties and solve problems. However, the lethal consequences of weapons cannot be overcome or resolved. They must be avoided. It is women's struggle to learn how to achieve this avoidance that may prove to be their greatest contribution to a culture of peace.

Women's efforts for peace have been numerous and have varied from actions on the ground and the practical application of nonviolence to conflict and struggle, to the development of theories on alternatives to armed force for national defense and international security. It is by raising these and other proposed alternatives to the level of public discussion, to achieve widespread knowledge of these possibilities, that we may find the means to persuade those in power to seriously consider the potential for less violent and more socially constructive security systems. This is essentially an educational task.

Some leaders have come to learn through educational efforts and through their own experience of the futility of weapons dependency. An increasing number of leaders, particularly those in their last years of public service, have come to see the urgent need for demilitarization and disarmament. But only those who are fully aware of the transformational requirements of a culture of peace understand the depth of the changes required for us to move beyond a weapons-based culture and military security to the commitment to nonviolence that is the heart of a culture of peace. Indeed, education of publics and their leaders may help to persuade the powerful to seek to reduce military weaponry, and may even lead to significant forms of disarmament that will greatly reduce the possibilities of war, but so long as weaponry in so many forms exists in so many societies, lethal violence by humans against humans will still be possible. The women who recognize this reality know that a more profound transformation, comparable to that pursued by recovering addicts, must be sought.

CONCLUSIONS

Weaponry is a destructive addiction perpetuated by the war system. A weapons-based security system dulls the critical faculties of citizens and anesthetizes their capacity to perceive the real threats to authentic human security. Toward such ends the European colonial and imperial powers encouraged drug addiction in prerevolutionary China. This causes a slow undermining of the general well-being and immediate, traumatic harm to the addicts, preventing them from confronting the obstacle to authentic human security. Addictions are often developed to fill a void, whether real or perceived, in the sources of well-being; and security is, at base, the expectation of well-being. As drug addicts "shoot" heroin into their veins, the culture of war "shoots" weaponry into our minds and politics, poisoning both. Both must be cured of this addiction.

Curing an addiction takes great strength of mind, courage, and love, qualities women are socialized to develop on behalf of others. Their actual and potential contributions to a culture of peace come in no small part from this socialization and what they have learned in fulfilling it. However, women's potential contribution to a culture of peace cannot be fully realized within the present weapons-dependent, patriarchal state system maintained through the coercive power of male elites. The liberation of the human family from the culture of war depends upon the transformation of that system. The transformational task can be achieved only through a genuine and mutual partnership between women and men in which power is shared equally and the perspectives, concerns, insights, and experiences of both women and men are constructively combined to overcome the weapons addiction. A global order must be devised and brought into being that is so committed to the fulfilment of human needs and the development of an interdependence based on equity and justice that the perceived and the real need for weapons will ultimately disappear: "lethal weaponry has no place in a culture of peace" (United Nations, 1994). That place can be filled only by real human security. Achieving that task requires deep learning to uproot the weapons culture from our minds and expunge violent force from all our relationships. This is the time to change. This is the time to choose.

ACKNOWLEDGMENT

Adapted from *Towards a Women's Agenda for a Culture of Peace*, edited by Ingeborg Breines, Dorota Gierycz, and Betty A. Reardon. 1999. Paris. United Nations Educational, Scientific and Cultural Organization (UNESCO), United Nations Division for the Advancement of Women (DAW).

BIBLIOGRAPHY

Reardon, B. A. 1993. *Women and Peace: Feminist Vision of Global Security*. Albany, NY: State University of New York Press.

Sivard, R. L., ed. n.d. *World Military and Social Expenditures.* Washington, DC (annual reports, various years).

United Nations Division for the Advancement of Women. 1994. *Report of the Expert Group Meeting on Gender and the Agenda for Peace.* New York: United Nations Division for the Advancement of Women.

CHAPTER 8

Gender, War, and the Search for Peaceful Coexistence

Diana Francis

INTRODUCTION

This chapter presents one woman's perspective on gender and the relationship between traditional constructions of masculinity and war. It also points to an alternative model of power that is open to women and men alike, as transformers of conflict and shapers of cooperative coexistence. What I write is informed by a lifetime of thought and activism at home and abroad, by many years of support for local peace actors in different parts of the world, and by a constant process of thinking and learning with others about culture and human nature, war and peace.

I will begin with a clarification of terms. By "gender" I mean the socially constructed and culturally entrenched roles of men and women, which exist in relation to one another, and which involve differentiation and discrimination on the basis of "sex" (biology). By "conflict transformation" I mean constructive ways of approaching conflict, which can include not only resolving conflict but also engaging in it nonviolently in order to bring about the change necessary for "positive peace"—a state characterized not only by the absence of war but by a common well-being that benefits a whole population. In line with the conflict transformation approach, I regard conflict not only as inevitable but as potentially positive, if conducted constructively. I see "violence" (the act of violating) as by definition harmful and believe that the use of violence to counter violence of any kind is likewise necessarily harmful and generates new violence. ("Force," which has the general meaning of strength, power, or impetus, is often used to avoid the term "violence," thus distancing the user from the violence of others.) "War" I define as the concerted, large-scale use of violence to conduct conflict and achieve social, political, and economic goals.

WHY HAS WAR FLOURISHED?

How is it that the violent coercion of war, with its acts of barbarity that shock and traumatize and flout all the norms of civilian life (civilization), continues to be justified? How is this possible, in an age when human rights are taken for granted in the received discourse of almost all societies; when capital punishment is widely, if not universally, regarded as uncivilized; when torture, where it is still in use by governments, is disowned; and when discrimination on the grounds of identity is generally (in theory if not in practice) outlawed? How is it that the killing of one person by another is a matter of shock and condemnation in day-to-day life—judged as a wildly aberrant act to be accounted for before the law, whatever its motivation—while killing in war is seen not only as acceptable but as heroic (when the killer is "one of ours" and "the other," by definition, worthy of death)?

How is it that we continue to commit immense resources of all kinds to a form of human activity that makes nonsense of the very notion of humanity (Glover, 2001), destroying lives and bodies, homes, lands and livelihoods, cities and infrastructure, and causing intense suffering and mass migration? In particular, how can we do this at a time when our species finds itself in extreme jeopardy on many fronts, confronted with the possibility of the collapse of economic systems; when resource scarcities loom, and the human population continues to expand while other species and habitats diminish; and when climate change threatens cataclysmic events that will affect us all?

And how is it that those who claim to practice and uphold democracy (at whose heart lies the principle of consent) with horrible monotony launch wars—the epitome of violent coercion—in democracy's name? In the words of one graffiti writer who lived in war-torn Yugoslavia and who cannot be quoted enough: "If war is the answer, it must be a very stupid question."

In the U.K., where I happen to live, on July 23, 2013, a 41-gun salute was arranged to celebrate the birth of a baby called George who was designated "Prince" and heir to the British throne. Why was this symbolization of killing power seen as a suitable way to greet him? Why is it regarded as fitting for military aircraft, belching noxious vapors, to fly overhead in formation on state occasions, when the British "royal family" appears on the balcony of Buckingham Palace, and why do the heads of other states preside over similarly wasteful and warlike absurdities?

The answer to all these questions is that our societies have inherited and perpetuate the ancient, deep-rooted cult of militarism, which is so deeply embedded in the dominant discourse of history and in present-day mores and systems of government and society that it ceases to be visible as such, being part and parcel of the equally taken-for-granted "banal nationalism" that makes jingoism and crude displays of weaponry seem normal and genteel (Billig, 1995).

DOMINATION AND CULTURAL VIOLENCE

Militarism is the crudest manifestation of what Riane Eisler calls the dominatory approach to relationships (Eisler, 1990), which stems from the "eat-or-be-eaten" worldview (Francis, 2010), whose adherents approach life as a struggle for survival, driven by the will to triumph over others. That culture of dominance gives rise to violence of many kinds, not all of them physical. Galtung defines violence as

avoidable insults to basic human needs, and more generally to *life*, lowering the real level of needs satisfaction below what is potentially possible. . . . The four classes of basic needs . . . are: *survival needs* (negation: death, mortality); *well-being needs* (negation: misery, morbidity); *identity, meaning needs* (negation: alienation); and *freedom needs* (negation: repression). (Galtung, 1990)

Such "insults to basic human needs" may be political, social, and/or economic, all too often enforced by the threat or use of physical violence .

According to Galtung, our lives are affected not only by actions but by the systems, institutions, or "structures" within which we live. And underlying or overarching both behavior and systems is the culture in which they exist. Violent actions and violent structures are the outcome of "cultural violence," or

those aspects of culture, the symbolic sphere of our existence—exemplified by religion and ideology, language and art, empirical science and formal science (logic and mathematics) that can be used to legitimize direct or structural violence. . . Cultural violence makes direct and structural violence look, even feel, right—or at least not wrong. (Galtung, 1990)

The way we regard things, the feelings we have about them, and our behavior in relation to them shape the way we live our lives. The most important assumptions we make are those most likely to be hidden from view, and therefore go largely unchallenged.

Violence against women, so commonplace in most societies, is a prime example of this pernicious dynamic. In many societies tradition (more in spite or regardless of religious precepts than in obedience to them) positions women as the chattels of men, to be dealt with as they see fit; laws and institutions reinforce their lowly status as beings of little worth, and daily behavior, involving verbal insults and physical assaults, enforced labor, and denial of economic rights, give concrete expression to the violence of thoughts, laws, and systems of power. And in circles of power in the societies where these norms persist, all this is seen as right and proper, not only by most males but, alas, by many females. (See Freire (1972) on the phenomenon of "internalized oppression," in which victims "approve of" and perpetuate their victimhood.)

I use this example of cultural violence not only because it is readily understood but also because it is intimately connected with the question of war. Most visibly in traditional cultures and more subtly in "modern" ones, patriarchal norms persist, in which men are born to be dominant over women and to seek dominance within their own hierarchies. Military violence is instrumental in the pursuit of domination and emblematic of it; witness the statuary of city squares around the world and a variety of imagery and artifacts in most, if not all, cultures. The apogee of masculinity is the warrior hero.

In an interview about male suicide (BBC Radio 4, *Today Programme*), psychologist Martin Seager articulated what he identified as three ancient rules of masculinity, adding up to a male script for life: men should be fighters and winners, men should be protectors and providers, and men should retain mastery and control. To fail in these is to fail as a man. Traditional female roles are subservient and instrumental in relation to this concept of masculinity: to be the mothers of heroes, to encourage and support warriors or become the victims of the violence of their opponents, reinforcing their power. As is widely recognized, the widespread incidence of rape in war is not a coincidence or an unfortunate side effect. Sexual prowess is an important element in traditional constructions of masculinity. Rape is not only the crude assertion of the perpetrator's virility and his dominance over the woman who is his victim; it is also a demonstration of his triumph over the males associated with the victim.

GENDER IN CONTEXT

I do not mean to suggest that wars are simply displays of masculinity and have no other causes. I do mean that gender as we know it, which positions men as dominant and characterizes them as aggressive and heroic, is fundamental to the culture of domination of which war is an expression.

At the same time, many men have specific motivations for joining armies—for instance, seeing a life in the military as one of service to their country or to just causes, or simply as one way of earning a living.

Furthermore, while the culture and machinery of militarism provide the setting and the means of war, greed also plays its part, as do the grievances of those who suffer its effects, whether that greed is for resources or for political control. Individual greed and political ambition, and policies aimed at economic and political hegemony or ideological control, give rise to oppressive relationships and unjust structures, and that "structural violence" is enforced by direct violence, which in turn engenders counter-violence. Greed and grievance are part and parcel of the system of domination (Berdal and Malone, 2000).

In recent decades, women have been drawn into the military, in some cases in fighting roles. That does not, however, alter the fact that war is based on male gender constructions. It means that women sometimes choose to join in a way of life that provides an alternative to the one they have been leading or would otherwise lead, or they see it as an opportunity to serve a cause that they believe in (being part of the culture that sees military solutions as just that). In most cases they serve in lowly positions, often in servicing roles—particularly sexual and domestic ones. Even in the most "modern" and nondiscriminatory armies they are in fact subjected to sexual harassment and discrimination (National Defense Research Institute, 2014), and often when they return to civilian life find it particularly difficult to be accepted back into society in ways that they would wish.

Although in some societies, during recent decades, public roles and private relationships have been changing, a glance at the photographs in a daily newspaper will indicate that patriarchy lingers on, and that women who, against the odds, reach positions of leadership do so by behaving like the males who usually occupy them. When women step into places traditionally reserved for men, they place themselves within the male paradigm and have to perform their roles accordingly. Sometimes they can modify the way in which the role is normally played, but often there is little or no room for maneuvering, and great courage, skill, and determination would be required to make a success of the role while playing it differently, whether for a man or a woman.

Nowhere is this more so than in national politics, in which militarism plays such a central role in many countries, underlying the very concept of the state as an entity holding a monopoly on violence (Weber, 2004). For presidents and prime ministers, going to war is often framed and regarded as proof of their fitness for office. British prime minister Margaret Thatcher (as a woman having a particular need to prove her capacity for dominance) saved her premiership for another term by going to war over the Falklands. Today, in the U.K. as in the United States, "strong action" (for instance, against the Assad regime in Syria) is frequently equated with a military. During the wars in Iraq and Afghanistan, where that meant not only air strikes, weapons supply, and military training, but also ground forces, British "war heroes" who were wounded or killed in action (not of course their opponents or the uncounted and countless civilians who have died) featured regularly in national news bulletins. Similarly, during last year's "celebrations" of the beginning of World War I, victory was associated with "sacrifice"—the tragic and untimely deaths of countless young men, the greater number of whom were "conscripts."

Thus society daily reinforces the assumption that, for men at least, fighting for "one's own" is a noble thing to do. The 2,000-year-old maxim of Roman poet Horace still reflects a deeply held view: *Dulce et decorum est pro patria mori* ("It is sweet and fitting to die for one's country."). The twist in the tail of this concept of what is fitting for a man to do is the principle underlying such fighting, which is that "might is right" or, conversely, that right is might. The power of brute violence, whether or not it is amplified by technology, is no basis for ethics.

NATURE AND NURTURE

The fact that masculinity has been constructed as it has does not prove that men are by nature more controlling, aggressive, or domineering than women, or that women are by nature more gentle and cooperative than men. It simply means that men, like women, are subject to the social pressures and requirements that go with prevailing, patriarchal gender constructions based on the old patriarchal model: a hierarchical system and culture based on the domination by half of the world's human population over the other half and on the idea of domination as such. And women are not the only losers. Not only are girls and women trapped and degraded by gender: boys and men are also imprisoned and diminished by it.

The impact of the norm of male dominance, with its connotations of physical prowess, is felt in the lives of boys and men from their earliest years (and indeed, weeks and months), through the behavior of those around them—in particular through their expectations that they will be brave ("boys don't cry") and will stand up for themselves, together with the implicit understanding that other qualities and abilities can never quite make up for deficiencies in this area. This indoctrination starts at home and in the playground; but when a boy grows into a man, he will still be expected to demonstrate his physical prowess—if not in fighting of one form or another, at least by performing well in contests of competitive sports, or by cutting a powerful figure in business or politics.

Mothers and other (mostly female) child carers play a powerful role in raising children and all too often reinforce traditional gender roles in doing so. Behavior in boy children that would bring swift reproof to little girls is frequently simply laughed at and even encouraged. Mothers as well as fathers all too often speak of rough boys as "real boys." My own son, when he was at secondary school, told me how he envied his sisters, because in a boy's world it was necessary always to compete and be tough, not even comforting those who are upset, let alone get upset oneself. I foresee little change for my grandchildren's generation. The social pressure to conform on gender remains huge. Little girls are encouraged to play with dolls or dress up as nurses, while the militarization of male children and adolescents continues, through toys, clothes, games, films and the like, and through the self-promoting presence of the military in schools (Everett, 2013), amounting to early military training as a road to future recruitment.

In the words of Tim Lynch, a veteran of Britain's war against Argentina in the Falklands, to make war acceptable and recruit fighters it is necessary only to

take a young man, desperate to establish an identity in the adult world, make him believe military prowess is the epitome of masculinity, teach him to accept absolutely the authority of those in command, give him an exaggerated sense of self-worth by making him part of an elite, teach him to value aggression, and dehumanize those who are not part of his group and give him the permission to use any level of violence without the moral restraints which govern him elsewhere.

THE PERSISTENT MYTH OF WAR AND HUMAN NATURE

Despite the pervasive encouragement of aggression in the socialization of young males, soldiers still need to be brutalized through initiation rites and military training in order to perform their designated roles. Killing fellow human beings does not come easily and is possible only when empathy is stifled. In his remarkable book *Humanity*, Jonathan Glover tells how a soldier could not obey an order to shoot a fleeing "enemy" because that man's trousers were falling down. That moment of fellow feeling made the act of killing him impossible.

The inhumanity of warfare does immense psychological damage to combatants. Statistics on the trauma of killing and the rate of postcombat suicides demonstrate this (Lendman, 2014). This phenomenon has long been under discussion in relation to the many studies on suicide among Vietnam War veterans (see, for example, http://www.globalresearch.ca/record-numbers-of-us-military-and-veteran-suicides/5322544). A former lieutenant in the U.S. Army, S. L. A. Marshall, after intensive research among fighting forces, wrote, "Fear of killing, rather than fear of being killed, was the most common cause of battle failure in the individual" (Baum, 2004). Conversely, according to Eisler (1995), there is a well-established connection between caring for others and the health of the carer.

Despite this evidence, it is argued that intergroup violence is an inevitable part of human life, since human beings are part of the animal kingdom, of "nature red in tooth and claw," and that the kind of innate sensibility that is suggested by the reluctance to kill and the psychological damage that results from doing so cannot therefore be powerful enough to dissuade us from deadly aggression. We do have much in common with other species and are remarkably like the apes in many respects, but our cooperative capacities exceed even theirs, with our highly developed linguistic ability playing a key role. In a Horizon program entitled *What Makes Us Human?* (BBC 2, July 3, 2013), anatomist Alice Roberts presents human science in

recent research and theory, which concludes that human beings' helplessness at the time of birth, and their dependency on others for many years
thereafter, leads to unique development in their social capacity. Relative to
those of any other species, human qualities stem far less from innate abilities and far more from knowledge, capacities, and attitudes acquired and
developed through social interaction. This gives us the power to communicate with infinite subtlety and create our own abstract thoughts, philoso-
phies, and cultures, and to articulate values and make moral distinctions
and choices. It is predominantly these capacities that shape our behavior.

Still, it is said, "history shows" that there have "always" been wars and
therefore our aggressive drives must exceed our cooperative tendencies.
According to historians like John Keegan (1994) and Riane Eisler (1990),
sociologists like Elise Boulding (2000), and archaeological anthropologists
like Brian Ferguson (2003) and Raymond Kelly (2000), that "always" is
wide of the mark, since the large-scale organized violence and the institution of war appeared relatively recently in the history of human social
behaviour, and much later in some parts of the world than in others. These
phenomena developed as societies became more structured and hierarchical. However, there have also been advanced and well-developed societies
that were nonhierarchical, characterized by gender equality and a cooperative culture in which warfare did not feature. The worldviews held in
different ages and societies have varied and these variations have had a
huge impact on the behavior of the people within the societies and the
systems they have developed.

Those different cultures themselves have changed and developed. The
executions and torture of the past, the common justification for the beating of women and children, and the enslavement of other human beings
have, mercifully, been recognized in mainstream opinion in many societies
as barbarous (albeit with shocking exceptions). This makes it all the more
remarkable that war continues to be justified in such societies; yet since
change is evidently possible, there is good reason to hope and there are
signs that the age-old enchantment with war is on the wane.

THE MEETING OF THE WAYS: THE "RESPONSIBILITY
TO PROTECT"

Life is not simple; nor are human beings. Categories and generalizations
are necessary in reasoning, but reality is more complex and mixed. Human
beings, of whatever sex or gender, embody a mixture of characteristics,
tendencies and motives, awareness and unawareness, ego and superego.
And although prevalent constructions of masculinity have encouraged the
tendency to dominate and to use physical violence and violent systems in
doing so, just as norms of human decency and kindness play a vital role
in day-to-day social life, in politics a discourse of justice and responsibility

runs alongside that of "the national interest," and compassion and a desire for justice can have some influence on political processes.

These kinder instincts and related language enter the discourse of military violence and play a role in encouraging its acceptance, not only in relation to particular wars but, more generally, providing moral cover for war as an institution. Indeed "Something must be done" all too quickly turns into a justification for "military intervention," whether by aerial bombardment or invasion, under the rubric of a "responsibility to protect" ("The Responsibility to Protect," 2015).

The threefold myth of war's capacity for good (Francis, 2004) is (1) that war is a means of last resort when all other options have been exhausted, whereas in practice the other options have often scarcely been tried by those who launch the wars; (2) that the intentions of those who intervene in this way are entirely altruistic, whereas they most often have some underlying strategic purpose; and (3) that the outcome of the "redemptive violence" of war will be the achievement of the good that was its purported goal.

We are rarely shown the evidence of the disastrous impact of military intervention, for instance, in Kosovo or in Libya, where mediation was cut short by Western military action and was reduced to violent chaos (Francis, 2001 and 2015). The Afghanistan war lasted too long to escape scrutiny and the aftermath of the Iraq war has been too terrible to be hidden. The "silver bullet" does not exist in reality, though this favorite metaphor for the instant achievement of a goal tells us all we need to know about the myth of violent power.

The *prevention* of lethal violence, while conflict is still tractable, is possible where the will and resources can be found to address its potential causes; likewise, peace *keeping* (essentially a policing function) can contribute to stabilization and make room for peace *building*, once some kind of stalemate or fragile peace has been achieved. Peace *making*, whether by violent or nonviolent means, is virtually impossible when violence is in full flood.

Miall et al. (1999) liken this closing down of opportunity for constructive action to the tight neck in the middle of an hourglass. Perpetrators are either mixed with or in close proximity to victims (as well as sometimes being inseparable from them morally, let alone philosophically); and where armies have not acted in the face of atrocities, it would seem to have been, at least in part, because they have not known how to do so. The Belgian general who pulled his troops out of Rwanda when the slaughter took place said as much. When the violent dynamic is at its most intense, the overwhelming likelihood is that suffering and brutality will be further intensified by additional violence. Then, as we have seen in Iraq and Afghanistan, resistance is very hard to overcome and those killed are replaced by others. Violence is like an unquenchable fire, ready to break out in any place.

This is at the heart of the case for nonviolence: you can't fight fire with fire. Adding to the carnage and intensifying already violent conflict, sending a country into utter lawlessness and civil war or another replacing one form of "ethnic cleansing" with another is not a way of helping, however desperate we may be to bring a swift end to suffering. One part of the "something" that can always be done is to address in all ways possible the human suffering occasioned by violence, through genuine humanitarian aid—providing adequate help for refugees, for instance, by supporting the countries where they take refuge and granting them asylum in our own. Another way is to engage in serious, intelligent, disinterested dialogue with all players (including other third-party countries that are seen to be "on the wrong side" but by the same token may have more influence where it is needed). A third alternative is to combine preparatory dialogue with concerted encouragement and, if it will help, pressure for the parties to take part in negotiations. These efforts will need to be mediated by representatives of a genuine "international community," such as the United Nations (rather than by the West describing itself as such), since most political conflicts in a given country are connected to regional interests and international alignments.

Such activities may be described as the use of "soft power," but the point is that they hold the genuine possibility of doing good. The challenge of large-scale political violence, whether home grown or international, is real. Horror and the desire to act are entirely proper to humanity. But surely there is also a responsibility to protect people from starvation, or from thirst, or from death by water-borne infection and other preventable diseases. The numbers of deaths caused by direct atrocities, though shockingly high, do not come near to equaling those caused by relentless deprivation, by ongoing domestic and street violence, or by the endemic human rights violations of some of the nations that are regarded by our governments as allies. These chronic and devastating ills are no less in need of redress and transformation, and most beneficial change has to be achieved with patience and determination through the combined efforts of governments and people and will involve a deep change in priorities and thinking as well as specific actions. Deconstructing rather than augmenting the machinery and dynamics of war is the only route to lasting peace.

AN ALTERNATIVE MODEL OF POWER

Having a different perspective on our place in the world and shifting our attention from military might to other forms of power would free our human and material resources for constructive action to create human security—inasmuch as it can be created. Acceptance of life's transience and our vulnerability (to the laws of nature as well as to each other) will be necessary if we are to maximize safety and increase the quality of each other's lives. Genuine international solidarity and peace building will become possible when a patriarchal worldview that sees things in terms of an endless struggle for domination is replaced with one that defines successful human life and endeavor in terms of acknowledged interdependence and creative cooperation. This orientation to life is more in line with current constructions of femininity as the counterpart to traditional masculinity, characterized by an acceptance of vulnerability; but all those who recognize their vulnerability will know that they can and must use it as a strength.

Women, being on average physically and socially vulnerable to men, have in many cultures a specific role assigned to them by society in which they use that vulnerability assertively. For instance, I have spoken to Naga women, in the far northeast of India, who carry—and act on—the social expectation that when violence has broken out between men, it is the women's duty to intervene, physically, to stop it. Their power takes the form of talking, listening, challenging, pleading, and mediating, as well as physically interposing themselves between the warring parties. It requires great courage and dauntless determination. Their action is accepted because they pose no threat. This is their protection. (Understandably, they sometimes resent the onus placed on them when men seem not to care about the impact of their aggressive behavior.)

This kind of power, whose use is not confined to women but is also chosen by many men (and indeed is probably used by everyone in some circumstances, albeit to differing degrees), is radically different from that suggested by the "eat-or-be-eaten" approach. Instead of separating "us" from "them," this kind of power springs from a sense of interdependence and the ability to identify, develop, and use to the fullest the connections between people, building a sense of solidarity and replacing hostility with understanding.

Just as the vulnerability of the fleeing man whose trousers were falling down created a human connection between him and the man who had been ordered to shoot him, so in many situations women are able to use assumptions of their harmlessness and vulnerability as protection to intervene in violent situations to end bloodshed. (In some cases, women use nakedness as a means to accentuate this vulnerability and to shame those using violence.)

The nuns who sat in front of tanks in the Philippines in an act of "people power" that hastened the downfall of dictator Ferdinand Marcos also reached out to the soldiers with gifts of flowers, cigarettes, and food (Deats, 2010). Those who came from all around Serbia to the capital Belgrade to demand that Slobodan Milosevic relinquish power when he refused to concede electoral defeat likewise ensured that they won over the police and the military who were on duty there (Ackerman and DuVall, 2000). Persuasion by unarmed people can overcome the power of armed might and can be exercised in many different ways, by the physically weak as well as by the strong, by the poor as well as by the rich, and by women as well as by men.

Instead of power *over* people and things, this is power *with* and *for* others, power to achieve shared goals. To be effective it requires both careful analysis and imagination, and a collectively elaborated, constantly revised and shared strategy. This is true of any nonviolent action, where the task in hand is the patient development of a just, respectful, and therefore peaceful society, with the norms required to prevent violent conflict in the future. It is true of the kind of pivotal resistance to tyranny that can pave the way for such peace building and of the character of action that can eventually bring some workable resolution to acute and destructive conflict, or achieve true reconciliation after it.

It is on this kind of imaginative, intelligent, empathic, and nonviolent power that the projects of conflict transformation and genuine peace building are based. It has a long way to go before it becomes the power of first resort by those currently "in power." It also has a long way to go in terms of the challenges it must address. The Arab Spring of 2011 too quickly turned to winter. All who care about peace must learn the lessons from that bitter experience. The astonishing large-scale movements that have demonstrated the efficacy of unarmed people power—in India (with Gandhi's leadership), the United States (led by Martin Luther King, Jr.), the Philippines (led by "base communities," Cori Aquino, and finally the Catholic Church), and the former Soviet Union (starting with the trade unionists in Gdansk)—have shown that mobilization is not the problem. The difficulty comes in sustaining the struggle to build peace and justice after initial success. This calls for careful, systematic, and painstaking preparation and continuation. It also requires tenderness as well as great courage. The emergence of a macho spirit will always be its downfall, wherever it takes place, even in the face of violence that is threatened or already under way, which will be intensified by counterviolence.

BEYOND GENDER TO THE HUMAN SPIRIT

Around the world many men and women are prepared to accept their own vulnerability and act to protect others or stand up for justice, even in the midst of threats and atrocities. For instance, some people took neighbors into their homes when they were threatened with death in Idi Amin's Uganda and in Kosovo before and during the NATO action there—just as people gave shelter to Jews in Europe when Hitler's men were looking for them to take them away to the concentration camps. Activists in Latin America during the worst years of tyranny there found the courage to protest against the disappearance of relatives, friends and neighbors, and young people from Peace Brigades International went to act as unarmed bodyguards for them.

During the civil war in Sri Lanka, people from the Sinhala and Tamil communities kept talking and unarmed international teams from Nonviolent Peaceforce worked to diffuse violence where they could. In the Indian state of Orissa people from different communities came together to demonstrate against intercommunal violence in 2008, when it was at its height.

There were also civil society activists who in 2008 stepped in as insider mediators to stop the spiraling postelectoral violence in Kenya. One woman who took a leading role in this vital intervention, Dekha Ibrahim, was at the heart of an earlier remarkable peace process, initiated with a small group of women in the early 1990s in her home district of Wajir in northern Kenya. A spate of open violence had claimed 1,500 lives in the region not long before, leaving hatred and suspicion between different clans and ongoing trouble over cattle raids.

Over time, this small group of women initiated dialogue that brought peace to the shared and vital marketplace, addressed the immediate problem of cattle raids, and eventually brought about a peace agreement between the clans. When that agreement was in place, they set up the Wajir Peace Committee to oversee its implementation, with representatives including clan elders, young people, government security bodies, parliamentarians, civil servants, Muslim and Christian religious leaders, and NGOs. This kind of partnership for conflict management became a model for similar initiatives throughout much of Kenya.

Working with clan elders was a highly unorthodox activity for the two young women who acted as mediators between the clans—one that was at first resisted. A remarkable film records the solemn meetings that they held and tells how they chose to use the symbol of an egg given to each of the clan leaders to keep safe, which representied the fragile and life-giving peace that they had agreed to protect from breaking. In an exquisitely touching and powerful moment, one of the elders, holding the egg he has been given with all the tenderness of a mother holding her child, speaks with reverence of its importance and his great sense of responsibility for the life and peace that it represents.

Those women and the men and women who joined them acted with remarkable power to bring peace to a region that had suffered for decades from violence. They did so with courage and determination, imagination and reasoning, in the moment and over the years to come. They did it because they cared about the common good and they did it in cooperation. To embrace this kind of power is in itself a liberation from fear and helplessness, and from the social and systemic pressure to prove strength of character through domination and violence.

The peacemakers of Wajir showed, as many others have done and will do, that culture is not immutable and that systems and relationships can change. They demonstrated what is possible when action changes thinking, which in turn leads to the creation of new structures in society that then go on influencing the way people think and act. The looming emergencies of climate change and economic collapse may sharpen minds and deepen understanding, and so accelerate the slow process of cultural change. Indeed, there are growing signs, from a movement of movements around the world, that change is already under way.

I have painted a bleak picture of governments, but they are not in themselves monolithic and are not all the same. Everywhere there are actual or potential allies for change. Some countries have already moved the focus of their international relations policy and activity from military to nonmilitary means of contributing to global affairs. They fund professional work in support of civil society peace building, work behind the scenes to help broker peace deals, and join with others to formulate and promote treaties on arms control. Such governments are no longer working to a macho model of "foreign policy" but rather to a human model of cooperation for the common good. There is therefore cause to hope that in time the global culture of international relations will change, along with global structures and behaviors. Constructions of masculinity that have had such a central influence can and will be transformed in this process, and new models of power will emerge, making way for the assumption of equality and interdependence between all people and paving the road to peace.

BIBLIOGRAPHY

Ackerman, Peter, and Jack DuVall. 2000. *A Force More Powerful: A Century of Nonviolent Conflict*. Hampshire, UK: Palgrave Macmillan.

Baum, Dan. 2004, July 12. The Price of Valor. *New Yorker*.

Berdal, Mats, and David Malone, eds. 2000. *Greed and Grievance: Economic Agendas in Civil Wars*. London: Lynne Rienner.

Billig, Michael. 1995. *Banal Nationalism*. London: Sage.

Boulding, Elise. 2000. *Cultures of Peace: The Hidden Side of History*. Syracuse, NY: Syracuse University Press.

Deats, Richard. 2010. The Global Spread of Active Nonviolence. Fellowship of Reconciliation, http://forusa.org/blogs/for/global-spread-active-nonviolence/6729

Eisler, Riane. 1990. *The Chalice and the Blade: Our History, Our Future*. London: Unwin Paperbacks.

Eisler, Riane. 1995. *Sacred Pleasure: Sex, Myth and the Politics of the Body*. San Francisco: Harper.

Everett, Owen, ed. 2013. *Sowing Seeds: The Militarisation of Youth and How to Counter It*. London: War Resisters International.

Ferguson, Brian. 2003, July/August. The Birth of War. *Natural History*, 28–34.

Francis, Diana. 2001. *Lessons from Kosovo/a: Alternatives to War*. London: Quaker Peace & Social Witness (available at www.dianafrancis.info).

Francis, Diana. 2004. *Rethinking War and Peace*. London: Pluto Press.

Francis, Diana. 2010. *From Pacification to Peacebuilding: A Call to Global Transformation*. London: Pluto Press.

Francis, Diana. 2015. *Faith, Peace and Power: 2015 Swarthmore Lecture*. London: Quaker Books, 2015, http://www.quaker.org.uk/shop/faith-power-and -peace-2015-swathmore-lecture

Freire, Paulo. 1972. *Pedagogy of the Oppressed*. London: Penguin.

Galtung, Johan. 1990. Cultural Violence. *Journal of Peace Research* 27 (3): 291–305.

Glover, Jonathan. 2001. *Humanity: A Moral History of the Twentieth Century*. London: Pimlico.

Keegan, John. 1994. *A History of Warfare*. London: Pimlico.

Kelly, Raymond. 2000. *Warless Societies and the Origin of War*. Ann Arbor: University of Michigan Press.

Lendman, Stephan. 2014. Record Numbers of US Military and Veteran Suicides. Global Research, http://www.phoenixcounsellingnw.co.uk/suicides-among -soldiers/ (accessed May 31, 2014).

Miall, Hugh, Oliver Ramsbotham, and Tom Woodhouse. 1999. *Contemporary Conflict Resolution*. Cambridge: Polity Press.

Moore, Keith. 2012, Fall. Performance, Masculinity, and Conformation, http://www .academia.edu/2562756/Performance_Masculinity_and_Conformation _How_Males_Learn_Manliness

National Defense Research Institute. 2014. Sexual Assault and Sexual Harassment in the U.S. Military. *Product Page*. http://www.rand.org/pubs/research _reports/RR870.html.

"The Responsibility to Protect." 2015. Office of the Special Advisor on the Responsibility to Protect. United Nations. http://www.un.org/en/preventgenocide/ adviser/responsibility.shtml.

Weber, Max. 2004. Politics as a Vocation. In *The Vocation Lectures*. Indianapolis: Hackett.

CHAPTER 9

Are Women the Peacemakers? Are Men the Warmakers? Exploring the Intersection of Gender and Militarization

Lynne M. Woehrle

INTRODUCTION TO THE LINKS BETWEEN GENDER AND MILITARIZATION OF LIVES

When we link the terms "gender" and "militarization" we often are trying to reference a social system relationship between being male and the integration of violence into a society. However, the relationship of these terms is much more complex than often thought.

To speak of men/war and women/peace is a false bifurcation that ignores the reality that men have actively resisted war as conscientious objectors and women have participated in war as soldiers. Such framing ironically shores up systems of thinking and cultural practices that have contributed to the oppression of women for thousands of years. It does so by embracing an archetypal division between the genders. This division has been used to justify patriarchy (male-centric power) built on stereotypes of women as needing protection provided by males. Violence statistics tell a very different story, one that suggests women might need protection from some men rather than finding their security enhanced by the presence of men in their lives.

Third-wave feminism dismissed the bifurcation of genders model (Baumgardner and Richards, 2000). Essentialism, the idea that being female involves enough similarity to make all women's experiences in common with each other, was fully rejected; there is no sense of broad solidarity merely based on the status of being a woman. Letting go of the theme of "as women we are all united" was a significant transition for the gender equity movement. It had begun to fall apart in the 1980s when essentialism was heavily critiqued as silencing women in marginal social positions (hooks, 1984). Third-wave feminists focused in different directions and worked to include men who were like them in positions of lost or shrinking power.

The wisdom of third-wave feminism is the recognition of the unquestionable interdependence of male and female. When "gender" became a code word for "women" the insight of a gender analysis was lost. A gender analysis invites a systemic view of the social categories built on the biological categories of male and female. A gender analysis pinpoints power hierarchies and intertwined relationships, how they are buttressed by rituals and social practices and why they tend to inscribe inequalities and stereotypes.

Male and female are created by society as discrete categories although biology tells us otherwise. Alternatively we could view male and female as not so distinct after all. A more accurate picture might show categories that overlap much more than most would think. This is the world where sex category is fuzzier. Some people fall biologically in a combined category, some fall socially in a combined category, and most spend an inordinate amount of time and resources making sure their category is clear. This concept of "doing gender" (West and Zimmerman, 1987) shows the funneling effect of the social system as depicted in Figure 9.1.

Studying women without men also provides significant (and often lost) insights, but it is not the same as studying systematically how the interconnections of male and female shape individual and group experience. To fully understand the war system and our potential for a peace system we need to turn to analyses of masculinity, femininity, and the combined gender system, which encapsulates everything on the male-female continuum as well as the surrounding social structures by which people live in their assigned category.

Pink and Blue Camouflage: Socialization into Militarism

The war system and the gender system are wound closely together— a fact exposed by many scholars (e.g., Reardon, 1985; Enloe, 2007; Riley et al., 2008). Everyday examples abound. Shockingly, toddlers' and small boys' disposable nighttime pants come covered in pictures of tanks and other weapons set on the background of a blue and grey camouflage pattern. It is pink and purple "camo" for little girls and blue, brown, or grey for boys. You do not have to go to a hunting store to find it. The images are

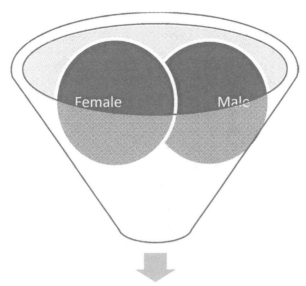

Male and Female continuum with crossover
mix and surrounded by society that funnels
their experiences.

Figure 9.1

Social Structures of Gender

woven into diapers, pants, shirts, tights, shoes, jackets, baby blankets, and more. It is so common that it is now such a subtle sign of militarization that few even notice its immensity and power of socialization. Gender analysis helps us unpack the complexity of this social norm. As Enloe (1983) argues in her first book on this subject, *Does Khaki Become You?*, the militarized culture deeply shapes women's lives and does not promise to pave a path to systemic equality—even when a woman serves as an admiral, captain, or other high-ranking officer.

Digging deeper we find that the war system is integrally bound up not just with sexism but also with racism and heterosexism. Daily micro-aggressions toward brown and black people categorize them as suspect, dangerous, and deserving of harsh punishment (Sue et al., 2007). Institutional practices of racial profiling and homophobia make use of degradation of the feminine to marginalize and emotionally harm social and cultural minorities.

Conversely, the conventional circular peace sign has become hypergenderized as well. It has been attached to the female dress code and nearly banned among boys. While it started as a symbol of counterculture it has been imbued with femininity—which reinforces the idea that to be male one must navigate the system of the military culture. While girls have broader choices of how female and how male to be, boys are tightly funneled toward the masculine. This makes sense in a militarized culture, which needs the next generation of fighters to step forward. Some of those may be female but the majority must be male in order to maintain the current militarized structure and the rationale that men go to war to fulfill their protector role.

It is for a purpose, argues Cohn (2013). The push of the system is to rationalize male control over power through control of resources and decision making. Cohn (2013) writes: "*If* men are believed to be stronger, more rational, more in control of their emotions, smarter, independent, tougher, better able to make and stick to a decision . . . *then* it might appear to make the most sense for men to be in charge" (p. 6, italics in original). Though tautological, for centuries the argument has been that men are stronger, better-equipped leaders, so therefore they should be in charge, and that because they are leaders it must be that they are good at it.

Theory on the Biological or Cultural Answers to Whether Boys Are More Violent and Better Soldiers

Long-standing "common knowledge" and academic scholarship both point to a biological divide between males and females. While we are focused on a continuum of male and female and recognized above that the model of discrete categories is biologically inaccurate because it leaves out so many people who range in between, it is useful to consider the question, how much of a biological basis is there for the gender performances that divide boys and girls into separate groups?

Diapers are only the beginning for a child. As they get inscribed with the practices of gender they also are learning their social roles in the military culture. This cultural analysis of violent responses to conflict is well grounded in social theory (Hedges, 2002; Mead, 2014[1940]). While there might be wisdom in the biological insights of "fight or flight" analysis and male hormonal needs, neither of these approaches explains why the instincts have led to the massive military-industrial complex that undergirds many economically complex societies. Nor does it explain why some societies grow to become dependent on the war habit and others do not. Getting beyond an individual response pattern, we need to look at the institutional structures that organize a violence-habituated social system.

Betty Reardon (1985) takes up this question of why we align women with peace and men with war. Her exploration of the issue focuses on a common root of militarism and sexism, which she argues is social violence. The fundamental source of the problem, she says, is within us. Approaching social relations with the goal of power at a cost to others leads to practices of inhumanity. Thus, she argues, "the major obstacle to disarmament is not political but psychosocial; it is fear" (Reardon, 1985, p. 6).

Chris Hedges (2002) has opened an important area of analysis in suggesting that gender categories are useful not only to society but also to the perpetuation of war. A war culture needs to hyperseparate the categories. There must be a warrior class and a protected class. Historically the line has been between genders. Later in this chapter we explore how this has begun to shift in some ways but not in others.

Riley et al. (2008) improve upon this developing model of why war exists by including racism and imperialism in their analysis of the war system. They propose that the new colonialism is the militarization of economic globalization; "that is, wars being waged through military and economic policy to advance and consolidate the profit-driven system of capitalism" (p. 3). Racialized systems of violence persist, whether in the "economic draft," the perpetuation of genocide, or the disproportionate representation of people of color in criminal justice systems around the world.

As we explore the social-biological debate regarding the production of war, we need to ask several important questions. Can the biological need for competition be proved, and if it can does that experience of competition require violence? Why does it require so much extensive training to convince a soldier to kill another human? And when a soldier does cross that line, watching or participating in the ending of the life of another, why does it leave the soldier so broken? A macro perspective on the discussion may help us see the need for an integrated approach. Biological bases such as fear seem to legitimately exist, but whether that fear leads to competition or cooperation is shaped by social practices such as sexism, racism, and homophobia. At the same time we discover that the social processes of discrimination and prejudice can often be interrupted through strategies that reduce or negate the need for fear (e.g., contact theory, dialogue groups, appreciative inquiry).

To hold up this genderized system we have managed to convince ourselves that power requires a winner and a protector. We focus solely on power as "power over," ignoring power that comes from collaboration. We have inscribed that protector status with a hypermasculinized identity. To fail to protect is labeled femininity, and women are generally placed outside the protector role except as peaceful mothers. Governments collect children's names for databases of future soldiers, and children are rewarded for "gender-appropriate" play, especially if they are boys.

Are We Somewhere in Between? Does It Matter for Peacemaking?

Social analysis often reveals that our observance of discrete categories is inaccurate and a continuum better explains social phenomena. The war culture is primarily a social process, but it reflects observable sex category behaviors. It is hard to know where biological factors end and socialization begins. More likely the two aspects of who we are (the biological and the social) exist together in layers. So, when needing to act out fears and concerns, boys turn to physical and large motor play while girls process through fine motor play and noncontact communication (see, e.g., http://everydaylife.globalpost.com/differences-gross-motor-development-boys-girls-early-childhood-18177.html).

A key question that this observation raises is, do boys biologically and culturally shy away from peaceful approaches to conflict and problem solving? Is their biological and sociological basis equally preparing them for nonviolent communication and interaction? Why do they pick violent play when they are children? Should we be raising children differently and is that possible without a shift away from patriarchy?

Biology is a tricky question in relation to violence. Researchers often look at how humans seek adrenaline-stimulating activities (exercise, roller coasters, etc.) but do not all have the same capacity or need for those experiences. It is also clear from studying twins that some biological basis exists for human habits and choices. But where biology leaves off and socialization takes over seems to be the crux of the conversation (see, e.g., Collins, 2009; Grossman, 1995). Can environment intervene and expand or reduce the biological basis of behavior? There is much agreement that learning matters, though not all scientists agree on what proportion of a person's reaction comes from the learning environment.

Multiple examples of individuals, groups, and societies where males choose the nonviolent path provide us with insight into our queries. When faced by the threat of Nazi Germany, leaders in Demark (predominantly male) did not seek battle. When challenging their authoritarian government, Chileans (mixed male and female leaders) won, but not through violent means. So the biology is not enough to determine a violent path. We must bring in socialization and examine the roles of fear and threat, along with images of bravery.

A highly militarized society funnels much of its economic, political, and social resources into the tools of militarization. War is costly, and often as war preparation increases, available spending on the social safety net is reduced (Kaufman and Williams, 2010, p. 2). This creates a change in the social contract between the government and the people. To justify its actions the government ramps up expenditures on "guns, not butter" socialization to get the public to accept the need for war. There are several gendered social myths that accompany war that are used to justify the need for war-based spending priorities.

IS GENDER ANALYSIS OF SOCIAL VIOLENCE ENOUGH?

The work of Riane Eisler (1987) helps us to recognize that gender socialization theory alone is inadequate to explain our militarized social system. She uses a gender analysis but not a continuum of male and female. Rather, she argues persuasively that that the polar opposite of our hierarchical and militarized society is not one that places women in the lead. It is not one that says that when women lead, peace will prevail. Her analysis shows a system of power that envelops gender divisions. The larger analysis focuses on the dominator versus the partnership society. Domination can be seen as the norm that shapes militarization, with the gender norms serving as a method of operationalizing the concept of power hierarchies. Partnership brings gender categories into positions of parity without normalizing a genderless social system (Eisler, 1987).

Patricia Hill Collins's research on race and sexual politics also charts the complexity of the relationship between gender and violence. She dissects the idea of racial liberation through strong black male leadership and finds that this leads to a culture of black patriarchy founded on the silencing and sometimes the sexual assault of black women who struggle to conform to male-led power hierarchies (Collins, 2005, chap. 7). Collins argues that since the watershed moment of Anita Hill's testimony before Congress, it has become increasingly clear that a black male patriarchy exists in parallel with (though somewhat different from) the society-wide white male patriarchy.

She focuses much of her interest on the ways in which power and control are based on the threat of sexual violence. In the black community, she notes, this evolves out of a complex yet blatantly violent past of slavery, with the lynching of black men and rape of black women in the postslavery society of the United States. Lynching, she argues became a public issue that symbolized the deeply embedded racism in the United States, whereas sexual violence against black women "has historically carried no public name, garnered no significant public censure, and has been seem as a crosscutting gender issue that diverts Black politics from its real job of fighting racism" (Collins, 2005, p. 217). This, suggests Collins, is why interrupting sexual violence within the black community is so difficult; its public discussion is seen as a threat to the black male path to social power. It also helps us to realize that achieving harmony and community does not always lead to the eradication of violence. Because of the larger system of violence and control based on racism and sexism, women of color find themselves in complex situations where they might live with one type of violence in order to join the fight against another. This is also an important way to make sense of the enduring question, if women are socialized to be peacemakers, when and why do they go to war?

SILENCING A GENDER CONTINUUM: MILITARISM AS A BLOCK TO GENDER CROSSING (AND HOW THAT CHANGED)

Women/Girl Soldiers: Are They Feminists?

It is a question worthy of discussion why some people seem drawn to make their mark on the world through nonviolent social change and others

seek change through violence. Much time and energy has been spent trying to identify key factors that produce violence-oriented individuals.
Social scientists have theorized that a "fight or flight" behavior pattern
was established in early human existence that we revert to in moments
of trauma and fear. Simplistic gender analysis takes this one step further
and aligns the male with the fight behavior and the female with the flight
behavior. Some psychologists have parsed this further and argued that
while physiologically males and females both adhere to "fight or flight" in
times of stress, research suggests that behaviorally females respond more
with a pattern of "tend-and-befriend" (Taylor, 2000). Sociologists in the
symbolic interactionist tradition have turned to theories of socialization
and their explanatory power regarding learned behavior and the influence
of environment (Mead, 1934; West and Zimmerman, 1987). These ideas
have also bifurcated behavior along gender lines: males are socialized to
fight through pressures of ideal-type masculinity, and females fear being
ostracized for stepping across gendered lines. The female ideal type in
this analysis achieves social power by learning to care for others and be a
"helper." Meanwhile rules of masculinity are pushing the boys to learn to
be doers and to seek public acclamation of their power.

So when women break through gendered barriers that restrict their
leadership roles in society and develop practices that fit in the so-called
male realm (e.g., serving as soldiers), does this act of crossing over make
them feminists? Does it help them to achieve equality? And if so, what are
the costs of that equality?

Even though women's service in militaries has expanded dramatically in recent decades, there has been resistance to having them serve
in decision making capacities. Much of the gatekeeping has centered on
preventing women from holding "combat" positions. This designation
has been somewhat mythical as women have served on front lines for
decades as soldiers, but usually in what were considered support roles.
Not having official combat experience has limited the ability of women
to rise through the ranks of power. Despite this many women have done
so. However, emerging data suggest that women striving for positions
of power in militaries have often experienced interpersonal violence
(especially sexual assault) (see, e.g., SWAN, n.d.). Even women just serving in the ranks are highly vulnerable to assault due to the misogynist
culture that surrounds them. In the United States the Academy Award–
nominated 2012 documentary film *The Invisible War* (directed by Kirby
Dick) has stirred awareness and prompted a push for better internal
processes in the military for identifying and addressing cases of sexual
assault. As a result of the attention paid, 2013 saw a record high number
of reported cases (not that the number of events went up but that previously they were so under-reported). The United States has also opened
combat service to women, though it is unclear whether this will improve

the overall safety of women in the U.S. military. An important related issue is the high rate of domestic violence in families of current and recently discharged soldiers.

A popular topic of study is the use of children in military forces. Until relatively recently the focus has been on boys, but increasingly it is acknowledged that girls are also recruited and forced into service. Women also join rebel groups seeking security because they have been arrested and sexually assaulted by government forces. Much of their service relates to their bodies as sexual objects. They may fight as soldiers but more often they are given low-status positions as "wives" of commanders, as cooks, or as nursing aides. Sexual assault of such women becomes routine and expected, with both men and boys participating (Mathers, 2013). More in-depth research is needed on this problem, and programs developed to serve them in the healing process will likely need to be specifically tailored to address the impact of sexual victimization. Being a girl soldier does not have the same impact as being a boy soldier. Girl/women soldiers may find themselves socially isolated because they have been raped. They may leave the ranks with sole responsibility for children conceived by rape. They are likely to be rejected by family members and spouses. They will typically re-enter societies structured on patriarchal values and find themselves with little or no opportunity to get ahead (Sonke Gender Justice Network, 2012).

Gender Violence: A Pillar of Military Masculinity

The depth of misogynist thinking and sexual assault in militaries around the world is astounding. As Cynthia Enloe (1983; 2007) has revealed, the military is often a willing supporter of prostitution near bases. Enloe (2007) explains that the hierarchical structure of patriarchy fits well with the hierarchical nature of militarized societies and the militaries that serve these societies. Another aspect of the use of sexual assault as a mechanism of power and control is the way it is implemented as an official strategy of war. Many scholars have studied extensively the attacks on civilian populations where rape and other forms of sexual assault have been used, often strategically with official sanction (Kaufman and Williams, 2010; Kuehnast et al., 2011; Mertus, 2000; Riley et al., 2008; Cohn, 2013). It has also become apparent that in some conflicts men are raped as a mechanism to gain power and control over them. Recent studies of Uganda have begun to unveil this phenomenon (Storr, 2011). That men are being raped does not undermine the gender analysis of militarism because it is clear that men are raped to place them in a subordinate position—or, as the rapist might say, to turn them into proverbial "women." Homosexuals in the military are also at risk for violence because they are seen as breaking the traditional gender boundaries.

Civilians and Refugees: Rape, Sex Trafficking, and Family Violence

Women and girls who are refugees are also considered highly vulnerable populations. War and refugee experiences make females likely victims of both sexual assault in camps and sex trafficking. The use of sexual assault in war is not new, but broad reporting, acknowledgment, and condemnation of it is relative recent. For example, at the Nuremburg trials rape was not on the list of "crimes against humanity," but in the tribunals after the war in Bosnia it was officially added to the list. It is not unusual for the reported number of women sexually assaulted or raped in a major conflict to surpass 100,000, and yet such numbers themselves are only general guides and are controversial. They are general guides because qualitative research finds repeatedly that women are hesitant to report themselves as victims due to fears of further victimization. They are controversial because it is hard to get viable data when the existing structure strikes fear in survivors, inflicts direct or indirect punishment on the survivors, and covers up systemic processes that support the practices of victimization. Sexual assaults committed by United Nations peacekeepers provide an example of our relative blindness to the idea that rape is about power holding, not about sex. The very forces that are looked to for protection find themselves enmeshed in the contradictions between masculine beliefs about power and access and the idea of human security and protection.

Rape during war can be part of an official military strategy, but it also happens on a more micro level (Kuehnast et al., 2011). A study by Sonke Gender Justice Network found that in the Democratic Republic of Congo (DRC) participants linked gender-based violence to high rates of unemployment leading to a sense of male disempowerment. The researchers pointed to the idea that rape became a tool to reinstate the sense of empowerment in men otherwise broken down by the hardships of war, emotionally wounded by treatment from enemies and from their own leadership, and plagued by a sense of total social dislocation (Sonke Gender Justice Network, 2012; cf. Chapter 12 in this volume).

Sex trafficking, which is a serious global problem, is another example of the importance of analyzing issues at the correct level (see Chapter 11 in this volume and Chapter 32 in Volume 2). Much of what was previously characterized as prostitution by individuals has been peeled back to find systematic networks of trade in human sex slaves. Economic insecurity is considered a key cause of sex trafficking vulnerability; because of this, conflict can be a catalyst for that vulnerability. Conflict happening in social systems with extreme economic inequalities, patriarchal values, and militaristic ways of dealing with difference sets the stage for abuse of marginalized populations. The norms of a region help determine if it is at risk for developing a market in sex trafficking. Viewing the problem as individualized cases of prostitution makes it possible for the larger underground network to form. High rates of unemployment impact the roles of both females and males in the sex trafficking industry. For girls and women the attraction is the prospect of potential employment (they are not told the details of the job at first), and for men it is the potential profit made from selling women they control into prostitution. The latter is exemplified by the practice by Serbian soldiers of selling Bosnian women into brothels across Europe during the war (Kara, 2009). Economic distress combined with cultural devaluation of women form the foundation of the sex trafficking industry. Power hierarchies found in both patriarchy and militarism support the market for gender-based violence.

An important related issue is the high rate of domestic violence in families of current and recently discharged soldiers. In December 2012 in the state of Wisconsin, a former soldier who was struggling with post-traumatic stress syndrome (PTSD) stalked his wife, who was an on-duty police officer, and shot her in the head using the sharpshooter skills he says he learned in the military. In his testimony about what led to the murder, he acknowledged his fear that she was gaining her own personal power by completing the police academy training and entering the working world. His fear of her self-actualization became the impetus to action. Notably, he had been very public about his struggles with PTSD but was seen as proactively addressing his issues. The case did raise discussions of the risks of PTSD but did little to spark conversation about the links between family violence and militarism. This echoes the conclusions of a report from the World Health Organization (WHO) released in 2005, which showed that relationships structured around highly controlling behaviors by the male were likely to also be characterized by physical violence by the male toward the female (Garcia-Moreno et al., 2005).

STRUCTURES OF LEADERSHIP AND GATEKEEPERS IN A MILITARIZED SOCIETY

It has been difficult to quell the use of sexual assault in militaries where it is viewed not as a weapon of war against an enemy but rather as an internal problem of a few bad apples. However, the high rates of sexual harassment, gender-based violence, and rape in military organizations around the world suggest that it is not simply an individual problem with case-by-case solutions. Public pressure can be used (e.g., as it has in the United States since 2012) to develop military practices and a military culture that eliminate the institutional supports for violence against women. Currently it is still more about cases and less about institutional culture, but the normative shift is in the shadows. In the United States in 2013 a change in the reporting and investigation processes for such cases has helped begin that change. The key lesson from feminist theory is that one way to maintain power is to sideline the problem as merely a case of individual failure rather than paying attention to patterns that help spot-light institutional practices. The change in the debate on the war front has likely been shaped by a shift to a less virulent form of patriarchy. In some places in our world deep discussions about gender stratification have led to a more covert form of patriarchy. While in a broad sense women still struggle to achieve social power, the norms have shifted to make direct violence related to male superiority less acceptable. As militaries have been exposed for sanctioning "strategic rape," public opinion has pushed for reform, noting that females, like males, need to be protected from undue harm in times of conflict.

The path to power for women in the military is complicated because it involves becoming part of a sharply hierarchical structure that has been built on the concept that masculinity equals the rejection of feminine char-acteristics. Full participation would likely require a major realignment of key structures and values. This would address the artificial bifurcation of male and female that informs all aspects of military life, from training to the development of policy and strategy. The U.S. invasion of Afghanistan is a case in point. It was widely argued by the policy makers that the United States needed to pursue intervention in Afghanistan to help address issues of gender-based violence on the ground. It is no secret that the Taliban enforces a highly patriarchal system that includes much violence against women. However, the "knight in shining armor" images promoted to the U.S. public suggested that the so-called West has addressed the problem of gender-based violence and could provide a healthy model for Afghani society. All this ignored that the Taliban were not based in Afghan culture, and that before the Soviet-U.S. war in Afghanistan (circa 1988) Afghan women were educated and serving in positions of leadership in their com-munities. It also ignored the high rates of gender-based violence within the U.S. military and in communities hosting U.S. military bases.

Sexual assault and harassment serve as unofficial but rampantly com-mon gatekeepers for women's advancement in the military. When women survive gender-based violence they find it difficult to address the issue, and it is not unusual for them to leave the institution as a result. This does not mean that they give up; rather, quite often they reach out. One poi-gnant example is the founding of the Service Women's Action Network (SWAN) by women veterans in the United States.

SYSTEMS NEEDED TO CONFRONT THESE ISSUES (MACRO, MESO, MICRO)

Since the late 20th century leaders on the global stage have been invest-ing quite a bit of energy into developing structures that address gender inequalities. One key focus has been developing norms and systems that reduce gender-based violence (GBV). While GBV is found in societies not at war, the risk level for women increases dramatically when political conflict breaks out (Mertus, 2000; Kuehnast ct al., 2011). Praxis (research and practice) has found that power inequalities between men and women encourage the use of violence to control women, who typically have less power. Several key interventions have worked to begin to shift the norms around women's vulnerability to GBV.

Millennium Development Goals

In the 1990s, as the new century loomed, there was energy to address social problems facing the world. At the Millennium Summit in September 2000 world leaders adopted the United Nations (UN) Millennium Declaration, which aimed to reduce extreme poverty. Eight goals were set with the deadline of reaching the targets set at 2015. Goal 2, "achieve universal primary education," and goal 3, "promote gender equality and empower women," both had the potential to shift patriarchal norms and alter the role of women in society (United Nations, n.d.). Goal 2 is a necessary condition of achieving goal 3. It is broadly agreed that educating girls and women has a tremendously positive impact on all areas of economic and social development. In a recent speech the UN Secretary-General, Ban Ki-moon, told the World Economic Forum (2014): "The United Nations gives girls a 'gold rating.' When you invest in their future, you are guaranteed results that multiply across society—on health, education, peace and the welfare of future generations" (United Nations News Centre, 2014). The power placed in girls has begun to change the dynamic in the family and across the nation. Females are not as easily victimized, and when they are there is a better forum for them to seek redress. The social norms are growing less accepting of the use of overt violence and sexist discrimination.

Increasingly violence is seen as a barrier to the success of girls and women. Building on global successes around the integration of women into discussions of conflict management and peace building spawned by Security Council Resolution (SCR) 1325, more recently groups have worked to connect the issue of GBV to global development goals. In March 2014 more than 6,000 women from 860 civil society organizations registered for the 58th meeting of the Commission on the Status of Women, organized by UN Women at UN Headquarters in New York. The theme of the meeting was "challenges and achievements in the implementation of the Millennium Development Goals for women and girls" (see http://www.unwomen.org/en/news/in-focus/csw) and an effort was made to shape the post-2015 development goals. One aspect of the discussions centered on including prevention of GBV in the future framework. This linking of issues is perhaps made possible by the establishment of UN Women as a coordinator of all UN-related activities that focus on women's needs and gendered social change (see Chapter 27 in Volume 2).

Security Council Resolution 1325

In 2000, building on legal understandings established with the criminal hearings after the Bosnia war, the UN Security Council adopted the first resolution on women, peace, and security. The resolution set out to mark

the disproportionate and unique impact of armed conflict on women; recognized the under-valued and under-utilized contributions women make to conflict prevention, peacekeeping, conflict resolution and peace-building. It also stressed the importance of women's equal and full participation as active agents in peace and security. (Peacewomen, n.d.)

Four additional resolutions (SCRs 1820, 1888, 1889, 1960) were passed in the next decade as a global movement crystalized around the idea that women were not adequately included and often were intentionally excluded from policy, diplomacy, and post-conflict economic recovery. The prehistory of this important resolution can be traced to the UN-sponsored Fourth World Conference in Bejing in 1995. According to Anderlini (2007), the conference produced a Platform for Action and Chapter E, "Women and Armed Conflict," added a new aspect to discussions about the core theme of women and development. Chapter E, rising from the lessons of Rwanda, Bosnia, and the peace work of women in Northern Ireland, South Africa, and the Middle East, called not just for the protection of women but for recognition of the positive peace roles they play around the world (Anderlini, 2007, pp. 5–6).

The shift in perspective that women might be valuable assets to peace building (prevention and recovery) work not just on the individual level but in all aspects stands as another marker of the slow but steady dismantling of patriarchy. What may be of intrigue is that it is the stereotypes of women as being better at caring and peace that first excluded women and now finds them at center stage in global mechanisms to shift from violent to nonviolent methods for solving conflicts. Although this broad cultural shift is happening, it takes slow and deliberate advocacy to get the actual institutional structures to change. In 2010, with little real change apparent one decade into the existence of SCR 1325, new pressure was placed on leaders to push for a system of implementation and evaluation. The National Action Plan (NAP) process was put in place. However, it remains a struggle to evaluate and enforce the principles of SCR 1325 in the face of reluctance or resistance.

National-Level Interventions in Military Policies and Practices

At the national level several strategies have been pursued to address in modest ways the negative impact of patriarchy on females. With decades of pressure on leaders to address the disempowerment of women, small strides have been taken. But they are small and not particularly impressive when viewed from a distance. Despite this, it is true that women's participation in most levels of government and business in most parts of the world has increased. Unfortunately, there has not been a parallel reduction in militaristic thinking in the large nations, although a handful of countries have eliminated their militaries in favor of a strictly national police force trained to act in national defense.

As discussed above, women have in some countries, including the largest military spender (the United States), been allowed to begin to move into combat roles and thus seek increasingly powerful positions in the military. But in general there remains discomfort with the idea of women as soldiers, as Jennifer Mathers (2013) argues, because "it challenges assumptions about appropriate roles for men and women within a society and about the nature of masculinity and femininity" (p. 125). Whether allowing women to serve in the military actually changes the individual or group status of females is not a question that has been clearly answered. As long as the military exists in tandem with patriarchal systems of power, it seems unlikely to be the change agent for women's empowerment. And in much the same way, as long as patriarchy continues to be buttressed by the military, and violence is considered a reasonable mechanism for dealing with difference or conflict, it seems unlikely that gender norms will change dramatically.

Civil Society Involvement in Solution Building

Social movement organizations have provided a vast range of opportunities for individuals to become more aware and active in addressing the issue of gender-based violence. A nearly century-old global organization, for example, Women's International League for Peace and Freedom (WILPF), has advocated for women's participation in policy and peacemaking from its inception (www.wilpfinternational.org). They also created the Peacewomen organization, which works specifically on tracking and assessing progress on SCR 1325 (Peacewomen, n.d.). U.S.-based Women's Action for New Directions was founded in the 1980s first as a women's peace political party and later became an NGO interested in demilitarizing the country and connecting peace issues to women's issues. The Women in Peacebuilding Program (WIPNET), part of the West African Network for Peacebuilding, founded in 2001, works to empower women and provide them with skills for more effective peace building (http://www.gnwp.org/members/wipnet). One of its founders is Leymah Gbowee, who found herself doing grassroots organizing of women in her home, Liberia, in order to move forward a peace agreement that would end the decade-long civil war. WIPNET realizes that it is not just about opening space for women to become involved, it is also about supporting them with training on how to get involved in peace building from the local to the national level. The Global Network of Women Peacebuilders (GNWP) is a coalition of women's groups and other civil society organizations from Africa, Asia and the Pacific, southern Asia, western Asia, Latin America, and Eastern and Western Europe that works on and advocates for the implementation of SCR 1325 (http://www.gnwp.org/). All of these organizations and many others see the intertwined nature of patriarchy and militarism, and link sustainable peace building with gender justice and women's/girls' empowerment.

Power Sharing in the Home

To unravel the well-knit duo of militarism and patriarchy is a key challenge in the pursuit of women's empowerment. Steps are being taken slowly on the international level, but much also must be done in nations and in households. In many states in the world, women live daily in a militarized home. This does not necessarily mean they always cohabitate with soldiers, though the case of military wives is a particularly important aspect of the militarized home. What it means is that they live in a cultural environment, with a set of family values that disempowers them and enforces their compliance with a patriarchal structure through the threat or application of interpersonal violence. Although in the United States marital rape has been illegal in all states since 1993, there continues to be debate about it as an enforceable crime. And although politicians may think that all sex in marriage is consensual (Redden, 2014), about one-third of domestic violence cases in the United States involve marital rape (RAINN, n.d.). In the 1980s Riane Eisler (1988) began to call for a "partnership society," an idea that fits well with the unlinking of power and patriarchy (see Chapter 24 in Volume 2).

ULTIMATELY GENDER ANALYSIS DEMANDS WE THINK OUTSIDE "THE BOX"

Ultimately it is not whether men or women have greater or less capacity for peacemaking or war making. It is that cultural expectations for power, habits around gender norms, and our failure to embrace both the differences and similarities between the needs of men and those of women set up a failure of the community as a whole to flourish. When one group succeeds only through the enslavement or colonization of another, it is not a successful society. Its norms of success have been set on the devaluation of human dignity.

For activists, theorists, and scientists to promote "women as peaceful" follows a familiar pattern in gender behavior but does not necessarily promote women's well-being. If being peaceful is characterized as weak, giving up, or giving in, this just perpetuates the false pairing of males and violence. It is not males but rather masculinity as circumscribed by militarism and a commitment to preserving patriarchy that links violence with power. While current history suggests that women more often than men stand on the side of practical peace building activities before, during, and after violent conflict, there is not adequate evidence that this is integral to the female nature. In fact, persistence at peacemaking within a patriarchal, militarized society may make women more vulnerable to victimization as they fulfill their expected roles. The challenge is to imagine the institution of powerful peacemaking roles—women emboldened to develop their cross-community ties, and men feeling safe in coming forward as survivors of sexual violence as well as in their role of perpetrators. It is far too simplistic to propose that masculinity is the problem. Rather, the root seems to lie in how we perceive the nature of power and its allowed use. Social-cultural norms can go a long way toward the prevention of inhumane violence. Furthermore, norms around the use of power and what defines power can contribute to a systemic shift. Imbuing those norms against violence with a commitment to gender, racial, and economic equality may provide the social system that supports our shared goal: to persevere.

BIBLIOGRAPHY

Anderlini, S. 2007. *Women Building Peace: What They Do, Why It Matters.* Boulder, CO: Lynne Rienner.

Baumgardner, J. and A. Richards. 2000. *Manifesta:Young Women, Feminism and the Future.* New York: Farrar, Straus and Giroux.

Cohn, C., ed. 2013. *Women & Wars.* Cambridge, UK: Polity Press.

Collins, P. H. 2005. *Black Sexual Politics.* London: Routledge.

Collins, Randall. 2009. *Violence: A Micro-sociological Theory.* Santa Barbara, CA: Greenwood.

Eisler, R. 1987. *The Chalice and the Blade.* New York: HarperCollins.

Enloe, C. 1983. *Does Khaki Become You?* Boston: South End Press.

Enloe, C. 2007. *Globalization and Militarism: Feminists Make the Link.* Latham, MD: Rowman and Littlefield.

Garcia-Moreno, C., H. Jansen, M. Ellsberg, L. Heise, and C. Watts. 2005. *WHO Multi-country Study on Women's Health and Domestic Violence against Women.* Geneva: World Health Organization.

Grossman, Dave. 1995. *On Killing: The Psychological Cost of Learning to Kill in War and Society.* New York: Little, Brown and Co.

Hedges, C. 2002. *War Is a Force That Gives Us Meaning.* New York: Anchor Books.

hooks, b. 1984. *Feminist Theory: From Margin to Center.* Cambridge, MA: South End Press.

Kara, S. 2009. *Sex Trafficking: Inside the Business of Modern Slavery.* New York: Columbia University Press.

Kaufman, J., and K. Williams. 2010. *Women and War: Gender Identity and Activism in Times of Conflict.* Sterling, VA: Kumarian Press.

Kuehnast, K., C. Oudraat, and H. Hernes. 2011. *Women and War: Power and Protection in the 21st Century.* Washington, DC: United States Institute for Peace.

Mathers, J. 2013. Women and State Military Forces. In *Women &Wars*, edited by Carol Cohn. Cambridge, UK: Polity Press.

Mead, H. 1934. *Mind, Self, and Society*. Chicago: University of Chicago Press.

Mead, M. 2014 [1940]. Warfare Is Only an Invention—Not a Biological Necessity. Reprinted in *Approaches to Peace: A Reader in Peace Studies*, edited by David P. Barash. 3rd ed. New York: Oxford University Press, pp. 20–23.

Mertus, J. 2000. *War's Offensive on Women*. Bloomfield, CT: Kumarian Press.

Peacewomen. n.d. About Women, Peace and Security, http://www.peacewomen .org/pages/about-1325 (retrieved January 27, 2014).

Rape, Abuse and Incest National Network (RAINN). n.d. Marital Rape, http://www.rainn.org/public-policy/sexual-assault-issues/marital-rape (retrieved January 27, 2014).

Reardon, B. 1985. *Sexism and the War System*. New York: Teacher's College Press.

Redden, M. 2014, January 15. GOP Congressional Candidate: Spousal Rape Shouldn't Be a Crime. *Mother Jones*, http://www.motherjones.com/ politics/2014/01/gop-congressional-candidate-richard-dick-black-spousal -rape-not-a-crime (retrieved January 27, 2014).

Riley, R., C. Mohanty, and M. Pratt. 2008. *Feminism and War: Confronting U.S. Imperialism*. New York: Zed Books.

Service Women's Action Network (SWAN). n.d. Careers at Risk, http://service women.org/blog/2013/03/23/careers-at-risk-2/ (retrieved March, 26, 2014).

Sonke Gender Justice Network. 2012. Gender Relations, Sexual Violence and the Effects of Conflict on Men and Women in North Kivu Eastern Democratic Republic of Congo, http://www.genderjustice.org.za/resources/cat_view/ 46-reports.html?limit=100&limitstart=0&order=name&dir=DESC (retrieved January 26, 2014).

Storr, W. 2011, July 16. The Rape of Men: The Darkest Secret of War. *The Observer*, http://www.theguardian.com/society/2011/jul/17/the-rape-of-men (retrieved January 27, 2014).

Sue, D. W., C. Capodilupo, C. Torino, J. Bucceri, A. Holder, K. Nadal, and M. Esquilin. 2007. Racial Microaggressions in Everyday Life. *American Psychologist* 62 (4): 271–286.

Taylor, S. 2000. Biobehavioral Responses to Stress in Females: Tend-and-Befriend, Not Fight-or-Flight. *Psychological Review* 107 (3): 411–429.

United Nations. n.d. Millennium Project, http://www.unmillenniumproject.org/

United Nations News Centre. 2014, January 23. At Davos Forum, Ban Seeks Business Help to Fight Gender Inequality, Climate Change, Hunger, http://www.un.org/apps/news/story.asp?NewsID=46988&Cr=mdg&Cr1 =#.UubYm7Tnbix (retrieved January 22, 2014).

West, C., and D. Zimmerman. 1987. Doing Gender. *Gender and Society* 1 (2): 125–151.

Women and Men in North Kivu, Eastern Democratic Republic of Congo, http:// www.genderjustice.org.za/resources/cat_view/46-reports.html?limit=10 0&limitstart=0&order=name&dir=DESC (retrieved January 25, 2014).

CHAPTER 10

Violence against Immigrant Women

Pilar Rodríguez Martínez

INTRODUCTION

We want to continue to contest the neglect of domestic violence against women, the tendency to dismiss it as a private matter. We need to develop an approach that relies on political mobilization rather than legal remedies or social service delivery. We need to fight for temporary and long-term solutions to violence and simultaneously think about and link global capitalism, global colonialism, racism, and patriarchy—all the forces that shape violence against women of color. Can we, for example, link a strong demand for remedies for women of color who are targets of rape and domestic violence with a strategy that calls for the abolition of the prison system? (Davis, 2000, p. 5)

Angela Davis, speaking of the experiences of women of color in the epigraph above, provides an inspiring analysis of violence against women, emphasizing that the violence that women suffer has historically been seen as a private matter. In fact, violence against women was discovered as a social problem only in the 1970s, when women tried to connect the suffering they experienced with the large social structures of domination. However, white and black women did not have the same analysis. Hegemonic, white, middle-class feminists connected violence directly and exclusively with patriarchy (Rodriguez, 2011). On the other hand, black women could not separate the inequities due to their being women and those due to race and class because, they argued, they experienced those inequities simultaneously. In the case of violence against immigrant women, "If one were to work only with gender issues at the expense of cultural and structural issues, such as poverty, racism, and immigration controls, the resultant gender analysis would be devoid of context and of the lived experiences of minoritised women"(Chantler and Gangoli, 2011, p. 358). Davis's work can help here, as she belonged to a movement that conceptualized problems of violence "as a 'web,' because the causes of violence, from interpersonal to global, are connected, as are the consequences" (Turpin and Kurtz, 1997, p. 12).

My approach in this chapter is similar to the one espoused by women of color (Grillo, 1995; Davis, 2000; Thompson, 2002; Richie, 2002) or the more recent intersectionality approach (Winker and Degele, 2011; Davis, 2008; Ken, 2008; Yuval-Davis, 2006; McCall, 2005). But it will be somewhat different because I don't confront exactly the same problems. I have called my view *peripheral feminisms* because it addresses the inequalities—and violence—that women from the margin suffer in the rich countries (Rodriguez, 2006). As formulated by Kimberlé Crenshaw, the intersectional approach detects the limitations in analyses of "additive" discrimination in gender and race, which assumes that the final inequalities are the sum of discriminatory practices suffered by white women and black men, which makes the inequalities suffered by black women invisible (Crenshaw, 1993). The problems I have to face are not only those of invisibility of the violence that immigrant women suffer (which are similar to the ones that Crenshaw and the intersectional approach detect), but also—and paradoxically—aproblematic hypervisibility (the spotlight shines on immigrant women, exacerbating their issues).[1] In this chapter I will explore this process of hypervisibility that has occurred since the 1990s in the rich countries. I will argue that it has some consequences for the kind of violence that immigrant women suffer and in the way they experience violence.

Let's begin by defining violence against women. The widely accepted definition comes directly from the declaration of the United Nations' Fourth World Conference on Women, held in Beijing in 1995. The conference established that "the term 'violence against women' means any act of gender-based violence that results in, or is likely to result in, physical, sexual or psychological harm or suffering to women, including threats of such acts, coercion or arbitrary deprivation of liberty, whether occurring in public or private life." I will work with this definition because it is the one that was used to collect data regarding violence against immigrant and native women. However, this definition considers violence in very narrow, reductionist terms. In this chapter I will talk about some other types of violence that immigrants suffer and I will focus on the social production of violence, which treats these constructs "in broad, inferential terms tied to general sociolegal currents such as class, race, ethnicity, or sexuality" (Alfieri, 1999, p. 1193).

A woman is an international immigrant if she was not born in the country where she lives.[2] Today in the Western countries not all the immigrant women come from poor countries; the movement of women between the rich countries has also increased. However, I will limit my focus to immigrant women coming from poor countries to live in Western ones, though not all of them are black women, nor are they all poor. The realities and lives of "immigrant women" are not homogeneous, nor are these women a monolithic group; much variation exists.

In this chapter I try to answer the following questions: Are the causes of violence against women the same for immigrants and natives? Is this the only violence that immigrant women suffer as immigrants? I have organized my remarks into three sections. I will first review some studies conducted in Western countries comparing the prevalence of violence against immigrant and native women. I will highlight the fact that there are no significant differences between migrants and natives with regard to the prevalence of domestic and interpersonal violence. However, since the 1990s, a considerable number of studies have tried to link violence against immigrant women with the culture of origin of those women. In the second section I take a critical look at these approaches. In the third section I try to specify some of the social conditions that define the contexts in which immigrant women from poor countries experience violence. Immigration laws and regulations, in my opinion, have played an important role in defining the social conditions that shape this experience.

THE ROLE OF THE SOCIAL STRUCTURE IN SHAPING VIOLENCE AGAINST IMMIGRANT AND NATIVE WOMEN

In Western countries, intimate partner violence, domestic abuse, and interpersonal violence have been most studied. There are a vast number of micro studies on violence among migrant populations, both qualitative and quantitative. However, researchers rarely compare the violence between the native population and immigrant population in a systematic way. In my opinion, this comparison is absolutely necessary if we want to know how migrant women experience violence compared to natives. I will then start by reviewing the results of the surveys conducted with sufficiently representative samples in three countries: Canada, the United States, and the U.K. I will also review the results of a European Union (EU)-wide survey about violence against women. Although these surveys do not share the same definitions of violence and the samples are not selected in the same way, all conclude that there is no difference in the prevalence of domestic abuse, intimate partner violence, or interpersonal violence between immigrant and native women.

In Canada, researchers found that there is little to no difference in the prevalence of spousal abuse between immigrant and native women. Farah

Ahmad et al. (2005) conducted secondary data analysis based on the General Social Survey (1999) in Canada, comparing Canadian immigrants to Canadian-born women. The prevalence of physical spousal abuse was not statistically different between the two groups when accounting for other variables. Using the same database, Ilene Hyman et al. (2006) found that the crude prevalence of intimate partner violence was similar among recent and nonrecent immigrant women. However, after adjustment, the risk for intimate partner violence was significantly lower among recent immigrant women compared with nonrecent immigrant women. Moreover, the country of origin (Asian, African, and Central and South American), age, marital status (single, divorced, separated or widowed), and having an activity limitation (physical/mental disability or health problem) were all associated with a higher risk for intimate partner violence. Janice Du Mont and Tonia Forte analyzing the data from the General Social Survey (2009) found that the prevalence of emotional abuse and physical/sexual violence was lower among immigrant women compared with Canadian-born women, and there were no differences between immigrant women and Canadian-born women in the physical and psychological consequences of physical or sexual intimate partner violence (Du Mont and Forte, 2012).

In the United States, the National Crime Victimization Survey (1992) estimated that there were no significant differences in the violence perpetrated by intimate partners across racial and ethnic boundaries. Black and white women and Hispanic and non-Hispanic women sustained about the same amount of violence by intimate partners (Bachman and Saltzman, 1995, p. 4). The National Violence against Women Survey (1995–1996) on the prevalence and incidence of rape, physical assault, and stalking did not find a significant difference between women based on their race. When data on African American, American Indian/Alaskan Native, Asian/Pacific Islander, and mixed-race women are combined, there is very little difference between white women and nonwhite women in the incidence of rape, physical assault, or stalking (Tjaden and Thoennes, 2000). Using the Conflict Tactics Scale, Rau Caetano et al. analyzed data from a multistage area probability sample representative of married and cohabiting couples from the 48 contiguous U.S. states (1995). They found that the 12-month rates of male to female partner violence were similar across whites, blacks, and Hispanics (Caetano el al., 2005, p. 401). As Joanne Klevens highlights in her overview of intimate partner violence among Latinos, other national and local population-based probability surveys have found higher, lower, and similar rates of intimate partner violence among Latinos compared to non-Latinos, but "differences in rates tend to disappear once income, urbanity, age, drinking impulsivity, and family history are controlled for" (Klevens, 2007, p. 112). In those studies, Latino victims of intimate partner violence tended to be younger, less educated, and more economically disadvantaged than non-Latino white victims, but these are the characteristics of the Latino population. In her review, Klevens concluded that Latinos share many of the same risk factors as non-Latinos, except that beliefs approving intimate partner violence and alcohol drinking patterns may not have much explanatory power for the prevalence of intimate partner violence among Latinos. Nevertheless, "although the core experience may be similar, intimate partner relationships must be understood within the context of a group's situation in our society. For many Latinos in the United States, IPV is often colored by experiences of immigration (frequently illegal), acculturation, and socioeconomic disadvantage" (Klevens, 2007, p. 119). Stella Resko reached the same conclusion when analyzing the Fragile Families Survey (1998–2000):

The findings from this study are consistent with previous research that shows a greater incidence of battering among women lower on the socioeconomic scale. The results are also consistent with previous research that has shown race/ethnicity is not statistically significant when economic variables are introduced into statistical models. (Resko, 2007, p. 274)

In the U.K. similar results were obtained after the results were analyzed of the computerized, self-administered questionnaire about interpersonal violence (domestic violence, sexual assault, and stalking)included in the British Crime Survey (2001). The interpersonal violence that women suffered was not found to be significantly associated with their ethnicity (white, black, or Asian). Sylvia Walby and Jonathan Allen detected some other risk factors associated with interpersonal violence: gender, lack of access to economic resources, low household income, the ability to find money on short notice, and the employment status of the victim. The lack of association in the case of ethnicity is interpreted as interesting: "There is little variation in inter-personal violence by ethnicity. This is an interesting finding because, since ethnicity is associated with variations in economic resources, it might have been expected to show parallel variations" (Walby and Allen, 2004, p. 74). I agree with Walby and Allen that this is an interesting finding. If we assume that ethnic groups in the U.K. have a lower socioeconomic status than the rest of the population, they should show a higher rate of interpersonal violence.

There are some other countries that have carried out national representative surveys with the same results as those. For example, in Australia the first national survey to measure the nature and extent of violence against women was undertaken in 1996. The survey found similar proportions of women born outside Australia (7.2 percent) and of Australian-born women (8.0 percent) reporting violence by a current male partner (Cunneen and Stubbs, 1997, pp. 31–32). In the Netherlands, the Dutch Department of Justice carried out a survey in the early 2000s of the ethnic communities. "Results regarding prevalence of 'domestic violence' (again adding up physical/sexual child abuse, psychological abuse, and intimate partner violence) turned out to be substantially *lower* for Moroccans and Turks" (Römkens and Lahlah, 2011, p. 83, italics in original).

Recently, the main results of an EU-wide survey about violence against women, conducted by the European Union Agency for Fundamental Rights (2014), have been made available The survey is based on interviews with 42,000 women across the 28 member states of the EU. A random probability sample of about 1,500 women per country were asked about their experiences of physical, sexual, and psychological violence, including incidents of intimate partner violence and sexual harassment. The report found some differences between those who are victims of physical and sexual violence and those who are not (differences related to age, educational level, income, and employment status and occupation). There are notable differences in the levels of experienced violence by heterosexual and nonheterosexual women, and among women with disabilities or health problems. Concerning citizenship, the survey differentiates between (1) citizens of the country of residence who have lived in the country all their lives; (2) citizens of the country of residence who lived in the country for 30 years or more (but not all their lives); (3) citizens of the country of residence who have lived in the country for less than 30 years; and (4) noncitizens of the country of residence. Given these differences in immigrant status, the report found the following:

The results indicate relatively small differences between the respondents based on the four categories as listed above and their experiences of various forms of violence. Women who are not citizens of their current country of residence have somewhat higher rates of physical and/or sexual violence since the age of 15 by partners and non-partners, but there are no notable differences with regard to other forms of violence examined (stalking and sexual harassment since the age of 15; and physical, sexual or psychological violence before the age of 15). (European Union Agency for Fundamental Rights, 2014, pp. 188–189)

From these results we can draw several conclusions. First, there are no significant differences in the prevalence of abuse between immigrant women and natives. And second, this kind of abuse is clearly linked to a lack of resources. The latter relationship must be interpreted with care: abuse may be the cause or the consequence of a lack of resources. In any case, the lack of resources explains some of the differences between immigrants and natives. As demonstrated by Yvonne Amanor-Boadu et al. (2012), immigrant women report higher levels of perceived risks and barriers in leaving an abusive relationship compared with natives. The lack of resources makes it difficult to deal with violence. This lack of resources also explains the fact that immigrant women are overrepresented in shelters and access social services at a higher rate than natives (Römkens and Lahlah, 2011, p. 84).

But these studies also have limitations. First, the way they selected their samples could exclude many immigrant women, especially undocumented immigrants. Second, the definition of violence used does not capture all the violence women suffer. For example, most of these surveys do not take into account the fact that women suffer violence in public places or at work. Also, they do not capture other possible types of violence that migrant women experience simultaneously (racism, discrimination due to their illegal status, etc.). Finally, the surveys do not give us an idea of the connotations that women attach to different types of violence.[3]

THE HYPERVISIBILITY OF VIOLENCE AGAINST IMMIGRANT WOMEN

In Western countries, immigrant women from poor countries have been historically neglected, even though more women migrate than men, as has been shown for the United States since the 1980s (Houstoun et al., 1984). Gender entered the analysis of migration during this decade, at the intersection of gender studies and migration studies. For example, in Silvia Pedraza's review about women and migration, she noted that the experience of immigration holds different benefits for women and men (Pedraza, 1991, p. 322). But in 1991, violence against immigrant women was not yet a subject of research. In fact, Pedraza makes no mention of violence against immigrant women as a separate category for analysis. Violence against immigrant women became a social problem and a subject of research in the 1990s, going hand in hand with the debates around the clash of civilizations thesis.

Current analyses about violence against immigrant women reproduce many of the constructs of hegemonic feminists as well as the tradition/modernity perspectives about women in migrations. For hegemonic feminists, violence against women is a means of controlling women and maintaining or enforcing male privilege (Rodriguez, 2011). On the other hand, it is often assumed that immigrant women, especially those from poor countries, come from traditional nonegalitarian cultures. As Mirjana Morokvasic points out, the tradition/modernity perspective has women in migration moving from more oppressive to less oppressive environments. As a result, immigration is seen as a liberating process where old cognitive modes are no longer operative in a modern environment. The improvement regarding gender was assumed to occur due to the "general improvement" resulting from migration—in particular from earning regular wages or being actively involved in the production process (Morokvasic, 2007, p. 72). The result of this combination of assumptions is that immigrant women experience a kind of gender violence that is *incomparable* to the one that natives suffer. As Alice Debauche remarks, in Western societies there is supposed to be a process of behavioral civilization, marked by a drop in the tolerance of violence but also by greater self-control and therefore fewer manifestation of violence. As a result, gender violence appears as something external, belonging to an *elsewhere* or a *before* (Debauche, 2011, p. 340).

Since the 1990s, analyses of violence against immigrant women have tended to assist in the "discovery" of some *incomparable* violence that women from the poor countries suffer. This includes the use of the veil, forced marriages, the Hindu practice of dowry, genital cutting, female infanticide, bride-burning, and—more recently—trafficking of women and international marriages. We can find this idea of incomparability in the definition of violence against women that is used. For example, in the introduction to Bradley's *Women, Violence and Tradition*, a book that "is intended to represent a snapshot, however small, of the concerns and experiences of black minority ethnic women in Britain" (Bradley, 2011, p. 29), the author states,

Violence against women emerges either as a result of specific practices such as female genital mutilation or in a domestic setting as a mechanism used by men (and in a small number of cases also women) to ensure women behave "appropriately" according to the so-called norms of their patriarchal culture. (Bradley, 2011, p. 4)

The problem with this definition is that it confuses violent conduct against women with the justification for such a conduct. So, even if it is not the author's intention, the analysis presented in this book reduces violence suffered by immigrant women to matters of religion, culture, and tradition, thereby excusing violent behavior and hiding the liability of the actors who abuse women. As Montoya points out,

Some forms of violence that should fall within broader categories of violence against women are referred to specifically (and problematically) because of their perceived cultural context. For example, "honor killings" and dowry deaths are particular forms of family-based or domestic violence. They are singled out, however, because they are often viewed, particularly by Western countries, as unique and a more "barbaric" form of violence, even though Western domestic violence leads to similar outcomes of death or maiming. It is no coincidence that increased emphasis on culturalized forms of violence has accompanied the rise in xenophobia and Islamophobia in Northern European countries: "When culturalized framings come to dominate discourse, they may serve to narrow the scope of what is understood as violence against women." (Montoya, 2013, p. 17)

As I stated earlier, this hypervisibility has become more prevalent since the 1990s. Let me add that it has come hand in hand with the publication of the Global Gender Gap by the World Economic Forum, which demonstrates, year by year, a strong correlation between those countries that are most successful at closing the gender gap and those that are the most economically competitive. If we consider violence against women to be an expression of gender inequality—as advocated by feminists of the hegemonic second wave—and we do not consider that such violence is exacerbated by a context characterized by a lack of resources, we end up with the conclusion that indeed women in poor countries suffer more violence than those in the rich countries because their cultures are particularly patriarchal. Within this discourse, we also learn that in rich countries, violence against women is something "abnormal." I paint this picture because analyses about violence against immigrants in the West go hand in hand with analyses about violence against native women. In rich societies "violence by member of dominant group is viewed as pathological, while that by member of minority groups is viewed as an aspect of their culture"(Debauche, 2011, p. 340).

Culture can be easily used as a racist or classist argument. For example, in the United States, this idea is presented by Kathleen J. Ferraro, who speaks about the reaction of the police when they confront the situation of violence against immigrant women: "Officers on patrol often referred to Mexicans, Indians, gay men, and people in the housing projects as 'low lifes,' 'scum,' or 'these kind of people.' Officers believed arrests were a waste of time and meaningless for these people because violence is a way of life for them" (Ferraro, 1989, p. 67). As Cecilia Menjívar and Olivia Salcido note,

Such notions not only serve to substantiate host governments' perceptions that domestic violence among immigrants is inherently a part of their culture—and thus nothing can be done about it—but also that domestic violence is higher among immigrants because they import it with them. (2002, p. 901)

To see culture as a cause of violence against immigrant women is always problematic, even if the analysis states that culture is not the main cause of violence. For example, in the review of research on violence against immigrant women quoted above, Menjívar and Salcido show that the incidence of domestic violence in not higher among immigrant women. However, the experiences of immigrant women are often *exacerbated* by language, isolation, contact with family and community, changes in economic status (entry into paid employment), legal status, and "the home country as a frame of reference." I will refer to those factors later. For now, I want to emphasize the analysis of culture as a frame of reference. When talking about the "home country as a frame of reference," Menjívar and Salcido state, "Often, women arrive from countries where domestic violence simply is not reported because of a lack of legal protection or cultural prescriptions that prevent women from reporting violence" (2002, p. 910). Like Menjívar and Salcido, most authors will state that in the case of immigrants, violence is often exacerbated because of the structural and legal context, but in the end they will also accept that there are some cultural factors that explain gender violence against immigrant women. In other words, they will say that immigrant and refugee families are at risk for domestic violence because of their migration history *and* differences in cultural values and norms (Pan et al., 2006, p. 36; Weil and Lee, 2004).

Depending on the country of origin of an immigrant group, some researchers will explain the violence women suffer—and their reaction to this violence—in light of such cultural factors "as prioritization of family and community over the individual and emphasis on the role of the woman in maintaining family unity. Other characteristics that have been identified are acceptance of spousal violence, traditional and evolving gender roles, and lack of legal protection for victims in the country of origin" (Ingram et al., 2010, p. 859). As Celeste Montoya highlights,

This phenomenon is harmful in a number of ways: it obscures the degree to which violence against women is rooted in structural causes; it serves to further marginalize already vulnerable groups by emphasizing an "us versus them" mentality based on perceived cultural superiority; and it undermines the seriousness of violence against women in all its forms perpetuating normalization. (2013, p. 20)

I do not want to say that culture does not matter in helping us to understand the justification of violence against immigrant or native women. But it is not the cultural ideas themselves, but the way that people connect these ideas in order to excuse (or not) the act of violence. I agree with Khatidja Chantler and Geetanjali Gangoli, who suggest that a cultural analysis needs to be comparative, because

even if we start by accepting that sexual jealousy in intimate heterosexual relationship in both white mainstream and minoritised communities is based on ideas of hurt, honour and shame, we might then begin to understand how its formulation may differ in both contexts. To illustrate, in white mainstream communities, these ideas may be more individualized or linked to ideas of individual masculinity while in some minoritised communities, they may be more community or family based, or based on ideas that women's behaviour can discredit familial pride and honour. (Chantler and Gangoli, 2011, p. 364)

In the same vein, in a paper I coauthored with Huzefa Khalil, where we analyzed the World Values Survey data, we showed that the justification for "a man to beat his wife" has to do with the values associated with gender equality *and* those associated with sexual mores. And these two sets of values change with the modernization process (Rodriguez and Khalil, 2013).

DRAWING BACK THE VEIL OF HYPERVISIBILITY

As noted by Smaïn Laacher (2008), the migration processes must be understood, first of all, as displacements. Migrations entail movements in geography and culture. The displaced are nationals without a nation, bearers of a nationality without a state, or a nation without territory; immigrants are humans who belong to one nation but whose existence is placed under the responsibility (in fact and law) of another nation (Laacher, 2008, p. 28). This situation disrupts the context in which immigrant women (compared to native women) suffer violence, the type of violence suffered, how they perceive the violence, and the possibilities they have of facing such violence. As Anannya Bhattacharjee notes, the idea of the private and the public does not have the same meaning for immigrants and natives. For example, the "home," which has been regarded as the most important place where domestic violence occurs against women (as portrayed by the hegemonic feminists of the second wave), does not have the same meaning for immigrant as it does for natives because the separation of the private and the public assumes that individuals are culturally homogeneous and citizens have a special relationship to the state. For Asian women, this relationship is different. For immigrants, "home" can mean the domestic sphere of the patriarchal and heterosexual family, but it may also mean an extended ethnic community separate and distinct from other ethnic communities; or their nations of origin, often shaped by nationalist movements and histories of colonialism (Bhattacharjee, 2006).

Citizenship (full membership in the community in which one lives) is omnirelevant for the immigrant population. It is not just a matter of formal legal status, "it is a matter of *belonging*, which requires *recognition* by other members of the community" (Glenn, 2011, p. 2, italics in original). Immigration laws and regulations are one of the many mechanisms that the state employs to create citizens. As Roberta Villalón synthesized, immigration laws and regulations permit the state to reaffirm its sovereignty, shape the state's nationhood (by setting citizenship ideals along racial, ethnic, gender, sexual, and class lines), and control the state's productivity (since they determine the number of foreign laborers who can legally join its workforce). They are critical tools for the inclusion and exclusion of persons and, respectively, for the struggle against or the re-creation of inequality (Villalón, 2010, pp. 36–38).

In fact, after the oil crisis of the 1970s and the crisis of the welfare state, rich countries have developed restrictive immigration laws and regulations to control the flow of immigrants from poor countries. As Cecilia Menjívar and Leisy Abrego point out for the case of Central American immigrants in the United States, immigration laws have normalized and cumulatively injurious effects. Menjíbar and Abrego use the concept of "legal violence" to capture the aggravation of otherwise "normal" or "regular" effects of the law, such as the immigrants' predicament that results from indefinite family separations due to increased deportations; the intensification in the exploitation of immigrant workers and new violations of their rights; and the exclusion and further barring of immigrants from education and other forms of socioeconomic resources for mobility and incorporation. All of these instances constitute forms of structural and symbolic violence that are codified in the law and produce immediate *social suffering*. (Menjívar and Abrego, 2012, p. 1384, italics in original)

Because immigration laws prioritize the labor market, they prescribe and limit the jobs that women from poor countries can engage in legally, depending on domestic necessities,[4] or, exceptionally, as refugees. The laws also recognize that women from poor countries can enter rich countries without a job, if they are sponsored by someone who has legal residence. Both admission categories, based on employment potential and family relationship, are a part of the multiple grounds of identity shaping violence against immigrant women, as long as they inform women's experiences of and responses to violence (Erez et al., 2009, p. 33).

In the case of "employment potential," we should take into account those immigration laws and regulations as gendered processes that have qualitatively transformed, and increased, the inequalities between poor and rich countries, and among women around the world. As Barbara Ehrenreich and Arlie R. Hochschild posit, "the lifestyles of the First World are made possible by a global transfer of the services associated with a wife's traditional role—child care, home-making, and sex—from poor countries to rich ones" (2003, p. 4). In their book *Global Woman*, the authors explain the increase in immigrants working as nannies, maids, and sex workers in the First World as a result of global polarization, increasing contact, and the establishment of a transcontinental female network. At the same time, white middle-class women are building careers that are molded according to the old male model. So immigrant women have become a part of the private solution that helps to mitigate some of the inequities between white men and women in the First World.

Saskia Sassen specifically connects the migration of maids, nannies, nurses, sex workers, and contract brides with the emergence of global cities and survival circuits, and the deepening misery of the global South (Sassen, 2003). On the one hand, in the global South we have assisted in the growth of mobilization of people (particularly women) into an alternative circuit of survival and profit in response to the effect of economic globalization (marked by unemployment, poverty, bankruptcies of a large number of firms, and shrinking state resources to meet social needs). On the other hand, the global cities of the North concentrate some of the global economy's key functions and resources, generating growth in the demand for highly paid professionals (men and native women), but also producing a direct demand for low-wage clerical and service workers and, indirectly, a demand for jobs associated with the consumption practices and lifestyles of high-income professionals. These not-so-attractive posi tions will be available for immigrants, especially immigrant women. They will become "the other workers" in the advanced corporate economy, a re-emerging "serving class" that works in a different employment regime, with or without documentation. As Sassen points out, "the image of the immigrant woman serving the white middle class professional woman has replaced that of the black female servant working for the white master in centuries past. The result is a sharp tendency toward social polarization in today's global cities" (Sassen, 2003, p. 262). In these global cities, types of abuse range from rape by employers and other physical and psycho- logical abuses, to exploitive or inhumane working conditions. As Nicola Piper points out, we should talk about *institutional forms of violence*,

carried out by the state vis-à-vis female migrant workers on both sides of the migration chain. In the context of the receiving state, violence consists of oppres- sive application of immigration laws whereby women workers are not provided options to find alternative employment . . . and are not treated as workers wor- thy of protection. . . . Thus, a situation is created where violence against women becomes part of the employment itself, as in trafficking and sex work, but also enabled by a state-sanctioned, or constructed, context that allows, and probably even furthers, the violence. (Piper, 2003, pp. 724–725)[5]

I have stated that as an exception to the spirit of the law, immigrant women can enter rich countries for (heterosexual)[6] family reunification and as marriage migrants. This "exception" has become the norm[7]since in most rich countries "illegal immigration is no longer a problem of illegal entry but a problem of illegal prolongation of an initially legal residence" (Tsoukala, 2005, p. 162). Since the 1970s, all countries recognize the impor- tance of family members in both attracting immigrants and promoting their successful settlement. Women from developing countries can rejoin family members from whom they were separated through the migration process or they can migrate, forming new families through international marriages. Recent data show the increase of international marriages in countries like the United States and Canada (Merali, 2008, p. 281). Some research concludes that the new couples do not differ much in race or education.[8]

In both cases, woman will not belong to the host country and they will not have recognition, at least in the beginning (for two to three years, depending on the country) (Merali, 2008, p. 282). They will depend, usu- ally, on their husband's immigrant status and, at least in the beginning, will not have the right to work. Referring to these women, Karolina Krzys- tek states, "The debates in Europe are strongly gendered and racialised, since the agents of this form of international migration are associated with negative stereotypes regarding minority cultures and religions and their image of women as traditional and submissive" (Krzystek, 2013, p. 126). In the previous paragraph I explored these ideas. Many immigrant women probably performed formal or informal paid work in their countries of origin before starting the process of family reunification, and in their countries of origin, their citizenship rights did not depend on their husbands.

In the new country, the immigration laws will define—and select women on the basis of—the type of relationship they must have with their partners: they must be formally married, and the person who sponsors them—usually the husband—must have sufficient economic resources to successfully carry out the process of reunification. The consequence of these laws and regulations is that women are formally tied to the status of the applying spouse because laws give the sponsoring spouse near total control over the woman's legal status. I do not want to suggest that domestic abuse that immigrant women suffer has its cause in this legal violence, but the two types of violence are connected when offenders use legal violence to beget violence against women. This is the way we should interpret the results of Edna Erez et al., from their analysis of 137 battered women who had immigrated to the United States from 35 countries across the globe:

The overwhelming majority of women (75%) described how men used immigrant status to force them into compliance. "He used my immigration status against me. He would tell me that without him, I was nothing in this country." Men threatened women in a number of ways with regard to immigration including that they would call ICE officials and report their immigration status (40%); get them deported (15%); withdraw their petition to immigrate or otherwise interfere with the naturalization process (10%); take away the children or deny their custodial rights (5%). One undocumented woman succinctly stated, "he makes threats to report me to the INS if I don't do what he wants." (Erez et al., 2009, pp. 46–47)

As Erez et al. point out, "This legal dependency intensifies gendered inequality, creates new ways for men to abuse and control their intimate partners, and entraps battered women" (Erez et al., 2009, p. 36). If they suffer abuse, they have to endure difficult relationships out of fear of losing their residence permit. And they risk being abandoned and left in an irregular situation if the spouse loses his status as resident. This situation is clearly exposed in *Violence against Latina Immigrants*. In this book, Roberta Villalón shows the crucial importance of resident status in cases of domestic abuse in order to seek justice and use public resources. She also demonstrates that in the United States the all-inclusive spirit of the Violence Against Women Act (1994) and the Victims of Trafficking and Violence Protection Act (2000)"work[s] within long-standing formal legal structures that prioritize men over women, married over nonmarried, heterosexual over nonheterosexual, American over foreign, and working, middle, or upper class over poor" (Villalón, 2010, p. 41).

Immigration laws and policies on family reunification also are part of the politics of belonging, defining, and manufacturing collective identities and value systems (who "we" are and what distinguishes "us" from the "others") in rich countries, as Saskia Bonjour and Betty de Hart (2013) clearly demonstrate in the case of the Netherlands. Reviewing the political debates and policies about "fraudulent" and "forced" marriages since the 1970s, the authors examine the ways in which gender and ethnicities interact with "other" transnational marriages and the women who engage in them. In this process, the migrant family has come to be represented as particularly problematic (immigrant women are denied agency and immigrant men are denied humanity and vulnerability). In doing so, politicians try to demonstrate their commitment to the norm of equality of men and women:

In both fields, love between two autonomous individuals is presented as the only valid grounds for entering into marriage. This is the "right" way: the "Dutch" way. Bi-national or migrant couples are represented as marriages on collective rather than individual, and material rather than romantic grounds and directly associated with fraud, abuse and violence. Denying the legitimacy of these marriages implies denying migrant spouses the right to enter and stay in the Netherlands. (Bonjour and de Hart, 2013, p. 72)

In the discourse of these politicians, arranged marriages are conflated with forced marriages, which in turn are conflated with fraud and violence; and in the course of the 2000s "imported brides" replaced migrant grooms as the most unwanted category. Bonjour and de Hart's analysis corresponds with Newsome's for international marriages in the United States:

Although there are no national figures on abuse of mail-order brides, authorities agree that domestic violence in these marriages can be expected at higher levels than in other marriages. . . .Mail-order brides do not complain for a variety of reasons—they do not know their rights, they are fearful of deportation, or they are isolated. (Newsome, 2007, p. 298)

Finally, this notion of immigrant room does not correspond at all with the notion of native men who kill immigrant women. As Chris Cunneen and Julie Stubbs (1997) concluded, analyzing the homicide victimization of Filipino women in Australia ages 20 to 39 (which was 5.6 times the rate for other Australian women in the same age of group),

A particular concern in the research is the way in which men who killed Filipino women were at times recast as the victims and that the women were seen as complicit in the violence which they experienced. It was apparent in some cases that the men who killed received considerable sympathy in media reports and from

the court. A significant part of this sympathy derived from the racial and gendered stereotypes about the nature of Filipino women. The women who were murdered were seen as undeserving of victim status, while the men who killed were
presented as *victims* of unscrupulous "Asian" women who abused the naivety of
western men. (Cunneen and Stubbs, 1997, p. 125)

SOME FINAL REMARKS

Returning to the epigraph at the start of this chapter, let us consider
the question posed by Angela Davis: "Can we, for example, link a strong
demand for remedies for women of color who are targets of rape and
domestic violence with a strategy that calls for the abolition of the prison
system?" It is clear that it will need to be reformulated for the case of immigrant women because they confront a problem of hypervisibility, not only
invisibility. The violence against immigrant women has much to do with
abusive men, but it is also related to a lack of resources, as is the case with
some native women. However, violence against immigrant women has also
become a racist and classist trope in rich countries. This means that immigrant women suffer an extra, symbolic violence, compared with natives.
The interactions between these kinds of violence still remain unexplored.

Moving toward other specific causes of violence against immigrant
women, I have considered the immigration laws and regulations. We have
seen that violence against women is only one of the many types of violence
that these women suffer. Immigrant women also suffer legal and institutional violence, both derived from immigration laws and regulations.
These have effects on their ordinary lives (as undocumented immigrants,
for example) and on the choice of jobs they can hope to have in rich countries. Violence against women (domestic abuse, interpersonal violence,
rape, etc.) is "colored" when men use legal or institutional violence to create more violence against them. However, it should also be colored when
the women are working in precarious jobs that increase the probability of
suffering exploitation, sexual harassment, and other violence.

Given this, let us now reformulate Davis's question and adapt it to the
specific case of immigrant women. I think Razack does it very well when
she talks about immigrant Muslim women in Norway:

How is it possible to acknowledge and confront patriarchal violence within Muslim
migrant communities without descending into cultural deficit explanations (they
are overly patriarchal and inherently uncivilised) and without inviting extraordinary measures of stigmatization, surveillance and control? (Razack, 2004, p. 131)

For Sherene H. Razack, you can't fight violence against Muslim women
with racism because racism is likely to strengthen patriarchal currents in
communities under siege. I would add that you can't fight violence against
immigrant women with symbolic, legal, and institutional violence.

ACKNOWLEDGMENTS

This chapter summarizes my background research on immigrant women and violence, developed at the Universidad de Almería in Spain (Area de Sociologia, and Centro de Estudios de las Migraciones y Relaciones Interculturales) and at the University of Michigan (Institute for Research on Women and Gender, and Institute for Social Research). I would like to thank the people in these institutions for the support they have provided, especially Huzefa Khalil, who, among other things, reviewed the language of the paper; and Silvia Pedraza, who read my first draft and suggested some changes. Also, I would like to thank the book editors, who have made suggestions along the way. When I started writing this chapter in the summer of 2013, I was not sure where to start. I would like to thank the authors I quote for helping me to draw a general picture on violence against immigrant women in the rich countries.

NOTES

1. I have described the social process that results in the "hypervisibility" of immigrant women as sexist and ethnocentric. For its formulation I took into account the work of several authors, especially those cited by Floya Anthias and Mira Yuval-Davis (1993). Indeed, in my dissertation I conducted a concrete proposal to analyze the sex-gender identifications of British and Moroccan immigrant women in Fortress Europe, which stressed that the social relations of sex-gender worked both in the intragroup level and between groups. In the intra-group level, we see the effect of sexism. Between groups, the social relations of sex-gender had the effect of Eurocentrism (Rodriguez, 2005).

2. The International Organization for Migration in 2007 reported that approximately 192 million people were living outside of their countries of birth.

3. I highlight the issue of connotations because in a recent study that I developed with immigrant prostitutes who had been abused in southern Spain, there were women who did not consider abuse as the most important form of violence they experienced in their lives. There was, for example, the case of an African who had come to Spain by boat. During the journey she had witnessed the death of several people, and when we asked about the kind of violence she had suffered in her life, she noted that the "only" violence she had suffered was the incident she experienced on the journey to Europe. This woman, like many undocumented migrants, prioritizes some violence over others.

4. The concrete tool that every country uses to select the entry and stay of people from developing countries varies. In the U.K. the state introduced in 2008 a "points-based migration system" to evaluate the level of economic desirability of migrants for the labor market; in France, special "skills and talents" visa will permit the entry of those with higher qualifications as of 2006. In Italy and Spain, the government uses a "quota system" based on shortages of the labor force in specific sectors of the economy. In Germany, efforts were made to formalize the employment of foreign workers in sectors with labor shortages such as domestic and care work. Also, regularization of undocumented migrants will take place. In all cases, migrant women

are mostly concentrated in those sectors of the labor market that are characterized by informality of employment (Krzystek, 2013; Campani et al., 2006).

5. Immigrant women suffer more than other collective labor from exploitation in temporary jobs, with no social security and no unions, regardless of the law (such as prostitution). As Shannon Gleeson highlighted after qualitative research with documented and undocumented Latino restaurant workers, the ever-present fear of deportation inhibits any formal confrontation, and leaves undocumented immigrants with a pragmatic and short-term understanding of their working life, rendering their working conditions temporary and endurable to them (Gleeson, 2010). If we think about maids, nannies, or sex workers, the lack of rights is more obvious because we are talking about jobs that still are not completely regulated (Leon, 2013; Holgado, 2008; Martin-Palomo et al., 2005; Oso, 2003). Survival in these circuits involves finding strategies and setting priorities. As I have noticed in my field work, one strategy that is used is spatial mobility.

6. A good piece of research about the control of sexuality by U.S. immigration laws can be *Entry Denied: Controlling Sexuality at the Border* (Luibhéid, 2002). She demonstrates that the sexual regulation at the border connects to sexual regulation within, and how such regulation punishes people who don't fit with the nation's heterosexual imperative: lesbians, homosexuals, prostitutes, pregnant unmarried women, etc. This situation is changing a bit, with some countries changing their regulations about same-sex and unmarried opposite-sex partners.

7. In fact, is not an exception if we consider that, "in the year of 2005, 1,122,373 immigrants were admitted to the United States on immigrant visas. Of these, 292,741 were spouses of US citizens or residents and 186,304 were children of US citizens or residents . . . those who entered based on employment status or as refugee or asylee in the same year numbered 246,878 and 142,963 respectively" (Abrams, 2007, p. 1635).

8. Polina Levchenko and Catherine Solheim demonstrate by analyzing the data from the American Community Survey (2008–2009). Spouses in Eastern European–U.S. couples were found to differ significantly by age, income, education, and number of previous marriages. A sample of U.S. husbands who married EE-born wives reported Eastern European ancestry; race, education, and marital status revealed within-couple similarities; and age and income revealed within-couple differences (U.S. spouses are nine years older and earn more than their EE-born spouses) (Levchenko and Solheim, 2013).

BIBLIOGRAPHY

Abrams, Kerry. 2007. "Inmigration Law and the Regulation of Marriage." *Minnesota Law Review* 91: 1625–1709
Ahmad, Farah, Maryam Ali, and Donna E. Stewart. 2005. Spousal-Abuse among Canadian Immigrant Women. *Journal of Immigrant Health* 7 (4): 239–246.
Alfieri, Anthony V. 1999. Prosecuting Race. *Duke Law Journal* 48 (6): 1157–1264.
Amanor-Boadu, Yvonne, Jill Theresa Messing, Sandra M. Stith, Jared Anderson, Chris S. O'Sullivan, and Jacquelyn C. Campbell. 2012. Immigrant and Non-immigrant Women: Factors that Predict Leaving an Abusive Relationship. *Violence against Women* 18 (5): 611–633.

Anthias, Floya, and Mira Yuval-Davis. 1993. *Racialized Boundaries*. London: Routledge.

Bachman, Ronet, and Linda E. Saltzman. 1995. *Violence against Women: Estimates from the Redesigned Survey*. Washington, DC: Bureau of Justice Statistics.

Bhattacharjee, Anannya. 2006. The Public/Private Mirage: Mapping Homes and Undomesticating Violence Work in the South Asian Immigrant Community. In *The Anthropology of the State: A Reader*, edited by Aradhana Sharma and Akhil Gupta. Oxford: Blackwell, pp. 337–356.

Bonjour, Saskia, and Betty deHart. 2013. A Proper Wife, a Proper Marriage: Constructions of "Us" and "Them" in Dutch Family Migration Policy. *European Journal of Women's Studies* 20 (1): 61–76.

Bradley, Tamsin, ed. 2011. *Women, Violence and Tradition*. London: Zed Books.

Caetano, Rau, Suhasini Ramisetty-Mikler, and Craig A. Field. 2005. Unidirectional and Bidirectional Intimate Partner Violence among White, Black, and Hispanic Couples in the United States. *Violence and Victims* 20 (4): 393–406.

Campani, Giovanna, Chiappellim Tiziana, Illundi Cabral, and Alessandra Manetti. 2006. *Mapping of Policies Affecting Female Migrants and Policy Analysis: The Italian Case*. Working Paper no. 6. WP1, Framework Program of the European Commission.

Chantler, Khatidja, and Geetanjali Gangoli. 2011. Violence against Women in Minoritised Communities: Cultural Norm or Cultural Anomaly? In *Violence against Women and Ethnicity: Commonalities and Differences across Europe*, edited by Ravi K. Thiara, Stephanie A. Condon, and Monica Schröttle. Berlin: Barbara Budrich, pp. 353–366.

Crenshaw, Kimberlé W. 1993. Demarginalizing the Intersection of Race and Sex: A Black Feminist Critique of Anti-discrimination Doctrine, Feminist Theory, and Antiracist Politics. In *Feminist Legal Theory: Foundations*, edited by D. Kelly Weisberg. Philadelphia: Temple University Press, pp. 383–395.

Cunneen, Chris, and Stubbs, Julie. 1997. *Gender, "Race" and International Relations: Violence against Filipino Women in Australia*. Sydney: Institute of Criminology.

Davis, Angela. 2000. The Color of Violence against Women. *Colorlines* 10: 1–5.

Davis, Kathy. 2008. Intersectionality as Buzzword: Sociology of Science Perspective on What Makes a Feminist Theory Successful. *Feminist Theory* 9 (1): 67–85.

Debauche, Alice. 2011. "They" Rape "Our" Women: When Sexism and Racism Intermingle. In *Violence Against Women and Ethnicity: Commonalities and Differences*, edited by Stephanie Condon, Monika Schröttle, and Thiara Ravi. Berlin: Barbara Buddrich, pp. 339–352.

Demleitner, Nora V. 2004. How Much Do Western Democracies Value Family and Marriage? Immigration Law's Conflicted Answer. *Hofstra Law Review* 32: 273–311.

Du Mont, Janice, and Tonia Forte. 2012. An Exploratory Study on the Consequences and Contextual Factors of Intimate Partner Violence among Immigrant and Canadian-Born Women. *BMJ Open* 2 e001728. doi:10.1136/bmjopen-2012-001728.

Ehrenreich, Barbara, and Arlie Russell Hochschild, eds. 2003. *Global Woman*. New York: Metropolitan Books.

Erez, Edna, Madelaine Adelman, and Carol Gregory. 2009. Intersections of Immigration and Domestic Violence. *Feminist Criminology* 4 (1): 32–56.

European Union Agency for Fundamental Rights. 2014. *Violence against Women: An EU-Wide Survey*. Luxemburg: Publications Office of the European Union.

Ferraro, Kathleen J. 1989. Policing Woman Battering. *Social Problem* 36 (1): 61–74.

Gleeson, Shannon. 2010. Labor Rights for All? The Role of Undocumented Immigrant Status for Worker Claims Making. *Law and Social Inquiry* 35 (3): 561–602.

Glenn, Evelyn Nakano. 2011. Constructing Citizenship: Exclusion, Subordination, and Resistance. *American Sociological Review* 76 (1): 1–24.

Glick, Jenifer E. 2010. Connecting Complex Processes: A Decade of Research on Immigrant Families. *Journal of Marriage and Family* 72: 498–515.

Grillo, Trina. 1995. Anti-Essentialism and Intersectionality. Tools to Dismantle the Master's House. *Berkley Women's Law Journal* 16: 16–30.

Holgado, Isabel. 2008. Trabajos y estrategias económicas de las mujeres migrantes. In *Mujeres, Trabajos y empleos en tiempos de globalización*, edited by Pilar Rodriguez. Barcelona: Icaria, pp. 87–114.

Houstoun, Marion F., Roger G. Kramer, and Joan Mackin Barrett. 1984. Female Predominance in Immigration to the United States since 1930: A First Look. *International Migration Review* 18 (4): 908–963.

Hyman, Ilene, ToniaForte, Janice Du Mont, Sarah Romans, and Marsha M. Cohen. 2006. The Association between Length of Stay in Canada and Intimate Partner Violence among Immigrant Women. *American Journal of Public Health* 96 (4): 654–659.

Ingram, Maia, Deborah McClelland, Montserrat Caballero, Maria Theresa Mayorga, and Katie Gillespie. 2010. Experiences of Immigrant Women Who Self-Petition under the Violence Against Women Act. *Violence against Women* 16 (8): 858–880.

Ken, Ivy. 2008. Beyond the Intersection: A New Culinary Metaphor for Race-Class-Gender Studies. *Sociological Theory* 26: 152–172.

Klevens, Joanne. 2007. An Overview of Intimate Partner Violence among Latinos. *Violence against Women* 13 (2): 111–122.

Krzystek, Karolina. 2013. Female Migrants and the Issue of Residence Rights. In *Paradoxes of Integration: Female Migrants in Europe*, edited by Floya Anthias, Maria Kontos, and Mirjana Morokvasic-Müller. London: Springer, pp. 117–132.

Laacher, Smaïn. 2008. *Femmes invisibles. Le urmots contre la violence*. Paris: Calmann-Lévy.

Leon, Margarita. 2013. A Real Job? Regulating Household Work: The Case of Spain. *European Journal of Women's Studies* 20 (2): 170–188.

Levchenko, Polina, and Catherine Solheim. 2013. International Marriages between Eastern European–Born Women and U.S.-Born Men. *Family Relations* 62: 30–41.

Luibhéid, Eithne. 2002. *Entry Denied: Controlling Sexuality at the Border*. Minneapolis: University of Minnesota Press.

Lutz, Helma. 1997. Limits of European-ness: Immigrant Women in Fortress Europe. *Feminist Review* 57: 93–111.

Martín-Palomo, M. Teresa, M. Jesús Miranda, and Cristina Vega, eds. 2005. *Delitos y fronteras: Mujeres extranjeras en prisión*. Madrid: Instituto de Investigaciones Feministas-Universidad Complutense de Madrid.

McCall, Leslie. 2005. The Complexity of Intersectionality. *Signs* 30 (3): 1771–1800.

Menjívar, Cecilia, and Olivia Salcido. 2002. Women and Domestic Violence: Common Experiences in Different Countries. *Gender and Society* 16 (6): 898–920.

Menjívar, Cecilia, and Leisy J. Abrego. 2012. Legal Violence: Immigration Law and the Lives of Central American Immigrants. *American Journal of Sociology* 117 (5): 1380–1421.

Merali, Noorfarah. 2008. Theoretical Frameworks for Studying Female Marriage Migrants. *Psychology of Women Quarterly* 32: 281–289.

Montoya, Celeste. 2013. *From Global to Grassroots: The European Union, Transnational Advocacy and Combating Violence against Women*. Oxford: Oxford University Press.

Morokvasic, Mirjana. 2007. Migration, Gender, Empowerment. In *Gender Orders Unbound? Globalisation, Restructuring and Reciprocity*, edited by Ilse Lenz, Charlotte Ullrich, and Barbara Fersch. Leverkusen Opladen: Barbara Budrich, pp. 69–97.

Newsome, H. B. 2007. Male Dominance: A Critical Look at the International Marriage Broker Regulation Act and Its Sufficiency in Curtailing Mail-Order Bride Domestic Abuse. *Campbell Law Review* 29: 291–309.

Oso, Laura. 2003. Mechanisms for Colombian and Ecuadorian Women's Entry into Spain: From Spontaneous Migration to Trafficking of Women. In *Gender and Insecurity: Migrant Women in Europe*, edited by Jane Freedman. Burlington, VT: Ashgate, pp. 55–76.

Pan, Amy et al. 2006. Understanding the Role of Culture in Domestic Violence: The Ahimsa Project for Safe Families. *Journal of Immigrant and Minority Health* 8: 35–43.

Pedraza, Silvia. 1991. Women and Migration: The Consequences of Gender. *Annual Review of Sociology* 17: 303–325.

Piper, Nicola. 2003. Feminization of Labor Migration as Violence against Women. *Violence against Women* 9 (6): 723–745.

Razack, Sherene H. 2004. Imperiled Muslim Women, Dangerous Muslim Men and Civilised Europeans: Legal and Social Responses to Forced Marriages. *Feminist Legal Studies* 12: 129–174.

Resko, Stella M. 2007. Intimate Partner Violence against Women: Exploring Intersections of Race, Class and Gender. Dissertation, Graduate School of Ohio State University.

Richie, Beth E. 2002. *Understanding the Links between Violence against Women and Women's Participation in Illegal Activity: Final Report*. Rockville, MD: National Institute of Justice.

Rodriguez, Pilar. 2005. Identificaciones de sexo-género de mujeres migrantes marroquíes y británicas en Almería. *Revista Española de Investigaciones Sociológicas* 110: 137–148.

Rodriguez, Pilar. 2006. Introduction. In *Feminismos Perifericos: Discutiendo las categorias de sexo, clase y raza (y etnicidad) con Floya Anthias*, edited by Pilar Rodriguez. Granada: Alhulia.

Rodriguez, Pilar. 2011. Feminism and Violence: The Hegemonic Second Wave's Encounter with Rape and Domestic Abuse in USA (1970–1985). *Cultural Dynamics* 23 (3): 147–172.

Rodriguez, Pilar, and Huzefa Khalil. 2013. Battery and Development: Exploring the Link between Intimate Partner Violence and Modernization. *Cross-Cultural Research* 47 (3): 231–267.

Römkens, Renée, and Esmah Lahlah. 2011. Particularly Violent: The Discursive Construction of Muslim Culture as a Risk Factor. In *Violence against Women and Ethnicity: Commonalities and Differences*, edited by Stephanie Condon, Monika Schröttle, and Thiara Ravi. Berlin: Barbara Buddrich, pp. 79–96.

Sassen, Saskia. 2003. Global Cities and Survival Circuits. In *Global Woman*, edited by Barbara Ehrenreich and Arlie Russell Hochschild. New York: Metropolitan Books, pp. 254–274.

Thompson, Becky. 2002. Multiracial Feminism: Recasting the Chronology of Second Wave Feminism. *Feminist Studies* 28 (2): 337–360.

Tjaden, Patricia, and Nancy Thoennes. 2000. *Full Report of the Prevalence, Incidence, and Consequences of Violence Against Women: Findings from the National Violence Against Women Survey: Research Report*. Washington, DC: National Institute of Justice.

Tsoukala, Anastassia. 2005. Looking at Migrants as Enemies. In *Controlling Frontiers: Free Movement into and within Europe*, edited by Didier Bigo and Elspeth Guild. Burlington, VT: Ashgate, pp. 161–192.

Turpin, Jennifer, and Lester Kurtz. 1997. Introduction: Violence: The Micro/Macro Link. In *The Web of Violence: From Interpersonal to Global*, edited by Jennifer Turpin and Lester R. Kurtz. Urbana: University of Illinois Press, pp. 1–28.

Villalón, Roberta. 2010. *Violence against Latina Immigrants: Citizenship, Inequality, and Community*. New York: New York University Press.

Walby, Sylvia, and Jonathan Allen. 2004. *Domestic Violence, Sexual Assault and Stalking: Findings from the British Crime Survey*. London: Home Office Research, Development and Statistics Directorate.

Weil, Jennifer, and Hwayun Lee. 2004. Cultural Considerations in Understanding Family Violence among Asian American Pacific Islander Families. *Journal of Community Health Nursing* 21 (4): 217–227.

Winker, Gabriele, and Nina Degele. 2011. Intersectionality as Multi-Level Analysis: Dealing with Social Inequality. *European Journal of Women Studies* 18 (I): 51–66.

Yuval-Davis, Nira. 2006. Intersectionality and Feminist Politics. *European Journal of Women's Studies* 13: 193–209.

CHAPTER 11

Trafficking in Women: Dynamics, Debates, and Disconnects

Maryann Bylander

INTRODUCTION

Unlike many of the topics discussed in this book, trafficking is not an area where women's experiences need to be brought to the fore. Over the past two decades, attention on the global problem of trafficking has increased dramatically, and much of its specific focus has been on trafficking in women. Thus in recent years we have seen an increase in academic studies published on trafficking, a growing number of anti-trafficking programs sponsored by the international community, and an impressive coverage of the issue by the media. And yet, what Kelly (2005, p. 236) aptly pointed out nearly a decade ago is still true: the increase in awareness and funding of anti-trafficking efforts has not necessarily led to a "deepening of the knowledge base." Rather, as was the case in the early 2000s, when the issue began to draw significant attention, the dominant discourse on trafficking (and particularly trafficking in women) tends to be more sensationalistic than empirical, more politicized than neutral, and more framed around Northern interests than around difficulties, desires, and priorities voiced by those who have experienced trafficking. Because of these orientations, the dominant discourse has a tendency to reproduce myths and false dichotomies, in turn limiting our ability to understand and successfully respond to human trafficking.

This chapter begins by making two overarching claims. First, what we *think we know* about trafficking is far greater than what we *actually know*. Second, what we actually know highlights how political and complex the terrain is. Thus, rather than mapping the issue of trafficking in women, as if it were a known landscape with easily distinguishable definitions, numbers, causes and solutions, this chapter is a map of disconnects, places where academic or mainstream public discourse on trafficking is challenged by empirical evidence. Specifically, I argue that four main disconnects are important to highlight for us to better understand knowledge gaps, research needs, and potential avenues for progressive change in anti-trafficking efforts.

1. *Definitions:* Forced dichotomies versus nuanced realities
2. *Scope:* Fuzzy math versus data-based evidence
3. *Patterns:* Global caricatures versus context-specific realities
4. *Action:* Reactive band-aids versus preventive approaches

In each of these areas, what we think we know about trafficking (or the dominant anti-trafficking approach) conflicts with the best evidence we have of experiences, patterns, and potential solutions. After discussing the disconnects noted above in greater detail, I conclude with some thoughts on where we have seen improvement and success, and suggestions for next steps in moving forward.

FORCED DICHOTOMIES VERSUS NUANCED REALITIES

One of the most pressing problems within the field is the lack of a clearly agreed upon definition of what constitutes trafficking. Despite over a decade of work trying to pin down the nature of trafficking, many institutions and actors still disagree on what qualifies, and how the term should be applied.

The most authoritative instrument, the United Nations (UN) Convention Against Transnational Organised Crime (adopted by the UN General Assembly in 2000), defines trafficking as

the recruitment, transportation, transfer, harbouring or receipt of persons, by means of the threat or use of force or other forms of coercion, of abduction, of fraud, of deception, of the abuse of power or of a position of vulnerability or of the giving or receiving of payments or benefits to achieve the consent of a person having control over another person, for the purpose of exploitation. Exploitation shall include, at a minimum, the exploitation of the prostitution of others or other forms of sexual exploitation, forced labour or services, slavery or practices similar to slavery, servitude or the removal or organs. (United Nations General Assembly, 2000)

The protocol further establishes that consent is irrelevant where it is made in the above circumstances (i.e., resulting from a position of vulnerability) and defines trafficking as present when children under the age of

18 are recruited, transferred, transported, harbored or retained for exploitive purposes even if other conditions noted do not apply.

Yet this definition still raises several key questions: What is exploitation? What qualifies as coercion, or a position of vulnerability? Even seasoned experts in the field disagree on these key operational distinctions. In an illustrative study, Hujismans and Baker (2012) found widespread disagreement among several dozen experts working in the field of anti-trafficking. Using case studies of instances of child migration in the Greater Mekong Subregion, the authors found that even among those working as experts in the field there is "considerable confusion about what, precisely, constitutes a case of child trafficking" (p. 924).

In trying to understand definitional challenges two main factors are particularly salient: the distinction between *choice* and *coercion* and the definition of *exploitation*. These concepts are at the heart of definitions of trafficking and how many international organizations differentiate undocumented labor migration from trafficking. Yet although pinning down a definition of trafficking requires a clear distinction between free and forced migration, and between exploitive and nonexploitive work, both are made problematic by the fact that neither choice nor exploitation is a dichotomous variable.

Trafficking versus Smuggling: Distinguishing Choice

According to the U.S. State Department, "The key component that distinguishes trafficking from smuggling is the element of fraud, force, or coercion" (U.S. Department of State, 2005). Here there is an assumption that we can easily categorize undocumented economic migrants (who resort to smuggling to seek work abroad) and trafficked persons (who are victims that have been misled or coerced into working abroad).

However, those who have worked with victims of trafficking suggest that these dichotomies do not adequately represent the complexity of the experiences of victims of trafficking (Kempadoo, 2005). Instead, the migratory process often begins in similar ways for undocumented economic migrants and for victims of trafficking. Many if not most victims of trafficking choose to migrate, often doing so for economic reasons or to find employment. In many cases they are aware of the kind of work they will be doing, and some if not all of the circumstances of the work. For example, in an International Organization for Migration (IOM) study of 55 Thai women trafficked into Japan, 85 percent of the women made clear decisions to migrate to Japan for jobs as sex workers, and the majority indicated they were not forced but chose to migrate as a way to help their families out of poverty (Caouette and Saito, 1999). Similarly, in interviews conducted with 147 Armenian trafficked women in Dubai, only 20 percent said they were "tricked" into migrating

(Grigorian, 2005). In Georgia, reports on trafficked women and undocumented economic migrants found that both groups of women made conscious (though constrained) choices to migrate (IOM, 2001). Thus the image of victims of trafficking as being fully coerced, while economic migrants are fully free has little relation to the realities experienced by victims of trafficking. Instead, what distinguishes victims of trafficking from undocumented migrants in many cases is not their decision to migrate, or even their decision about the choice of their work sector, but the fact that at some point during the migration process their freedoms or mobility become restricted. In other words, "if the process goes well, it is migration; if it does not, it is trafficking" (Bangladesh Thematic Group, 2004, p. 13).

Moreover, this dichotomy obscures the fact that many economic migrants, as well as trafficking victims, describe their migrations as forced—not explicitly through the actions of an individual, but structurally, due to the lack of meaningful alternatives at home. In contexts of conflict, environmental degradation, poverty, a lack of employment opportunities, or natural disaster, migrations are often constrained choices, made in a situation where they are neither fully voluntary nor clearly compelled. Thus, drawing a clear line between those who migrate with full freedom, knowledge, and choice and those who migrate due to coercive elements is difficult at best.

Exploitation

Similarly, although there are well-established indicators that identify exploitive and slavery-like practices, operationalizing exploitation remains a political and empirical challenge. Most commonly international organizations working in the field of trafficking consider exploitation as involving one or more of the following:

- Threat of physical/sexual violence
- Physical/sexual violence
- Withholding of passports
- Controlled movement
- Threats to family
- Withholding of salary (Surtees, 2005; U.S. Department of State, 2005)

While this may seem relatively clearcut, there are two particular challenges in distinguishing exploitation. First, exploitation is hardly a dichotomous variable. It resides on a continuum that ranges from inadequate pay and emotional abuse to physical abuse and assault, and many migrant workers experience one or more elements of exploitation on a regular basis. In fact, there are many who argue that the exploitation of migrant labor is a key feature of the global capitalist economy. As Anderson and Andrijasevic (2008) aptly point out, "low-waged migrant labour is permitted and sought by employers, precisely because it can be exploited. How to draw a line in the sand between 'trafficked' and 'not trafficked but just-the-regular-kind-of-exploitation migrants?" (p. 141). Whether legal or not (and migrant or not), workers in the least desirable economic sectors often experience violence, confinement, deception, overwork, exploitation, and some form of coercion (Anderson and Andrijasevic, 2008; Kahale, 2003; Chaiyarachta, 1996; Satterthwaite, 2005). Moreover, exploitation is not simply something migrants face in work abroad. Many have also experienced exploitation in their home countries, and in some cases, exploitation at home may even be a cause of migration. Thus, relying on exploitation as a key feature that sets apart two clearly distinct groups (victims of trafficking versus non-trafficked migrants) can be seen as reproducing a false binary that has little bearing on the lived experiences of migrant workers or trafficking victims.

Second, in the field of trafficking the definition of exploitation is political—and is often underpinned by individual, state, or organizational positions in a feminist debate centered on sex work. Though international institutions and organizations vary in their specific definition of trafficking, the UN Protocol (as well as the U.S. government) specifically distinguishes prostitution as exploitive. As a result, women working in the sex sector are routinely deemed trafficked, even if there is no element of deception, coercion or force, due to what is seen as the inherently exploitive nature of their work (U.S. Department of State, 2005). By this interpretation of "exploitation" the destination sector of employment is central to defining a woman as trafficked. Women who knowingly contract with third parties to migrate as domestic workers are not necessarily trafficked, but those who contract to enter the sex sector are. Several advocacy organizations hold to this view, making their work as much about ending prostitution as about stopping global trafficking in women. This viewpoint is also part of how the United States has worked to combat trafficking. In 2003, the Bush administration authorized the Trafficking Victims Protection Reauthorization Act (TVPRA), which stipulated that the government could not fund organizations that advocated, supported, or otherwise promoted the legalization of prostitution (Desyllas, 2007). According to media reports, organizations that forcibly removed women from prostitution were given funding preference (Desyllas, 2007).

Other feminist groups, including many that are based in the Global South, argue that women who choose to migrate for sex work should not be necessarily labeled as victims of trafficking. Instead, they argue that sex work is a valid form of work that should be afforded legitimacy and protection, and that sex work is similar to other forms of "emotional labor" such as child care, massage, and service work where caring and feeling are required (Chapkis, 1997). Exploitation in the sex industry might exist as it does in all other employment sectors, yet it is not a necessary outcome of prostitution (Kempadoo and Doezema, 1998; Kempadoo et al., 2010). For these groups, the political posturing by the U.S. government and others contributes to an "alarmist victim discourse" that can dismiss the agency of sex workers, migrants, and victims of trafficking (Piper, 2005). Moreover, others argue that this discourse diverts much needed attention from the structural causes of trafficking (Katsulis et al., 2010) and can even disadvantage the women it is aiming to support (Dewey, 2010).

Regardless of one's standpoint on sex work and its legitimacy, the immense grey areas between *free* and *forced* and between *work* and *exploitation* are centrally problematic for discussions of trafficking. While definitions and labels necessarily treat both choice and exploitation as dichotomous variables, such distinctions rarely resonate with the lived experiences of migrants and victims of trafficking. Rather, many migrants (in particular those from the developing world) would argue that their migrations are structurally constrained by a lack of viable options at home, and that various forms of exploitation are a constituent feature of their experiences abroad.

Taken together, these challenges mean that our conversations about trafficking often use a singular term to speak about different concepts and contexts. For example, while some advocacy organizations view all migrant sex workers as victims of trafficking (eschewing the notion that their consent to such exploitation is meaningful), others would use the term to characterize the much narrower group of those truly deceived and forced into the sex sector. Still others would include even more broad-based definitions of exploitive work and constrained choice, labeling much of the low-paid and dangerous work done by undocumented migrants as slavery or trafficking. Both choice and exploitation exist on a continuum, where, depending on the definitions and moral judgments one makes, many migrants can be labeled as either undocumented migrants or victims of trafficking.

FUZZY MATH VERSUS DATA-BASED EVIDENCE

The muddled and often inconsistent definitions noted above result in what are best described as "slippery statistics" (Gozdziak and Collett 2005). Despite two decades of persistent attention to the problem of trafficking, we still have few reliable indicators as to its extent, what kinds of patterns are most prevalent, and how they shift over time. Instead, there continue to be sensationally high estimates of global trafficking reported and re-reported, often removed from the contextual caveats that originally framed estimates. Moreover, both media and academics tend to reproduce unsubstantiated estimations that trafficking (and particularly sex trafficking) is increasing over time (e.g. Beyrer and Stachowiak, 2003).

For example, the United States Trafficking in Persons report of 2012 estimated that "as many as 27 million men, women, and children around the world are victims of what is now often described with the umbrella term "human trafficking" (U.S. Department of State, 2012, p. 7). Yet the best data we have come nowhere near justifying these kinds of numbers. In their 2012 report on global patterns in trafficking, the United Nations Office on Drugs and Crime (UNODC) notes that between 2007 and 2010 some 43,000 victims of trafficking were detected in 118 countries around the world. Similarly, while UNODC estimates that there are 250,000 victims trafficked into Europe per year (UNODC, 2009), in 2010 EU member states recorded just over 9,500 victims (Eurostat, 2013).

Certainly, the very nature of trafficking is that it is hidden. Therefore, we can expect that many cases will never be identified or captured by statistics and that our estimates will necessarily be much higher than the number of victims we can identify. However, even a cursory look into the disparities between estimates and the methods (or lack thereof) by which numbers are produced invites skepticism. In 2003 the United Nations Educational, Scientific and Cultural Organization (UNESCO) began a project comparing estimates of trafficking by various institutional and state actors, and found a striking range. In some cases, estimates differed by a factor of 5, most of them actually unsubstantiated by data. In a compelling article describing the production of numbers in more detail, Jordan (2011) documents how numbers of sex workers in any given context are often re-reported in estimates of trafficking victims, highlighting the conceptual conflation between sex workers and trafficking victims.

Given the way that numbers are so routinely inflated and provided without evidence, it is no wonder that scholars in the field suggest that the bulk of trafficking-related research wouldn't meet the academic standards that are taken for granted in other social scientific areas of inquiry (Salt, 2000). In fact, as a result of the increasing recognition that statistics have been inflated and politically generated, the past decade has seen many international actors reducing their estimates of the number of trafficking victims. The United States' estimate of victims in the country has been revised down at least twice, from 45,000–50,000 in 1999 to 18,000–20,000 in 2003, to 14,500–17,500 in 2004 (Gozdziak and Collett, 2005). Some critics argue that even these numbers are too high.

GLOBAL CARICATURES VERSUS CONTEXT-SPECIFIC REALITIES

A third disconnect is that much of the data we have on trafficking do not easily align with the common mythologies about what victims of trafficking are, where they come from, and why they leave their home communities. The most reproduced caricature of trafficking suggests that victims of trafficking are primarily women; come from poor, vulnerable regions;

are kidnapped or sold, transported long distances (often into developed countries in the Global North); end up in work in the sex trade; and are more likely to come from places where women's rights are threatened or limited.

In certain contexts, some of these images may align closely with real patterns. However, trafficking is highly context specific and varies significantly by region, country, and even community. Thus, broad-based statements attempting to describe the dynamics of global patterns of trafficking (including its root causes) are often misguided and represent only one of many truths. To understand trafficking is to understand that there are few truly global patterns and not just a single, easily delineated global solution. Several particularly common caricatures and the varied realities behind them are described next in more detail.

Patterns: Women, Children, Sex

The bulk of research and media attention suggests that trafficking is primarily a problem of women and children being exploited in the sex sector, where they are controlled and deceived by male traffickers. However in much of the world, the data we do have on trafficking suggests a more diverse and complex picture. First, while women do make up the largest proportion of identified victims of trafficking in most contexts, significant numbers of men have been identified as victims of trafficking, and this gender breakdown varies across regions. In particular, what we know suggests that trafficking among men is more prevalent in Europe, Central Asia, and the Americas than in other parts of the world (UNODC, 2012). In the United States, for example, in 2008 the Department of Health and Human Services certified 286 victims of trafficking, 45 percent of whom were male (U.S. Department of State, 2009).

Moreover, even these findings are likely skewed by our bias in *looking for* trafficking among women and within the sex sector. Currently, disproportionate numbers of advocacy organizations, nongovernmental organizations (NGOs), and funding work specifically in combating trafficking for the purposes of sexual exploitation. As a result, it is likely that that trafficking among women and for the purposes of sexual exploitation is more often detected, while trafficking among men in forced labor is likely underestimated and less often detected (UNODC, 2012). In line with this, in a recent study by UNODC researchers found that though women make up the majority of victims of trafficking globally, their share of the total has somewhat decreased over the past decade, as has the share of cases of trafficking that were for the purposes of sexual exploitation. Alongside this shift the share of detected cases of trafficking for forced labor has doubled over the past four years (UNODC, 2012). To what extent this reflects a real change, and to what extent it reflects an increasing recognition that men (and women outside the sex sector) can experience trafficking is unclear. However, it seems likely that at least part of the increase in our detection of male victims relates to the increased efforts to locate them.

Clearly, situations of male forced labor can be just as dehumanizing and dangerous as those involving women and/or sex work. For example, recent research into the fishing sector in Thailand has documented widespread abuse and exploitation of men working on fishing boats that travel internationally (IOM, 2011). Reports have documented extensive abuse and physical violence, including men being thrown overboard or killed by boat captains. Wages are routinely withheld, and there are clear rights violations across the sector. Moreover, because of the nature of the work at sea, even when violence is of a lesser degree workers have limited or no mobility and cannot escape abusive conditions (IOM, 2011). Although these and other situations of labor trafficking among men have been occurring alongside trafficking in women and sex trafficking for decades, until recently research has rarely focused on these situations. Part of the problem of missing men in trafficking research relates to the dominant narrative of trafficking as equated with women, and specifically with exploitation in the sex sector.

Similarly, the global image of children as particularly likely to be victims of trafficking appears to vary by context. While children make up the majority of victims of trafficking detected in Africa and the Middle East, they make up a much smaller percentage of those detected globally (UNODC, 2012). Again, context mediates the types of trafficking that are most commonly detected, and perhaps experienced among both adults and children. In Europe and Central Asia, statistics suggest that the majority of trafficking is for sexual exploitation, whereas in Africa, the Middle East, and Asia a greater proportion of trafficking is for the purposes of forced labor or other purposes. Trafficking for the purposes of begging, organ removal, and other forms of exploitation also varies widely by context (UNODC, 2012). While this may be explained by differing policy/protection contexts that shape the potential to detect various forms of trafficking, it is also likely that context mediates the composition of trafficking flows.

Another global myth is that trafficking primarily takes place on a long-distance, global scale—with the Global North as a primary destination. Again, while we have little reliable data, UNODC's research suggests that almost half of victims worldwide were trafficked within their regions of origin. Although the most highly publicized movements are from the Global North to Europe and the United States, movements are at least as if not more likely to take place within regions (Kelly, 2002; Kelly, 2005; UNODC, 2012). Even in Europe, Eurostat report notes that most major flows of trafficking in persons are taking place within Europe, not from Africa or Asia into Europe. Moreover, significant levels of trafficking occur within countries; domestic trafficking accounts for over a quarter of all detected cases of trafficking in persons (UNODC, 2012).

Finally, it is worth noting that women are not only implicated in patterns of trafficking as victims; they are also perpetrators, a reality that academics, policy makers, and the media have been slow to draw attention to. In fact, in comparison to other criminal activities, the high level of women's participation in trafficking is striking (UNODC, 2012). Reports suggest that it is particularly likely for women to be involved in the trafficking of younger girls and other activities that have high risks of detection, and that women's involvement in crimes of trafficking varies significantly by region (UNODC, 2012). In parts of Southeast Asia (notably Thailand and the Philippines) nearly a quarter of those prosecuted or convicted of trafficking are women, while in other regions this number is significantly lower (UNODC, 2012). In some contexts, most identified traffickers share the nationality of those they traffic, while in others perpetrators are primarily citizens of destination countries or nationals of a third country (UNODC, 2012).

Causes: Poverty, Vulnerability

There is a widespread acceptance that poverty and vulnerability are fundamental root causes of trafficking, and that this is true globally. However, evidence suggests that the relationship among poverty, vulnerability, and trafficking is not so straightforward, and that it may vary significantly across contexts (Danailova-Trainor and Laczko, 2010).

First, while it is likely that poverty plays a role in predisposing individuals to trafficking, trafficking victims identified do not primarily originate from the poorest countries or the poorest areas within a country (Danailova-Trainor and Laczko, 2010). In fact, the countries that have been identified by UNODC as top origin countries for victims of trafficking are primarily considered lower- to upper-middle-income countries: Albania, Belarus, Bulgaria, China, Lithuania, Nigeria, Moldova, Romania, Russian Federation, and Thailand. Importantly, many of them have high levels of human development, even after adjusting for gender equity (Danailova-Trainor and Laczko, 2010). At least from a global perspective, the countries where trafficking appears to be most common are not all places where women's rights are most limited. Thus, the commonly cited idea that the "greatest likelihood of trafficking occurs where women and girls are denied property rights, access to education, economic rights, and participation in the political process (Shelley, 2010, p. 16) does not appear to be a powerful explanatory story on a global level. While it is likely that certain forms of gender inequality exacerbate vulnerability for women, and thus raise their risk of vulnerability to trafficking, these connections warrant further examination.

Poverty does appear to play a key role in many patterns of trafficking, but in a way that is more nuanced and complex than is often suggested. For example, data from the IOM suggest that trafficking may be more closely related to relative deprivation than it is to absolute poverty. This has been repeatedly shown to be the case in studies of labor migration, where research suggests that being or feeling relatively poor is a more important predictor of international migration than poverty itself. Given that trafficking and economic migration often begin in similar ways, this should hardly be surprising. Though limited studies have explored this concept among trafficking victims, there is evidence to suggest that the poorest of the poor are not necessarily more at risk of trafficking (Surtees, 2008). For example, in a study of young Romanian women Lazaroiu and Alexandru (2003) found that individuals who were "at risk" of trafficking were not the most objectively poor in their communities, but rather perceived themselves as poor. Similarly, data from the IOM database on trafficking shows that less than half of assisted persons reported that they were "poor" (Danailova-Trainor and Laczko, 2010).

The data we have point to a less commonly identified driver of trafficking: unemployment. In particular, there is some qualitative evidence of a relationship between the number of trafficking victims originating in a country and its level of female youth unemployment (Danailova-Trainor and Belser, 2006). UNODC reports that there is a positive correlation between unemployment rates in destination countries and the number of victims of trafficking (of that origin) in destination countries. For example, UNODC found that as unemployment rates in Russia and the Ukraine went down, the share of Russian and Ukrainian victims of trafficking detected in the Netherlands also declined. Similarly, as the gross domestic product (GDP) in Russia went up, Germany recorded decreasing victims of trafficking from Russian origin. Comparable results have been found in other trafficking patterns (Thais in Germany, Indonesians in Japan).

Again, these patterns vary by context. The drivers of trafficking and factors that put women, children, and men at risk are highly context specific. In some places population displacement puts women and children at risk for trafficking, and in others government policies that encourage migration may put individuals at risk (IOM, 2008) In some places research has suggested that those with greater mobility may even be less susceptible to trafficking (Hauser, 2005). Conversely, limited or costly opportunities for migration can cause would-be migrants to move outside formal channels and put them at risk of trafficking. Finally, external factors such as conflict, the erosion of social protection systems, natural disasters, land degradation, and even development itself can be causes of trafficking (Danailova-Trainor and Laczko, 2010).

REACTIVE BAND-AIDS VERSUS PREVENTIVE APPROACHES

The last disconnect I discuss in this chapter relates to anti-trafficking approaches. There is no shortage of funding or political will to combat trafficking. The U.S. government alone has given approximately $447 million in foreign aid to combat and eliminate trafficking over the past decade (Danailova-Trainor and Laczko, 2010). However much anti-trafficking work has been focused on *responding* to trafficking, rather than shifting the contexts and policy environments that enable trafficking to occur. The focus on short-term gaps and solutions has arguably done little to solve the problem of trafficking, at times leading to further harm for trafficking victims, migrants, and would-be migrants from the developing world (Danailova-Trainor and Laczko, 2010).

Typically, anti-trafficking programs are located in source countries and are aimed at detecting and prosecuting traffickers, raising awareness about of trafficking as a potential outcome of migration (as a preventive measure), and protecting those deemed "at risk" for trafficking or victims who have been repatriated after an experience of trafficking. There are several key disconnects with the mainstream approach. First, oversimplifications that equate migration with trafficking have been known to cause harm or have unintended side effects. For example, in Nepal Hausner (2005) notes that early anti-trafficking campaigns were interpreted by local communities to mean that migration would necessarily result in trafficking, which was likely to result in HIV—links that were clearly not valid for all migrant workers. These messages led to some young women being prevented from migrating, even from crossing the border for legitimate jobs or to be reunited with family. Given the conflict at the time, migration was an important livelihood strategy and may have made young women better off in key ways. In Hausner's words, in Nepal it is

not the act of migrating that makes women and girls vulnerable to trafficking, it is the separation from social structures which might otherwise protect them. Woman migrating with caring guardians may be better off than those in the village. . . . Assuming that migrants are somehow more vulnerable than residents of a village involves a somewhat colonial logic that mobile populations are ungovernable, falling outside of sedentary social structures. (Hausner, 2005, p. 7)

Thus, while anti-trafficking measures tend to link trafficking with migration, Hauser argues that this approach is both inappropriate and potentially harmful in places where migration is an important livelihood strategy.

In line with this, the best evidence we have suggests that after their return or rehabilitation, many victims of trafficking seek to return to the destination countries where they were trafficked (Demir and Finckenauer, 2010). Although some see these instances of repeat trafficking (or retrafficking) as a result of stigma, shame, and difficulty reintegrating, there is also evidence to suggest that it may have more to do with the lack of job opportunities in source communities, and other push factors that make it difficult to make a decent living locally (Surtees, 2005; IOM, 1997; Caouette and Saito, 1999). The mismatch between prevention, rescue, and rehabilitation programs that seek to stop migration (or encourage local reintegration) and the desires that many victims of trafficking have for further migration has led some scholars to argue that there is a need to move beyond a focus on stopping movement, and shift to a focus on stopping exploitation. The Global Alliance Against Trafficking in Women (GAATW) argues that this is a key shift needed in anti-trafficking work:

In effect, most people who are trafficked have deliberately left home in order to make a living elsewhere: the criteria used by government agencies to distinguish between the different groups often appear inappropriate and even discriminatory, for while efforts are nominally made to protect people from being trafficked, the main emphasis of most governments when it comes to migrants is to "control" and limit migration and does not involve assisting or protecting migrants. Indeed, the narrow focus on trafficking seems in many countries to act as a justification for not taking action to end all the abuse to which migrant workers in the informal sectors of the economy are subjected. (GAATW, 2007, p. 12)

Given this, a solution proposed by some contemporary scholars and activists is to shift anti-trafficking efforts from being primarily located in source countries (where they often seek to limit movement) to being primarily located in destination countries, where they could target demand or recognition (Andrijasevic and Anderson, 2009). These kinds of campaigns could encourage consumers or employers to ensure their production lines are not using trafficked labor. This has been attempted to some extent with the sex sector, particularly with U.S. backing, yet there have been more limited attempts to do this outside of the sex sector. However, because demand-focused approaches target the structural problems of inequalities and human rights violations among migrant workers more broadly, many see these campaigns as powerful alternatives to the narrow, reactive strategies that characterize anti-trafficking efforts today (Andrijasevic and Anderson, 2009).

MOVING FORWARD

To this point, this chapter has focused on disconnects and challenges in the field. Yet none of these challenges should be taken as minimizing the real harm, risk, and costs of trafficking and the exploitation of migrant workers. No doubt, human trafficking is among the most egregious violations of human rights. It is a critical legal, economic, health, and social crisis, not only affecting the victims of trafficking but also significantly limiting the potential for economic development of the communities and nations where trafficking victims originate (Danilova-Trainor and Laczko, 2010). The lost wages and potential remittances of victims of forced labor alone are estimated to add up to US$21 billion (ILO, 2009). Moreover, there are tremendous social costs to trafficking. Trafficking can contribute to the spread of HIV (UNDP, 2007), lead to the neglect of or lack of care for children, and potentially create stigma around migration, leading to the marginalization of return migrants (Danilova-Trainor and Laczko, 2010).

Thousands of women (and men) are victims of trafficking. Just as important, there are even greater numbers of women (and men) who may not clearly fit the definition of victims of trafficking but who experience labor exploitation and human rights violations in the course of migration, or who understand their migration experiences as compelled or coerced by a lack of meaningful alternatives. To date, research and advocacy have had limited success in addressing these rights violations. Rather, the field of trafficking is still characterized by ideological debates over the legitimacy of sex work, a patchy knowledge base, and a lack of proactive responses aimed at root causes. In the words of Antonio Maria Costa, Executive Director of UNODC, with regards to trafficking "the crisis we face of fragmented knowledge and disjointed responses shames us all" (UNODC, 2009, p. 7).

Yet despite these challenges the past decade has also witnessed compelling and positive shifts in more productive directions. From a policy perspective, there is greater awareness and pressure on countries to sign on to, create, and implement anti-trafficking legislation, pressure that has led to some moderate success. Since the early 2000s the number of countries that have worked toward implementing the UN Trafficking in Persons Protocol has doubled, and convictions for crimes of trafficking are slowly increasing (UNODC, 2009; UNODC, 2012). Moreover, over time there has been increasing attention placed on the structural causes of trafficking and attempts to better understand (and tackle) root causes. Both academics and policy makers are increasingly recognizing the complexity involved in preventing trafficking, and are focusing on raising awareness about the deeper drivers of trafficking, including joblessness, corruption, environmental destruction and degradation, armed conflict, and international debt.

Also promising is that over recent decades there has been increased activism and vocal engagement from feminists, sex workers, and activists in the Global South, as well as male victims of trafficking. Much of this activism has been transnational, seeking to mobilize the voices of those actually at risk of trafficking or with experiences of exploitation abroad. These dialogues have productively added to Northern voices, which historically have proposed a singular idea of what trafficking is and what should be done about it.

Finally, with a greater diversity of voices there have been increasing debates about the need to shift to a human rights perspective and move away from using victim discourse to discuss trafficking and anti-trafficking efforts. Herein lies perhaps the most productive shift in the field. Increasingly, scholars and activists are recognizing the power in using a broader framework to address problems of trafficking—one of labor rights, migration, and human rights (Desyllas, 2007). In line with this approach, there has been an emerging consensus among international actors as well as scholars that a potential avenue to protect migrant workers is better migration policies—part of which means more open migration regimes and a focus on protecting the rights of all migrant workers. The former point is more controversial than the latter. Although there is some clear dissent to the idea of more open borders as a means of reducing the worst forms of trafficking (primarily among those who argue that more opportunity for migration will mean less oversight and more opportunity for exploitation), those who advocate for more open borders as a means of mediating the worst forms of trafficking argue that when migrants have access to legal institutions, it is less likely that they will experience exploitive outcomes (Wickramasekera, 2002).

In conclusion, there is still a significant need for research, advocacy, and action to combat global trafficking. Specifically, there is a need for the media to ask more inclusive questions; for policy makers to focus on preventive rather than reactive approaches; for activists to highlight the needs and voices of those in the Global South; for scholars to demand, produce, and reproduce more sound empirical evidence; and for us all to recognize that trafficking, while one of the worst forms of human rights abuse, also has much to teach us about the broader rights violations of migrants throughout the world.

BIBLIOGRAPHY

Anderson, Bridget, and Andrijasevic, Rutvica. 2008. Sex, Slaves and Citizens: The Politics of Anti-Trafficking. *Soundings* 40: 135–145.
Andrijasevic, Rutvica, and Bridget Anderson. 2009. Anti-Trafficking Campaigns: Decent? Honest? Truthful? *Feminist Review* 92 (1): 151–165.
Bangladesh Thematic Group on Trafficking. 2004. *Revisiting the Human Trafficking Paradigm: The Bangladesh Experience. Part I: Trafficking of Adults.* Geneva: International Office for Migration.
Beyrer, Chris, and Julie Stachowiak. 2003. Health Consequences of Trafficking of Women and Girls in Southeast Asia. *Brown Journal of World Affairs* 10 (1): 105–117.
Caouette, Therese, and Yuriko Saito. 1999. *To Japan and Back: Thai Women Recount Their Experiences.* Geneva: International Office for Migration.
Chaiyarachta, Charles R. 1996. "El Monte Is the Promised Land": Why Do Asian Immigrants Continue to Risk Their Lives to Work for Substandard Wages and Conditions? *Loyola of Los Angeles International and Comparative Law* 19.
Chapkis, Wendy. 1997. *Live Sex Acts: Women Performing Erotic Labor.* New York: Routledge.

Danailova-Trainor, Gergana, and P. Belser. 2006. *Globalisation and the Illicit Market for Trafficking Victims: An Empirical Analysis of Supply and Demand.* ILO Working Paper 53. Geneva: International Labour Organization.

Danailova-Trainor, Gergana, and Frank Laczko. 2010. Trafficking in Persons and Development: Towards Greater Policy Coherence. *International Migration* 48 (4): 38–83.

Demir, Oguzhan Omer, and James Finckenauer. 2010. Victims of Sex Trafficking in Turkey: Characteristics, Motivations, and Dynamics. *Women & Criminal Justice* 20 (1/2): 57–88.

Desyllas, Moshoula Capous. 2007. A Critique of the Global Trafficking Discourse and U.S. Policy. *Journal of Sociology & Social Welfare* 34 (4): 57–79.

Dewey, Susan. 2010. Invisible Agents, Hollow Bodies: Neoliberal Notions of "Sex Trafficking" from Syracuse to Sarajevo. In *Sex Trafficking, Human Rights and Social Justice*, edited by Tiantian Zheng. London: Routledge, pp. 102–116.

Eurostat. 2013. *Trafficking in Human Beings.* Eurostat European Commission, Methodologies and Working Papers. Luxembourg.

GAATW. 2007. Collateral Damage. The Impact of Anti-Trafficking Measures on Human Rights around the World. Bangkok: Global Alliance Against Traffic in Women.

Gozdziak, Elzbieta M., and Elizabeth A. Collett. 2005. Research on Human Trafficking in North America: A Review of Literature. *International Migration* 43 (1/2): 99–128.

Grigorian, Hilda. 2005. *Human Trafficking in the Republic of Armenia.* Washington, DC: World Bank.

Hausner, S. 2005. The Movement of Women: Migration, Trafficking and Prostitution in the Context of Nepal's Armed Conflict. Kathmandu: Save the Children USA.

Hujismans, Roy, and Simon Baker. 2012. Child Trafficking: "Worst Form" of Child Labour, or Worst Approach to Young Migrants? *Development and Change* 43 (4): 919–946.

ILO. 2009. The Cost of Coercion. Global Report Under the Follow-up to the ILO Declaration on Fundamental Principles and Rights at Work, ILO Geneva.

IOM. 1997. *Trafficking in Women to Japan for Sexual Exploitation: A Survey on the Case of Filipino Women.* Geneva: International Office for Migration.

IOM. 2001. *Hardship Abroad or Hunger at Home: A study of Irregular Migration from Georgia.* Geneva: International Office for Migration.

IOM. 2008. *World Migration Report 2008: Managing Labour Mobility in the Evolving Global Economy.* Geneva: International Office for Migration.

IOM. 2011. *Trafficking of Fishermen in Thailand.* Bangkok: International Office for Migration.

Jordan, Ann. 2011. *Fact or Fiction: What Do We Really Know about Human Trafficking?* Issue Paper 3. American University, Washington College of Law, Center for Human Rights and Humanitarian Law.

Kahale, Salme. 2003. *Exploratory Study on Foreign Domestic Work in Syria.* Damascus: International Office for Migration.

Katsulis, Yasmina, Kate Weinkauf, and Elena Frank. 2010. Countering the Trafficking Paradigm: The Role of Family Obligations, Remittances, and

Investment Strategies among Migrant Sex Workers in Tijuana, Mexico. In *Sex Trafficking, Human Rights and Social Justice*, edited by Tiantian Zheng. London: Routledge.

Kelly, Liz. 2002. *Journeys of Jeopardy: A Review of Research on Trafficking in Women and Children in Europe*. Geneva: International Office for Migration.

Kelly, Liz. 2005. You Can Find Anything You Want: A Critical Reflection on Research on Trafficking in Persons within and into Europe. *International Migration* 43 (1/2): 235–255.

Kempadoo, Kamala. 2005. Introduction. In *Trafficking and Prostitution Reconsidered*, edited by Kamala Kempadoo. Boulder, CO: Paradigm.

Kempadoo, Kamala, and Jo Doezema, eds. 1998. *Global Sex Workers: Rights, Resistance, and Redefinition*. New York: Routledge.

Kempadoo, Kamala, Jyoti Sanghera, and Bandana Pattanaik, eds. 2010. Trafficking and Prostitution Reconsidered. In *New Perspectives on Migration, Sex Work, and Human Rights*. 2nd ed. Boulder, CO: Paradigm.

Lazaroiu, Sebastian, and Monica Alexandru. 2003. *Who Is the Next Victim? Vulnerability of Young Romanian Women to Trafficking in Human Beings*. Bucharest: International Office for Migration .

Piper, Nicole. 2005. A Problem by a Different Name? A Review of Research on Trafficking in South-East Asia and Oceania. *International Migration* 43 (1/2): 203–233.

Salt, John. 2000. Trafficking and Human Smuggling: A European Perspective. *International Migration*, Special Issue 2000 (1): 31–56.

Satterthwaite, Margaret L. 2005. Crossing Borders, Claiming Rights: Using Human Rights Law to Empower Women Migrant Workers. *Yale Human Rights & Development Law Journal* 8.

Shelley, Louise. 2010. *Human Trafficking: A Global Perspective*. New York: Cambridge University Press.

Surtees, Rebecca. 2005. *Second Annual Report on Victims of Trafficking in South-Eastern Europe*. Geneva: International Office for Migration.

Surtees, Rebecca. 2008. *Trafficking of Men—A Trend Less Considered: The Case of Belarus and Ukraine*. IOM Migration Research Series No. 36. Geneva: International Office for Migration.

UNDP. 2007. *Human Development Report 2007/2008: Indicators*. New York: United Nations Development Programme.

UNESCO. n.d. Trafficking Statistics Project, http://www.unescobkk.org/culture /diversity/trafficking-hiv/projects/trafficking-statistics-project/ updated -data-comparison/ (accessed August 15, 2013).

United Nations General Assembly. 2000. Protocol to Prevent, Suppress and Punish Trafficking in Persons, Especially Women and Children, Supplementing the United Nations Convention against Transnational Organized Crime.

UNODC. 2012. Global Report on Trafficking in Persons. Vienna: United Nations Office on Drugs and Crime.

UNODC. 2009. *Global Report on Trafficking in Persons*. United Nations Office on Drugs and Crime and UN Global Initiative to Fight Human Trafficking.

U.S. Department of State. 2005. *Trafficking in Persons Report*. Washington, DC: U.S. Department of State.

U.S. Department of State. 2009. *Trafficking in Persons Report*. Washington, DC: U.S. Department of State.

U.S. Department of State. 2012. *Trafficking in Persons Report 2012*. Washington, DC: U.S. Department of State.

Wickramasekera, Piyasiri. 2002. *Asian Labour Migration: Issues and Challenges in an Era of Globalization*. Geneva: International Migration Programme, International Labour Organization.

CHAPTER 12

Wartime Rape: A Case Study of the Democratic Republic of Congo

Mariam M. Kurtz and Mwamini Thambwe Diggs

A certain number of soldiers must prove their newly won superiority—prove it to a woman, to themselves, to other men. In the name of victory and the power of the gun, war provides men with tacit license to rape.
— Susan Brownmiller (1975, p. 33)

In a Bukavu hospital in the eastern Democratic Republic of the Congo (DRC), a new patient was telling others about what the Rwandan militias did to her. She had been raped by about 15 of them. Another woman seated nearby asked, *"That's what you call being raped? That's what you call suffering?"* She started to explain her story, of how she was kidnapped while in the field with her baby on her back with a group of other women and girls from 7 to 70 years old. While they were walking to their base, her baby had started crying. They asked her to quiet the baby. She explained to the armed men that the only way to stop the baby from crying was to breastfeed him, but they refused to let her.

Later she told them she needed rest and was thirsty. They stopped and asked her to kneel down and open her mouth. They urinated in her mouth and then forced her and the others to walk. She was forced to obey or she would have been killed. As she continued walking, her baby kept on crying; they stopped and told her that they knew a way to stop the baby from crying. She couldn't see what they were doing behind her back to the baby, but he was still crying. They told her to keep walking. She began to walk but felt restrained. She couldn't see the baby on her back; she was beaten to keep walking. She tried to walk and could not hear her child crying anymore. She didn't know they had tied a rope around her baby's neck and her efforts to walk forward were actually strangling him. After they killed her baby, they kept her in their camp and raped her every day. She could not tell how many men had raped her because she had simply stopped counting after she had seen more than 10 different men on top of her.

At the main hospital of Bukavu or Goma, all the stories about rapes are similar. Some women looked at certain patients and told them that they were lucky because the rapes inflicted on them were not as severe as the violence inflicted on other women.

Margot Wallstrom, the Special Representative of the UN Secretary General on sexual violence in conflict, described the DRC as "the rape capital of the world." The United Nations News Service reports 48 women are raped in the DRC every hour. Recurrent conflict in the DRC is the primary factor that caused the number of rape cases to increase in the country. Reports from the popular press, peer-reviewed publications, and multinational and nongovernmental organizations (NGOs) describe the number of rapes in the DRC as in the tens of thousands in a country with an estimated population of 70 million (Peterman et al., 2011). Between January 2005 and December 2007 alone, for example, Maltese International, an NGO that provides medical and social support in South Kivu, registered 20,500 women and girls as victims of rape.

Wartime rape is not new; it has been used in various wars throughout history, from the ancient Greek and revolutionary wars, to the wars of religions, knights, and pilgrims, and in the first and second world wars. What draw much recent attention to the problem is that often these rape victims become HIV/AIDS victims. Traditionally, armed conflict has been considered a catalyst for HIV transmission. Sexual violence against women with a lack of preventive and curative health services often means it is associated with HIV (Anema et al., 2008). Studying seven countries affected by conflict (DRC, southern Sudan, Rwanda, Uganda, Sierra Leone, Somalia, and Burundi), however, Spiegel et al. (2007) call that assumption into question. Their study concluded, "Despite wide-scale rape in many countries, there are no data to show that rape increased prevalence of HIV infection at the population level" (p. 2187; see also Anema et al., 2008).

This chapter explores rape in the DRC from the time of the Great African War in the 1990s as a case study. We will examine several efforts by scholars to explain why DRC is the "rape capital of the world" and why wartime rape is perceived as a threat to public health.

During war rape, women are victims of the worst violence, which includes physical and mental torture; after the rape, they became victims again—this time of rejection by their communities and, more precisely, by their families. It is hard to tell which is worse for them (Diggs, 2012, p. 74). Moreover, many of these women became AIDS victims as well. Rape in the DRC is used to humiliate a woman as well as every member of her family. Many cases reported to the national police claimed that sons were forced to rape their mothers or sisters, and that husbands were forced to rape their daughters or wives in front of the entire family. Indeed, rape as a tool of war in the DRC is more common than death by arms (Diggs, 2012).

WHY WOMEN ARE VICTIMS OF RAPE IN WARTIME

The United Nations (UN) estimates that at least 200,000 women have been raped in the DRC since the beginning of war in 1998. Human Rights Watch claims there were about 16,000 women raped in 2008 alone in the DRC. There are many explanations about rape in wartime and why rape is used as a weapon of war. Structural violence and social practices are among the factors that could explain wartime rape in the DRC. The DRC is among the patriarchal societies in which men control through domination and, in some situations, the application of force, subjecting women to men on a daily basis. In these contexts, women are distrusted, despised, and dominated by men. The social structure in patriarchies thus gives power to the men while at the same time devaluing women, so that they become a disadvantaged group in the society (Taylor and Miller, 1994).

Unequal gender arrangements in the DRC were enforced, with men in control, and when the war broke out, men from both sides of the war became warriors while women became enemies (Gottschall, 2004). Injustice and inequality embedded in the structure make women and girls vulnerable even in peacetime (Leatherman, 2011; cf. Chapter 3 of this volume), but that structural violence also lays the groundwork for physical violence in times of war. As Brownmiller put it (1975, pp. 13–14), "Man's structural capacity to rape and women's corresponding structural vulnerability are as basic to the physiology of both our sexes as the primal act of sex itself." Indeed, a recent quantitative transnational study of sexual violence rates by Yodanis (2004, p. 670) found that a structure of gender inequality is associated with a culture of violence against women. The educational and occupational status of women is correlated with the prevalence of sexual violence in a country, with a high status of women corresponding with lower rates of sexual violence. Gendered structural inequality in certain societies such as the DRC is providing the structural conditions for rape, which then become exaggerated in wartime. These structures, however, are socially constructed.

Masculinity and femininity have been treated by many as "natural," Cynthia Enloe (2000, p. 3) notes, but today "there is mounting evidence that they are packages of expectations that have been created through specific decisions by specific people" (cf. Skjelsbæk, 2001, p. 50). Constructivists emphasize the role of norms, rules, beliefs, ideas, and principles that shape expectations of social behaviors in the social structure and give men power.

Biosocial pressure cooker theory describes rape in wartime as just like rape in peacetime, in that rape is driven by the desire of men to apply their dominance over women (Gottschall, 2004; see also Barstow, 2000; Sajor, 1998; and Stiglmayer, 1994). Pressure cooker theory suggests that "war rapists are the victims of irresistible biological imperatives and that the chaos of war time milieu encourages men to vent their urges to terrible effect" (Gottschall, 2004, p. 130).

Most researchers do not see rape—especially militarized rape—as the result of a natural sex drive, however, and instead describe it as a form of aggression (Brownmiller, 1975; cf. Baaz and Stern, 2009). Gottschall (2004, p. 133) claims that when aggressive behavior occurs among soldiers exposed to wartime environments, they are encouraged to become hostile to civilians identified with the enemy, which could lead to a high rate of rape. Biosocial theories fail to prove rape is a biological factor because, in many conflicts, many soldiers do not rape (Gottschall, 2004).

The cultural pathology perspective on rape draws from psychoanalysis, looking at the developmental and national history features that could be causal factors regarding sexual assault. Military culture that fosters a hostile attitude toward women often reinforces behavior or feelings of entitlement to rape. The availability of pornography before the war, when seen as normal, means that men are predisposed to dehumanize women. Cultural pathology theory helps us to understand rape in wartime as an outcome of cultural themes of masculinity that become exaggerated and militarized in times of war.

Various studies demonstrate that military sexualized violence is constructed through global discourses that define the military as masculine and heterosexual (Connel, 1995; Ehrenreich, 1997; Enloe, 1990; Enloe, 2000; Enloe, 2005; Enloe, 2007; Goldstein, 2001; Higate and Hopton, 2005; Morgan, 1994; Shepherd, 2007; Stern and Nystrand, 2006; Whitworth, 2004). In this context, to attempt to show that women are weak and vulnerable and therefore need a militarized masculinity to keep them safe, women and the "feminine" are stereotypically associated with the need for protection and with peacefulness and life giving, while "masculinity" is associated with protecting, warring, and killing (Baaz and Stern, 2009, p. 499; Enloe, 2000).

Rape is a strategy, just like the use of other means of warfare such as bombs, bullets, and propaganda "that the military could use to accomplish its strategic objectives; rape is a tactic executed by soldiers in the service of larger strategic objectives" (Gottschall, 2004, p. 131). Rape diminishes resistant civilians, demoralizing, humiliating, and emasculating enemy soldiers to show they have failed in their duty to protect. Here rape serves a collective interest rather than the specific interest of soldiers, and its suffering does not target only victims but the entire community. "In war rape is an assault on both the individual and her family and community" (Swiss and Giller, 1993, p. 612).

Rape attacks the very root of the targeted culture, affecting its ability to remain coherent and to flourish. By raping a woman, a soldier splits the family atom, the fundamental component of every society. A raped woman may become pregnant by the enemy, and may also suffer grievous physical and psychological trauma or death (Baaz and Stern, 2009).

Children of rape are a source of conflict among their families because they are permanent reminders of what happened during the war. Many of these children are abandoned or killed right after delivery. Rape could take a woman's life or cause her to be disowned by her shamed family and husband. Survivors face horror and live with the physical and emotional trauma of the injuries caused by rape. However, women continue their role of caring for their children, including those born of rape and they suffer because their society regards them as "damaged goods, living symbols of a nation's humiliation and bearers of 'enemy' children" (Leatherman, 2011, p. 49).

This violence degrades the ability of a culture to replenish itself through sexual reproduction. This can be referred to as "genocide rape," the aim of which is to destroy the people and their culture. This could happen by spreading HIV/AIDS or by making women forcibly pregnant so that the society will be full of the "enemy's" children, who remind people of the horror and affect the integrity of their culture (Hyun-Kyung, 2000, p. 20; Allen, 1996; Barstow, 2000). Genocide rape functions to violate the group as well as the individual (De Vito, 2007). The *Akayesu* Trial Chamber observed that rape as genocide can be understood as a particularly "effective tool of genocide" and a way to inflict serious bodily or mental harm on a group (in De Vito, 2007, p. 376). It also can be strategically counterproductive, resulting not in a cowed and crushed population but in a galvanized and vengeful confederation of civilians and soldiers.

Men who are aware of their having AIDS may attempt to rape women as a strategy of war, infecting the women with a virus that could eventually kill them. The Congolese Women against Sexual Violence campaign claimed that among the 80 percent of women who were raped in the first six months of the year, 30 percent of them were HIV infected (Leatherman, 2011).

Rape destroys social interaction between the survivors and their community; the stigma has forced some of these women to move to areas where no one knew them, and some were rejected by their husbands (Leatherman, 2011).

Thus, rape as a strategic act of war is a theoretical perspective that has considerable support in the studies of wars in the Congo. It was deliberately used to undermine or even destroy "enemy" populations and in fact has had devastating effects on target populations and their cultures.

IS RAPE FRUSTRATION, AGGRESSION, OR DESPERATION?

In Baaz and Stern's (2009) study of Congolese soldiers' discourse, 193 soldiers from 49 different armed groups were interviewed to study their view of rape and to distinguish what makes them view it as "evil" and "lust." They argue that some of the rapes are driven by a desire for sex and others are an effort to destroy the enemy. Still other rapes are driven by the belief that raping a woman will help a man gain strength for the fight.

Baaz and Stern (2009) established a link between rape, poverty, frustration, power (by having a gun), and the craziness of war. Soldiers' narratives that they elicited in their study demonstrate that rape is also caused by frustration, anger due to poverty, and neglect (p. 511). Baaz and Stern's (2009) interviews revealed that the soldiers in the DRC thus situated rape as a "general wish to destroy" that arises from "suffering" and "frustrations." In the soldiers' narratives, poverty and a general feeling of neglect (including "not being loved" by one's wife and being "cheated" by superiors) and frustration play an important role in explaining—even partly excusing—this kind of sexual violence. Failed notions of "the provider" and "the sexually potent fighter" thus haunt the "sense" made of rape here (Baaz and Stern, 2009, p. 511).

This crime intersects with other crimes. For example, a sex slave named Christine keeps the skulls of her kids in a piece of cloth. Every time she tells the story she opens the cloth because she doesn't want to forget. She wants people who are listening to her story to understand that it is not fiction but the daily reality of women residing in the eastern Congo. Christine was kidnapped by an armed group and used as their sex slave. The kidnappers hid the children from her for days; she begged them to give her kids back to her or at least to let her see them. She knew that something had happened to them. Finally, she asked the chief of the camp if he would ask his soldiers to bring her children to her. The man laughed and told her that lately she seemed happy eating meat, which she had cooked for all of them. That was the meat of her children. The man showed her where he threw the rest of their body parts near the village. She dug at the location and found the heads of her children and kept the skulls to never forget the nightmare she lived.

Human Rights Watch argues that the FARDC soldiers were involved in crime because it integrated some of the rebel groups who were involved in sexual violence and because of the failure to provide basic needs of its army such as equipment, salaries, and food for its soldiers. "Lack of support does not only hamper the FARDC's military power, it is also contributes to the general climate of violence as FARDC soldiers prey upon the local population for survival" (Baaz and Stern, 2009. p. 501).

The U.S. Congressional Research Report on Sexual Violence in African Conflict (2010) claimed that "military troops are poorly paid, and troops deployed in conflict areas are not provided adequate food or supplies, which is thought to encourage looting and other abuse" (Arieff 2011). About 60 percent of attacks were mostly military gang rapes that took place in homes in front of families accompanied by looting in South Kivu (Leatherman, 2011, p. 119). As Miller (quoted in Gurr, 1970, p. 33) contends, "frustration produces instigation to various responses, one of which is aggression." When the basic categories of human needs such as welfare needs, which include food, shelter, water, medical treatment, and schooling (Galtung, 1990, p. 309) are not met people can become aggressive.

When more than 6,000 rebels in the DRC were integrated into the FARDC as part of an effort to end the conflict in the eastern DRC (Voice of America report), the CNDP was created secretly within the FARDC. The leader of the CNDP, Laurent Nkundabatware, was recruiting Tutsis into the national Congolese army while he was a general. In May 2004, the CNDP officially separated from the national army and started a war against the government. The multiple mix between the national army and the different armed groups make the army uncontrollable.

Gang rapes make up 59.3 percent of the rapes in the eastern DRC (Bartels et al., 2010). Every armed group present on Congolese soil has perpetrated gang rapes, including the Congolese army. Among the largest perpetuators of sexual and other kinds of violence in the conflict zone, the FARDC, CNDP, the Congolese police (PNC), ADF-NALU, the Lord's Resistance Army from Uganda, the FDLR from Rwanda, the Mai Mai, M23 and UN soldiers.

The dominant discourse in Baaz and Stern's (2009) interviews of 193 Congolese soldiers from 49 groups defined the role of women in the military as belonging to the "feminized sphere" of the armed forces, which they described as cooking, health, social services, and administration, while males belong to the "masculine sphere," which implies courage and level-headed, tough killers (Baaz and Stern, 2009).

They dismissed women soldiers' femininity as it is understood in the "civilian sphere," sometimes perceiving women soldiers as "men" and at other times "casting them as sexualized opportunists, instead of as soldiers or ('they are only hookers looking for clients'); and finally by denying women soldiers are real soldiers who can handle warfare" (Baaz and Stern, 2009, p. 505). However, the image of the macho male, virile, and aggressive soldiers whose sexual desire is barely controllable was also portrayed in those interviews.

Women who are victims of rape are labeled as "dirty" or "damaged goods." Patriarchy demands the purity of women's bodies secured through controlling and limiting their sexual activity (Zabeida, 2010). In the DRC, for example, some victims of rape who discussed their experiences with their husbands after the incident claimed they were allowed to stay in the house but the husband took a second spouse and the victim of rape became more of a servant. Being rejected by one's husband is not the worst outcome. Some children would refuse the affection of their mother after the rape because of the community teaching that rape is a betrayal. Some women in the community would not show sympathy to the victim but would say that the victim encouraged the abuse (Diggs, 2012, pp. 71, 72).

Women are believed by some to have a responsibility to protect their virginity in order not to be viewed by society as impure or contaminated (Cheldelin, 2011, p. 29). Survivors of rape are stigmatized; some of these women were forced to move to areas where no one knew them. Some were rejected by their husbands when they found that their wives had been raped. A man in Bukavu, for example, said he would rather have a wife who cheated than a wife who had been raped. He said that when a cheating woman comes back to her husband, it means that he has conquered her, but taking back a woman who had been a victim of rape is like taking a poor person under his wing (Diggs, 2012, p. 71). Rape survivors were outcast and excluded from society (De Vito, 2007). Cheldelin notes (2011, p. 29) that in a patriarchal system women are valued "most for their reproductive identity and virginity." Therefore, "rape in war also comes as a consequence of social definition of men's honor and purity of women in their community" (Zabeida, 2010, p. 24). Women are required to follow socially established codes of behavior because it brings honor to the men (Zabeida, 2010, p. 24).

WARTIME RAPE AS A PUBLIC HEALTH ISSUE

It has been reported that in the past 10 years there has been widespread rape by armed combatants in Burundi, Sierra Leone, Rwanda, the DRC, Liberia, Sudan, and Uganda. International organizations have perceived rape as the major cause of HIV transmission in conflict settings (Anema et al., 2008). Throughout the history of the region rape has been used as weapon of war, and after 1990 rape in wartime became a threat to health due to the AIDS/HIV epidemic (Aginam, 2010).

The impact of AIDS does not end at the personal level of suffering and death. "HIV/AIDS has the effect of destabilizing society and the state by destroying structures of governance that ensure human security" (Gamharter, 2007). The Commission on Human Security addresses health challenges to human security in three categories: global infectious disease, poverty-related threats, and violence and crisis. HIV/AIDS fits into all of these categories. Ayele (2011) claims that the threat of rape causes women and girls to become afraid of performing their daily tasks such as collecting wood and water, and as a result thecommunity faces the challenge of food insecurity and inadequate family nutrition.

The victim of rape could suffer severe psychological problems such as posttraumatic stress disorder (PTSD), displayed in the form of depression, heightened fear, anxiety, anger, feelings of isolation, phobia, withdrawal, flashbacks, panic disorder, and substance abuse. The physical manifestations of PTSD include suicide, self-injury, sleep disorders, headaches, and gastrointestinal disorders. There are no resources to support the victims; for example, adequate psychological counseling is not available in resource-poor countries (Ayele, 2011). In Kivu only a few hospitals have specialists who can operate on women suffering with fistula (an abnormal connection or passageway between two epithelium-lined organs or vessels). Panzi Hospital, Saint Joseph, and E-Africa are among the few hospitals that could provide service to women who need fistula repair surgery.

Johnson et al. (2010) conducted a survey of 998 adults over 18 years of age in the eastern DRC looking at the prevalence of sexual violence and its association with depression and PTSD: For example, 67.7 percent of women who claimed to be subjected to sexual violence during conflict met symptom criteria for major conditions such as major depressive disorder (MDD).

Findings show that the victim's age at the time of the sexual assault has an impact on the extent of the psychological effect and subsequent adjustment.

Older women have been found to have more difficulty adjusting to the trauma most likely due to fear of stigma while children tend to suffer from long-term and greater symptoms of PTSD, while those who suffered the repeated sexual assaults have greater distress and severity and frequency of PTSD symptoms. (Johnson et al., 2010)

Most incidents of mass rape during conflict that are committed at the victim's home or in front of the family and community members have even more severe psychological consequences and can lead to chronic and infectious illnesses. Physical conditions associated with mass rape include injury, HIV/AIDS and other sexually transmitted disease (STD), recurrent infections, fistula, cervical cancer, forced pregnancy, miscarriage, infertility, chronic sexual dysfunction, and death.

The winner of many awards, including the UN Human Rights prize, the Clinton Global Citizen Award for Leadership in Civil Society, and the Human Rights First Award, Dr. Denis Mukwege, founder of the Panzi Hospital in Bukavu, tells of a 14-year-old girl from Shabunda region who was gang-raped by multiple armed groups from Rwanda for two years, before being brought under his care. The doctor discovered that her internal genital organs were damaged due to gang rape. She had a fistula from the multiple rapes and from giving birth at her young age. The doctor performed reconstructive surgery and repaired her organs. The 14-year-old claimed she was raped by an armed group from neighboring Rwanda. She spent months recovering at the hospital, where she felt safe.

After months in the hospital she started to regain her self-esteem. She began arranging her hair and talked about how beautiful she was. Then it was time to depart. Three years later, she was brought back to the same hospital, and this time she was in a coma. She had been massively gang-raped again. This time she had an infection in her genitals and she was HIV positive. She was re-examined and the damage was much more extensive compared with the first visit. Her fistula could not be repaired this time. She was forced to live the rest of her life incontinent.

Many of the women who are rape victims in the DRC suffer physical injuries, including broken bones, wounds, and concussions while resisting rape. Victims are often raped with guns, knives, bottles, or sticks, causing damage to genital and anal body parts. A review of the medical record at HEAL Africa Hospital in Goma between 2006 and 2008 indicates that 74 percent of hospitalized children under 18 years old were assaulted by a family member as opposed to the military, whereas adults are mostly assaulted by the military (Kalisya et al., 2011). Children tend to delay seeking medical attention for 72 hours on average, and they are more likely to get pregnant but less likely to be HIV positive.

INTERVENTION

Rape as war booty, genocide, or gendercide, can no longer be deemed a "natural" part of war. As Cheldelin (2011, p. 28) reports, "No rape charges were brought at the Nuremberg trials of prominent Nazis after the Second World War, and the Tokyo trials did not deal with the enslavement of Korean women forced to serve as prostitutes for Japanese soldiers."

It was not until February 2001 that the International Criminal Tribunal for the former Yugoslavia (ICTY) prosecuted three veterans of the 1992–1995 war for the systematic and savage rape, torture, and enslavement of Muslim women in 1992 in the town of Foca in southeastern Bosnia. ICTY was the "the first international criminal tribunal to enter convictions for rape as torture and for sexual enslavement as a crime against humanity" (United Nations– ICTY, n.d.). Amnesty International calls the verdict a significant step for women's rights: "Sexual enslavement in armed conflict is now legally acknowledged as a crime against humanity and perpetrators can and must be held to account." But this is still happening in the DRC; as many as 500,000 women have been raped in the DRC since it plunged into an ongoing civil war in 1996 (Calvert, 2011).

Bergoffen (2001) argues that the verdict has opened a new chapter in international law. She explains the factor that makes the verdict significant: "First, the decision to prosecute. Second, the condemnation. Third, the classification of rape as torture, a crime against humanity. Of these three factors, the condemnation is the most dramatic" (p. 116).

Rape in wartime poses threats to the economy, national and international security, and health; therefore, it requires a multidimensional approach, as Ayele (2011) suggests. Governments, UN agencies, and NGOs should cooperate to end the rape crime. Various measures should be taken to combat rape in wartime by raising the awareness of soldiers and civil society to help them understand that rape is a war crime and a violation of human rights. In addition to prosecuting the perpetuators, the International Tribunal has held responsible the officers who carry out the act or who order it, and the people in power who fail to prevent rape (Goldstone, 2002).

To deal with war crime such as rape a mobile court system was created in the DRC. These mobile courts are making judgment easier because the aggressors don't have to go to court; instead the court comes to them. This system made possible the arrest of Colonel Daniel Ibibio Mutware in February 2001. Colonel Mutware had sent his men on a punitive expedition against the civilians. Mutware was sentenced to 20 years in prison for sending his troops to rape, beat, and rob civilians in Fizi.

The mobile court system is an effective way of dealing with rape crimes in the DRC, so it is important to keep it viable. Therefore, a climate of trust between the judge and the victims and between the judge and the perpetrators should be given priority in order to create a state of trust between the court and the aggressor. All aggressors should have jail time based on their crimes, and not on an influential person whom they know. Also, the court system should involve female judges to deal with crimes of humanity from a female perspective (Diggs, 2012, p. 123).

A former chief prosecutor of the United Nations International Criminal Tribunal in Rwanda, Justice Richard Goldstone advises that women should be among the judges involved in war crime trials as a strategy to address rape during wartime. In his 2001 lecture at Case Western University School of Law he said,

Men had written the law in an age when rape was regarded as being no more than an inevitable consequence of war. . . . Tribunals have advanced that substance of international humanitarian law through defining rape, sexual violence and sexual slavery and broadening the categories of international crime under which judicial bodies can prosecute gender crime.

Thus, the ICTY and the sister tribunal for Rwanda have changed the landscape of international humanitarian law and brought huge progress to women's rights. Tribunals managed to bring the "explicit charges of wartime sexual violence, and to define gender crimes such as rape and sexual enslavement under customary law" (United Nations–ICTY , 2014).

BIBLIOGRAPHY

African Rights, London. 1995. Rwanda Death, Despair and Defiance, http://www.opengrey.eu/item/display/10068/439901 (retrieved September 21, 2012).

Aginam, Obijiofor. 2012. Rape and HIV as Weapon of War, http://unu.edu/publications/articles/rape-and-hiv-as-weapons-of-war.html

Aginam, Obijiofor. 2010. Global Health Governance, Intellectual Property and Access to Essential Medicines: Opportunities and Impediments for South-South Cooperation. *Global Health* 4 (1), http://unu.edu/wp-content/uploads/articles/000/012/887/aginam-ghg-south-south-cooperation.pdf

Allen, Beverly. 1996. *Rape Warfare: The Hidden Genocide in Bosnia-Herzegovina and Croatia*. Minneapolis, MN: University of Minnesota Press.

Allen, C. 1999. Warfare, Endemic Violence & State Collapse in Africa. *Review of African Political Economy* 26 (81): 367–384, http://www.tandfonline.com/doi/abs/10.1080/03056249908704399 (retrieved September 21, 2012).

Anema, Aranka, Michel R. Joffres, Edward Mills, and Paul B. Spiegel. 2008. Widespread Rape Does Not Directly Appear to Increase the Overall HIV Prevalence in Conflict-Affected Countries: So Now What? *Emerging Themes in Epidemiology* 5 (11): 1742–76. http://www.biomedcentral.com/content/pdf/1742-7622-5-11.pdf

Arieff, A. 2009. Sexual Violence in African Conflicts. Congressional Research Service Report for Congress, http://assets.opencrs.com/rpts/R40956_20101130.pdf (retrieved September 30, 2012).

Ayele, Missale. 2011. Public Health Implications of Mass Rape as a Weapon of War. Georgia State University, School of Public Health, ScholarWorks @ Georgia State University, http://scholarworks.gsu.edu/cgi/viewcontent.cgi?article=1170&context=iph_theses

Baaz, M. E., and M. Stern. 2009. Why Do Soldiers Rape? Masculinity, Violence, and Sexuality in the Armed Forces in the Congo (DRC). *International Studies Quarterly* 53 (2): 495–518, http://onlinelibrary.wiley.com/doi/10.1111/j.1468-2478.2009.00543.x/full (retrieved September 19, 2012).

Barstow, Anne Llewellyn. 2000. *War's Dirty Secret: Rape, Prostitution, and Other Crimes against Women*. Cleveland, OH: Pilgrim Press.

Bartels, Susan, et al. 2010. Patterns of Sexual Violence in Eastern Democratic Republic of Congo: Reports from Survivors Presenting to Panzi Hospital in 2006. *Conflict and Health* 4 (1): 9, http://www.conflictandhealth.com/content/4/1/9/abstract (retrieved September 21, 2012).

Bergoffen, Debra. 2001, February 22. Toward a Politics of the Vulnerable Body. *Hypatia* 18 (1): 116–34.

Brownmiller, Susan. 1975. *Against Our Will: Men, Women and Rape*. New York: Fawcett Books.

Calvert, Mary F. 2011, September. The War on Congo's Women. *Mother Jones*, http://www.motherjones.com/photoessays/2011/09/congo-rape-epidemic/congo-rape-soldiers

Carpenter, R. C. 2007. Born of War: Protecting Children of Sexual Violence Survivors in Conflict Zones, http://books.google.com/books?hl=en&lr=&id=

PxTEvHSR_vUC&oi=fnd&pg=PR7&dq=rape+war+rwanda&ots=HuO uiM_Bpw&sig=CU01ZuzOSxewApwZoBkb9WeCoP0 (retrieved September 21, 2012).

Cheldelin, Sandra I. 2011. Victims of Rape and Gendercide: All Wars. In *Women Waging War, and Peace*, edited by Sandra I. Cheldelin and Maneshka Eliatamby. New York: Continuum, pp. 12–34.

Cheldelin, Sandra I., and Maneshka Eliatamby, eds. 2011. *Women Waging War, and Peace*. New York: Continuum.

Connell, R. W. 1995. *Masculinities*. Berkeley, CA: University of California Press, 2005.

Couillard, Valérie. 2007. The Nairobi Declaration: Redefining Reparation for Women Victims of Sexual Violence. *International Journal of Transitional Justice* 1 (3): 444–453, http://ijtj.oxfordjournals.org/content/1/3/444 (retrieved September 29, 2012).

Csete, J., and J. Kippenberg. 2002. *The War within the War: Sexual Violence against Women and Girls in Eastern Congo*. Human Rights Watch, http://books .google.com/books?hl=en&lr=&id=E-XsrFDyBsEC&oi=fnd&pg=PA1&dq =women+rape+war+congo&ots=fIHpAsJB_h&sig=D3beQojDw3LaFTGw n9SZ3S1Enn0 (retrieved September 19, 2012).

De Vito, Daniela. 2007, December 4. Rape as Genocide: The Group/Individual Schism. *Human Rights Review* 9 (3): 361–78. doi:10.1007/s12142-007-0054-y.

Dégni-Ségui, R., and UN Commission on Human Rights Special Rapporteur on the Situation of Human Rights in Rwanda. 1996. *Report on the Situation of Human Rights in Rwanda*. United Nations.

Diggs, Mwamini Thambwe Mwamba. 2012. *The Untold Story of the Women and Children of the Democratic Republic of the Congo: Analysis of Violence in Eastern DRC*. Houston, TX: Strategic Book Publishing.

Ehrenreich, Barbara. 1997. *Blood Rites: Origins and History of the Passions of War*. London: Virago.

Ellsberg, Mary, and Lori Heise. 2005. *Researching Violence against Women: A Practical Guide for Researchers and Activists*. Geneva: World Health Organization.

Enloe, Cynthia. 1990. *Bananas, Beaches and Bases: Making Feminist Sense of International Politics*. Berkeley: University of California Press.

Enloe, Cynthia H. 2005. "What if Patriarchy Is 'the Big Picture'? An Afterword." In *Gender, Conflict, and Peacekeeping*, edited by Dyan Mazurana, Angela Raven-Roberts, and Jane L. Parpart, 280–83. New York: Rowman & Littlefield.

Enloe, Cynthia H. 2007. *Globalization and Militarism: Feminists Make the Link*. Lanham, MD: Rowman & Littlefield.

Farwell, N. 2004. War Rape: New Conceptualizations and Responses. *Affilia* 19 (4): 389–403, http://aff.sagepub.com/content/19/4/389.short (retrieved September 21, 2012).

Galtung, Johan. 1990. Cultural Violence. *Journal of Peace Research* 27 (3): 291–305.

Gamharter, Katharina. n.d. Access to Affordable Medicines and the HIV/AIDS Pandemic: Facing a New Challenge in International Security Law, http:// www.esil-sedi.eu/sites/default/files/Gamharter_0.PDF (accessed April 7, 2014).

Gamharter, Kathatrina. 2007. Access to Affordable Medicines and the HIV/AIDS Pandemic: Facing a New Challenge in International Security Law. Paper at

2nd ESIL Research Forum, Budapest, 28–29 September 2007, http://www
.esil-sedi.eu/sites/default/files/Gamharter_0.PDF.

Goldstein, Joshua S. 2001. *War and Gender: How Gender Shapes the War System and Vice Versa*. Cambridge, UK: Cambridge University Press.

Goldstone, R. J. 2002. Prosecuting Rape as a War Crime. *Case Western Reserve Journal of International Law* 34: 277, http://heinonlinebackup.com/hol-cgi-bin/get_pdf.cgi?handle=hein.journals/cwrint34&section=28 (retrieved September 30, 2012).

Gottschall, J. 2004. Explaining Wartime Rape. *Journal of Sex Research* 41 (2): 129–136, http://www.tandfonline.com/doi/abs/10.1080/00224490409552221 (retrieved September 19, 2012).

Gurr, Ted Robert. 1970. *Why Men Rebel*. Princeton, NJ: Princeton University Press.

Hamilton, H. 1999. Refugee Women, UNHCR and the Great Lakes Crisis, http://www.freewebs.com/hbhamilton/Women%20Refugees%20Great%20Lakes.pdf (accessed December 10, 2002; retrieved September 21, 2012).

Higate, Paul, and John Hopton. 2005. War, Militarism, and Masculinities. In *Handbook of Studies on Men and Masculinities*, edited by Michael S. Kimmel, Jeff Hearn, and Raewyn Connell. Thousand Oaks, CA: Sage, pp. 432–447.

Hynes, H. P. 2004. On the Battlefield of Women's Bodies: An Overview of the Harm of War to Women. In *Women's Studies International Forum*, vol. 27, pp. 431–445, http://www.sciencedirect.com/science/article/pii/S0277539504000457 (retrieved September 19, 2012).

Hyun-Kyung, C. 2000. Your Comfort versus My Death. In *War's Dirty Secret: Rape, Prostitution and Other Crimes against Women*. Cleveland: Pilgrim Press, pp. 13–25.

Jackson, D., and K. Payne. 2003. *Twa Women, Twa Rights in the Great Lakes Region of Africa*. Minority Rights Group International, London, http://www.chr.up.ac.za/chr_old/indigenous/documents/Uganda/Themes/Gender%20Equality/Report%20on%20Twa%20Women.pdf (retrieved September 21, 2012).

Johnson, Kirsten, Jennifer Scott, Bigy Rughita, Michael Kisielewski, Jana Asher, Ricardo Ong, and Lynn Lawry. 2010. Association of Sexual Violence and Human Rights Violations with Physical and Mental Health in Territories of the Eastern Democratic Republic of the Congo. *Journal of the American Medical Association* 304 (5): 553–562.

Juma, L. 2007. "Shadow Networks" and Conflict Resolution in the Great Lakes Region of Africa. *African Security Studies* 16 (1): 1–17, http://www.tandfonline.com/doi/abs/10.1080/10246029.2007.9627630 (retrieved September 21, 2012).

Kalisya, Luc Malemo, Paluku Lussy Justin, Christophe Kimona, Kavira Nyavandu, Kamabu Mukekulu Eugenie, Kasereka Muhindo Lusi Jonathan, Kasereka Masumbuko Claude, and Michael Hawkes. 2011. Sexual Violence toward Children and Youth in War-Torn Eastern Democratic Republic of Congo. *PloS One* 6 (1): e15911.

Kang, Hyun Yi. 2003. Conjuring "Comfort Women": Mediated Affiliations and Disciplined Subjects in Korean/American Transnationality. *Journal of Asian American Studies* 6 (1): 25–55, http://muse.jhu.edu/journals/journal

_of_asian_american_studies/v006/6.1kang.html (retrieved September 30, 2012).

Kippenberg, J. 2009. Soldiers Who Rape, Commanders Who Condone: Sexual Violence and Military Reform in the Democratic Republic of Congo. Human Rights Watch, http://books.google.com/books?hl=en&lr=&id=E7IJz0P U3jwC&oi=fnd&pg=PA1&dq=Soldiers+Who+Rape,+Commanders+Wh o+Condone&ots=fc6RrM_tHG&sig=0eMfKiic7KejcLoHm1RvVXcwWYE (retrieved September 21, 2012).

Kumar, K., and D. Millwood. 1996. Rebuilding Post-War Rwanda. Steering Committee of the Joint Aviation of Emergency Assistance to Rwanda, http://www .grandslacs.net/doc/0744.pdf (retrieved September 21, 2012).

Leatherman, J. L. 2011. Sexual Violence and Armed Conflict. Polity, http://books. google.com/books?hl=en&lr=&id=xkHOsFgV9BEC&oi=fnd&pg=PR1&d q=Leatherman+2011+women+inequality&ots=X_ffzdW4AL&sig=Pi2kwu gFfp1vfzlXpUgiQyY4R-Q (retrieved September 29, 2012).

Mills, E. J., S. Singh, B. D. Nelson, and J. B. Nachega. 2006. The Impact of Conflict on HIV/AIDS in Sub-Saharan Africa. *International Journal of STD & AIDS* 17 (11): 713–717, http://ijsa.rsmjournals.com/content/17/11/713.short (retrieved September 21, 2012).

Morgan, H. J. 1994. Theater of War: Combat, the Military, and Masculinities. In *Theorizing Masculinities*, edited by Harry Brod and Michael Kaufman. Thousand Oaks, CA: Sage Publications, pp. 165–182.

Morris, M. 1995. By Force of Arms: Rape, War, and Military Culture. *Duke Law Journal* 45: 651, http://heinonlinebackup.com/hol-cgi-bin/get_pdf.cgi? handle=hein.journals/duklr45&section=27 (retrieved September 21, 2012).

Mukamana, Donatilla, and Petra Brysiewicz. 2008. The Lived Experience of Genocide Rape Survivors in Rwanda. *Journal of Nursing Scholarship* 40 (4): 379–384, http://onlinelibrary.wiley.com/doi/10.1111/j.1547-5069.2008.00253.x/ abstract (retrieved September 30, 2012).

Mukwege, D. M., O. Mohamed-Ahmed, and J. R. Fitchett. 2010. Rape as a Strategy of War in the Democratic Republic of the Congo. *International Health* 2 (3): 163–164, http://www.sciencedirect.com/science/article/pii/S187634 1310000446 (retrieved September 21, 2012).

Palmero, Tia, and Amber Peterman. 2011. Undercounting, Overcounting and the Longevity of Flawed Estimates: Statistics on Sexual Violence in Conflict. *Bulletin of the World Health Organization* 89 (12): 924–925, http://www.who.int/ bulletin/volumes/89/12/11-089888.pdf (retrieved September 29, 2012).

Peterman, Amber, Tia Palermo, and Caryn Bredenkamp. 2011. Estimates and Determinants of Sexual Violence against Women in the Democratic Republic of Congo. *American Journal of Public Health* 101 (6): 1060–1067.

Prunier, G. 2011. *Africa's World War: Congo, the Rwandan Genocide, and the Making of a Continental Catastrophe.* New York: Oxford University Press, http:// books.google.com/books?hl=en&lr=&id=kp93kUfdhC0C&oi=fnd&pg=P R5&dq=women+rape+war+congo&ots=mpV-FZh8AW&sig=T08sfQtrvdS 5dGZWOOEaJmYk6BQ (retrieved September 19, 2012).

Puechguirbal, N. 2003. Women and War in the Democratic Republic of the Congo. *Signs* 28 (4): 1271–1281, http://www.jstor.org/stable/10.1086/368319 (retrieved September 19, 2012).

Rehn, E., and J. Sirleaf. 2002. *Women, War, Peace*. United Nations Development Fund for Women, http://147.96.1.15/info/ucmp/cont/descargas/documento7201.pdf (retrieved September 19, 2012).

Russell-Brown, S. L. 2003. Rape as an Act of Genocide. *Berkeley Journal of International Law* 21: 350, http://heinonlinebackup.com/hol-cgi-bin/get_pdf .cgi?handle=hein.journals/berkjintlw21&section=21 (retrieved September 30, 2012).

Sajor, I. L., ed. 1998. *Common Grounds: Violence against Women in War and Armed Conflict Situations*. Quezon City, Philippines: Asian Center for Women's Human Rights.

Shanks, Leslie, and Michael J. Schull. 2000. Rape in War: The Humanitarian Response. *CMAJ: Canadian Medical Association Journal* 163 (9): 1152–1156, http://www.ncbi.nlm.nih.gov/pmc/articles/PMC80250/ (retrieved September 21, 2012).

Sharlach, L. 2000. Rape as Genocide: Bangladesh, the Former Yugoslavia, and Rwanda. *New Political Science* 22 (1): 89–102, http://www.tandfonline. com/doi/abs/10.1080/713687893 (retrieved September 21, 2012).

Shepherd, Laura J. 2007. "Victims, Perpetrators and Actors" Revisited: 1 Exploring the Potential for a Feminist Reconceptualisation of (International) Security and (Gender) Violence. *British Journal of Politics & International Relations* 9 (2): 239–56.

Skjelsbæk, Inger. 2001. Is Femininity Inherently Peaceful? The Construction of Femininity in War. In *Gender, Peace, and Conflict*, edited by Inger Skjelsbaek and Dan Smith. Oslo: International Peace Research Institute; London: Sage, pp. 47–67.

Sow, N. 2006. Gender and Conflict Transformation in the Great Lakes Region of Africa. *International Alert Report*, http://www.glow-boell.de/media/de/ txt_rubrik_2/Ndeye_Sow_FGmai6.pdf (retrieved September 21, 2012).

Spiegel, Paul B., Anne Rygaard Bennedsen, Johanna Claass, Laurie Bruns, Njogu Patterson, Dieudonne Yiweza, and Marian Schilperoord. 2007. Prevalence of HIV Infection in Conflict-Affected and Displaced People in Seven Sub-Saharan African Countries: A Systematic Review. *Lancet* 369 (9580): 2187–2195.

Stern, Maria, and Malin Nystrand. 2006. *Gender and Armed Conflict*. Stockholm: Sida. http://www.sida.se/contentassets/bc275fc0cb754d469e546b449a0807bd/ gender-and-armed-conflict_1689.pdf

Stiglmayer, Alexandra. *Mass Rape: The War against Women in Bosnia-Herzegovina*. Lincoln: University of Nebraska Press, 1994.

Swiss, Shana, and Joan E. Giller. 1993. Rape as a Crime of War: A Medical Perspective. *Jama* 270 (5): 612–15.

Taylor, A., and J. B. Miller. 1994. *Conflict and Gender*. Cresskill, NJ: Hampton Press.

Turshen, M., C. Twagiramariya, et al. 1998. *What Women Do in Wartime: Gender and Conflict in Africa*. London: Zed Books, http://www.cabdirect.org/ abstracts/19981805198.html (retrieved September 21, 2012).

United Nations–ICTY. n.d. Crime of Violence, http://www.icty.org/sid/10312 (accessed April 7, 2014).

United Nations News Centre. n.d. New UN Statistics Show Alarming Rise in Rapes in Strife-Torn Eastern DR Congo, http://www.un.org/apps/news/story.asp?NewsID=45529#.Uy8V1eddV7E

United Nations News Service. 2010, April 27. Tackling Sexual Violence Must Include Prevention, Ending Impunity—UN Official. *UN News Service Section*, http://www.un.org/apps/news/story.asp?NewsID=34502#.Uwd-oUJdVhU

United Nations News Service. 2011a. UN News—DR Congo Mass Rape Verdicts Send Strong Signal to Perpetrators—UN Envoy. *UN News Service Section*, http://www.un.org/apps/news/story.asp?NewsID=37580&Cr=sexual%20violence&Cr1=#.UGbcmHORti4 (retrieved September 29, 2012).

United Nations News Service. 2011b. UN News—DR Congo: UN Report Details Suffering of Rape Victims, Recommends Reparations. *UN News Service Section*, http://www.un.org/apps/news/story.asp?NewsID=37672&Cr=&Cr1=#.UGbcSnORti4 (retrieved September 29, 2012).

United Nations News Service. 2012. UN News—Interview with Margot Wallström, Special Representative on Sexual Violence in Conflict. *UN News Service Section*, http://www.un.org/apps/news/newsmakers.asp?NewsID=55#.UGbcwnORti4 (retrieved September 29, 2012).

Urwin, G., and J. Stearns. 2011. Dancing in the Glory of Monsters: The Collapse of the Congo and the Great War of Africa. PublicAffairs, http://books.google.com/books?hl=en&lr=&id=2jfKMaQmqnoC&oi=fnd&pg=PP8&dq=rape+great+lake+africa&ots=65zTpEJxck&sig=iITzlGVyxiT5lQikg6EJ4V-a-yA (retrieved September 21, 2012).

Voice of America. n.d. DRC Army Integrates Over 6,000 Rebels, VOA. http://www.voanews.com/content/a-13-2009-01-29-voa59-68795517/361109.html (retrieved September 29, 2012).

Wakabi, W. 2008. Sexual Violence Increasing in Democratic Republic of Congo. *Lancet* 371 (9606): 15–16, http://www.lancet.com/journals/lancet/article/PIIS0140-6736(08)60051-3 (retrieved September 19, 2012).

Warrilow, F. 2008. The Right to Learn: Batwa Education in the Great Lakes Region of Africa. Minority Rights Group International, http://www.ecoi.net/file_upload/1002_1229179469_mrg-batwa.pdf (retrieved September 21, 2012).

Whitworth, Sandra. 2004. *Men, Militarism, and UN Peacekeeping: A Gendered Analysis*. Lynne Rienner Publishers.

Wood, E. J. 2006. Variation in Sexual Violence During War. *Politics & Society* 34 (3): 307–342, http://pas.sagepub.com/content/34/3/307.short (retrieved September 21, 2012).

Wood, S. K. 2004. A Woman Scorned for the Least Condemned War Crime: Precedent and Problems with Prosecuting Rape as a Serious War Crime in the International Criminal Tribunal for Rwanda. *Columbia Journal of Gender & Law* 13: 274, http://heinonlinebackup.com/hol-cgi-bin/get_pdf.cgi?handle=hein.journals/coljgl13&section=13 (retrieved September 21, 2012).

Yodanis, Carrie L. 2004. Gender Inequality, Violence against Women, and Fear: A Cross-National Test of the Feminist Theory of Violence against Women. *Journal of Interpersonal Violence* 19 (6): 655–675, http://jiv.sagepub.com/content/19/6/655 (retrieved September 29, 2012).

Zabeida, Natalja. 2010. Not Making Excuses: Functions of Rape as a Tool in Ethno-
       Nationalist Wars. In *Women, War, and Violence: Persona Perspectives and
       Global Activism*, edited by Robin M. Chandler, Lihua Wang, and Linda K.
       Fuller. New York: Palgrave Macmillan, pp. 17–30.
Zraly, Maggie, and Laetitia Nyirazinyoye. 2010. Don't Let the Suffering Make
       You Fade Away: An Ethnographic Study of Resilience among Survivors
       of Genocide-Rape in Southern Rwanda. *Social Science & Medicine* 70 (10):
       1656–1664.

CHAPTER 13

Women's Roles in Everyday Armed Violence and Cease-Fire Pacts in a Caracas Barrio

Manuel Llorens, Verónica Zubillaga, and John Souto

VIOLENCE IN THE INNER-CITY BARRIOS[1] OF CARACAS

Lethal violence has grown progressively in Venezuela during the last two decades, reaching rates that put it among the deadliest countries in the world. In 1998 the country had a rate of 20 homicides for every 100,000 inhabitants, and by 2011 that rate had grown to 50 for every 100,000 (Sanjuán, 2012). Caracas in particular appears to be one of the most dangerous cities in the world, with a homicide rate 10 times higher than that of Mexico City or Sao Paolo (UNODC, 2011). A large part of this violence occurs among young armed males, mostly in what is called *la culebra* (the snake) in slang in the context of Caracas's barrios. It is a term often applied to the *enemy* and *the situation of conflict that is settled with death*, and that is prolonged in a chain of revenge and of more deaths. Young, disempowered men are the main victims and perpetrators of armed violence.[2] But *la culebra* is only a result of the concomitant environment pervaded by a chronic lack of justice, the evident police corruption, the lack of opportunities for youth when they grow up, and the widespread, uncontrolled availability of handguns, all of which characterize the lethal violence nowadays experienced in Caracas.

Indeed, the widespread presence of lethal weapons in youths' immediate environments and the dynamics of armed violence in their communities produce a sense of complete helplessness, as we have pointed out elsewhere (see Zubillaga, 2009). Very early in their lives, youths incorporate the sense of living in a world of pure antagonism, where the strongest one rules. In this context, in order to survive, it becomes necessary for them to arm themselves and become personal vigilantes in their territories (Zubillaga, 2009). They are responding to the extremely inhospitable social conditions in which they grow up, where tens of thousands are involved in a dynamic of armed violence (Wacquant, 2007). In this sense *la culebra* is a result of state abandonment and the associated widespread availability of guns.

We have been working as community psychologists and researchers in a Caracas barrio named *Catuche* for more than three years, researching a cease-fire achieved by what have been called "peace commissions" formed by groups of women who belong to two rival sectors (each with its corresponding group of armed youths) whose chronic state of armed conflictivity had produced more than a hundred murders over the years. The cease-fire is significant for many reasons. Its effectiveness (it has held up for six years without any homicides); the fact that it was a mobilization issued, proposed, and set up by the community; it shines as a contrast to a city that has become more and more violent; and finally, it was generated by the work of a group of women.

The women—mostly mothers, but also sisters, cousins, aunts, and grandmothers of the young men involved in armed confrontations—called out for a cease-fire and organized themselves to set up a series of negotiated agreements that have transformed this community. The relevance of these events led us to form a long research relationship with the community; the complexity of the dimensions that form the dynamics of this everyday armed violence and the cease-fire has continued to demand our attention.

In this chapter we will try to reflect upon the roles women play in the dynamics of violence in this inner-city barrio in Caracas, as well as the impact it has had on their lives. Indeed, the effects of this social urban violence on women's lives and the role women play in these dynamics are two questions that are as yet unanswered in the scholarship (Gay, 2005; Koonings and Veenstra, 2007). So we ask, how have they, as mothers, resisted—and at the same time contributed to—the reproduction of violence in their neighborhoods?

EVERYDAY ARMED VIOLENCE AND ITS EFFECTS

As mentioned before, violence has continually grown in Venezuela during the last two decades. This is reflected in Catuche, where reports of violence date back to the early 1980s but acquire larger dimensions in the 1990s, leading up to the state of complete warfare that prompted the creation of the comissions of Convivencia.[3]

Catuche is a barrio that stretches along one of Caracas's many brooks. Caracas is in a valley surrounded by mountains that form many small rivers and creeks. In a populated city these brooks have many times served as the vacant space where poor city dwellers build their improvised ranchos[4] and where many impoverished slums began. Catuche has the particularity of occupying the beds of a small river that runs through the central area of Caracas, very close to the city center and the main government buildings.

This barrio, like all others, is divided in geographical sectors. These sectors tend to create strong bonds and a sense of identity among their members. In this case two neighboring sectors, Portillo and La Quinta, lodge two small communities, each with approximately 100 families. Between the youngsters of these two sectors a rivalry began many years ago, one that led to a continuous armed confrontation that has produced many deaths.

In interviews with members of each sector many painful deaths of loved ones are recalled, many close encounters with death are described. For example, Elisa told us, "seven cousins from my family were murdered, two of my aunt's boys were murdered on the same day, at the same time . . . one was 19 and the other 23 and two twin brothers of my uncle."

The great majority of these homicides were results of the ongoing armed conflict between the groups of young men of these respective sectors, which produced not only death, but a constant state of uneasiness that directly affected everyday life. Public spaces became part of the battleground, making it difficult to circulate freely; explicit lines were established that delineated territories; relationships were altered; a state of constant danger became part of the necessary planning of daily routines; and loss and fear became parts of everyday life. Virginia told us:

They meet up in the plaza and boom-boom! Shots, they killed each other . . . you couldn't live here in those times, you couldn't sleep; you'd come home from work and had to check: "are there shots or not?". It was horrible. My house is full of gunshots, the windows too. My roof is made of zinc[5] so I was terrified that the bullets would fall inside. Every time the kids went out, someone got shot here or there. That was driving me crazy, you couldn't go in and out of your house . . . I was angry that nobody did anything.

In the women's narratives the emotional scars of violence were evident. The interviewees presented the symptoms described in other populations severely traumatized by armed conflicts, such as a hypervigilance, constant startling, anxiety, rumination on feelings of pain and rage, re-experiencing the traumatic episodes, time collapse, perpetual mourning, and unresolved loss (Volkan, 1997; Volkan, 2004; Volkan, 2006).

Often, the recalling of painful episodes triggered a series of emotional responses that blurred the possibility of organizing the experience in time, as tends to happen in post-traumatic states. For example, after one of those conversations, Nancy told us, "It's like it were happening all over again, what we lived in those times." And Virginia replied, "In my home everybody says, 'Virginia is screwed,' because I remember all the time, the anniversary of each death."

Significantly enough, when we tried to organize the episodes into a time frame, it was hard to establish a timeline. When recalling the dates of different events of the community life, the women identified as the main reference points either the birth dates of their children or the dates of significant murders.

The confrontation dates back at least two decades. In the 1980s some of the women interviewed described their relationships with an armed gang from one of the sectors. They spoke of the gang with nostalgia, remembering their friendship with many of the young men, now disappeared: either dead or in jail. Not only were they described as friends, but also as "Robin Hood" types who had helped to "protect" their sector from dangerous outsiders (Hobsbawn, 1965).[6] But when they described the dynamics of violence in their neighborhoods a big difference was emphasized: the confrontations of the 1970s and early 1980s were mainly fistfights; from the 1990s onward, the proliferation of guns and heavier arms had significantly altered the intensity and lethality of the confrontations.

Curiously enough, none of the community members interviewed, neither women nor men, could pinpoint the beginning of the confrontation. Different episodes and dates were mentioned by all. Some spoke of the beginning of the 1990s, but older members remembered the murders of family members dating back to the beginning of the 1980s. A violent rivalry with the other sector was described as an inevitable path to fatality, despite the absence of any concrete reason for its beginning. Through the years however, an accumulation of loss and trauma brought on by the aggressions of the young men from the other sector marked a seemingly unalterable direction.

THE PEACE COMMISSIONS

Catuche is also noteworthy for its history of local organization. A web made up of community residents and university and religious organizations has developed groups of community intervention in different areas—such as housing, family counseling, and children's education—that have had a significant impact through the years.[7] A number of women were active in these processes and consider these experiences to be very significant in their lives. When recalling these efforts one of the women told us:

The emotion, because first of all, I never imagined that I was going to own an apartment in my own barrio. And I used to say: "when is that husband of mine going to buy me a house, my God, when am I going to be able to get out of here!" . . . I wanted to live in some decent place, because I was afraid of living in the slums. . . . What convinced me was that they didn't come to talk about politics, they didn't talk to me about that, it was something spontaneous, they showed you the project, how the buildings were going to be.

The women spoke of the terrible deprivation of their original houses, which lacked running water (which they took from the contaminated brook), electricity, space, and safety. As in the quotation above, they speak of their hopes of living decently and attribute the possibility of attaining such a life to the efforts of their men. But the community process made many of the women protagonists of their own change and fostered in them a hope for a better life.

We believe that this experience of transforming life conditions, the strengthening of the web of collaborative relationships, and the community organizations that helped to lead these efforts are important antecedents to the creation of the Peace Commission.

There had been numerous attempts throughout the years to resist violence in Catuche. Protest marches and previous accords had been implemented without any significant results. In August 2007 armed confrontation had once again reached a climax, when a large group of young men of La Quinta searching for a youngster, in an act of revenge, assaulted Portillo during the night. The women of Portillo described the episode:

We thought we were going to die that day.

Barbara: Exactly, I thought that they were going to kick down my door and enter and kill everybody because it was ugly, let's be real, I think even the bravest peed in their pants. All the mothers had to take their children under their beds.

The shootings went on all night, until the 18-year-old they were looking for was found and murdered.

But something significant happened afterward. In the midst of her pain, the mother of the slain boy called on the other women of her sector and pleaded to convince the young men of her own community not to seek revenge for the death of her son. Instead she asked to lay the grounds to protect her only son who remained alive (the 18-year-old was her second son to be shot dead) and to speak with the neighboring sector to plead for a truce. She recalled:

I was at the funeral and said to myself: "This can't go on! We don't need no police, we have to fight ourselves! I'm gonna do it! I'm gonna do it! We can't allow any more deaths." And my son was buried and he didn't have one month dead when I came here and told my older sister: "Damn it, we can't continue like this, we have to fight! Let's talk to Doris! Let's speak at Fe y Alegría and see what they tell us."

Her act defied the chain of revenges. Her plea had an impact on the women of the neighboring sector. Through the mediation and contacts made by Doris, the community activist who worked at the community center of Fe y Alegría, the women of both sectors agreed to a meeting. It was the first meeting with women from the warring sector any of them remembered during their lives.

Significantly, when the young men of La Quinta were asked about the possibility of meeting with the women of the neighboring sector to talk, they responded, "You don't need to talk with us, you need to talk with the gossiping old hags." This expression, which can have many interpretations, implies, among other things, that the women play an important part in the dynamics of violence. Gossips and rumors are mentioned time and again as a significant piece of the logic of violence. When one youngster is singled out by the rumors to have offended a member of the neighborhood, the men are called on to execute revenge. The women took this answer at face value, and unlike in previous attempts to stop the violence, the accords were made not directly with the youngsters, but between the two groups of mothers.

The first meeting was set up. As a symbolic act, the women of Portillo were met by the women of La Quinta in the middle of the path that unites the two sectors and they walked together up to the community center of Fe y Alegría. Doris and Yaneth, the two community activists of the center, organized the meeting with a predefined order of communications. Along with the two groups of mothers and the two community activists, two men with a history of community work were part of the meeting. The group's first gesture was to hold hands and pray together. Then the women began to speak of their personal experiences. The stories of fear and pain for their lost friends and relatives were shared. One of the women of La Quinta told us:

We thought that they were coming to fight. . . . We thought that and they did too, and we also thought that if they came here to shout at us we weren't going to let them do it, but first we were going to listen. And the truth is that in the end we came out hugging each other, crying, because we all had the same problem. The same problems that we were living here was what they were living there, like sleeping with the mattress on top, locked in, scared to go out even to buy what you needed, all the same, so the meeting was beautiful after all.

The emotional significance of this meeting continues to have a resonance for those who participated. It had a transformational effect on the participants' lives and on their collective power to stand up against violence. Elisa, who has become an active participant of the commissions, expressed it like this: "I think we hadn't woken up. Before, there was a murder, we buried him, it hurt of course, we wept, we mourned. But that was it, then came another killing and we buried the next one . . . but now we've woken up." It also served to create an agreement about the need to reach a negotiation with the youngsters on both sides and to coordinate efforts toward the implementation of a cease-fire. A peace commission was set up in each community comprised of mothers from each sector. An agreement was worked on and discussed in subsequent meetings until a definitive version was presented by the mothers to the youngsters of their own communities. The agreement was negotiated with them and, when they finally accepted, they were asked to sign the written accords as a symbolic act. The accords include rules such as a prohibition against participating in public acts of defiance against the other community and a prohibition for the youngsters involved in the regular confrontations against crossing into the other sector.

When one of those rules is broken, the commission meets and decides on the consequences. Mainly they summon the youngster to meet with the women and remind them of the importance of the accords, and when they feel the youth "went too far" they threaten that they will report him to the police. On occasions the leaders of their groups are recruited as allies to help enforce the rules.

So the commissions have solidified a tradition of community organization and propelled a group of women to take a stand against violence and to lead a series of agreements and implement a group of procedures that have been very effective in containing a state of violence that had lasted 30 years. The bravery and wisdom of these women have touched a chord in the wider society and they have become a symbol of resistance to gun violence in the country. Their testimony has begun to appear in the media (Barrios, 2013a; Barrios, 2013b; González, 2010; Mosegue, 2011).

A LEGACY OF VIOLENCE

Our research allowed us to register the powerful testimony of Catuche but has also allowed us to deepen our understanding of the complexities of the process, showing not only the stupendous achievements of the commissions, but also the ambiguous nature of the resistance to violence and the evident precariousness of the agreement due to the extremely harsh conditions in which the people live and the lethal violence that pervades Caracas's daily life.

It is useful to understand some of the dynamics of the armed confrontation that we heard about in Catuche, which, as research on violence has suggested, are framed in terms of stereotypical gendered notions. In particular we suggest that the notion of *respect*, related to masculinity, reflects many of the arguments the young men and the women interviewed employed to explain the reasons for the violence they are engulfed in.

Researchers from different latitudes have described persistent violent conflicts in different regions based on "cultures of honor," where the value of masculinity depends on defending one's honor, when at stake, at any costs. In regions where there are territorial conflicts and an absence of the rule of law, it is common to find violent conflict handed down through generations of men (Cohen et al., 1996; Bosson et al., 2009; Vandello et al., 2008). Similarly, Bourgoise (2010) and Sennet (2003) have described how respect becomes an essential value for inner-city young men who are excluded from other sources of recognition and how violence can become the way to defend and get respect.[8]

The same has been described in Venezuela by researchers who have recorded life stories of young males involved in violent lifestyles[9] (Zubillaga, 2005; Zubillaga and Briceño-León, 2001). Their lives of economic and social exclusion underline a precariousness of self-worth that makes social recognition scarce (Sennet, 2003; Hardy and Lasloffy, 2005). We found this to be true in Catuche. The young men of one sector, for example, complained in one interview that the youngsters of the other sector passed through their territory at any time they pleased, and that that made them look dumb and weak. They were ambivalent about continuing to avoid violence because they risked being seen as wimps and losers by others.

But even though these cultural imperatives are heavily centered on men's relationships, women also play an important part. We found that women spoke ambivalently about men's violent actions.

When speaking of the past in one group interview, for example, the women from one of the peace commissions spoke with longing about their youth and the male friends of a gang they hung out with. María said:

They took care of this. And we were always playing with them. . . . They took their drugs and had their guns and all that, but the respect we had for them was so high that sometimes they were caught right here in the barrio [by the police]—and we went out to defend them, and we hid them because those were gente![10] Even though they had their problems outside, they took care of us.

In the other sector, the women told us how they helped to stash the guns and firepower of the young men. On one occasion, facing the imminent threat represented by the young armed men from the neighboring sector, amidst their helplessness they spent days helping the youths from their own sector to build Molotov bombs; they felt it was the only way to defend themselves from their neighbors, and the young males were the only ones doing anything to protect them.

Gender dynamics were evident in the logic that led to much of the violence. The women we interviewed not only complained often of the machismo and violence of the men, but at the same time appealed to those codes when looking to confront a youngster. Doris, the community activist at Fe y Alegría, is a very effective communicator who often had to organize, invite, mediate, challenge, and confront the youngsters and the women to advance negotiations of conflicts. When confronting young men, she usually rebuked them, telling them to "act like a real man" or not to "behave like a whore."

So even though the women suffered from the violence and even though they weren't the protagonists of it, they participated indirectly and supported violence through their actions and their consent. The reasons for this are multiple and layered. First of all, the conditions of poverty, exclusion, lack of opportunities for the youth and chronic lack of justice play a part. Inhabitants of Catuche have had little access to public services in general, but their relationship with the police and the justice system has been particularly traumatic. In our interviews the lack of access to justice was dramatic, as were the episodes of police brutality witnessed and suffered by the women. It seems that when the police appeared, they were more of a menace than a solution to the threats the youths faced (Zubillaga et al., 2013).

The growing presence of guns in the community has helped to magnify the lethality of the confrontations, the fear, and the need to find some sort of protection. The lack of access to decent jobs and income operates as a basic material condition that opens the gate for the acceptance of drug trafficking and other illegal activities. The progressive and continuous exposure to violence seems to have naturalized it, turning it into something inevitable that you just have to try to avoid but that is impossible to end.

TRAUMATIC TRANS-GENERATIONAL TRANSMISSION

Along with the state's dereliction in pacification (Wacquant, 2007), the chronic lack of justice that fosters the cycle of violent revenge implied in *la culebra*, and the constant presence of weapons, the emotional consequences of repeated violent losses is, we believe, a significant piece of the puzzle.

The tracks of loss and trauma were all over our conversations. We often spoke about the pain of the violent losses of their children and brothers. Indeed, the women spoke of the losses of young men as a shared grief. María put it this way:

Look, sometimes we speak about one's children, because we have lost our children, but one is also in grief for the other kids because you saw them grow, we shared with them and then it also hurts the same. Sure, it's not the same pain like the mother's pain, but we have also cried all those deaths, as they have also mourned the death of our children. We have shared the pain. The one who has lost a child knows what it is like, the one who hasn't, doesn't, and may God release him from knowing. Because right now it is the contrary, now we the mothers we bury our children, and that is not what it should be. Sons should bury their mothers and that's the way it should be. These are truly hard moments we shared and we have cried together and suddenly we have laughed remembering things from their childhood. You know what I mean? But it was not easy for us to get through this.

Dozens of exchanges were about the violent events that led to someone's death or their personal close encounter with it. The trauma of violence was greatly increased by their experience during the floods of 1999 that devastated Catuche. Many lost their homes and survived life-threatening times.

As mentioned in the section on the emotional consequences of violence, the conversations where the women talked about traumatic episodes were recurrent. For example, it was common for them to say afterward, "It's as if I were reliving it again right now, as if time had not passed." This symptom of the traumatic reliving of the experience, along with a host of other ones, was evident and turned many of our encounters into moments to share and reflect back on sadness, fear, and rage.

We found much of what researchers such as Volkan (1997) have described as the traumatic sequelae common in social groups that have survived war or violent persecution, which include hyperarousal, increased group cohesion and increased identification with the in-group, and "fight or flight" response, which lead to an "us versus them" polarized perception. Volkan speaks of an "ethnic tent" with an increased sense of we-ness as common among groups who have been severely threatened. Group loyalty also increases, and small symbolic facts that differentiate the in-group from their neighbors become all too important.

Some of the more difficult aspects of the emotional consequences of these violent deaths of loved ones are the rage and hate they produce and the fact that these emotions are too much to bear in the absence of justice or other modes of coping with this grief (Rosaldo, 2004). In one group interview, after a few mothers mentioned how they have empathy for the women of the other sector, Virginia burst out, saying:

It's a lie that I cared that they killed that other kid, God forgive me, but they didn't care either. What did one of the thugs that killed Milagros,[11] a girl only eight years old, say? He said that the kid shouldn't have been on the street waiting for bullets at that hour. That's what he said. Or am I wrong? They didn't care about our pain, so we don't care about their pain. Let's be clear about this, we're in this now because yeah, thank God, but this is bullshit! I don't kid myself, I see things as they are, because that's how they are!

Her comment was enlightening: she dared to say what the other women might also be struggling with but didn't dare speak of, at least to us. They preferred to talk about how the commissions had brought peace and how they had worked to eradicate violence. But until then they had not talked about the grudges they continued to hold against those who had murdered their loved ones. They had felt inhumanely treated by life in general and specifically by the members of the other sector, and they consequently responded with hate and rage. The victimization suffered was upheld as proof that entitled their sector to avenge their pain. A competition over who has been hurt more often arises, and a list of grievances is made that forges what Volkan has called the "egoism of victimization" (2006). When these feelings came up, empathy was impossible and the dehumanization of the other was a common result.

Borders, territory, and minor differences, explains Volkan (2004), tend to become all important in social groups in conflict and faced with a sense of threat: "psycho-spatial borders and other tangible distinctions assume a new intensity of symbolic significance" (p. 73). The lines drawn to separate the sectors were emphasized by Virginia, as she described the ways she taught the children of her sector to maintain an allegiance to their group and an antagonism toward the other one:

OK we have peace, we don't want any trouble, but it's not like we're going to get together with them because there are deaths on both sides. It's not like we're going to live together, right? That's what I've told the kids over and over again so they understand what is what. We don't want any more deaths, let them go out, pass through their sector, but it's not like we're going to live together.

The pain the men and women had gone through was evident every time we talked about the past. Their struggles with unresolved loss came up again and again. As Virginia mentions in the quote above, these feelings are passed on to the children. Volkan (1997) defines trans-generational transmission as occurring

when an older person unconsciously externalizes his traumatized self onto a developing child's personality. A child then becomes a reservoir for the unwanted, troublesome parts of an older generation. Because the elders have influence on the child, the child absorbs their wishes and expectations and is driven to act on them. It becomes the child's task to mourn, to reverse the humiliation and feelings of helplessness pertaining to the trauma of his forebears. (p. 43)

Perpetual mourning is present in Catuche, the wounds of violent conflict continue to influence family and intergroup relationships, and the rage of impunity leaves the hurt unresolved.

Volkan (1997) also describes how each side of a violent conflict tends to create its own version of how it has been victimized, which then entitles them to act to restore their honor. These stories of *chosen traumas* generally leave out or minimize each group's responsibility in the violence, and these stories serve as powerful symbols of identification through which allegiances, a sense of entitlement to revenge, and group values are passed on to younger generations.

It seems meaningful that the women's traumatic conversations tended to be about their losses and victimization. On occasions the women spoke of the difficulties of handling their sons or nephews when they misbehaved. But hardly any mention was made of the severe violence committed by some of their youngsters. On one occasion, Virginia came late to the community center and asked to talk to one member of our team—one of the researchers who is a psychologist. It was evident she had drunk too much rum. She began to speak about her fears, about the way she felt concerning the fact that she had the power to condemn somebody just by speaking harshly about her or him to her son, a respected drug dealer in the barrio who won't hesitate to use his gun. She talked about the burden of having to deal with her son's violent lifestyle. But it was on these marginal occasions that we had a glimpse into the experience of guilt. We believe that it is a particularly difficult emotional issue and that the impossibility of tolerating that guilt and the consequences of looking at one's sector's own responsibility is part of the cycle that keeps the pain unresolved.

THE ASCENDANCE OF MOTHERS

It is undoubtedly noteworthy that in the midst of a historic confrontation that has left so much bereavement, the women were capable of leading a process that consolidated a truce. It is almost ironic that a violence perpetrated and sustained by men has been undone and negotiated away by the women. We argue that it is crucial to understand the place of gender, in this case women specifically in their role of mothers, in the dynamics of violence in Catuche and the ways they contribute to reproduce violence as well as their strength in negotiating a peaceful coexistence. We also believe that the same structural and cultural conditions that sustained the dynamics of violence are, in some ways, also present in the dynamics that made the commissions possible, and that these conditions continue to be present and therefore continue to create tensions that could again lead to violence.

As mentioned before, when word got around to the young men of La Quinta that Andrea, the mother of the young man murdered in Portillo, had called upon the women of her sector and pleaded not for revenge but to go up to the other sector to talk, they answered, "They don't need to talk to us, they need to talk to the *viejas chismosas.*"[12] So the petition to talk was delivered to the women of La Quinta and not to the men. It was then that the women, specifically the mothers, took on the challenge to listen, talk, and negotiate a series of agreements that led to the creation of the Commissions of Convivencia.

Motherhood has been studied in depth as a particularly revered role in Latin-American culture (McLean et al., 1995; Fuller, 1995). In Venezuela, in particular, the idealization of the mother has been studied by anthropologists and social psychologists (Vethencourt, 1974; Hurtado, 1998; Moreno et al., 1998). Vethencourt (1974) coined the term "matricentrada," or "mother-centered," to describe the central role motherhood has in constructing identities and relationships in the Venezuelan family. In a patriarchal culture, where women clearly have less access to power, motherhood is a route to a place of recognition and a sense of power, at least in the intimate sphere. In life stories Moreno and his team (Moreno et al., 1998; Moreno and Luna, 2002) have described how motherhood becomes the central reference for organizing life experience, not only for the women but also for men.

This is consistent with our findings in Catuche. For example, Jairo, one of the most renowned drug dealers in the barrio, is described as defending his mother over everything else. When she appears and slaps him in public, he bows his head. Even though the codes of manhood demand that a male save face and defend himself from any aggression, this episode is not considered by anyone to be offensive or an act of cowardliness, but rather a sign that he honors his ties to his mother and is a "man of respect."

Undoubtedly this is a crucial piece that explains how these mothers were able to summon the armed youngsters and convince them to sign an agreement to end the confrontation with the other sector. All heard the plea of the mother in mourning. One youngster clearly expressed how the bond he has with his mother is what allows the commission to have a restraining effect on his behavior: "To tell you the truth, I did this 'cause I respect my momma . . . to be clear, you understand. . . . Because the commission in itself is not something I believe in. . . . I don't support it, you understand?"

Loyalty is a central regulatory mechanism in human relationships. Boszormenyi-Nagi (1973) studied such mechanisms in family functioning. We believe that in a context deprived of institutionalized justice, these mechanisms acquire greater importance. It is through these calls for loyalty and ascendance that a son can feel the need to vindicate his mother's or his community's suffering through violence.

Loyalty is at the heart of the us-them confrontation. When one youngster gets into a problem with the men of the other sector, his friends, as they explained to us in the interviews, feel compelled to come to his defense. Even if their friend was in the wrong, they might complain to him in private, but in public their call is to be loyal to their friend. As one of them told us, "Will gets in trouble and I'm always with Will, his problem is also mine, why? Because I'm not going to leave him, because he is the one who is with me."

Mother-son loyalty is also a prized value. This creates a particularly difficult scenario for the mother when the youngster transgresses a norm outside the house. Her loyalty to her son can push her to protect him unconditionally; to confront him in front of others can be interpreted as disloyalty. But the union of the women has helped to create and sustain new commitments in the community. The commissions have opened up a new possibility. The women mentioned how they identify with each other through their experience of motherhood. The pain of a mother who has lost her son is the pain of all the women, so intensely felt as to have a powerful resonance in the women from the other sector.

The commission unites the ascendance of all the mothers when rebuking a young man who has violated one of the agreements. The women spoke of how they gathered strength from the presence of the other women, even when having to confront their own son. Acting as a group sends a very strong message that is hard to ignore.

When one of the women faces a difficult situation because of an unruly son, she can talk about it at the commission, hear other opinions, and deal with her dilemma through other perspectives. When a youngster transgresses one of the agreements, the commitment to the commission and its goals competes with the code of mother-son loyalty and gives the women strength to establish firm limits. In many cases the women spoke of taking a step aside and letting the rest of the women do the talking. One expressed it in this way:

I acted many times like a neutral party; I'm not going to get into this because my son is the one causing trouble. I had to keep quiet, because I am a part of the commission . . . many times people told me, but you're his mother! But in those moments I'm part of the commission, I'm not his mother; if I acted like his mother I would have had to quit because then it would not make any sense.

It is important to underline that much of the power of these bonds is linked to the affective and caring relationships these women have cultivated with their sons, nephews, and neighboring young men. The women constantly spoke of the affection for the youngsters, even the ones that had grown up to lead violent lifestyles. They remembered their interactions with them when they were young, and they appealed to those ties when trying to speak and negotiate with them. They could speak about them with contempt, but often salvaged the humanity of the intimate moments shared along the way. This emotional bond creates bridges that allowed them to talk to the males even in times of distress. It is what has been called the *ethics of caring*, and we believe it to be crucial in the power they have to appeal to young men who have grown up in exclusion (Lister, 2005). In accordance with feminist relational models of development (Baker Miller et al., 2010; Westkott, 1989), the women of Catuche often describe themselves through their relationships. They value the affective bonds and attachments, constantly referring to relationships to explain their actions.

This approach helps to open space for empathy amidst the apprehension. It also serves to rehumanize them or to counteract the devaluation of the lives of men. Perhaps this element, which may seem subtle, is the most dramatic distinction between the commissions and the formal justice and penal system, which tends to dehumanize and stigmatize these young men and increase the devaluation they have already internalized.

It seems that the relational capacity of the women has been central to the process of working through the emotional sequelae of violence and re-establishing a tender bridge. Even though they still have difficulties dealing with guilt, their ability to listen to the other sector's pain, to register the loss of the other, has been key. In Judith Butler's (2006) words:

Certain faces must be admitted into public view, must be seen and heard for some keener sense of the value of life, all life, to take hold. So, it is not that mourning is the goal of politics, but that without the capacity to mourn, we lose the keener sense of life we need in order to oppose violence. And though, for some, mourning can only be resolved through violence, it seems clear that violence only brings on more loss, and the failure to heed the claim of precarious life only leads, again and again, to the dry grief of endless political rage. (p. xix)

THE FRAILTY OF THE COMMISSIONS

The structural conditions, the cultural dispositions and practices, and the emotional tensions that contributed to breed the violence have not disappeared from Catuche, so the prospects for peaceful coexistence are continually threatened and demand a continuous active resistance. In a recent episode the lack of proper housing prompted a family member from Portillo to invade a space by the brook and start building a shack. But this new home has taken up some of the space of the walkway that unites the sectors, which in turn has made it more difficult for the garbage truck to circulate through Catuche and pick up the garbage. This set off new tensions and disagreements between the women of the communities. Appeals to settle the disagreement through armed confrontations by their sons was mentioned on several occasions. The issue was resolved, but the episode evidenced the frailty of the truce.

The women are faced daily with structural violence, material deprivation, and dangerous situations that require careful handling. The cease-fire seems fragile. Not surprisingly, the women constantly complain of feeling tired and overwhelmed by the scope of the responsibilities and difficulties they have to face. Our close relationship with Doris meant offering a place to voice her anxiety about many of these close encounters with violence and community conflict. Time and again she spent hours sharing with us the details of the most recent episode.

The commissions and the mothers of Catuche serve as a moving testimony to the strength of an active and mobilized community in effectively dealing with violence in a country that seems to be cornered by the amount of guns, the degree of conflict, and the deterioration of the police and the judicial system. But at the same time their experience is problematic.

We feel that it is problematic because it builds on the cultural tendency to lay responsibility for taking care of practically all relational matters dealing with family and community on women's shoulders. The power and reverence of motherhood has a dark side: women are made responsible and left alone to deal with practically all of the family's needs. A big part of the commissions rests on the mothers' actions and disposition to serve as supervisors, mediators, and disciplinarians. This also means they are taking over the responsibilities of the state. One of the most recent episodes involving the commission is that two men have commented on their interest in becoming collaborators. This has been celebrated as good news, but at the same time it has come with rumors and murmured jokes about these two men's sexuality and manhood. The machismo that endorses violence also restricts the possibility of recruiting more men to pursue more caring options, thus leaving women to haul the whole weight on their shoulders.

Not only do these conditions add injustice to the lives of the women of Catuche, they also make the agreements dependent on the energy of a group that often complains of fatigue. The testimony of Catuche can shed light on the dynamics that can help our society rebuild its social fabric, but these actions must be supported by strong institutional response and investment in ameliorating living conditions and, evidently, the state's strong engagement with the pacification of social relations.

ACKNOWLEDGMENTS

The research on which this article is based was conducted with financial support from the Open Society Institute and the Consejo de Desarrollo Científico Humanístico y Tecnológico de la Universidad Católica Andrés Bello. During field work we had the support of Gilda Núñez and, in different periods, Ignacio Lucart, Valentina Larrazabal, and Diana Castellanos.

NOTES

1. Caracas, like many other Latin American cities, arose with notorious divisions within the urban areas, where the middle- and upper-class sectors are settled in the *urbanizaciones* and the poor in the *barrios* (referred to as *favelas* en Brazil and *villamiserias* in Argentina). The latter represent spaces of self-construction and silent struggles where those excluded from wealthier areas attempt to improve life conditions in the midst of relegation (Bayat, 2000). It is estimated that the residents of Rio de Janeiro favelas make up 18.6 percent of the city's population (Koonings and Veenstra, 2007). While Rio's favelas make up one-fifth of the population, in Caracas half of the population live in barrios.

2. This fact and some of the cultural givens that frame these confrontations have been the focus of analysis of local researchers (Zubillaga, 2008; Zubillaga, 2009; Zubillaga and Briceño-León, 2001).

3. *Convivencia* is used more frequently than "peace" in Catuche and, literally meaning "living together," is close to the actual nature of the commissions.

4. It is the name given to the lower-income houses built by the barrio inhabitants.

5.   Sheets of zinc are commonly used to build the roofs in lower-income houses.

6.   According to E. Hobsbawn (1965), the social bandit, whose most classic icon is Robin Hood, is regarded as a benefactor in his community and, hence, enjoys local protection from neighbors—against, for example, the police or their enemies (Hobsbawm, 1965, p. 17). Some of the women we interviewed depicted this image of the benefactor when speaking about this gang, especially with regard to their role as community vigilantes.

7.   These groups have included the "Christian Communities," which are small groups that meet to discuss the Bible. They have been organized by a local Jesuit organization, Fe y Alegría, and they were the starting point of a community process in the 1990s where local problems such as violence and housing began to be addressed and treated as "collective problems" and thus to be solved by community organization. This led, to illustrate the strength of this everyday silent movement, to the creation of the *Consorcio Social Catuche*, which, in alliance with universities and local government, mapped and took a census of the barrio. Then, together, the community, university, and local government built two apartment buildings that replaced many precarious houses (Virtuoso, 2004). This project received the *Premio Nacional de Investigación en Vivienda* (National Prize for Research in Housing) in 1995, and in 1996 it was considered among the 100 best housing practices at the United Nations World Conference on Habitat (Baldó and Villanueva, 1996).

8.   An archeology of the notion of *respect* reveals certain parallelisms with what represented the notion of *honor* in traditional Mediterranean societies. Indeed, honor as an ideal value orients social actions in these societies; it is mostly a request for dignity (Pitt-Rivers, 1965). One aspect that allows us to distance ourselves from the notion of *honor* and prefer that of *respect* (it is also the notion used by young people themselves) is that although the two are associated with a fundamental question, the notion of respect as well as that of honor reveals a subject that claims an estimated value attached to one's personhood in his own eyes and in the eyes of others. However, the subject of *respect* is freed from blood ties; it is not the value of the family lineage that is claimed (as in the honor claim), but the recognition of the autonomous subject (Vidal, 1999). The reputation built, claimed, or defended is not the one of the family group, but that of the individual.

9.   We use the term "violent lifestyles" to refer to youths who are routinely involved in armed confrontations with peers, and who also participate in illegal trafficking networks and/or organized crime. When speaking of a "lifestyle," we refer to a course of action that is related to both *doing* and *being* during a biographical period of time and in certain places. We do not speak of "violent youth," that is, as if they were inherently violent individuals, and this is in order to emphasize the possibility of transformation of lifestyle due the change of social life conditions and the possibility of forging self-existential projects that would allow them to get self- respect and social recognition.

10.   The Spanish expression used is ¡*eran gente!* which literally means "they were people!" and implies that they were humane and worthy of respect.

11.   Milagros was the woman's niece.

12.   *Viejas chismosas*: "the old women who gossip."

BIBLIOGRAPHY

Baker Miller, J., I. Pierce Stiver, J. Jordan, J. Surrey, C. Brooks, and J. Clements. 2010. Enfoques feministas de la teoría de la personalidad. In *Teorías de la Personalidad*, edited by R. Frager and J. Fadiman Mexico City: Alfaomega.

Baldó, J., and F. Villanueva. 1996. La conferencia mundial de las NNUU (Hábitat ii). *Sic*, 587 (59): 292–295.

Barrios, D. 2013a, August. Vecinos de Catuche Frenan el Hampa en Seco: Mujeres toman el bando para evitar refriegas entre bandas. Diario Últimas Noticias, http://www.ultimasnoticias.com.ve/noticias/actualidad/sucesos/video--vecinos-de-catuche-frenan-el-hampa-en-seco.aspx (downloaded on September 15, 2013).

Barrios, D. 2013b, August. La Paz del Sector Catuche Trasciende Fronteras. Diario Últimas Noticias, http://www.ultimasnoticias.com.ve/noticias/ciudad/parroquias/la-paz-del-sector-catuche-trasciende-fronteras.aspx (downloaded September 15, 2013).

Bayat, A. 2000. From Dangerous Classes to Quiet Rebels: Politics of the Urban Subaltern in the Global South. *International Sociology* 15 (3).

Bosson, J., J. Vandello, R. Burnaford, J. Weaver, and A. Watsi. 2009. Precarious Manhood and Displays of Physical Aggression. *Personality and Social Psychology Bulletin* 35: 623–634.

Boszormenyi-Nagi, I., and G. Sparke. 1973. *Invisible Loyalties: Reciprocity in Intergenerational Family Therapy*. New York: Harper Row.

Bourgoise, P. 2010. *En busca de respeto: vendiendo crack en Harlem*. Buenos Aires: Siglo Veintiuno.

Butler, J. 2006. Precarious Life: The Powers of Mourning and Violence. London: Verso.

Cohen, D., R. Nisbett, B. Bowdle, and N. Schwarz. 1996. Insult, Aggression and Southern Culture of Honor: An "Experimental Ethnography." *Journal of Personality and Social Psychology* 70: 945–960.

Fuller, N. 1995. Acerca de la polaridad marianismo machismo. In *Lo Femenino y lo Masculino: Estudios Sociales sobre las Identidades de Género en América Latina*, edited by G. Arango and M. Viveros. Bogota: Ediciones UniAndes, Universidad Nacional de Bogotá.

Gay, R. 2005. *Lucía. Testimonies of a Brazilian Drug Dealer's Woman*. Philadelphia: Temple University Press.

González, D. 2010, April 11. Escudo contra la violencia. *El Nacional-Siete Días*. Caracas, pp. 1–2.

Hardy, K., and T. Laszloffy. 2005. *Teens Who Hurt: Clinical Interventions to Break the Cycle of Adolescent Violence*. New York: The Guilford Press.

Hobsbawn, E. 1965. *Primitive Rebels: Studies in Archaic Forms of Social Movement in the 19th and 20th Centuries*. New York: W. W. Norton.

Hurtado, S. 1998. *Matrisocialidad*. Caracas: Ediciones de la Biblioteca-Ediciones de la Facultad de Ciencias Económicas y Sociales.

Koonings, K., and S. Veenstra. 2007. Exclusión social, actores armados y violencia. *Foro Internacional* XLVII (3): 616–636.

Lister, R. 2005. *Feminist Citizenship Theory: An Alternative Perspective on Understanding Women's Social and Political Lives*. Families & Social Capital ESRC Research Group Working Paper No. 12.

Mclean, J., C. Gilligan, and A. Sullivan. 1995. *Between Voice and Silence: Women and Girls, Race and Relationships*. Cambridge, MA: Harvard University Press.

Moreno, A., J. C. Brandt, A. Campos, R. Navarro, M. Pérez, W. Rodríguez, and Y. Varela. 1998. *Historia de vida de Felicia Valera*. Caracas: Fondo Editorial conicit.

Moreno, A., and L. Luna. 2002. Buscando Padre: Historia de vida de Pedro Luis Luna. Caracas: Universidad de Carabobo.

Mosegue, M. 2011, November. Madres acueden al diálogo como sus únicas armas. Diario Correo del Orinoco, http://www.redapoyo.org.ve/index .php?option=com_content&task=view&id=414 (downloaded April 10, 2012).

Observatorio Venezolano de la Violencia. 2011. *Informe Nacional de la Situación de Violencia y Criminalidad 2011*. Caracas: OVV.

Rosaldo, R. 2004. Grief and a Headhunter's Rage. In *Death, Mourning, and Burial: A Cross-Cultural Reader*, edited by Antonius C. Robben. Malden: Blackwell Publishing Ltd.

Sanjuán, A. 2012. Seguridad Ciudadana en Venezuela. Conference presented at Woodrow Wilson Center, May 30, 2012.

Sennet, R. 2003. *El Respeto: Sobre la dignidad del hombre en un mundo de desigualdad*. Barcelona: Anagrama.

UNODC. 2011. *Global Study on Homicide 2011: Trends, Context, Data*. Vienna: UNODC.

Vandello, J., E. Cohen, and S. Ransom 2008. U.S. Southern and Northern Differen ces in Perception of Norms about Aggression: Mechanisms for the Per- petuation of a Culture of Honor. *Journal of Cross-Cultural Psychology* 39: 162–177.

Vethencourt, J. L. 1974. La estructura familiar atípica y el fracaso cultural del vene- zolano. *Sic*, 362, Centro Gumilla.

Virtuoso, J. 2004, August 29. José Virtuoso, S. J.: Catuche . . . Aventura, ideal . . . una realidad que emerge (entrevista). *Últimas Noticias*, Caracas, p. 10.

Volkan, V. 1997. *Blood Lines: From Ethnic Pride to Ethnic Terrorism*. Boulder, CO: Westview Press.

Volkan, V. 2004. *Blind Trust: Large Groups and Their Leaders in Times of Crisis and Ter- ror*. Charlottesville, VA: Pitchstone.

Volkan, V. 2006. *Killing in the Name of Identity: A Study of Bloody Conflicts*. Charlot- tesville, VA: Pitchstone.

Wacquant, L. 2007. *Parias Urbanos: Marginalidad en la ciudada a comienzos del milenio*. Buenos Aires: Manantial.

Westkott, M. 1989. Female Relationality and Idealized Self. *American Journal of Psy- choanalysis* 3: 239–250.

Zubillaga, V. 2005. La carrera moral del hombre de respeto y armas: Historias de vida de jóvenes y violencia en Caracas. *Revista Venezolana de Psicología Clínica Comunitaria* 5: 3–39.

Zubillaga, V. 2008. La culebra: una mirada etnográfica a la trama de antagonismo masculino entre jóvenes de vida violenta en Caracas. *Akademos* 10 (1): 179–207.

Zubillaga, V. 2009. "Gaining Respect": The Logic of Violence among Young Men in the Barrios of Caracas, Venezuela. In *Youth Violence in Latin America. Gangs and Juvenile Justice in Perspective*, edited by G. Jones and D. Rodgers. New York: Palgrave Macmillan.

Zubillaga, V., and R. Briceño-León. 2001. Exclusión, masculinidad y respeto: algunas claves para entender la violencia entre adolescentes en barrios. *Nueva Sociedad* 173: 34–48.

Zubillaga, V., M. Llorens, J. Souto, and G. Núñez. 2013. *Violencia Armada y Acuerdos Comunitarios de Convivencia: Pistas para la Acción*. Caracas: Amnistía Internacional.

CHAPTER 14

When Daughters Are Unwanted: Sex Determination Tests in India

Madhu Purnima Kishwar

Technologies such as amniocentesis and ultrasound, used in most of the world primarily for detecting fetal abnormalities, are used in large parts of the Indian subcontinent for determining the sex of a fetus so that the mother can have an abortion if the fetus in the womb happens to be a female. The rapid spread of these tests has resulted in sex-selective abortions of hundreds of thousands of female fetuses.

The magnitude of the problem can be gauged by noting that Dr. Sunil Kothari, who runs a major ultrasound and abortion clinic in Delhi, in an interview on the BBC admitted to having performed 60,000 such tests. He declared with total conviction, "This is the best way of population control for India." There are thousands of doctors all over the country who are engaged in the same type of medical practice as Kothari—some operating openly and some in a clandestine manner.

The full demographic impact of the spread of this technology is likely to show up dramatically in the all-India census for the year 2001. India has had a lower proportion of females than of males in the overall population for at least a century. The 1901 census recorded 972 females per 1,000 males in the country's population. By 1991, the sex ratio had come down to 929 females per 1,000 males, indicating a deficit of nearly 30 million females in the total population. Selective abortions of female fetuses following sex determination tests are likely to further accelerate the deficit of females.

There are important regional differences in son preference and devaluation of daughters. As the census figures testify, sex ratios are much lower in the northwestern areas of the subcontinent. Traditionally, the states in the south (e.g., Kerala) and in the northeast (e.g., Manipur) have recorded either evenly balanced sex ratios or sex ratios in favor of females. In the northwest sex ratios have been far more imbalanced against females among specific land-owning communities (such as Rajputs, Jats, and Gujjars) and relatively more balanced among the landless poor, or among the artisanal groups. In Bihar, there is a sharp north-south divide. Among the land-owning Hindu peasant communities of the north, the sex ratio is in favor of males. However, in South Bihar, among the predominantly tribal population, the sex ratio is in favor of females.

An alarming aspect of the deficit of females is that, over the last few decades, the prevalence of low sex ratios has spread both horizontally and vertically. Areas in the south and the northeast (which earlier recorded sex ratios slightly in favor of females) now have almost all shifted to a deficit of females and are slowly moving toward the all-India pattern. Lower-status groups, which not too long ago had favorable sex ratios, are beginning to emulate higher-status groups in rural areas and are recording a decline in the proportion of their respective female populations. Thus the culture of overvaluing male lives at the cost of female lives is not merely a legacy of traditional norms, as is often believed, but is a widespread "modern" phenomenon.

SEX-SELECTIVE ABORTION

Many women's organizations and other concerned citizen groups have responded to the epidemic of abortions of female fetuses by demanding a ban on sex determination tests. The state of Maharashtra was the first to outlaw these tests. It passed the Prenatal Diagnostic Techniques (Regulation and Prevention of Misuse) Act of 1988 after a government-sponsored study found that in most cases gynecologists were performing amniocentesis solely to determine the sex of the fetus; only a tiny proportion of all tests were for detection of genetic disorders. Nearly all of the 15,914 abortions during 1984–1985 at a well-known abortion clinic in Bombay were undertaken after sex determination tests (SDTs) indicated the fetus was female. Such clinics are not confined to big cities. They have sprung up in small towns and villages as well.

Three other states—Punjab, Haryana, and Gujarat—also banned these tests because their clinics were indulging in aggressive campaigns to encourage people to abort female fetuses. Billboards with offers such as "Pay 500 rupees now and save 5 lakh of rupees later," playing on the anxieties of parents about having daughters, had become a common sight in these states.

THE INEFFECTIVE BAN

However, the law remained a dead letter and the clinics continued to mushroom and thrive in all these states. The only difference the new law made was that huge signs that had earlier read, *Ladka Ya ladki jaanch karaiye* ("Find out if it's a boy or a girl") were replaced by thinly veiled messages such as *Swasth ladka ya ladki?* ("Healthy boy or girl?") and *Garbh mein bacchhe ki har prakar ki jankari* ("Everything you want to know about the child in your womb").

Doctor-client complicity ensured that the clinics flourished despite the ban. A magazine reported that in a small town like Sirsa in Haryana at least 100 tests were being performed every day. Doctors in the town declared openly, "Earlier, we used to give our findings in writing. Now we will simply tell them the sex of their child verbally. Who can stop us from doing that?" Dr. M. R. Bansal of Sirsa, who had hit the headlines with his display jars containing female fetuses preserved in formalin, declared that the ban would only result in doctors' "hiking their fees" and, as a result, "the poor will suffer" (Jain and Singh, 1994).

Before the ban, an amniocentesis test cost anywhere between 70 and 600 rupees. After the new law, an amniocentesis could still be had for 1,500 to 2,000 rupees at average-quality clinics. Another, less invasive and safer sex determination test, ultrasound, is now easily available for 800 to 1,500 rupees.

Despite the dismal failure of new state laws to curb female feticide, some women's organizations continued to demand comprehensive all-India legislation and even more stringent provisions to deal with the problem. In August 1994, Parliament enacted another law, also called the Prenatal Diagnostic Techniques (Regulation and Prevention of Misuse) Act, in response to their pressure. This law prohibits any genetic counseling center, laboratory, or clinic from performing any of the prenatal diagnostic (PND) techniques unless it registers under this act. They must also satisfy one or more of the criteria that the law establishes for determining if the test is permissible:

- The age of the pregnant woman is above 35 years;
- The pregnant woman has undergone two or more spontaneous abortions or fetal losses;
- During her pregnancy, the pregnant woman had been exposed to substances potentially harmful to the fetus such as certain drugs, radiation, infections, or exposure to certain dangerous chemicals;
- The pregnant woman has a family history of mental retardation or physical deformities.

The doctor who conducts the tests is required not only to explain the possible side effects and risks involved, but also to obtain the pregnant woman's consent in writing.

In an attempt to ensure that the results of these tests are not used in deciding to abort a female fetus, the law states that "no person conducting

PND procedures shall communicate to the pregnant woman concerned or her relatives the sex of the fetus by words, signs or in any other manner." Likewise, the law bans advertising in any manner whatsoever the availability of PND procedures as a means of determining the sex of the fetus. Any person violating this law can be sentenced to imprisonment for a term that may stretch to three years, and with fines that may extend to 10,000 rupees. A medical practitioner convicted by the court for flouting the law may lose his membership in the State Medical Council for a period of two years for the first offense, and permanently for any subsequent offense.

The act does not limit penalties to the medical fraternity. It considers the woman's family even more culpable. The normal practice is that a person is believed innocent unless proven guilty. But this is not the case for this law: "The court shall presume unless the contrary is proved that the pregnant woman has been compelled by her husband or his relatives to undergo the PND test and such persons shall be liable for abetment of offence" and held punishable. As an indication of what the law considers improper use of the PND test, it stipulates that "every offence under this Act shall be non-cognisable, non-bailable and non-compoundable."

The Maharashtra Act had exempted from punishment any pregnant woman who underwent this test. However, the central legislation states that any person who seeks the aid of a genetic lab or clinic for conducting PND tests on any pregnant woman is punishable with imprisonment up to three years and a fine of up to 10,000 rupees. Unless the pregnant woman herself can prove that she was compelled to undergo the test, she is not exempt from punishment. In case of a second offense, the term of imprisonment can go up to five years and the fine up to 50,000 rupees.

With such a draconian law, one would imagine that people would be too frightened to conduct or undergo such tests. This is far from the case. Delhi, the seat of the central government, has thousands of clinics with facilities for carrying out prenatal SDTs.

Several women's organizations have demanded that the law be made even more stringent. They want genetic tests to be permitted only in government hospitals. They have also demanded that all ultrasonography equipment be registered with the government to prevent its misuse.

It is time that we face the fact that the laws that have been enacted to prohibit prenatal sex determination will not work given the political and administrative levels of functioning in our country. The more stringent a law attempting to prohibit consensual behavior, the greater the likelihood that it will be used primarily for extorting bribes by officials in return for looking the other way. The police know the locations and activities of sex determination clinics and collect regular bribes from the doctors as protection money, just as they do from brothel owners, since prostitution is also banned. Similar issues arise in the selective enforcement of the laws against drug smuggling, or brewing illicit liquor. In fact, the moment any activity is declared illegal, the police develop a vested interest in encouraging people to undertake it—for that brings them enormous amounts of extra income.

In banning SDTs we run the risk of criminalization of the medical profession. The popular demand for these tests will ensure that many doctors will be willing to do the tests in return for higher payments. Part of that money will be used to buy police protection. In addition, if clinics go underground, it will become impossible to monitor clinic functioning and safety, and women who go for these tests will be exposed to even greater risks. The emergence of a police-doctor nexus has dangerous implications for the well-being of any society. As it is, large numbers of Indian doctors commit unethical practices. This easily and profitably flouted law will further strengthen the hold of such people on the profession.

Moreover, the technology needed for performing these tests is easily available and relatively inexpensive; just about anyone can set up such a lab if he or she so desires. There is no way to police these mushrooming clinics, especially since many doctors have begun to use portable ultrasound machines that they carry in their cars to perform the tests in people's homes. Since ultrasound is a valuable technique for a whole range of other diagnoses of the internal organs, there is no way the use of ultrasound can be banned altogether.

New innovations in this field will make it even easier to choose the sex of children. Recent research indicates that it may soon be possible to prevent the very conception of female children by manipulating male sperm to ensure that a mother desirous of having a son will conceive only a male child. Things are likely to move in this direction in the near future, making any attempt to ban sex-selective birth even more impossible.

PRO-SDT ARGUMENTS

Sadly enough, many people feel that sex-selective feticide can serve as an important part of India's answer to overpopulation. Most families in India keep producing children until they feel they have the required number of sons. In the process, several daughters may be born before the desired number of sons arrive. Therefore, it is argued that if families could ensure the birth of a son or two without risking the birth of too many unwanted daughters, it is likely that they would have more of an interest in smaller families.

Many people even argue that as women become scarcer their lives will be more valued. One reason such bodies as the medical associations have failed to take a stand against these tests is that most doctors involved in this business are convinced that they are providing an important social service, that they are doing "noble work". Dr. Pai, a pioneer in providing cheap and safe SDTs and sex-selective abortions in Bombay, speaks on behalf of many in his profession when he says, "Happy and wanted children is what we desire. . . . Unwanted babies must be aborted." A woman doctor, Sudha Limaye, head of the Obstetric and Gynaecology Department of Bokaro General Hospital in Bihar, is reported to have said, "Our priority is population control by any means. Amniocentesis should be used as a method of family planning and be made available to everyone at a minimum cost or even free."

Some studies have revealed that most parents obtain SDTs only after the birth of one or two children. For instance, the data so far collected by Ritu Juneja of Delhi University in her doctoral research on prenatal gender selection show that the majority of parents come for SDTs only if they already have one or two daughters. In her sample she found that 40 percent of women came for SDTs after the birth of one daughter, 29 percent after two daughters, and the rest after three or more daughters. In her sample she did not find a single case of a woman using a SDT for her first pregnancy. Her respondents saw SDTs not just as a family planning (keeping families small) measure but also as a way of "balancing" (having children of both sexes in) their families. However, the desire to "balance" the family through SDTs is far more pronounced in families that have only girls than in those with only sons. Juneja came across only one woman who had undergone two sex-selective abortions with a view toward having a daughter after two sons. However, Sunil Khanna's (1995) study indicates that among a certain community SDTs are resorted to even in the case of a first pregnancy. This is unlikely to be a general pattern.

Many argue, what is wrong with helping people achieve their desired family size? Most of those who are pro-choice and want women to have autonomy tend to support a woman's right to abort. Why, then, do some of these very same people object to sex-selective abortion, especially if the woman herself is averse to producing more than one or two daughters? If we do not want the government to prevent women from aborting unwanted children, how can we remain consistent and support the government when it tries to prevent women from aborting unwanted daughters?

PERPETRATORS OR VICTIMS?

Most of those supporting the laws against SDTs claim that women are being socially coerced into getting rid of daughters; they are not viewed as free agents. Therefore, banning sex-selective abortions does not amount to encroaching on a woman's right to decide how many children she should have. However, several studies have revealed that in large parts of the country and in many communities, a mother's aversion to having more than one daughter is no less strong than that of male family members. Investigations have revealed that many women go for these tests on their own initiative; they are not mere victims of coercion, although other forms of constriction of choice may be salient considerations.

A recent M.Sc. thesis by Meenu Sondhi titled "The Silent Deaths: A Study of Female Foeticide in Delhi" found that most of the women clients coming to SDT clinics that were included in her study were highly educated and from well-off families. Several of the interviewed women suggested that SDTs must be legalized since this technology is an advance in science and maximum use should be made of it. Some talked about the social pressure to produce a son. Others pointed out the need to "balance" their families since they already had a daughter. Although the doctors performing the tests and subsequent abortions claimed that they provided this service only to those women who already had two daughters, the researcher found that several of the women who opted for the test already had a son (Chandra, 1990).

All these socioeconomic factors make it virtually impossible to enforce such a ban in a country where the police are unable to enforce the law impartially and effectively even for those activities that people agree are harmful, such as the manufacture of spurious medicines. Few of the parties involved in SDT tests and subsequent abortions, or their families and neighbours, view themselves as doing anything wrong. Abortion is legal in India and is frequently advocated as a family planning measure. Aborting female fetuses to limit family size has a widely observed legitimacy. It is socially sanctioned among several communities. A law can work only when at least some people have an interest in enforcing it and see in it some benefit for themselves.

WHEN WOMEN ARE SCARCE

This brings us to some vital questions. Is there any truth in the argument that the killing of unwanted girls will ultimately help make the lives of those daughters who are allowed to live any better? Is greater scarcity of women likely to lead to the surviving women becoming more valued?

From what we know of the existing low-sex-ratio regions, it appears that the market law assigning a higher value to items lower in supply does not appear to operate in this realm. Communities with low sex ratios tend to be more misogynistic, while those with high sex ratios tend to allow for greater female autonomy and dignity. Compare the lives of Jat and Rajput women with Nair women of Kerala or Meitis of Manipur, and the point becomes obvious. Seclusion and *purdah*, disinheritance of women from property, low female literacy rates, poor health, and low employment rates are all characteristic of low-sex-ratio regions, as is a greater incidence of domestic violence against women. In contrast, among the high-sex-ratio regions and communities, women do not live under as many crippling restrictions, have more secure inheritance rights, are rarely forbidden the right to earn independent incomes, and tend to have higher literacy levels and relatively better health. They also tend to have better opportunities for political participation at the local level.

If women's own lives are so negatively affected by discrimination against their daughters, why then are women so wrapped up in the culture of son preference? Aversion to having daughters is a culturally conditioned choice rooted in certain economic and political power relations within the family and community. For instance, a study done in a Punjab village (Horowitz and Kishwar, 1984) found that both peasant women and landless agricultural laborers displayed an overwhelming preference for boys and a serious dread of having daughters. Some women wanted no daughters at all. Even those who mentioned that daughters provide valuable support to their mothers, share their problems, and give a helping hand in domestic work still did not want any daughters. Two of the 15 peasant women interviewed got sterilized after they gave birth to two sons because neither they themselves nor their families wanted a daughter. One of these women said that because she had eight sisters and had suffered so much as a result, she herself never wanted to give birth to a girl. Almost all the women said girls are unwanted because they are a burden. One of them reported that her own mother had died within days after the birth of her fifth daughter because her husband had become very unhappy at the birth of yet another daughter.

Even among the agricultural laborers, 9 out of 14 stated a clear preference for male children. Not one of them said she preferred a girl, but their reactions to the births of daughters was not as adverse as it was among peasant women. However, most of these women did clearly admit that, from their own point of view, daughters would be good for them; they felt daughters would be more emotionally supportive and help them more than the sons.

DREAD OF DAUGHTERS

Why is it that women dread having daughters?

- Their own lives as women and what they saw of their mothers' lives give them an aversion to producing others to suffer like them.
- Their own status in the family is downgraded and they become vulnerable to more abuse every time an unwanted daughter is born to them or if they fail to produce a son. A woman often even seems to become incapable of breastfeeding her girl child when she herself has an insecure place in the family. If the birth of a girl child makes her life more miserable, there is reason for her to hate that child, and even to wish it dead.
- Most women do not envision their daughters having a better life than they themselves have experienced.

- As distinct from the mother's own interest, the family as an economic unit sees these daughters as burdensome on account of dowry and limited employment opportunities for women.

Thus we find that women's responses to their children are not a matter of unconditional nurturing and caring but are determined in part by their own perceived interests. Motherhood gets expressed in a variety of ways, depending on the woman's own situation in the family.

Since in our culture men and women are expected to subordinate their individual interests to that of the family, it is to be expected that ultimately women themselves see their own interests as indistinguishable from the family's interests, and consequently become actively involved in favoring male children at the cost of daughters, just as they ignore their own health and nutritional needs but seldom those of their husbands.

WHY ARE WOMEN DEVALUED?

The culture of self-neglect and self-depreciation is more prevalent among women of certain communities and regions. One can identify some of these areas by their low sex ratios. Misogynist attitudes are much stronger in the northwest plains of India, for example, because this region has been a frontier area for centuries. It has witnessed constant warfare, facing outside invaders as well as experiencing fighting among the diverse groups inhabiting this area. The people of this area have come to pride themselves on their marital traditions. They adopted more stringent forms of female seclusion and *purdah* that went far beyond those practiced in other parts of India.

In this region, ownership of land was the hallmark of higher status and there was a constant drive toward acquiring more and more land. Since maintaining possession of land was so precarious, the importance of males was enhanced considerably in comparison to areas that did not experience so many invasions. The land-owning communities in the northwest came to value physical strength and skills in wielding weapons, equating "manly" qualities with aggressiveness and virility far more than is healthy for any society.

In such a situation, women came to be valued primarily as the bearers of sons and were seen as liabilities in most other contexts. The fiercely patrilineal family and kinship structure that evolved made it mandatory for daughters to be sent away to the husband's family after marriage. Not only were daughters a constant source of anxiety because of their assumed need for greater protection against an outside world full of enemies, they were also seen as an economic drain because they take away wealth rather than add to it.

The establishment of British rule brought an end to internecine warfare as well as to external invasions but exacerbated land hunger even more. The most important and far reaching of the changes introduced by the British involved the revision of land ownership patterns. Cultivators ended up as tenants of a much more interventionist and rapacious state. With the creation of these new tenancy rights, women's rights in the land were disregarded and bypassed. Even among communities where women were the primary workers on the land, in the process of converting communal property rights of the clan into individual property rights, women were almost completely excluded.

Labor power is more valued in societies with surplus land and scarce labor. As land becomes scarce and population pressure increases, a woman's labor power loses its value and possession of land becomes the all-important asset. If ownership of land is vested mostly or exclusively in the hands of men, women begin to be treated as mere dependents and considered liabilities rather than assets.

Take the case of certain tribal communities that until the 19th century practiced shifting cultivation combined with hunting. In tribal groups, families highly value their daughters because women's labor is the mainstay of agricultural operations. Men's labor plays a peripheral role in their rural economy. Consequently, most tribal girls fetch a bride price instead of requiring a dowry. They are not perceived as a burden on the family and their births are far from dreaded, as is evident from their sex ratio figures. According to the 1971 census, there were 1,041 females for every 1,000 males among the Hos in Bihar. The comparable figures for females from the 1971 census for other northern states are Punjab and Haryana (874), UP (883), and Rajasthan (919).

However, people in these communities were forced to become settled agriculturalists by the British, and their communally owned land was parceled out to individual families, the title vesting with the male head. The impact of the British forcing tribals to switch to sedentary agriculture is documented at length in my study of women of the Ho tribe in Singhbhum District, Bihar (Kishwar, 1987). It shows how the society was compelled by outside forces to fall in line with the culture of son preference even though these communities did not traditionally devalue daughters, as is evident from their sex ratios.

The new ownership patterns introduced by the British were crystallized in the Chotanagpur Tenancy Act of 1908, which conferred exclusive rights to men as the owners of cultivatable land; widows and unmarried daughters were allowed only limited usufructory rights. For instance, as soon as a daughter marries, she loses even the right to be maintained from her father's land; she does not inherit land as a son does. Even if an unmarried daughter is raped or has a brief sexual affair with a man, she loses her right to live off the family land, in the same way as she would if she were to get married.

A tribal woman cannot claim a share in her husband's land in her own right even if she is the one cultivating it while he may have migrated elsewhere for employment. She is allowed only to claim a right through her son, if she has one. If a man has no sons, the land he cultivates will revert to his brothers and their sons after his death. A man is assured of his right over the land in his lifetime, but his wife's position is not so secure.

A woman's ability to hold on to the land is also determined by the age of her sons at the time of her husband's death. Women who have only daughters or baby sons tend to be relatively powerless in case her relatives decide to use strong-arm methods to deprive her of land share. The land of such widows is often snatched away from them through force or fraud. Thus, women are pressured into a situation of son preference for their own protection.

Another reason for son preference is that the outside world of education and employment is extremely male oriented and male dominated. Therefore, if tribals have to seek a foothold in the mainstream economy, they can do so only through sons.

Most of the 37 women I interviewed in the course of my study of a Ho village stated that they personally preferred daughters. One of the women, Jasmati Sundi, explained this preference in response to my question as to whether she wanted a son or a daughter:

I want a daughter even though having a son will improve my position vis-á-vis my husband's land. Even if I have a son, my husband may throw me out before the son is grown up enough to defend me. If he does allow me to stay on, what do I need a son for? If our land goes to his uncles or cousins after we die, what do I care? If we don't have a daughter who will give us some affection and care when I am old? A son and a daughter-in-law will never do that. When my mother was sick I cared for her, none of my brothers looked after her.

That the culture of son preference has largely been imposed on the Hos by patriarchal land relations dictated from above becomes evident when one considers the attitude of Hos toward children born out of wedlock. Daughters born out of wedlock are not as unwelcome as are sons, even in cases where the father refuses to acknowledge responsibility for the child. A baby boy whose father does not accept him runs a higher risk of being killed or allowed to die through neglect than does a girl. A boy's life is not seen as being worth much if he is not going to inherit land, since that is seen as a male's most important function in life. Also, if an unmarried woman is saddled with a son, she will find it more difficult to get married because a prospective husband would not like another man's son in the house as a possible claimant to the land, whereas a stepdaughter is welcome because she is seen as an additional worker on the land. In addition, she can earn a bride price for the family.

INCREASING LAND HUNGER

At the heart of these battles is the growing land hunger among the peas-
antry, both tribal and nontribal. Land hunger is leading to constant conflicts in villages. The relatively more powerful families are constantly on
the lookout for opportunities to usurp the land of less powerful families.
Often the influential families get widows' land surreptitiously transferred
in their own names by bribing local officials. They push out those women
who have no adult male family members to protect their land. Given the
corruption and lawlessness of the government machinery in India, those
who cannot resist aggression and physical force tend to lose their land.
There is a popular saying in the north: *Jitney ladke utne lath, jitney lath utna
kabza* ("The more the sons, the more your capacity to wield batons [vio-
lence]—and the number of batons decides how much land a family controls"). As the scale of violence increases in society, and its importance in
controlling and gaining access to new resources is enhanced, daughters
are seen more and more frequently as liabilities.

The increase in insecurity bolsters the ideology of keeping women
housebound. In many parts of India, working outside the home is seen as
a sign of a family's low social and economic status. Refusing to let women
work outside the home does not save women from drudgery, but rather
ensures that they stay confined to all the unpaid jobs on their family farm:
field labor, harvesting, weeding, caring for family livestock, basic home
processing of farm produce, housework of all kinds, and care of children.

While they may play an important role in producing food, women are
usually not allowed to engage in other economic activities that might give
them access to cash, such as the marketing of produce, which involves
exposure to and contact with the world of commerce and men. Since cash
is highly prized in rural areas, and women have few opportunities to earn
cash, this is another way that women are kept dependent and why they
are usually considered an economic liability rather than an asset.

SUMMING UP

If we want to stop the killing and neglect of women, it is not enough
to simply pass a law and hope that it will succeed in countering all those
social and economic forces that make women's lives appear expendable.

However, when I argue that a legal ban on female feticide won't work,
I do not mean to imply that we should leave things as they are, or that
the resultant scarcity of females will inevitably raise the value of female
lives. What I am suggesting is that we stop looking for quick fixes and
instead face the problem squarely. There is no way to ensure the healthy
survival of baby girls unless families find them worth nurturing. That is
indeed a complex challenge that allows for no easy short-term solutions.

As Ravindra (2014) demonstrates, all the hard work put in by activists in Maharashtra has not led to the curbing of SDTs. If anything, the practice has grown and spread. The real challenge before us is to figure out ways in which the value of daughters can be enhanced in the eyes of their own families.

ACKNOWLEDGMENT

Reprinted with permission from *Manushi: A Journal about Women & Society*, issue No 86, Jan.–Feb., 1995. http://www.manushi.in/articles.php?articleId=1064#.U59MWY1dXR1 (accessed June 16, 2014).

BIBLIOGRAPHY

Chandra, Sharmila. 1990, October 28. *Indian Express Magazine*.

Horowitz, Berny, and Madhu Kishwar. 1984. Family Life—The Unequal Deal: Women's Condition and Family Life among Agricultural Laborers and Small Farmers in a Punjab Village. In *In Search of Answers: Indian Women's Voices from Manushi*. London: Zed Books, pp. 69–103.

Jain, Minu, and Harry Singh. 1994, July 24–30. Foetal Divide. *Sunday Magazine*.

Khanna, Sunil K. 1995. Prenatal Sex Determination: A New Family Building Strategy. *Manushi* 86: 23–29.

Kishwar, Madhu. 1987, January. Toiling without Rights: Ho Women of Singhbhum [in three parts]. *Economic and Political Weekly* 22 (3–5).

Ravindra, R. P., and P. M. Lata. n.d. Names Are Important. Letters to Manushi, http://www.manushi-india.org/pdfs_issues/PDF%20files%2071/letters_to_manushi.pdf (accessed June 16, 2014), pp. 43–44.

CHAPTER 15

Banalization of Violence as a Self-Protection of the Psychism

Miriam Gutiérrez-Otero

In their desert of tears, forgotten, we are allowing
"Town of Shadows"

—Miriam, July 17, 2000

HISTORIC CONTEXT OF THIS RESEARCH

Ciudad Juarez, Chihuahua, is located in north Mexico, at the border with the United States, right across from El Paso, Texas. It has been known as "the most violent city of the world" for two years in a row, as of 2009. To show the magnitude of this problem it seemed important to me to expose the facts—not only to tell the facts but to name the violence, deepening its analysis to try and reach a better understanding of the problematic.

In 2009, there were 191 murders for every 1,000 people (El Universal, January 11, 2010), which means 2,667 murders throughout the year (McKinley, 2009, p. A1), over 1.5 times the number in 2008 (1,550 murdered people). In 2010 there were 3,622 homicides (Toledo, 2012), declining in 2011 to 2,086 (Toledo, 2012). This means that there were hundreds more killings in Juarez than in countries at war, such as Iraq, even without counting the innumerable kidnappings, disappearances, extortions, and armed robberies. It should not be forgotten as well that Ciudad Juarez was an arena where femicides and female assassinations took place.

All of this cruelty and spilled blood that started at the border had to reach the center of the country for the nation to react and from there to believe what was actually happening when these murders began to appear. In Nuevo Leon, Michoacan, Durango, Tamaulipas, Sinaloa, Guerrero, Morelos, and Veracruz, just to name a few. Only then did they come to question the state of things, to grasp the degree of violence and the horror the country was living in.

We start out with the fact that the border is a "no man's land" literally. It is 3,185 kilometers (1,979 miles) in length, a place where everything that is that is "outlawed" is favored, and thus a "lawless town," where justice as such does not exist and many make it "by their own hand." Delinquency finds a "shelter" here thanks to corruption and impunity, to a lack of law enforcement. The population, in such a situation, tries to live on the margins—tries to keep on living, working, and doing their daily activities, trying to ignore (i.e., trivialize) what is going on, in order to preserve their reason and of course their lives. Some people react—too late—when one of their loved ones or relatives is literally "touched" by this violence, whether physically, economically, or sexually., Psychologically we have all experienced it in some way, though many may try to calm themselves and their own, violence is present there and here, and from what I have been able to verify throughout these years, it is omnipresent. Maybe that is why it has been "assimilated" in some way and has come to be a part of Ciudad Juarez's daily life.

At this point one should ask, how do people do it? How do all of us who live in this city do it? How do we ignore and/or trivialize the violence happening around us? How does a mother calm herself and ease her child's anxiety sufficiently to go to preschool and assure him or her, and herself, that "they will be back well," safe and sound? "We know we go out but we don't know if we will be back" (Ajo and Ravelo, 2003, p. 19)— this asseveration, the title of an article, is a daily truth in Ciudad Juarez, not only for women working in factories, but for everyone: men, women, kids, teenagers, and elderly. We are all here, as some may say—though many will refuse to admit it—"until the bullets reach us."

Before continuing, I must point out that it is very interesting to observe the significant slippage in French phonetics between "la mer morte," the "dead sea" of which Saint Augustine writes in *The City of God*, and "la mère morte," the "dead mother." "The sea" is male gendered in Spanish and Italian, but feminine in French—"la mer," which phonetically slips into "la mère," though, of course, there are many similarities in language. I avail myself of this metonymy—even though in English it is not evident—since it allows me to explore the potential connections.

I invite you into a journey, a journey to the recent past—a sinister journey, without a doubt. I invite you to revisit the wounds, still open, of this city of the desert, which is bleeding, becoming lifeless, dying little by little and day by day—a city that it is not only like the dead sea Saint Augustine made reference to (La Cité Dieu, 1960, p. 417), where the fruits contained ashes inside and vanished in the hands of those who harvested them, but is more like a dead mother: instead of receiving life from her, you harvest the dead bodies of men, women, young people, and children. The sand is bloody, giving off a foul odor, having lost her fertility already, her creative virtue of giving life.

Let's hear from a witness: "It was a bloodbath. I saw two dead bodies piled up on the sidewalk, three more dumped a few meters away, one of them with its brains out, afterwards they said that there were two others inside of the Federal and Municipal Police units" (Diario Digital, 2010).

I invite you to meditate deeply about the banalization of violence that is observed in the population of Ciudad Juarez. For this it will be necessary to walk through different doors along a dark tunnel and descend to different levels, the only light shining upon is that from not giving up our capacity to think despite the violence we find along our way, along the tunnel.

FIRST DOOR: ENTRANCE TO HELL

This is a parallel connection of two cases, with names and last names, one Mexican, one French. First there is 23-year-old Elsa Jurado, mother of a 3-year-old child, former psychology student of the Universidad Autonoma de Ciudad Juarez, burned alive with gasoline inside her car, out of which she managed to walk to ask for her neighbors' help. This happened in her home's parking lot at Fovissste Chamizal III, in Ciudad Juarez, Chihuahua, on July 6, 2006. When they heard the screaming her neighbors came out and tried to put out the fire. She died three days later as a consequence of the third-degree burns over 70 percent of her body (Aguilar and Castro, 2006, p. 6; Rodriguez and Cabullo, 2006, pp. 3b, 9b). Second, there is Sohane Benziane, a 17-year-old girl, who on October 4, 2002, was burned alive with gasoline in Cité Balzac Vitry Sur Seine. She was found in a dumpster on Banlieue Parisienne, with third-degree burns covering 80 percent of her body. The person responsible was Jamal Derrar, a 19-year-old boy (Kaci, 2006; M. K., 2006; Vigoureux, 2006).

In the Mexican case there were no manifestations, citizen participation, or a notice on behalf of the university community, official or unofficial. In other words, nothing happened. It seemed to me, at that moment and even now, inconceivable that nobody did anything, that in the citizen population this crime did not even generate repulsion. Manifestations against violence and insecurity started around the end of 2009 and beginning of 2010, when a good part of the population already had suffered a murdered, kidnapped, disappeared, or extorted friend or relative. Thousands of murders had to happen before the citizens of Ciudad Juarez call for a stop to the injustice, the impunity, and the reestablishment of a state of law. It gives the impression of a wounded, armless, legless, eyeless people parade, after a war where everyone has lost a member of their family, has been damaged in some way or has lost a loved one. Ciudad Juarez is the arena and theater of the war against drug trafficking, and everyone in the parade there is war wounded.

In Ciudad Juarez and the state of Chihuahua, politicians have trivialized the violence, but they have done it in a conscious way, in order to downplay the importance and magnitude of the violence, justifying it by arguing, among other things, that the people who have been murdered during different periods are "prostitutes," "drug dealers," or "delinquents," even in the cases of public junior high school and university students and teachers, and other people who work honestly, when it is evident that there is no trustworthy evidence to prove that the affirmations by the authorities are true. Said another way, it is as if just because a person works in prostitution, for example, she deserves being murdered—this according to the authorities' hierarchy of values, as if this were an excuse. However, this argument used by municipal and state authorities has not been enough to erase their inefficiency in the face of the murder wave, or to convince those of us who think, who live in this city, who do not let ourselves be swayed by false explanations. On the other hand, they forget that regardless of the activity a person performs, human rights are inalienable; they have to prevail, and these include the rights of life and justice. All of this clearly reveals a lack of social responsibility.

Given these conditions, we start to observe a loss in the capacity of surprise among the general population and listen to the people who, instead of reacting with an exclamation, scream of their repulsion over the severely violent acts that happen every day, such as kidnappings, violations, and decapitations. We begin to hear the "classic" expression "oh, another one," "another dead one," "another raped woman," or "another violated and murdered kid," as if it were just "one more piece" or one more object that is going to be forgotten in the anonymity of dead objects. It is then that we observe the banalization of violence not because violence is not violent even if it seems excessive, but because it becomes necessary to remove this burden not only to be able to live with it, but also to be able to sleep with it on a daily basis. If it weren't for this ability, people would go mad. This loss in the capacity of surprise on the part of the people who live here, which foreign people wonder about, is itself a severe symptom of the population's alienation from being poisoned with so much violence and impunity. It is the disavowal in the Freudian sense of the term. It is as if they have been anesthetized, as if they have had their conscience and empathy anesthetized, as if they have become unable to feel, to sympathize, to really "put themselves in the place of the other."

Thus, on one side we have a lack of social responsibility on behalf of the authorities and on the other, albeit an echo of the first, the loss of the capacity of surprise. Both attitudes have allowed this city to keep bleeding. . . . In the case of Elsa Jurado, the former psychology student, nobody knew anything else, neither the person responsible for the murder nor the legal measures that should have been undertaken by this being an intentional murder. It took five years to learn something new about this case. In

2011 the person responsible for the murder was arrested. Francisco Luna Sanchez received a sentence of 30 years in prison after the criminal judge of the Bravos Fourth Judicial District found him criminally responsible for murder (la red noticias, 2011; la opcion de Chihuahua, 2011). There is a child who has been orphaned and a family damaged for life in a severe psychological way. In the same way they have been left in the "cold case" file for five years, and this is nothing more than a "dead file," with hundreds of unresolved murders of men and women who keep on waiting. On one side justice is done and impunity is stopped; on the other the public ministry, forensic services, and judicial police can afford to do the pertinent investigations and not dedicate themselves only to pick up the dead, literally, and place a number on the corpse (although someone has to do so).

But what are the differences between French and Mexican society specifically in these two cases of young women burned alive?

In the French case of Sohane Benziane, it was a crime that shook the entire nation. It gave rise to an impassioned debate about the relationships that rule between men and women in the "cités" throughout France, in the poor immigrant neighborhoods. "Her death has become a symbol of the most extreme violence against women," Jean Paul Content, lawyer of Sohane's family, affirmed (BBC News Europe, 2006). It gave birth to the movement "Ni putes ni soumises" ("Not prostitutes nor submissive"), which took place in 23 stages, crossing all of France and ending in a 30,000-person demonstration on March 8, 2003, in which we came out to the streets to express our indignation and reprobation of this incident. Of course, it is also questionable that this movement used as a "flag" Sohane's case, more than to become acknowledged, but for taking its political strength to national and international levels.

In France people are individualists but there is a political life; as a matter of fact they are strongly politicized citizens. They participate in political parties beginning in their youth; it should be enough of an example that sometimes universities are taken over by student political parties and that on May 1, Labor Day, thousands of citizens march of their own will to fight for legitimate demands. There is also a respect for the law and a demand that it be served. There is, as a manner of synthesis, a state of law.

As to Sohane's case, despite the fact that the judge's decision took three years, six months, one week, and six hours to be determined, the penalty against Sohane Benziane's murderer was exemplary: 25 years in criminal seclusion for acts of torture and barbarism, having implied death without the intention of giving it (Kaci, 2006; M. K. 2006; L'Humanité, 2006; Vigoureux, 2006).

The postponement of the trial was due to how complicated the case was; during the search for testimonies and reconstruction of the facts, many of the witnesses backed down. The trial also observed fraternal support for the murderer, with applause and shouts of solidarity during the reconstruction of the facts, in the neighborhood where he lived. The complication resided in how to handle and make French law viable since it implied a clash of cultures as it it involved French with a particular Arabic-Muslim ascendancy, in which the woman has no rights and must obey every order men give her. They have a social statute of "trading objects" that is related specifically to what Pierre Bourdieu refers to as "the social construction of bodies." In this regard, it is illustrational that the book *Male Domination*, in which when studying society Kabile, who lives in Argelia, explains, "The private space is the female space, the public space is the male space" (Bourdieu, 1998, pp. 64–66). Bourdieu calls our attention as well to what masculine means for this society. In *Virility and Violence*, he shows us the two title traits are equivalent for Kabile society and allows us to read it backward: without violence there is no virility, he writes.

The male privilege does not cease to be trap and finds its counterpart in the permanent tension and contention, sometimes taken to the absurd, imposing in each man the duty to reassure his virility in every circumstance. . . . Virility then, understood as the reproductive, sexual, social capacity, as the ability for combat and exercise of violence (in a revengeful way most of all) is fundamentally a burden. In opposition to women, whose honor, essentially negative, can only be defined or lost, being her virtue virginity and faithfulness successively, the man "real man" is the one who feels obliged to rise up to the statue of the of the possibility of increasing his honor in the search for glory and distinction on a public sphere that is offered to him. (Bourdieu, 1998, pp. 68–69)

Meanwhile, Sauvadet adds in his text about "the young men 'de la cité': how do they form a group?" [Les jeunes "de la cité": comment forment-ils un groupe?], highlighting the risks young mean in "les cités" take, and the dangers to which they are submitted to—both men and women, each according to gender, and he says that "taking up public space, young girls weaken their respectability and endanger young boys (brothers, cousins) forcing them to protect their 'virtue' with the purpose of affirming their manly skills, already threatened by the work inactivity and poverty" (Sauvadet, 2006, p. 7).

Bourdieu allows us, through his lectures, if not to justify, at least understand on the one side the attitude of the young murderer where he feels obliged to defend with violence his honor and, of course, his manhood—in this case, extreme violence. On the other hand, it allows us to understand the fraternal support of his neighborhood when they applaud during the reconstruction of the facts, given that his action was some kind of "legitimate" defense, at least for these Arabic Muslims, as if they said to themselves, "I would have done the same thing" by applauding his actions. If he had not done that, he would have lost his honor as a manly man in front of his group of friends, his public image, and on the inside he would have been left worthless. Jamal Derrar "bit the bait" of the Arabic-Muslim social trap about his manhood; he will now be in prison for 25 years, but in front of his group, in which he has an identity, he increased his honor, obtaining glory and distinction in a public sphere.

On the other hand, in the Mexican case, in Ciudad Juarez specifically, there is no political life. I mean that the citizens' political participation is basically nile; there are no public manifestations, despite there being less individualism. However, there is no law: instead there is impunity and corruption, an absence of workers rights particularly in the factories, where the staff are exploitable objects and human rights are mostly absent.

Trying to investigate the causes of this citizen apathy, we must highlight, as we did in *Sexual Violence in Ciudad Juarez: A Preliminary Study* (Gutiérrez-Otero, 2006), the fact that people who come to the border share at least four characteristics that affect the absence of political life and demand for every citizen's rights; also the border has some common characteristics with Mexican tourist spots such as Quintana Roo, that make them more vulnerable to social issues. This affects the city and its population, but it specifically hits those unprotected: women, boys, and girls. These characteristics are the transitory character, the low level of integration as a society, the uprooting of the people, and the anonymity.

To try to give a clearer idea we will revisit Elena Azaola in "Homage to the Dead Women." Here she talks about the anomie and she mentions that once primary links are broken, and they are not replaced by new links, a crisis results, producing a weak affiliation. "The anomie does not only alter the boundaries of transgression but also . . . the perception of their mere existence. There is no transgression where the rules have been appropriate and sanction is weak" (Azaola, 2003, p. 122).

Of these two cases, Ciudad Juarez's and Vitry Sur Seine's, we can say— along with the philosopher Antonio Muñoz Ortega—that the law, to be respected, needs to be validated. This means that the law requires of its own application to maintain its sense, known as the concretization of law on punishment. If this principle is not accomplished there is a loss in the deep meaning of the law.

SECOND DOOR: THE DARKNESS OF THE DECAPITATED

The second point is the highlighting of the extreme sensation that decapitation conveys, which is directly related to our own dismemberment or to our torn, incomplete image in the mirror, but in another; and since it is the other, with the small *o* (minuscule *a* to Jacques Lacan), the one in the imaginary axis, it resends us an image of our completeness; the decapitated then reminds us that we too can be dismembered, and this is extremely violent for anybody's psychism, bordering on the unthinkable. Lacan (1966) talks about dismemberment, the body's fragmentation, the mutilation, castration, as well as the devouring, previous to the mirror phase properly said; the image of the decapitated comes in as a privileged image; it also symbolizes castration and, of course, dismemberment (Lacan, 1966, p. 104).

The "Covert of the Psychism," or Psychic Self-Protection

What are the self-protection mechanisms the psychism uses in extreme situations?

It is important to point out that there are different levels of defense mechanisms. The psychism has several covert or self-protective procedures, and these are used according to the situation that occurs and the personality structure. These self-protection mechanisms are used on the three basic personality structures that Lacanian psychoanalysis acknowledges: neurosis, perversion, and psychosis. Let's say that these mechanisms are in the listed order, from the most "flexible" in neurosis to the most archaic in psychosis.

Furthermore, it should be highlighted that people who commit a homicide—murder by the fire of a gun, fire as in burning a person alive, or decapitation—also draw upon psychism self-protection, but they do it through the cleavage of oneself.

Dehumanization

Those who decapitate cut out the last human trace in the other, but in that same motion they also cut out the last human trait in themselves. Dehumanizing in order to kill, in their imagination they reduce the other to the category of animals—pigs, cows, rats—to be able to execute the action of removing another human being's life. And by doing so, they fall within the thin boundaries of sadism and violence, but also the boundaries of sanity and insanity. To be responsible for decapitation, one needs to dissociate or split oneself in order to "not be there" (see Lifton, 1997; Lifton, 2000; Tanner, 2013). Let's remember the Ku Klux Klan (KKK) executioners, who wore white sheets and masks. It is interesting to observe how *they transform into others*, which means they are not themselves; they cross-dress—through different clothing, a hood, or even another name—into the executioners of a command.

This transformation into another is interesting because it tells us about the scission of the ego—"it is not me who is the one killing," or it is me but transformed into another—but this is really about dividing, splitting oneself, being another, and that other is the one who is murdering, not me; that other is the one who executes, not me. We can also add that the dead person is another "not me"! It is to say that the possibility of the sinister looming over oneself is also eliminated.

Walking over Dead Human Bodies

This also requires scission of the ego—first to think, or rather not to think, they are or were humans, the corpses as themselves, in another time, reaching depersonalization—but to see them as animals or inanimate objects. Moreover, the stopping of thought and memory would mean that the "device" that records into the thought memory is for that not only to happen in a subjunctive hypothetical time but rather not to have ever happened in the past subjunctive (Gutiérrez-Otero, 2003). I will revisit this further on.

Dismemberment and decapitation are also used as extreme images in the tragedy of *the Bacchae*, a divine punishment. In Dionysius against Pentheus, his cousin, who is killed at the hands of the Bacchae, but specifically in the hands of Agave, his mother holds her son's head as a hunting trophy. "Manifest justice come, come armed with a sword to kill with one gash on the throat, the godless, lawless, without justice, Equion's offspring, born from the earth!" (Euripides, 1991, p. 391).

David Ayala highlights, "Violence where the victim is murdered, is extreme violence where murder is the last link in a sinister chain" (Ayala, 2010, p. 19).

However, we see that the sinister has no limits in this frontier; thus, the passage through literature, mythology, and psychoanalysis became necessary to think—thanks to rendering it distant—of the dismembered, decapitated, literally castrated bodies, placed there in the middle of the streets, hanging outside schools, as inanimate torn objects, as garbage and a means of spreading terror.

We could talk about a triggering of the "covert of the psychism" or a psychic self-defense mechanism. Following up on our idea, the restoration of the prohibition of thinking becomes in this way a strategy of the covert of the psychism, the non-registration of the trauma (Gutiérrez-Otero, 2003, p. 231).[1] Psychosis, for me, would be the "psychism's last resource" in which no other "covert" procedure would have worked.

To develop this idea I take as a trauma example incest in children. How can traumatic experiences lived during early childhood and that will have a determinant importance in the future, leave no mnemonic inscription, no cognitive imprint in the psychism of the incest and/or sexual abused children? What is the origin of conscious memories and what is the origin of the effacement of these remembrances in the memory or in the psychism? What is the cause of a memory's "paralyzation" or the paralyzation of the "recording" in the memory?[2]

Freud writes that "the psychic formations submitted to repression in hysteria are not memories properly said, since nobody puts its memory to work without a good reason"(Freud, 1956 [1897], p. 173).

Freud (1973b [1899]), in his text about concealing memories, questions his assumptions; he started off from the idea—as we all do—that what is important is conserved in the memory. However, he realizes the psychism works a different way; Freud shares with us his inquiries, writing, "It is necessary to first question why exactly what is significant is repressed and what is indifferent is what is conserved" (Freud, 1973b [1899], p. 117).

Freud offers a meta-psychological explanation; he talks about the forces acting in opposite directions, reaching a compromising solution: "Since precisely the important components of the impression are those that were harmed, the substitution memory should be unprovided of this important element; therefore he will be simply banal" (Freud, 1973b [1899], p. 117). On the other hand, forgetting, or the psychical mechanism of forgetfulness, will consist in the "unbinding" of displeasure (Freud, 1984 [1898]).

It is as if a device that would confuse the imprints and mix the origins of memories was released in the psychism! Such a device would consist in the detention of all "printing appliances," the memory being an integral part of this apparatus, and the ego would be "the writer," "the pen, the writing tip," as Monique Schneider would say (2002–2003). Nonetheless, to imprint something in the memory, in the psychism, it is necessary to first have invested and to have reasons to want to invest it; to make a perception reappear it is necessary that this has been linked to a satisfaction experience. However in traumatic experiences "nobody puts its memory to work for no good reason" (Freud, 1956 [1897], p. 173). There will be a non-investment or perhaps we should say a "counter-investment" (Freud, 1996 [1920], p. 301) that will debilitate all psychic systems; for the experience not to be inscripted, the subject "will not be there." He will be there like an anesthetized or psychically paralyzed person, intellectual level included; the judgment will stop and pretend that the experience "never happened" or "did not appear."

In *The Defense Psychoneuroses*, Freud writes, "it exists, however, a kind of defense much more energetic and much more efficient that consists in the ego rejection (verwirft) of the unbearable representation[3] at the same time as its affection, and it is conducted as if the representation had never happened to the ego" (Freud, 1973 [1891], p. 12).

Furthermore, he highlights the price to pay for the "usage" of this radical defense: "But, in the moment this takes place, the person is in a psychosis that cannot be classified as more than a 'hallucinatory confusion'" (Freud, 1973 [1894], p. 12).

If the ego, having rejected both parts of the perception—the representation and affection, so that *there is nothing left but a hole in the memory*, that would be at the same time an injury to the ego, because it is a tearing of the ego from the inconciliable representation.

We retake the thread of our reflection; the event is erased from the memory but imprinted on the body, and it too will have a kind of memory, which we may call "bodily memory."[4] This "bodily memory" would be the physical inscription of sensory prints, such as odor, touch, sight, hearing, taste, and kinesthetic prints.

Moreover, we highlight the fact of disappearing from the place where the prints should be inscripted, of missing prints, over the fact of erasing them to make them disappear. There we find three moves to know: the inscription that remains at a conscious level, the effacement that would be done by the ego's scission as a defense mechanism; and finally, the disappearing that would be a result of the ego's scission.

We take the active meaning of the word "efface" and the passive meaning of the phrase "being effaced" or eliminated. The trauma would have "something of the un-inscriptible" (Schneider, 2003). It would have a "no-inscription of the traumatic seduction characteristic" (Schneider, 1992, p. 40)—the non-investment of oneself. It is necessary that this occur at a narcissistic level to be inscripted. If we follow up Freud in *The Interpretation of Dreams,* there would be no representation sustained more than for desire: "it is the motion that we call desire: the reappearance of perception is the accomplishment of desire, and the total investment of perception starting from the need is the shortest path to the accomplishment of desire" (Freud, 1967 [1900a], p. 481). Desire is linked to the first experiences of satisfaction. In consequence, if there is no investment, there will be neither a representation nor mnemonic prints.

It would be necessary that this episode had been invested from the beginning, to have been able to save some of the prints in the memory. In order to re-find the deleted prints, I think it would not be enough to re-invest the past; but perhaps it would be necessary to re-invest the injury, re-invest the place where the prints where inscripted: re-invest the body.

In relation to the impossibility of inscribing a traumatic event, M. Schneider (2002–2003) highlights in her seminar, while doing an analysis of discomfort in culture (Freud, 1971 [1929]), Freud's position and the radical traumatic experience, humankind's disgrace or the disgrace of being a human, that would reflect, by the act itself of becoming a victim, the human misery, as in war (Freud, 1971 [1929], p. 36). She says, "the inscription somehow stops. It is precisely the impression that you cannot do." It would "rupture the power of writing that was caused by extreme misfortune, . . . a kind of global destruction of psychic abilities" (Schneider, 2003).

THE METONYMY OF HOLES

At this point that I would like to deepen, I conceive the trauma of incest as a "hole" that works inside of what I call the metonymy of holes: I think that violation and incest, as sexual traumas, work through a bodily anchorage of the hole in the psychism.

Freud (1973) in *The Defense Psychoneuroses* says—as we have highlighted before—that the ego rips the inconciliable representation and in consequence a piece of reality; therefore, the representations could manifest in the hallucinatory form. Such tearing would leave what I call a "hole," where eventually there could be a hallucinatory re-investment. But precisely this tearing would leave its mark, both on the side of the thought and on the bodily side—the representations that will not be there, not only repressed, "forgotten," but having disappeared, having been effaced or annulled, due to the scission (cleavage). That will then leave a hole in the thought, and in relation to the amount of affection, there would be a kind of "anchorage" to the body on the side of the real, at least in prostitution and drug addiction in relation to incest and/or sexual abuse suffered in childhood. This "bodily anchorage" would have an inscription of the hole as a characteristic, and this could have several manifestations.

On the side of the non-symbolizable, since there is no representation, there is no mnemonic, cognitive record besides the holes as the only inscription in the "bodily" memory and the "cavity" and the "print of no print" (Press, 1997, pp. 56–59) in the memory, in the thought.

The hole in the psychism would be to me, as Schneider affirms, "the inscription of a hole that annuls the thought" (Schneider, 1999, p. 26), but at the same time it would be a constituent part like the gear of a clock, like the "galleries of a charcoal mine"—all linked together, in chain, by contiguity that would represent this metonymy of holes, until ending in a sort of annulment "earthquake" of the subject, where the complete psychism would suffer some sort of major "short circuit."

Nevertheless, short circuits would be cumulative; the holes in the body would "touch" and "trigger" in the sense of the thought holes and vice versa. That is to say, there would be a direct communication among all the holes, as in mines. As a "communicating vessel" a hole in the body would always make reference and be linked to a hole in the thought. As a matter of fact, if we think of the subject as a territory, the metaphor would be the jungle that would end up becoming, from a desert—abandoned, burnt, worn out, "short-circuited"—a complete desert, where the drought will have won the complete territory; that is, the metonymy of holes would go in the sense of dead pulsion!

THIRD DOOR: THE FIGHT OF THE DEVIL AGAINST DEATH, AND THE INTERNMENT TO THE CHILD'S UNCONSCIOUS

What do you want to be when you grow up?

Preschooler 1: I want to be a drug dealer!
Preschoooler 2: I want to be a hit man!
Sigmund Freud in *The Interpretation of Dreams* (Freud, 1993 [1900b], p. 143) said that to ask a child what he or she dreamt of was like asking a goose, because children do not implicate that much difficulty in their understanding. Freud tells us about the child's dreams, that they are "brief, clear, coherent, easy to understand, univocal, and, with all, indubitable" (Freud, 1993 [1915–1917], p. 115). Dreams are an accomplishment of desires and, in the case of adults, an accomplishment of sexual, infantile, and repressed desires.

What particularly interests me here is the children's choice of the *ominous figure* of the drug dealer or hit man. Beyond simple appearances, beyond a simplistic explanation such as "they learn by imitation" or "they want to be superheroes," this figure they identify themselves with, I dare to affirm, is a demonic figure.

Preschool kids—if not all, then at least the ones from Ciudad Juarez— know what a drug dealer and a hit man are; they do not confuse either with a superhero; they are very smart; they know where the corpses are thrown, where the bullets are and their calibers too, where the heads of the decapitated have appeared, where the "narco-pits" have been found, as well as the "narco-blankets" and what the "charging dues for the space" is. Some of us have had to learn the entire spectrum of terms from the "narc-world" inventory.

Monique Schneider (2002) explains that the identification with the devil is preferable to the demiurge of identification with the dead. Identification with the semi-god or semi-devil is a place of absolute transcendence. She questions why having a power is having a destruction, an annulment power, power to murder discreetly or not, power to annul?

Monique Schneider (1985) in *Father, Can't You See . . . ?* [*Père, ne vois tu pas . . . ?*] explains an accident little Sigmund Freud had when he split his chin and had to go to the doctor, Doctor Pur, but not without a scolding first. Freud, while facing the doctor, had a sensation of *Unheimlich*, the sinister, because the doctor was missing an eye. The one-eyed doctor, this mutilation in his look, would inhabit his unconscious for 38 years, since the conditions under which they met for the first time were "traumatic and hemorrhagic" circumstances. as the author notes. In this borderline experience in front of the savior and righteous doctor, little Freud literally disfigured, had risked losing all of his teeth according to his own comment, and looked for the insurance of his completion.

Monique Schneider asserts that in a traumatic situation the character's transference becomes necessary, as an "instant deportation in the being of the other," and affirms

Freud seems to take into account a desire that he at first held back, in an unsustainable scene, as if directed against him, as if the doctor had intervened as a giver of the right of life and death. Not being able to continue inhabiting in a threatened position, lived as in a place of death, the kid had emigrated to the place from which death finds itself enacted and applied, it is only running away rapidly, in the memories linked to the dream of the novelties in the front, of the victim's position towards the executioner's position, that he assures, in half-blindness, this "blindness of the non-blind" of which the studies about hysteria talk—a relative domain of the scene. (Schneider, 1985, pp. 127–128)

In the same way, the Unconscious is the one talking in the kid who says he wants to be a drug dealer when he grows up . . . seeing his position as a child or as a grown man in the future, threatened by death, the child does not want to be the dead one! It is for this reason that he rapidly migrates in his identification—if necessary, to the devil himself—who is in the place of life, the safest place, the place from where death is decreed and executed, the place of the one who ordains who lives and who must die: the child, to secure the domain of the scene and most of all the anguish that this generates in the face of being the dead one or himself dead. The child dies in the position of a kid but lives by transferring himself to the place where death is decreed, the place of the drug dealer. This identification with the devil or the drug dealer becomes the only chance of survival for the child.

In the effort of repairing—after the lived trauma—the psychism tries to rewrite the event through repetition, to give sense—as in playing or dreaming—to something unavailable. But in certain cases, such as rape, incest, and murder, the psychism tries to disappear, to make up, in order to "welcome"—if we can say that—this violence in the interior of the psychism. The implication here is disappearing violence or effacing oneself!

THE EXIT FROM HELL: EXORCISING THE DEVIL

In order to exorcise the devil it is necessary to conjure him, with his same powers. My bet here is to bring back the personal and collective traumatic experience; make a narrative of the wounds, the still open wounds, the loss of the meaning of law, of justice, the plenitude of the person; and revert the reification processes. The intention of my writing is to bring back the memory of the trauma to the community, to then work it out and tell it as an inclusive part of the story and not a hole in the same, as if "that"—murders, massacres, kidnappings, decapitations, fires, women burnt alive—had never existed, allowing others, as always, to make up the story, "their" story . . . and that because we do not want the official story to say that in Ciudad Juarez they were all killed because they were all drug dealers, children included. We want the story to be told differently; we do not want to keep seeing ourselves in the same cheating, hallucinating mirror that deforms the reality of the facts.

Re-historicize then from everyone's wounds, so we do not bleed out through the holes from different traumas. Rebuild the bridge of truth and justice for everybody, the state of law, of life. Stop and heal the wounds and relive Ciudad Juarez. Get back the capacity of surprise in the face of violence, like any other foreigner.

The banalization of violence seems to me a "covert" or self-protection of the psychism, or, to say it in a harder but clearer way, banalization of violence is a way of survival!

ACKNOWLEDGMENTS

My gratefulness to Sylvia Aguilar, research assistant and psychology student in the Universidad Autonoma de Ciudad Juarez for the translation of this article from Spanish to English. All the translations from French that appear in this text are mine.

NOTES

1. Gutiérrez-Otero (2003). Original text in French. All translations to Spanish are mine.
2. I retake some reflections from my doctoral thesis to explain the concepts I try to elucidate here.
3. Original term "inconciliable" modernized to "irreconcilable" based on the footnote of the translator page.
4. I use the term "bodily memory" to distinguish it from the psychic memory. To note a bodily anchorage, M. Schneider on her behalf explains that "the wound would not be a memory." I take this up again further on.

BIBLIOGRAPHY

Aguilar, Sonia, and Salvador Castro. 2006. Intentan quemar viva a una mujer. Arroja hombre combustible al vehículo que tripulaba Elsa Aglae Jurado Torres y le prende fuego; sospechan de su expareja. *Norte de Ciudad Juárez*, Sección B, July 7, 2006.

Ajo, Mirna, and Patricia Ravelo. 2003. "Sabemos que salimos pero no sabemos si vamos a regresar": Vulnerabilidad y percepción del riesgo entre mujeres trabajadoras de la maquila de Ciudad Juárez. *Género y salud en cifras* 1 (3): 19–24, www.mujerysalud.gob.mx (accessed June 20, 2006).

Ayala, David. 2010. Erotismo de vida, erotismo de muerte o cuando la sexualidad se torna en violencia. In *Perspectivas socioculturales de la violencia sexual en México y otros países*, edited by M. Gutiérrez-Otero and O. L. Bustos Romero. Ciudad Juárez, México: Universidad Autónoma de Ciudad Juárez, pp. 21–63.

Azaola, Elena. 2003. Homenaje a las mujeres, muertas en Ciudad Juárez. In *La memoria de las olvidadas: Las mujeres asesinadas en Ciudad Juárez*, edited by R. M. Álvarez de Lara. Serie Ensayos, 14. México: UNAM, Instituto de Investigaciones Jurídicas, pp. 119–135.

BBC News Europe. 2006, April 8. French man jailed in torture case, http://news .bbc.co.uk/2/hi/europe/4891474.stm (accessed December 1, 2009).

Bourdieu, Pierre. 1998. *La Domination Masculine.* Paris: Seúil.

Consejo Ciudadano para la Seguridad Pública y Justicia penal A. C. 11 enero 2010, www.seguridadjusticiaypaz.org.mx (accessed January 20, 2010).

Diario Digital. 2010, April 24, www.diario.mx/local/

El diario. 2006, July 7, 3b, 9b.

Eurípides. 1991. Las bacantes. In *Tragedias (III)*. España: Biblioteca Clásica Gredos, pp. 323–409.

Freud, Sigmund. 1973 [1894]. Les psychonévroses de défense. In *Névrose, psychose et perversion*, translated by J. Laplanche. Paris: PUF Originally published in 1894 *Neurol. Zbl.*, 13 (10): 362–364 and *Neurol. Zbl.*, 11: 402–409, pp. 1–14.

Freud, Sigmund. 1956 [1897]. Lettre 61 2-5-1897. In *La Naissance de la psychanalyse*, translated by A. Berman. Paris: PUF Originally published in London: Imago Publishing 1950, pp. 173–174.

Freud, Sigmund. 1984 [1898]. Sur le mécanisme psychique de l'oubli. In *Résultats, idées, problèmes*, translated by J. Altounian., A. Bourguignon, et al. Paris: PUF. Originally published in 1898 *Mschr. Psychiat. Neurol.*, 4 (6): 436–443, pp. 99–107.

Freud, Sigmund. 1973 [1899]. Sur les souvenirs écrans. In *Névrose psychose et perversion*. Paris: PUF Originally published 1899 *Mschr. Psychiat. Neurol.*, 6 (3): 215–230, pp. 113–132.

Freud, Sigmund. 1967 [1900a]. *L'interprétation des rêves*, translated by I. Meyerson. Paris: PUF. Originally published in Leipzig and Vienna: Franz Deuticke.

Freud, Sigmund. 1993 [1900b]. La interpretación de los sueños. In *Obras Completas*, Vols. IV and V, translated by J. Etcheverry. Buenos Aires: Amorrortu. Originally published in Leipzig and Vienna: Franz Deuticke.

Freud, Sigmund. 1993 [1915–1917]. *Octava Conferencia de introducción al psicoanálisis (1915–1917): Sueños de niños.* In *Obras Completas*, Vol XVIII, translated by J. Etcheverry. Buenos Aires: Amorrortu Originally published in *Der Traum*, Leipzig and Vienna: Heller, 1916, pp. 115–124.

Freud, Sigmund. 1996 [1920]. Au-delà du principe de plaisir. In *Œuvres complètes*, Vol. XV. Paris: PUF Originally published in Leipzig, Vienna, and Zurich: Internationaler Psychoanalystischer Verlag, 1920, pp. 273–338.

Freud, Sigmund. 1971 [1930]. *Malaise dans la civilisation*, traslated by CH. Et J. Odier. Paris: PUF Originally published in Leipzig, Vienna, and Zurich: Internationaler Psychoanalystischer Verlag, 1930.

Gutiérrez-Otero, Miriam. 2003. *Les vicissitudes de la symbolisation de la Loi de l'interdiction de l'inceste. Discours des enfants qui l'ont subi.* Doctoral thesis, Paris University 7, Denis Diderot.

Gutiérrez-Otero, Miriam. 2006. *La violencia sexual en Ciudad Juárez: Un estudio preliminar.* USA. Center for Border Health Research.

Juárez es la ciudad más violenta del mundo. 2010. January 11. *El Universal.* http://www.eluniversal.com.mx/notas/650956.html (accessed January 20, 2010)

Kaci, Mina. 2006, April 10. Sentence exemplaire dans l'affaire Sohane. *L'humanité*, www.l'humanite.fr (accessed December 10, 2009).

Kaci, Mina. 2006, April 20 Gros plan sur le meurtrier de Sohane et sa bande. *L'humanité*, www.l'humanite.fr (accessed December 10, 2009).

Lacan, Jacques. 1966a. L'agressivité en psychanalyse. In *Ecrits*. Paris: *Éditions du Seuil*, pp. 101–124.

Lacan, Jacques. 1966b. Le stade du miroir comme formateur de la fonction du Je telle qu'elle nous est révélée dans l'expérience psychanalytique. In *Ecrits*. Paris: *Éditions du Seuil*, pp. 93–100.

La opcion de Chihuahua. 2011, March 4. Dan 30 años de prisión a asesino que le prendió fuego a su víctima. http://laopcion.com.mx/n/id_101646.html (accessed February 17, 2015).

La red noticias. 2011, March 4. Dan 30 años de prisión a feminicida http://www
.larednoticias.com/noticias.cfm?n=58562 (accessed February 17, 2015).

Le littré. Dictionnaire de la langue Française. Edition numérique.

Le nouveau petit Robert. 1993. *Dictionnaire de la langue française.* Paris: Le Robert.

Lifton, Robert Jay. 1997. Doubling: The Faustian Bargain. In *The Web of Violence:
From Interpersonal to Global,* edited by Jennifer Turpin and Lester R. Kurtz.
Chicago: University of Illinois Press, pp. 29–44.

Lifton, Robert Jay. 2000. *The Nazi Doctors: Medical Killing and the Psychology of Genocide.* New York: Basic Books.

M. K. 2006, April 9. De la dimension sexiste du crime. *L'Humanité,* http://www
.humanite.fr/node/100589 (accessed December 10, 2009).

McKinley, James C. Jr. 2009, January 23. Two Sides of a Border: One Violent,
One Peaceful. *New York Times,* http://www.nytimes.com/2009/01/23/
us/23elpaso.html?_r=3&hp (accessed January 30, 2009).

Press, Jean. 1997. Caractère(s), traumatisme(s), somatisation(s). *Revue française de
Psychosomatique* 11: 49–70.

Rodriguez, A., and G. Cabullo. 2006, July 7. Prenden Fuego a una mujer viva en El
Chamizal II *El diario,* 2006.

Saint Augustine. 1960. siècle IV *La cité Dieu. Livres XIX–XXII: Triomphe de la cité
céleste,* edited by Desclée de Brouwer. Suisse: Bibliothèque Augustinienne
(1960).

Sauvadet, Thomas. 2006. Les jeunes de la cité: comment forment-ils un groupe?
Socio-logos: Revue de l'association française de sociologie [En ligne], 1 2006, mis
en ligne le 11 juin 2006, http://socio-logos.revues.org/55 (accessed May
10, 2010).

Schneider, Monique. 1985. *Père, ne vois tu pas . . . ?* Paris: Denoël.

Schneider, Monique. 1992. La séduction traumatique. *Revue du collège de Psychana-
lystes, 45: Violences et subjectivation,* pp. 35–46.

Schneider, Monique. 2002–2003. *Séminaire des archives Husserl 2002–2003: Le traite-
ment de l'altérité; la rencontre freudienne de l'antisémitisme et la question des
différences.* A l'Ecole Normale Supérieure, séminaire du 16 janvier 2002 et
du 19 mars 2003.

Tanner, Samuel. 2013. Dynamiques de participation d'une bande armée dans des
crimes de masse. In M. Cusson, S. Guay, J. Proulx and F. Cortoni, *Traité des
violences criminelles. Les questions posées par la violence, les réponses de la science.* Montréal: Hurtubise, pp. 333–67.

Toledo, Victor, R. 2012, February 3. Quince rosales en Salvárcar. *La jornada,.* http://
www.jornada.unam.mx/archivo_opinion/autor/front/96/31129/y/
homicidios-dolosos-Jurez (accessed February 19, 2013).

Vigoureux, Elsa. 2006, March 30. Les bourreaux de Sohane, www.lenouvelobs.com
(accessed December 10, 2009).

CHAPTER 16

Sharia Law and Its Implications for Women's Status and Rights

Saira Yamin

INTRODUCTION

This chapter examines the relationship between Sharia or Islamic law and the status of women in Muslim societies. It explores how Sharia has been incorporated in legal and social structures and institutions and reflects on implications for women. It finds that the interpretation and uses of Sharia are not uniform across the Muslim world and that it has been used either as a tool for progressive reform or conversely for the suppression of women. It illustrates that in some Muslim societies where patriarchal norms and traditions are pervasive, women are subjected to injustice through judicial or extrajudicial means sometimes through misrepresentation of Sharia. The chapter presents evidence to suggest that transformative change for women is possible through legal reform in compliance with Sharia.

SHARIA'S SCOPE AND INFLUENCE

Sharia, a religious framework, encompasses both a legal and a personal moral code influencing the lives of about 1.6 billion Muslims living across the world, in varying degrees. In a number of Muslim states, Sharia serves as a legal or a parallel legal system governing personal status laws—pertaining to family relations such as marriage, alimony, divorce, child custody, inheritance, and religious freedoms. Sharia also guides gender relations in Muslim societies either formally, when it is incorporated into the law, or informally, when it is embedded in tradition, is the cultural norm, and carries no legal implications. Sharia also addresses crime and punishment and is a source of legislation on adultery, fornication, and rape in several Muslim countries. While the breadth of Sharia as a legal and moral code of conduct extends far beyond the areas identified above, this research focuses on how Muslim women's rights and status are affected by it, especially since it has been a subject of considerable controversy around the world, in non-Muslim and sometimes also in Muslim societies.

It is often suggested that Sharia law serves as a vehicle for the oppression of women. In the West in particular, Sharia is widely viewed as an embodiment of "misogyny, intolerance, and harsh punishment" (Sacirbey, 2013). The theory and practice of Sharia with respect to a number of very important matters have drawn considerable criticism. Examples include the legal weight of a woman's testimony (half that of a man); polygamy rights accorded to Muslim men; a woman's share in inheritance (half that of her brother); and the Hadd laws, where the onus of proof rests on the rape victim, failing which she is treated as an adulterer and subject to harsh punishment. All of these elements of Sharia practiced in some countries legally and extralegally present evidence of discrimination and injustice against women.

Human rights activists charge that Sharia legislation affecting both women and men in a number of Muslim states is in violation of universal human rights norms and laws. Consider, for instance, stoning as a punishment under Sharia law for adultery and fornication in Iran, Mauritania, Nigeria, Pakistan, Qatar, Saudi Arabia, Somalia, Sudan, the United Arab Emirates, and Yemen (Redpath, 2013). While there is some comfort in the knowledge that in most of the aforementioned states stoning as a legal punishment has rarely if ever been executed (Redpath, 2013), legislation must be reformed to protect women (and men) from inhumane punishments and to prevent its extrajudicial practice. In Pakistan, for instance, despite the existence of such legislation, stoning has only taken place in tribal communities without legal sanction (Redpath, 2013). The only Islamic country other than Somalia (essentially an ungoverned state) where stoning has been executed legally is Iran. Iran is believed to have stoned between 70 and 150 convicted adulterers since 1980, the highest global record (Fantz, 2013; Al Arabiya News, 2013). It has been reported that a majority of those condemned to stoning in Iran are women (Hoseini, 2010). Before stoning became part of the penal code in Iran at least 10 people had been subjected to it extrajudically, demonstrating that legislation made far more people vulnerable—especially women (Hoseini, 2010). However, in a recent development, Iran has amended this law, a positive step toward the eradication of an inhumane practice (Al Arabiya News, 2013). But while Iran is demonstrating its willingness to reform its legal structure, Afghanistan is considering signing the punishment into law, which prompts the question why some Muslim states, even if in minority, are inclined to incorporate such harsh punishments in their penal codes (Hodge and Totakhil, 2013).

Ironically, stoning is not mentioned in the Quran but does appear in the Torah and Old Testament (Alasti, 2007; Mohd Noor and Ghazali, 2008). The Quran does, however, prescribe flogging as a punishment for adultery or fornication for men and women both. While flogging is not much less brutal than stoning, it is a rare practice in the Muslim world. Saudi Arabia, Nigeria, and the former Sudan are the only countries where flogging has been observed (Mohd Noor and Ghazali, 2008; also see Quran 24:2; ABC News, 2007). On occasion, those who defend stoning have falsely suggested that it is based on Quranic teachings, demonstrating their ignorance on this issue (Hodge and Totakhil, 2013). Generally, however, most advocates of stoning such as tribal communities, religious extremists, and politicians with vested interests have suggested that there is precedent in the life of Prophet Muhammad (Alasti, 2007). Within the community of Muslim scholars there is disagreement concerning similar precedents in the life of Prophet Muhammad. The scholarly contention on the issue is significant given that under the principles of Sharia all religious doctrines must be standardized through scholarly consensus or ijma (for an in-depth narrative on this debate see Mohd Noor and Ghazali, 2008; see, for example, Farooq, 2011, Chapter 4). Thus, when consensus on an issue doesn't exist, to claim it is within the confines of Sharia law is false.

DEFINING THE PROBLEM AND SCOPE OF RESEARCH

The relationship between Sharia law and women's rights and status is very complex. While the role of Sharia is important in an analysis of women's status in Muslim societies, a consideration of its influence in isolation from a range of other pertinent factors inhibits clarity on the issue. To be sure, the legal rights and obligations of women emanating from religious sources, when sanctioned by the state, play an important role in their empowerment or, conversely, their social vulnerability. However, there are other, equally important factors shaping women's lives, such as the role of state institutions and societal structures in providing gender-equitable opportunities for self-actualization and in promoting participatory and inclusive policies; cultural and traditional influences; and socioeconomic development levels; to name a few. These dynamics are critical in an analysis of a Muslim woman's positioning in society, in the community, and within the family. They are important elements of an environment that enables and empowers her to live a life with a fair sense of dignity, security, self-sufficiency, and agency, forming multiple layers of a complex and dynamic process defining the trajectory of her rights and status.

An examination of the nexus between Sharia law and the status of Muslim women, numbering roughly about 800 million around the world, also suggests that it is not possible to make generalizations about the relationship. I base my argument on the premises that: (1) the experiences

of Muslim women and the status of their human rights have been vastly
different through history, and (2) the interpretation and uses of Sharia
vary widely by state as well as by the juristic school of thought. Religious scholars have argued, for example, that the variations in popular,
scholarly, and official understandings of Sharia demonstrate "a lack of
consensus among Muslims and should deter generalizing about Islam"
(Hajjar, 2004). Although about 49 Muslim majority states around the
world (Desilver, 2013) rely on the Sharia to varying degrees, Muslim
women living in regions such as Asia Pacific, the Middle East, and Africa
must not be taken as a monolithic group. They may have a common
religious faith, but a number of variables affect women's lives, in relative degrees, for better or for worse. The history, politics, culture, and
socioeconomic context of a state, as well as community and clan subcultures, also have a bearing on women's positioning in society and sometimes far outweigh religious influences.

Consider also that millions of Muslim women live as religious minorities scattered across all continents in secular states or those following
other religions. They also live in Muslim states where Sharia is not incorporated into the law.[1] Their social positioning is difficult to compare even
though large numbers of Muslim women residing in these societies abide
by Sharia as a moral and legal code in their personal and private lives to
some extent. For example, Muslim marriages are usually solemnized by
an Imam (religious leader) or a Qazi (religious arbitrator) in accordance
with Sharia. The Islamic marriage contract is usually signed in addition to
the registration of marriage under the civil laws of the land. Personal matters such as marital relations, hygiene, dress code, diet, fasting, and praying are also commonly practiced under the precepts of Sharia depending
on individual and family choices.

Interestingly in recent years, some Western countries including the
United Kingdom and Canada have permitted the establishment of unofficial Sharia law tribunals for personal dispute resolution in keeping with
the demands of Muslim communities. The U.K. is believed to have 85
Sharia courts (Bingham, 2009). These serve as religious councils operating in mosques and provide guidance in the resolution of marital,
domestic, and business disputes. While the tribunals are informal and
their judgments may be superseded by an official court of law, they are
legal in accordance with the British Arbitration Act of 1996 (McSmith,
2009). In Ontario, Canada, informal Sharia courts are also permitted,
under the Canadian Act of 1991, for Muslims seeking to settle their personal disputes (Brown, 2004; Sturcke, 2008). Regardless of the recourse to
Sharia in many matters by Muslim women (and men) in Western societies and elsewhere, by virtue of the rights and opportunities accorded to
them by state institutions, their status is generally on par with the societal mainstream.

There are, however, instances where the culture and values of immigrants in Western societies have interfered with the rights and liberties given to women as citizens. Honor killings are a case in point. It is important to clarify that the practice is not in compliance with Sharia law. It is a centuries-old cultural custom and various manifestations have been reported in a number of non-Muslim societies as well, including Italy, India, Israel, Sweden, Brazil, Ecuador, and Uganda (see, for example, Mayell, 2002 and Moussaoui, 2007). This research hopes to clarify commonly held misperceptions regarding Sharia and its conflation with misogynistic cultural practices deeply entrenched in a number of societies.

While this chapter discusses the sources of Sharia and identifies various divergent and patriarchal interpretations and their implications for women, it is beyond its scope to assess the validity of the differing opinions of various schools of Islamic jurisprudence. However, I argue that while Sharia serves as a recognized body of Islamic law, when there is divergence in understanding and practice across different states, then it is reasonable to challenge its interpretation and application. Injustice meted out to women in the name of Sharia law often stems from extra-Islamic conditions. In instances where disagreement in scholarly opinion is evident, it is imperative that the Muslim community of scholars work toward universal Islamic consensus or ijma. The process of ijma is a requirement for standardizing Sharia law; it is based on a collective understanding of evidence available in the primary sources of Sharia: the Quran and Sunnah (the teachings and sayings of the most revered messenger of Islam, Prophet Muhammad) (Abusulayman, 1987).

The urgent requirement for ijma, a pivotal source of Sharia, on a host of issues pertaining to women's rights and status is crucial for the progress and welfare of Muslim women in general. The findings of this research suggest that there are many areas of concern where various schools of thought stand opposed in the interpretation and application of Sharia. The study highlights a few conflicting interpretations and uses of Sharia, drawing attention to both regressive and progressive interpretations. It argues that societal reform is an inherent element of Sharia and should be upheld in fulfillment of women's greater rights and empowerment across the Muslim world, a process set forth with the advent of Islam. Regrettably, however, women's progress and development have been obstructed by patriarchal norms, traditions, and structures and unresponsive state institutions.

SOURCES AND INTERPRETATION OF SHARIA LAW

"Sharia" literally means "path" or "way" in Arabic. The term is commonly used with reference to "Islamic law" and is widely considered to refer to divine law. However, some scholars rightly argue that while Sharia is a religious law, it should not be seen strictly as divine law because it is heavily reliant on human judicial reasoning and interpretation, a process that started many decades after the revelation of the Quran and Prophet Muhammad's demise. Sharia primarily draws on four sources. Of these, two are primary and foundational: (1) Quranic text and (2) Sunnah, the conduct and sayings of Prophet Muhammad. Sharia has evolved on the basis of human interpretation of these two sources, mostly by men (Imam, 2003).

The process of interpretation draws on two inherently dynamic practices—the secondary sources of Sharia. They are known as "ijma" (consensus) and "ijtihad" (use of human reasoning) based on qiyas (precedents and analogy), an equally important part of ijtihad (Hasan, 2003; Abusulayman, 1987). The judicial interpretation of Sharia is called "fiqh," or Islamic jurisprudence. Because fiqh is a process that relies substantially on human reasoning, Sharia is subject to change and adaption. While human reasoning opens up space for manipulation, the process of ijma, or universal religious consensus, serves as a check against the potential of misuse. Ijma is a precondition for the use of ijtihad, or reasoning, and is the third most important source of Sharia after the Quran and Sunnah. Regrettably, however, despite the importance of consensus there is lack of uniformity in the interpretations of the teachings imparted in the Quran and Sunnah across various schools of Islamic thought as well as between individual scholars within these schools. Thus contrary to the spirit of Sharia, under the circumstances there is no one Islamic law (Vikør, 2005).

The lack of uniformity in the understanding of Sharia is very evident in a number of rulings pertaining to women's rights and status. As aptly noted by one scholar, Sharia "is surrounded with confusion between theory and practice, between theological and legal meanings, between internal and external perspectives, and between past and present manifestations" (Otto, 2010). Therefore, it is not unreasonable to argue that Sharia has been tainted and exploited by patriarchal interpretations and vested interests.

Sharia's evolution, based on a very complex process of interpretation of the Quran and Sunnah, has predominantly been inspired by four schools of Sunni jurisprudence—Hanbali, Maliki, Shafi'i, and Hanafi—and a fifth, Shiite school: Jafaria. The schools have been named after the scholars who developed fiqh from the eighth century onward (Otto, 2010, p. 20). Many scholarly books on Islamic jurisprudence produced in the first two centuries of the evolution of this process were replete with case studies and rules (Otto, 2010). The literature was drawn from the Quran and *Ahadith* (the traditions of Prophet Muhammad's life collected and preserved by his companions). However, the prominent fiqh scholars' opinions often differed on many issues, including the sources of Sharia, their scope, and their legal validity, leading to the emergence of various distinct schools of thought (Otto, 2010).

The four schools of Sunni jurisprudence present a range of moderate to very conservative interpretations of the law and serve as guidelines in varying degrees in the affairs of governance in many Islamic countries. In most countries, Sharia is applied selectively, with adoption of only a few of its components, while a few rely on Islamic law as a comprehensive guide for the legal and justice system. Saudi Arabia provides an example where Sharia is the absolute law of the land. The kingdom follows the Hanbali school, the most orthodox among them, also used in Afghanistan, particularly under the former Taliban regime. The Hanafi school, considered the largest and most influential, is also the most moderate and progressive. It is followed by some majority Sunni states in Central Asia, Egypt, Pakistan, India, China, Turkey, the Balkans, and the Caucasus (Council on Foreign Relations, 2014). The Maliki school is influential in North Africa and the Shafi'i school in Indonesia, Malaysia, Brunei Darussalam, and Yemen (Council on Foreign Relations, 2014). The legal systems of these countries are also influenced by European-style common and civil law while they also use Sharia in some aspects of governance. Shia Muslims follow the Jafaria school, mostly in Iran, the only state with a Shia majority. Shia minorities in other countries—most notably Pakistan, India, and Iraq—follow the same school of thought (Pew Research Center, 2013). Shias remain a minority in the Muslim world, comprising about 10–13 percent of the global Muslim population (Pew Research Center, 2013).

IMPLICATIONS FOR WOMEN

An analysis of Sharia's implications for women's rights must be premised in the knowledge that the two primary and foundational sources of the law, the Quran and Prophet Muhammad's Sunnah, are replete with evidence that Islam supports equality between men and women. However, by virtue of gender differences in social functions and allocation of responsibilities, particularly the financial obligations on men as primary providers, it is often argued that men have been granted a superior status and authority over women under Sharia. This view, however, does not carry significant weight when examined in a comprehensive assessment of gender roles and relations prescribed in the Quran and modeled by Prophet Muhammad (Saleh, 1972). Saneya Saleh suggests that the Quran addresses both men and women very frequently in equitable terms as "believing men and believing women." She draws a number of references from the Quran, the foundational base of Sharia, and argues, for instance, that it is quite balanced in the rights and duties of men and women; explicit in entitling the genders to equal earnings and rewards; and that there are vastly more indicators of their equality than their inequality (Saleh, 1972, pp. 36–37). Taj Hashmi, a male scholar of Islam, has argued, "It would be a mistake to assume that the Quran has given men a higher status than women and hence women are disqualified to be leaders in society. In fact, there is nothing in the Quran which disqualifies women as rulers" (Hashmi, 2010). He justifies his position by referring to Chapter 27 of the Quran, where Queen Sheba of Yemen is praised as a "competent and powerful ruler" (Hashmi, 2010).

There are many examples of women in leadership and decision making roles in the times of Prophet Muhammad, the dawn of Islam (Hashmi, 2010). These include women in the Prophet's family who fought battles alongside him, shielded him, and killed enemies. Among them his aunt Safiya, Asma bint Yazid, Nusaybah bint Kaab, and Khawla bint a-Zawar are counted among warriors and soldiers of Islam (Hashmi, 2010). Drawing on Prophet Muhammad's teachings, eminent Islamic jurist Dr. Jamal Nasir underscores that the Prophet supported women in the role of teachers both for women and men (Nasir, 2009, p. 17). Widely quoted in the Muslim world is a story about Prophet Muhammad being asked three times about the one person to love the most. He gave the same reply each time: "Your mother." Such is the status of women in Islam.

LAWS OF INHERITANCE

A number of Sharia laws discriminating against women are often cited to suggest that women are not considered equal to men. The laws of inheritance, where a woman acquires only half the share of her brother, is one element of the debate on gender equality. The Quranic injunction pertaining to inheritance appears in the fourth chapter of the Quran titled "An-Nisa," meaning "women." It reads as follows:

Say: Allah directs (thus) about those who leave no descendants or ascendants as heirs. If it is a man that dies, leaving a sister but no child, she shall have half the inheritance: If (such a deceased was) a woman, who left no child, Her brother takes her inheritance: If there are two sisters, they shall have two-thirds of the inheritance (between them): if there are brothers and sisters, (they share), the male having twice the share of the female. Thus doth Allah make clear to you (His law), lest ye err. And Allah hath knowledge of all things. (Quran 4:176)

While this verse is apparently discriminatory, Saleh (1972) offers a contextual explanation reminding one of the conditions in pre-Islamic Arabia whereby the aforementioned revelation radically challenged tradition by according women the right of property through a share in inheritance. In defense of the verse, Saleh adds quite persuasively that Islam provided women the right to inheritance and property in unequivocal terms six centuries before they were extended to them in Europe. Thus, she contends that the advent of Islam in pre-Islamic Arabia "elevated the status of women" and, contrary to popular beliefs, the low status of women in a number of Muslim societies is rooted in "other cultural sources."

Yet another rationale for the laws on inheritance provided by Hamasamy (1958) suggests that an unequal share in inheritance is culturally acceptable in the Muslim world because traditionally the man is the primary provider of the family. From this perspective the man is viewed as deserving a greater financial share. While this assertion may be correct with respect to certain segments of Muslim society, it cannot be applied universally as it disregards situations where women either contribute financially to the maintenance of the family or are the sole breadwinners. Additionally, the view that men necessarily play the role of the sole provider of the family points to another complexity emanating from the use of the term "qawamuna" appearing in verse 4:34 of the Quran. The term is sometimes interpreted to mean that men are the providers or protectors of women, but the same term has been interpreted by many religious scholars to signify men's authority over women (and ergo their superiority). The interpretation supports and promotes the notion that women have an unequal status in Islam. Consider one anonymous interpretation of the verse confirming this view and compare it to various similar or contrasting interpretations offered by other prominent sources, provided below. (Note that the italics in each interpretation of the term "qawamuna" cited here have been added by this author and are not in the original.)

1. Men have *authority over women* since Allah has made men superior to women because men spend their worldly goods on their wives. (Anonymous)
2. Men are the *protectors and maintainers of women*, because Allah has given the one more (strength) than the other, and because they support them from their means. (Ali, Yusuf, Quran)
3. Men are *in charge of women*, because Allah hath made the one of them to excel the other, and because they spend of their property (for the support of women). (Pickthall, Quran)
4. Men *are in charge of women* by [right of] what Allah has given one over the other and what they spend [for maintenance] from their wealth. (Sahih International, Quran)
5. Men are the *ever upright (managers) (of the affairs) of women* for what Allah has graced some of them over (some) others and for what they have expended of their riches. (Ghali, Quran)

The range of interpretations of the term "qawamuna" sheds light on the differences of opinion on whether the term assigns to men (1) greater responsibility and obligation in financial affairs, (2) charge of protection of women by virtue of their financial responsibility and strength, (3) greater authority by virtue of financial responsibility, (d) charge of women owing to their (men's) superiority, and so on. Many more interpretations by prominent scholars, not given here, form part of the debate on the meaning of "qawamuna" and the status and obligations of men and women toward each other and their families.

In a striking contrast to the aforementioned interpretations of verse 4:34 of the Quran, Dr. Riffat Hassan, a prominent feminist Islamic scholar, argues that it is addressed to both men and women and that "qawwamun" means "breadwinner," or the one who provides livelihood (Hassan, 1999). Hence, the question of superiority or authority of one over the other is an ambiguous one. Hassan draws attention to a preceding verse in the same chapter of the Quran (4:32) cognizant of women's earning potential being on par with that of men to substantiate her rationale: "To Men is allotted to what they earn and to women what they earn." One could argue therefore that verse 4:34 needs to be interpreted within the broader context of women's financial contributions to the household, especially in the contemporary era. In spite of Hamasamy's thoughts on gender roles and responsibilities in the Muslim world, there is dire need for reform whereby men and women are accorded equal rights of inheritance under the law.

Owing to the lack of agreement on the precise meaning and context of "qawamuna" and the fact that women are often equally burdened with financial responsibilities as men, scholars have called for challenging juristic interpretations that are partial toward women at the level of fiqh—a product of human interpretation of the primary sources of Sharia. Ziba Mir-Hosseini (2006) suggests that it is a mistake to equate fiqh with Sharia as is often done in popular, scholarly, and legal discourses. In her words, "What Islamists and others assert to be a Sharia mandate (hence divine and infallible) is the result of fiqh, juristic speculation and extrapolation (hence human and fallible)" (Mir-Hosseini, 2006).

Relevant to the interpretation of verse 4:34 of the Quran, Bernard Weiss, an Islamic scholar, contends that the interpretation of Sharia rests on human understanding and must accommodate societal norms (Weiss, 1998). Therefore, reform under ijtihad and ijma must continue with respect to social and cultural change. The lack of reform on women's rights can be attributed to a huge gap in the practice of Sharia, which should ideally be, and in principle is, a dynamic process. Ijtihad and ijma provide for ongoing interpretation of the foundational sources of Sharia in view of the contemporary societal context. Muslim women activists have been trying to explore reform through ijtihad (Vikør, 2005), but the process of reformist ijtihad has been more or less dormant within the Islamic community of scholars. Regrettably, Islamic jurists have resisted challenging the interpretations of classical Islamic fiqh produced by the prominent schools of Islamic jurisprudence many centuries ago.[2]

THE RIGHT OF POLYGAMY

As stated earlier, there are a number of Quranic injunctions on the rights of men and women that have led to divergence in scholarly opinion (fiqh) on the issue. Polygamy in Islam, the right given to a man to take up to four wives, is another important consideration in an assessment of gender equality in Islam. The Quranic verse supporting polygamy also appears in the fourth chapter of the Quran titled An-Nisa ("women"). It reads:

And if you fear that you will not deal justly with the orphan girls, then marry those that please you of [other] women, two or three or four. But if you fear that you will not be just, then [marry only] one or those your right hand possesses. That is more suitable that you may not incline [to injustice]. (Quran 4:3)

While there appears to be agreement within most schools of thought regarding the permissibility of polygamy under Sharia, the Shafi'i school argues that this provision is conditional (Mashhour, 2005, p 569). Because the Shafi'i stance, a prominent school of fiqh, lays emphasis on the restrictive nature of this clause, one could argue that consensus (ijma) does not exist and therefore the law's conformity with Sharia is questionable. At another level, Mashhour argues that since Quranic teachings subscribe to a gradual process of reform, the abolition of polygamy (as in the case of slavery) was an intended objective implicit in the limitation imposed on the number of marriages (Mashhour, 2005, p. 2).[3] Alexandre argues that in pre-Islamic Arabia it was customary for men to take as many wives as they wanted without any legal obligation to take care of them, and "Verse 4.3 of the Qur'an was innovative and radical at the time, especially considering the laissez faire state of polygamy before the Qur'an was revealed to the Prophet" (Alexandre, 2007).

There is also the scholarly contention that polygamy is conditional on being "just" and is therefore discouraged (Kidwai, 1976, p. 103). Drawing on this angle, Saleh argues that while a man can take up to four wives, his right to do so is conditional on his ability to act justly with all wives and his capacity to provide for them and all their dependents (Saleh, 1972, p. 39). From this it is inferred that while Islam permits polygamy, it does not encourage it because the conditions are difficult, almost impossible to fulfill for most men.

A verse appearing later in the same chapter appears to validate the opinion that monogamy is preferred to polygamy. It reads as follows: "Ye are never able to be fair and just as between women, even if it is your ardent desire" (4:129). Imam Shafi'i of the prominent Shafi'i school claims that the verse underscores the principle that polygamy should be restricted under the law (Mashhour, 2005, p. 569). This view has been upheld by modern Islamic jurists, including Nasir, who emphasizes both conditions for polygamy: justice as well as the provision of maintenance of all wives

(Nasir, 2009, p. 25). Those who advocate polygamy do not often consider the significance of these conditions. However, on an optimistic note, a number of Muslim states have sought to restrict the practice, discussed subsequently in this chapter. Notable among them is Tunisia, regarded as a feminist state model; it has effectively prohibited polygamy under Sharia law (Sharia Controversy, 2012).

Yet another juristic perspective on the practice of polygamy maintains that it is permissible only in exceptional circumstances. This is based on the rationale that the relevant Quranic verse (4:3) was revealed after the murderous battle of Uhud, when a large number of Muslim men had died leaving behind orphans and widows, girls, and women requiring physical and financial protection (Kidwai, 1976, p. 103). Saleh and Alexandre concur that polygamy was permitted only in conditions of hardship and the Prophet's main concern was that women and children not be left homeless and destitute during the early period of great wars in defense of Islam (Saleh, 1972, p. 39; Alexandre, 2007). The reasoning is persuasive, especially in consideration of the fact that verse 4:3 of the Quran, permitting polygamy, begins with reference to the protection of orphan girls.

Prophet Muhammad himself is considered a feminist by some. His first wife, Khadija, was a widow, twice married before, and 15 years his senior. She was 40 at the time of their marriage and had been the one to propose to him. He did not take any other wife in her lifetime, and they remained married for well over two decades until her death. All but one of the Prophet's wives were either widows, divorcees, or prisoners (whom he freed from captivity through payment of ransom money). In the Muslim world, it is widely believed that Prophet Muhammad married them not to legitimize sexual relations or satisfy his needs, but primarily to provide disadvantaged women protection in accordance with societal norms and needs.

The lack of consensus on the issue of polygamy and its conditions and restrictions has left it open to debate and therefore much criticism. In view of the ambiguity in Islamic jurisprudence, it is useful to consider additional Quranic injunctions very clearly disapproving of injustice against girls and women, still vulnerable in many Muslim and non-Muslim societies. For example, the Quran's position on the issue of infanticide is very clear, particularly female infanticide, a common form of postpartum birth control in pre-Islamic Arabia, and still in practice today in many parts of the world. The Quran specifically condemns the practice of female infanticide and infanticide in general. Consider the following verses.

"On the Day of Judgment 'When the infant girl buried alive is asked,' for what crime she was killed." (Quran, 81:8–9)

"And when the good news is given to any of them of a daughter, His face turns dark and he is filled with grief. With shame does he hide himself from his people because of the bad news he has had! Shall he retain her on (sufferance and) contempt, or bury her in the dust? Ah! What an evil (choice) they decide on?" (Quran, 16:58–59)

"Most surely they became losers, who, in their folly and ignorance, killed their own children and made unlawful what Allah had provided them as sustenance, falsely ascribing prohibitions to Allah." (Quran, 6:140)

"Do not kill your offspring for fear of want: for it is We who provides for them and for you as well. Indeed their killing is a heinous excuse." (Quran, 17:31)

These verses are lucid examples of the gender-sensitive, equitable, and progressive spirit of Islam, and I maintain that essentially Sharia provides women equality and protection against injustice. However, its interpretations are sometimes taken out of the historical context and are often selective. They are therefore misunderstood. The historical evolution of Sharia also shows that ijtihad, a process that is inherently responsive to societal change, has stalled within the scholarly Islamic community. The discontinuation of this dynamic and the resistance to reform in Islamic jurisprudence has placed women at a considerable disadvantage. The utility of ijma (consensus) and ijtihad (human reasoning) in addressing contemporary social issues has a pivotal place in Islamic jurisprudence. However, the substantive lack thereof, beyond the works of the aforementioned classical schools of Islamic thought, has contributed to regressive legislation in a number of states. As a matter of fact, the founders of the prominent schools of Islamic jurisprudence had advised their followers that their interpretations should not be viewed as infallible and be examined, challenged, and rejected if necessary.[4]

Evidence suggests that the lack of universal consensus on women's rights and status in Islamic jurisprudence has created the space for states and nonstate actors to misuse Sharia to preserve and perpetuate extrareligious misogynistic practices such as stoning and honor killing. However, this chapter notes that Sharia has also been used as a tool for reform and elevation of the status of women in society. The following section provides evidence to elaborate on the role of the state in the interpretation and uses of Sharia—both good and bad practices—affecting women. It also identifies socioeconomic and cultural factors contributing to the manipulation of Sharia.

SHARIA AND THE STATE

A recent survey by the Pew Research Center (2013) found that the percentage of Muslims who want Sharia to be the official law of the land ranges from as little as 8 percent (in Azerbaijan) to an overwhelming 99 percent (in Afghanistan). While there is considerable variation here, "solid majorities" in the Muslim world "favor the establishment of Sharia."[5] Very importantly, the survey notes that Muslims are most comfortable with

using Sharia in the private sphere for the settlement of family and property disputes (Pew Research Center, 2013). That being said, in principle,
Islam as a religion is widely accepted as a complete way of life in Muslim societies. Unfortunately, however, due to the widespread authority
commanded by Sharia, ruling elites in many countries have used it as an
instrument of state power (Hajjar, 2004, p. 237). There is often a close relationship between those who wield power and use religion as a means to
preserve, consolidate, and legitimize it and right-wing religious groups—
the self-styled "godmen" and "only" true Muslims whose understanding
of Sharia is claimed as the unassailable truth.

The nexus between the state and right-wing religious groups creates
the political space for the latter to intervene in affairs of governance and
to perpetuate misogynistic practices in the name of Sharia. In Muslim
societies, it is a political faux pas and virtually taboo to question Sharia
law because it is considered divine, even when citizens do not approve of
the way it is manipulated and exploited by the powers that be and their
allies. When state authorities in the Muslim world (more often authoritarian than democratic) use religion as an opportunity to justify their rai-
son d'être, it empowers the religious right wing at the expense of other
segments of society who risk persecution and threats to their security
if they question the utilization of Sharia. Regrettably, religion has been
hijacked by highly conservative and patriarchal religious and political
elites in parts of the Muslim world. In addition, enlightened debate on
the need for reform through ijtihad and ijma has also been thwarted. This
is particularly unfortunate.

In many countries across the Muslim world, feminist activists, progressive voices, and liberal religious clerics are harassed, persecuted, and even
assassinated. Some might argue that the state is guilty of tacit support of
those responsible. Examples include the persecution of Egyptian feminist
activist Dr. Nawal El Saadawi, a state minister for health who wrote many
books on the subject of women and Islam. Her public expression of women's
rights and her revolutionary book *Women and Sex* called for social equality
between men and women and openly condemned practices such as female
genital cutting (FGC), also known as female genital mutilation (FGM) or
female circumcision. FGC is very common in Egypt but has no foundation
in Sharia, although it is often misperceived as having religious roots. It is
a centuries-old pagan tradition also practiced by many Coptic Christians
in Egypt and is quite widespread in Africa. FGC is believed to reduce a
woman's sexual libido and considered a means to prevent illicit sexual
relations. The Egyptian religious orthodoxy reacted to El Saadawi's activism by leveling charges of apostasy against her in 2001 (Bald, 1998, p. 132).
An Islamist lawyer challenged her in a civil affairs court in Cairo, hoping
to have her divorced from her Muslim husband on the claim that her writings on the veil and Islamic inheritance laws were grounds for her ouster

from the Muslim community (Bald, 1998, p. 132). El Saadawi was forced to flee Egypt in 1988 in the face of death threats.

Likewise, Tunisian religious scholar and thinker Tahir al-Haddad, who wrote extensively on the need for reform in Islam and equality of the sexes, also faced criticism and persecution (Hijab, 1988, p. 23). Haddad's seminal text on the status of women *Imara'tuna fil Sharia wal mujtama*, meaning "our women in law and society," is considered one of the first feminist works in Arabic literature. It assessed the status of women in Tunisia and advocated for the expansion of women's rights, challenging the interpretations of Islamic jurists. It argued that Prophet Muhammad's model did not suggest that societal progress was in its final stages and that Sharia provided an "inexhaustible source of reform" for women (Hijab, 1988). In Nigeria, Yemen, Egypt, Lebanon, and elsewhere in the Muslim world harassment and threats against feminist activists are common (Imam, 2003; *Economist*, 2013).

Hajjar (2004) argues that many Islamic countries have incorporated Sharia law in their legal regimes through strategies to create more space for exercise of their authority. Thereby, a state may use religion by "according its authorities and institutions semi-autonomy from the national legal regime, the latter under the direct control of the state." She argues that sometimes the state embraces religion as the grounds for its own authority and pursues the enforcement of religious law. This is perhaps most evident in Iran and Saudi Arabia, both modern-day examples of theocratic Islamic states. Afghanistan under the Taliban regime was also a theocracy. Given the ambiguity surrounding the human rights of women under President Hamid Karzai's nearly decade-long regime, it appears that the country is still very vulnerable to a misogynistic orientation. With its weak institutions and the primacy of the Taliban ideology across vast stretches of territory, the prospect that the state may elicit the support of the religious right is quite plausible (see, for example, Barr, 2013). Many Islamic states, particularly those with weak and ineffective institutions, also depend on religious rights groups to provide public services that they are unable or unwilling to provide.

Imam notes that the nexus between the state and the religious right often paves the way for the incorporation of Sharia into the legal framework (Imam, 2003). The state's dependence on religious rights groups is apparent in a number of African countries, particularly in Nigeria (Imam, 2003). The alliance of ruling elites with the religious right has facilitated the "Sharianization" of patriarchal practices through extralegal means, particularly in the country's recent history (Imam, 2003). This phenomenon is pervasive in northern Nigeria, where the imposition of dress codes on women, attempts to force them to sit in the back of public vehicles, and intrusions into private homes to stop music and dancing are now widespread, although they have no legal or religious basis (Imam, 2003). Apparently, these measures are enforced by nonstate actors, "young men vigilantes," sometimes with the open support of a state government (Imam, 2003).

THE DRACONIAN HUDOOD ORDINANCES OR HADD LAWS

Pakistan was placed on a theocratic trajectory during former military dictator General Muhammad Zia ul Haq's 11-year regime (1977–1988). Zia sought to Islamicize the state to strengthen his ties with right-wing religious groups and infuse religious legitimacy to his dictatorial rule. He intended a complete transformation of a secular state system by enforcing his version of Nizam-e-Mustafa, a comprehensive vision for a state based on Sharia. Under the new system, the draconian Hudood Ordinances were enacted, involving various manifestations of institutionalized discrimination. Blasphemy and Zina laws under the Hudood Ordinances were particularly discriminatory toward religious minorities and women, sections of society that religious right-wing groups sought to suppress and control. The Zina laws governing adultery, fornication, rape, and prostitution required a woman to produce four witnesses if she reported sexual violence. Failure on her part to do so was interpreted as guilt. Hence, she could face capital punishment (for adultery) or imprisonment (for fornication) if she sought justice as a victim of rape in a court of law without witnesses (Khan, 2003, p. 76).

The Quranic verse forming the basis of the Zina laws actually protects women from false sexual accusation by stating that whoever makes an allegation of zina, or illicit sexual intercourse, must produce witnesses or face harsh punishment. But the interpretation of the verse has been blatantly distorted, and rather than providing protection to women it makes them vulnerable to false accusations. The verse reads as follows:

And those who launch a charge against chaste women and produce not four witnesses (to support their allegations)—flog them with eighty stripes; and reject their evidence ever after: for such men are wicked transgressors. (Quran 24:4)

This Quranic injunction speaks clearly in favor of women. However, the Pakistani state placed the onus of proof on the woman under Zina laws and treated the matter as an offense against the state (Khan, 2003). The Hudood Ordinances or Hadd laws are also in place in many Nigerian states using the Sharia penal code where, similar to the practice in Pakistan, if a woman is raped, unless *she* can produce four witnesses she runs a high risk of being charged with illicit sexual intercourse (Imam, 2003). A Nigerian woman is particularly vulnerable to being treated as an offender if she becomes pregnant. That more women than men are convicted of zina (illicit sexual relations) in Nigeria reveals the discriminatory nature of the legal and justice system (Imam, 2003). While these heinous laws are widely viewed as representative of Sharia, it is noteworthy that the Hudood Ordinances have been adopted in only three Islamic countries—Pakistan, Nigeria. and Saudi Arabia—suggesting that it is an uncommon facet of Islamic state institutions, although these frameworks put millions at risk of injustice (Rizvi, 2003).

POLYGAMY AND THE ISLAMIC STATE

Statistics on the incidence of polygamy in Muslim societies are not readily available. While the practice is permissible under Sharia law, it is not the norm but the exception in most Muslim societies. Even in countries where it is practiced, it would not be incorrect to speculate that monogamous marriages are significantly more prevalent. It appears that the concept of polygamy under Sharia, or rather polygyny (a clearer reference to the gender-specific nature of the law), is greater cause for controversy than the practice itself. The controversy is rooted in the lack of knowledge that polygyny is conditional on a number of factors that are virtually impossible for a man to fulfill, and is permissible only in exceptional circumstances to provide protection to widowed women and orphans. Thus, polygyny is inherently an instrument for the welfare of women rather than a prerogative given to men to satisfy their sexual desires.

It is encouraging to note that a number of Islamic states have sought to restrict the practice of polygyny under Sharia in a number of ways. In Tunisia, for example, polygamy has been banned for both men and women and is punishable by imprisonment or a fine or both (Hijab, 1988; Mashhour, 2005). In Morocco, the practice is restricted under certain conditions and is forbidden if unequal treatment of wives is a concern (Hijab, 1988). In Yemen also, polygamy is restricted and permitted only under court orders if the wife is unable to produce children or is incurably ill (Hijab, 1988). Likewise, in Algeria, the practice is permitted only on the grounds that equal treatment of wives is considered likely, and is subject to the prior consent of the first wife (Hijab, 1988). In Indonesia, permission for polygamy must be granted by a court under the condition that the wife is unable to perform her responsibilities, is infertile, is physically disabled, or suffers from an incurable disease (Government of Australia, n.d.). Prior consent of the first wife is also required by a court of law in Indonesia (Government of Australia, n.d.). In Pakistan, polygamy is restricted and permissible only with the permission of the court as determined by an Arbitration Council involving representatives from the families of both the husband and wife to determine the necessity of the second marriage (Zafar and Associates, 2014). Written approval of the first wife must also be sought by a Pakistani man for legal permission to marry a second time (Zafar and Associates, 2014). Regrettably, however, although there is a legal penalty for taking a second wife without obtaining permission, the second marriage is not legally invalidated if it is not granted (Zafar and Associates, 2014).

These models suggest that in a number of states Sharia has been interpreted to provide protection to women and that there is space for reform and social justice within Islamic law. It is noteworthy that Turkey, a predominantly Muslim country, has also banned polygamy, albeit under a secular legal framework.

TUNISIA'S PERSONAL STATUS CODE FOR WOMEN

The Tunisian Personal Status Code (PSC) is exemplary in its use of Sharia as a reform tool promoting gender equality and social justice. It was issued in 1956 by the Tunisian founding father and former president Habib Bourguiba and has helped to foster an egalitarian family structure. The prohibition of polygamy and extrajudicial divorce, and equal rights of divorce to both men and women under the Tunisian PSC, provide evidence in this regard (Hijab, 1988). Tunisia is the only member of the Arab League that has incorporated such sweeping reforms into the state law (Think Africa Press, 2013). When President Ben Ali came into power in 1987, he carried on the process of feminist reform initiated by Bourguiba, including protection for divorced women in the form of financial maintenance (Think Africa Press, 2013). Outside of the family realm women were given civil, social, political, and economic rights, including the right of employment without the consent of the husband (Think Africa Press, 2013).

Tunisia's historical narratives suggest that Bourguiba viewed the empowerment of women as an essential element of the country's posturing among civilized nations; in accordance with the needs for social justice; and in moderate alignment with the Islamic world (Hijab, 1988). Thus, under Bourguiba, the "emancipation of women became one of the fulcrums of Tunisia's modernist politics" (Think Africa Press, 2013). While he faced some opposition from religious leaders, they had been considerably "weakened and discredited" during the struggle for independence and the space for their resistance had been reduced (Hijab, 1988). Nevertheless, Bourguiba worked with religious scholars to ensure that the PSC remained within the confines of Sharia and didn't spark controversy (Hijab, 1988). Hence the Mufti, the highest religious authority in Tunisia, was satisfied that Sharia remained a source of legislation in the country, unlike Turkey, which had abolished Sharia courts altogether under the leadership of Mustafa Kemal Ataturk (Hijab, 1988).

Both Bourguiba and Ben Ali took institutional measures to protect and promote state feminism through the establishment of the Tunisian women's organization, Union Nationale de Femmes Tunisiennes (UNFT), a women's affairs research center, Center for Research Studies, Documentation and Information on Women (CREDIF), and a special secretary of state and ministry for women and family affairs (Think Africa Press, 2013).

However, analysts have noted that during both regimes state authoritarianism was instrumental in silencing dissenting voices (Think Africa Press, 2013). This is a plausible insight given that in the wake of the Arab Spring revolutions, the transition to democracy in Tunisia has witnessed the popular rise of the Islamist movement al-Nahda. From an optimistic perspective, however, feminist activism and women's visibility in the movement for democracy has been in full swing prior to, during, and after the Jasmine Revolution. As a matter of fact, Tunisia was the epicenter of the Arab awakening and women were the first to take to the streets calling for an end to decades-old autocratic rule. From academic bloggers to movie stars, Tunisian women such as Lina Ben Mhenni and Hend Sabry will be remembered for their leadership roles in the Arab Spring revolution.

THE STATE AND WOMEN'S TESTIMONY IN ISLAM

Earlier in this chapter scholarly contention over the issue of the legal testimony of women was mentioned as an oft-cited example of gender inequality in Islam. Many in the Muslim community, including jurists and laypersons, argue that women are legal minors because the Quran explicitly states that one man's testimony is equal to those of two women. The Quranic verse forming the basis of the debate reads as follows:

And call in to witness two witnesses, men; or if the two be not men, then one man and two women, such witnesses as you approve of, that if one of the two women errs the other will remind her. (Quran 2:280)

Religious consensus (ijma) on the status of women as legal minors does not exist. Scholars opposing the stance that a woman is a legal minor under Sharia law present a number of arguments, including the historical socioeconomic context of the verse, the respect accorded to women's intellect by Prophet Muhammad, leadership roles played by women since the early days of Islam, and a comprehensive assessment of women's capabilities in the larger Quranic context. Because the aforementioned verse pertains to a woman's testimony in commercial transactions, it should be interpreted within the sociohistorical context, bearing in mind that at the time of the revelation of the verse, two women were recommended as substitutes for one man because women were a lot less familiar with business procedures than men (Badlishah and Masidi, 2009; Hashmi, 2010). The context of the verse has been elaborated further to suggest that it was advised that the agreement be in writing. Further, the need for documentation makes the requirement for two women as witnesses a rational one, given that there were not as many women as men who could read and write. Sadly, this remains the reality today in a number of Muslim and non-Muslim societies.

Relying on human memory as a reliable source of evidence in a contractual agreement is not recommended even in the modern era, and therefore it is not unreasonable to argue that this verse is not discriminatory per se. It does not exclude women from the process; it is cognizant of ground realities and offers practical guidelines on the ethics of commercial transactions in a very primitive societal context. Hashmi (2010) takes issue with Muslim jurists for applying disproportionate emphasis on the aforementioned verse pertaining to testimony. He notes that there is only one among nine verses on the subject stipulating that one man's testimony is equal to two women's (Hashmi, 2010). The Prophet's Sunnah also suggests that he had relied on a woman as the sole witness of a rape to pass judgment regarding the punishment of the crime (Ali, 1992). The Prophet regularly consulted his wives on several important matters, demonstrating his respect for their intellectual capacity and equality. For instance, he sought and accepted the counsel of his wife to make peace with the Quraish tribe at Hudaibiyah (*Dawn*, 2010).

Echoing the thoughts of Qamaruddin Khan, a scholar in Islam, Hashmi (2010) raises the objection that if women's mental and intellectual capacities were not equal to those of men, they could serve neither as judges nor as government officials, nor could they be competent guardians of their own children. To be sure, there is ample evidence that women in Muslim societies have served as judges as well as heads of states. In recent history and in the contemporary era a number of Muslim stateswomen such as Benazir Bhutto of Pakistan, and Sheikh Hasina and Khalid Zia of Bangladesh have demonstrated their mettle as democratically elected heads of state. While there is a minority who have questioned their leadership capacity on the basis of their gender, the democratic mandates given to them in two of the most populous, predominantly Muslim countries, and the fact that all three women were democratically re-elected for a second term attests to their capability. Regrettably, religious extremists and radical elements within the Islamic community continue to be hostile to and a threat toward women in leadership roles. A case in point is Benazir Bhutto's assassination in December 2007. The Pakistani Taliban claimed responsibility for the heinous crime on the grounds that a woman could not be head of an Islamic state. Although the Taliban's extremist movement has spread across the country, their views do not represent those of the public mainstream in Pakistan.

The engagement of women judges and lawyers in a number of Muslim states also challenges the notion that women are legal minors under Sharia law (Hijab, 1988). A hadith stating, "You may take half of the spirit of Islam from women" also supports a woman's appointment as a judge if she possesses the scholarly wherewithal as a man in a similar capacity (Ali, 2011). In Arab states, women judges serve in civil courts in Algeria, Bahrain, Egypt, Iraq, Palestine, Tunisia, Morocco, and former South Yemen (Ali, 2011; Taylor, 2010; UNESCO, 2006). Palestine is widely believed to have appointed the first female judge in a Sharia court in the Middle Eastern region (Prusher, 2009). Khouloud al-Faqeeh, the first female judge to have this distinction, maintains that in Islam a "*Sharia* judge has to be a Muslim, rational adult—not necessarily a man" (Prusher, 2009). She says male judges understand this but insist that it is traditional for men to be in this profession (Prusher, 2009). Women judges serve in Malaysia's civil courts and Sharia courts (Badlishah and Masidi, 2009; Taylor, 2010). Indonesia, the world's largest Muslim country in terms of population, has over 100 female judges in Sharia courts (Badlishah and Masidi, 2009; Taylor, 2010). In Bangladesh, although many women have served as judges, a woman has recently been appointed a judge in the Supreme Court, a remarkable milestone in the country's exemplary quest for the empowerment of women (*Daily Star*, 2011). In Pakistan, women are appointed as judges in courts of law, and the Federal Shariat Court (an important institution that determines whether the laws of the land comply with Sharia) has ruled that a woman can be appointed a judge in Islam (Federal Shariat Court, n.d.). The Grand Sheikh of al-Azhar, widely considered the highest authority in Sunni Islamic thought, Mohamed Sayid Tantawy has also ruled that there is no restriction in the Quran and Sunnah that bans a woman from holding a judicial position in a court of law (Ali, 2011).

Despite the aforementioned evidence in favor of women's intellectual status putting them on par with men, a number of schools in Islamic jurisprudence, including Shafi'i, Maliki, and Hanbali, do not support the notion that women qualify as judges. This is based on the reference to men as the protectors or providers ("qawamuna") of women (Quran 4:34). As discussed earlier, scholars have argued that the word "qawamuna" has been misinterpreted to mean that men have superiority and authority over women (Badlishah and Masidi, 2009). Clearly, however, consensus on the issue of a woman's incapacity to serve as a judge does not exist within and across the schools of fiqh, as there are minorities within the Malikis and the Shafi'is who have opposed the discriminatory stance (Badlishah and Masidi, 2009). Thus, the Hanafi school has conceded that if women's services are required, then they may be appointed as judges (Badlishah and Masidi, 2009). The orthodox Hanbali school, followed in Saudi Arabia, is the only one with the unanimous view that women are not qualified as judges (Badlishah and Masidi, 2009). Female judges are banned in Saudi Arabia and Iran (UNESCO, 2006). However, because so many women serve as judges in many Muslim countries in civil as well as Sharia courts, the argument that they are legal minors is unsupported.

CONCLUSION

Sharia or Islamic law is often regarded as unfavorable to women. The study finds that the relationship between Sharia and the rights and status of women in Muslim societies is a complex one. Muslim women themselves are not a homogenous group; therefore, their position in society and its relationship with Sharia cannot be explained without consideration of other, context-specific influences. It also finds that women's social vulnerability in Muslim societies cannot be explained on religious grounds, as the understanding and application of Sharia is not uniform across the world. Further, Islamic law has been used both as a tool for reform and as regressive legislation. However, evidence suggests that Sharia is fundamentally progressive, gender equitable, and gender sensitive. Regrettably, it is sometimes misused by states as an instrument of power. In such cases, governments often co-opt the religious right to bolster their legitimacy. Governments may also rely on religious rights groups to provide public goods and services they are unable or unwilling to provide. The nexus between ruling elites and the religious right can be a source of perversion of Sharia in both its interpretation and its implementation, legally and extralegally.

Women in some parts of the Muslim world have also suffered on account of the discontinuity in progressive juristic interpretation (ijtihad) of Islamic thought, one that is responsive to the evolving societal context. Additionally, the requirement for scholarly religious consensus (ijma), a pivotal source of Sharia, on a range of issues pertaining to women does not exist. As long as there is scholarly dispute on the interpretation of Quranic text and Sunnah (teachings of Prophet Muhammad), it cannot be standardized as Sharia law, but it sometimes is incorporated into the legal framework to the detriment of women. A thorough analysis of women's status in Muslim societies demonstrates that Sharia law is not the primary determinant of their positioning. Factors such as the state's unique socioeconomic, cultural, political, and historical contexts are also important sources to consider. Both societal and state institutions play an important role in fostering an enabling environment for women. This is possible with the application of Sharia, especially by opening the doors of ijtihad to elevate women's status to put them on par with men—a process that was initiated with the advent of Islam.

NOTES

1. For a list of countries where Sharia is not incorporated in the legal framework of the state, see Council on Foreign Relations (n.d.).

2. For a detailed discussion on the closing of the practice of ijtihad in Islam, see Farooq (2011, Chapter 4). Also see Mashhour (2005).

3. It is worth noting that while slavery is not prohibited in the Quran it is very clearly discouraged, and based on the interpretation of fiqh schools, it is considered illegal under Sharia law. See, for example, Leipert (2011).

4. Refer to Imam (2003), who mentions that "Imam Hanbal urged 'do not imitate me, or Malik, or al-Shafi, or al-Thawri and derive directly from where they themselves derived.' Imam Malik, the founder of the school of fiqh accepted in

Nigeria, cautioned that 'I am but a human being. I may be wrong and I may be right. So first examine what I say. If it complies with the Book and the Sunnah, then you may accept it. But if it does not comply with them, then you should reject it.'"

5. The survey by the Pew Research Center involved 38,000 face-to-face interviews in more than 80 languages. For detailed statistics by region and country see Pew Research Center (2009).

BIBLIOGRAPHY

ABC News. 2007, November 29. Two Cases Shed Light on Floggings in Muslim World. ABC News, http://abcnews.go.com/International/story?id=3927504&page=2 (accessed May 22, 2014).

Abusulayman, Abdulhamid A. 1987. *The Islamic Theory of International Relations: New Directions for Islamic Methodology and Thought.* Herndon, VA: International Institute of Islamic Thought.

Al Arabiya News. 2013, May 30. Iran Amends Law on Stoning for Adultery. Al Arabiya News, http://english.alarabiya.net/en/News/middle-east/2013/05/30/Iran-amends-law-on-stoning-for-adultery-.html (accessed May 22, 2014).

Alasti, Sanaz. 2007. Comparative Study of Stoning Punishment in the Religion of Islam and Judaism. *Justice Policy Journal* (Center on Juvenile and Criminal Justice) 4 (1): 1–38.

Alexandre, Michèle. 2007. Lessons from Islamic Polygamy: A Case for Expanding the American Concept of Surviving Spouse So as to Include De Facto Polygamous Spouses. *Washington and Lee Law Review* (Washington and Lee University School of Law): 1461–1481.

Ali, Asghar. 1992.*The Rights of Women in Islam.* Selangor: IBS Buku Sdn. Bhd.

Ali,Yousuf. 2011. The Appointment of Muslim Women as Judges in the Courts: A Textual Analysis from Islamic Perspective. In *2nd International Conference on Humanities, Historical and Social Sciences.* Singapore: IACSIT Press.

Ali, Yusuf, trans. 1992. *The Quran, Surat An-Nisa* [The Women]. Available online at: http://quran.com/4/34

Badlishah, Nik Noriani Nik, and Yasmin Masidi. 2009. *Women as Judges.* Sisters in Islam.

Bald, Margaret. 1998. *Banned Books: Literature Suppressed on Religious Grounds.* New York: Facts on File.

Barr, Heather. 2013, December 10. In Afghanistan, Women Betrayed, http://www.nytimes.com/2013/12/11/opinion/in-afghanistan-women-betrayed.html?hpw&rref=opinion&_r=0

Bingham, John. 2009, June 29. At Least 85 Sharia "Courts" Operating in Britain, Says Civitas Report. *Telegraph,* http://www.telegraph.co.uk/news/religion/5675166/At-least-85-Sharia-courts-operating-in-Britain-says-Civitas-report.html (accessed May 22, 2014).

Brown, DeNeen L. 2004, April 27. Canadians Allow Islamic Courts to Decide Disputes. *Washington Post.*

Council on Foreign Relations. 2014. Islam: Governing Under Sharia, http://www.cfr.org/religion/islam-governing-under-Sharia/p8034 (accessed May 22, 2014).

Daily Star. 2011, February 23. SC Gets Ist Woman Judge, http://archive.thedailystar
.net/newDesign/news-details.php?nid=175201

Dawn, The. 2010, July 30. Women Judges and Sharia, http://www.dawn.com/
news/839595/woman-judges-and-Sharia (accessed May 22, 2014).

Desilver, Drew. 2013, June 7. World's Muslim Population More Widespred
Than You Think. Pew Research Center, http://www.pewresearch.
org/fact-tank/2013/06/07/worlds-muslim-population-more-widespread
-than-you-might-think/ (accessed May 22, 2014).

Economist. 2013, November 18. Arab Women's Rights: Not Yet Sitting Pretty,
http://www.economist.com/blogs/pomegranate/2013/11/arab-
womens-rights?fsrc=nlw%7Cnewe%7C11-18-2013%7C7020120%7C134053
218%7CNA (accessed May 22, 2014).

Fantz, Ashley. 2013, June 3. Iran Aims to Keep Stoning as Adultery, Rights Group
Says. CNN World, http://www.cnn.com/2013/06/03/world/meast/
iran-stoning/ (accessed May 22, 2014).

Farooq, Mohammaded Omar. 2011. Toward Our Reformation: From Legalism to
Value-Oriented Islamic Law and Jurisprudence. In *Ist International Institute
of Islamic Thought.*

Federal Shariat Court. n.d. Leading Judgements/Reports, http://federal
Shariatcourt.gov.pk/3.html (accessed May 22, 2014).

Ghali, Muhammad Mahmood, trans. n.d. *The Quran, Surat An-Nisa* [The Women].
Available online at http://quran.com/4/34

Government of Australia, Refugee Review Tribunal. n.d. Country Advice Indonesia. *Refworld,* http://www.refworld.org/docid/4f46182b2.html

Hajjar, Lisa. 2004. Domestic Violence and Sharia: A Comparative Study of Muslim
Societies in the Middle East, Africa and Asia. In *Women's Rights and Islamic
Family Law: Perspectives on Reform,* edited by Lynn Welchman. London: Zed
Books.

Hamasamy, L. S. 1958, June. The Role of Women in the Development of Egypt.
Middle East Forum, 24–28.

Hasan, Ahmad. 2003. *The Doctrine of Ijma': A Study of the Juridical Principle of Consensus.* New Delhi: Kitab Bhavan.

Hashmi, Taj I. 2010. *Women and Islam in Bangladesh: Beyond Subjection and Tyranny.*
New York: Palgrave.

Hassan, Riffat. 1999. Feminism in Islam. In *Feminism and World Religion,* edited by
Arvind Sharma and Katherine K. Young. Albany, NY: State University of
New York Press, p. 264.

Hijab, Nadia. 1988. *Woman Power: The Arab Debate on Women at Work.* Cambridge:
Cambridge University Press.

Hodge, Nathan, and Habib Khan Totakhil. 2013, November 25. Afghanistan Considers Reinstating Public Stoning for Adultery. *Wall Street Journal,* http://
online.wsj.com/news/articles/SB10001424052702304281004579219724141
928740 (accessed May 22, 2014).

Hoseini, Farshad. 2010. *List of Known Cases of Death by Stoning Sentences in Iran
(1980–2010).* Statistical Report, International Committee Against Execution.

Imam, Ayesha. 2003, September 17. Women, Muslim Laws and Human Rights
in Nigeria (interview by Mary Johnson Osirim). In *A Keynote Address*

by Dr. Ayesha Imam. Washington, DC: Woodrow Wilson Center for International Scholars.

Khan, Shahnaz. 2003. The Moral Regulation of the Pakistani Woman. *Feminist Review*, 75–94.

Kidwai, Mushir Hosain. 1976. *Women under Different Social and Religious Laws: Buddhism, Judaism, Christianity, Islam.* Seema Publications.

Leipert, David. 2011, November 16. Ending Slavery the Sharia Way. *Huffington Post*, http://www.huffingtonpost.com/dr-david-liepert/slavery-and-Sharia_b_1088473.html

Mashhour, Amira. 2005. Islamic Law and Gender Equality: Could There Be a Common Ground? A Study of Divorce and Polygamy in Sharia Law and Contemporary Legislation in Tunisia and Egypt. *Human Rights Quarterly* (Johns Hopkins University) 27 (3): 562–596.

Mayell, Hillary. 2002, February 12. Thousands of Women Killed for Family Honor. *National Geographic.*

McSmith, Andy. 2009, June 30. The Big Question: How Do Britain's Sharia Courts Work, and Are They a Good Thing? *The Independent*, http://www.independent.co.uk/news/uk/home-news/the-big-question-how-do-britains-Sharia-courts-work-and-are-they-a-good-thing-1724486.html (accessed May 22, 2014).

Mir-Hosseini, Ziba. 2006. Muslim Women's Quest for Equality: Between Islamic Law and Feminism. *Critical Inquiry* 32 (4): 629–645.

Mohd Noor, Azman, and Mohd al-ikhsan Ghazali. 2008. Interpreting and Understanding the Command of God: Authority of the Sunnah as a Source of Law in the Case of Stoning to Death of a Convicted Adulterer. *Shariah Journal* 16 (Special Edition): 429–442.

Moussaoui, Naima El. 2007, December 18. Talking about Honor Killings. *Common Ground News Service*, http://www.commongroundnews.org/article.php?id=22317&lan=en&sid=1&sp=0 (accessed May 22, 2014).

Nasir, Jamal J. Ahmad. 2009. *The Status of Women under Islamic Law and Modern Islamic Legislation.* Boston: Brill.

Otto, Jan Michiel, ed. 2010. *Sharia Incoporated: A Comparative Overview of the Legal Systems of Twelve Muslim Countries in Past and Present.* Amsterdam: Leiden University Press.

Pew Research Center. 2013, April 30. *Religion & Public Life Project*, http://www.pewforum.org/2013/04/30/the-worlds-muslims-religion-politics-society-exec/ (accessed May 22, 2014).

Pew Research Center. 2009, October 7. Mapping the Global Muslim Population. *Religion and Public Life Project*, http://www.pewforum.org/2009/10/07/mapping-the-global-muslim-population (accessed May 22, 2014).

Pickthall, Muhammad, trans. n.d. *The Quran, Surat An-Nisa* [The Women]. Available online at http://quran.com/4/34

Prusher, Ilene R. 2009, May 13. New Female Judge Transforms Islamic Court, http://www.csmonitor.com/World/Middle-East/2009/0513/p06s20-wome.html (accessed May 22, 2014).

Redpath, Rhiannon. 2013, October 16. Women Around the World Are Being Stoned to Death. Do You Know the Facts? *PolicyMic*, http://www.policymic.com/

articles/68431/women-around-the-world-are-being-stoned-to-death-do
-you-know-the-facts (accessed May 22, 2014).

Rizvi, Majida. 2003, October. Pakistan: Interview with Justice (retd.) Majida Rizvi:
Women Living Under Muslim Laws. Newsline.

Sacirbey, Omar. 2013, July 29. Sharia Law in the USA, 101: A Guide to What It Is
and Why States Want to Ban It. *Huffington Post*, http://www.huffington
post.com/2013/07/29/Sharia-law-usa-states-ban_n_3660813.html
(accessed May 22, 2014).

Sahih International. n.d. *The Quran, Surat An-Nisa* [The Women]. Available online
at http://quran.com/4/34

Saleh, Saneya. 1972, March. Women in Islam: Their Status in Religious and Traditional Culture. *International Journal of Sociology of the Family* 2 (1): 35–42.

Sharia Controversy: Is There a Place for Islamic law in Western Societies? 2012,
January 3. *Global Researcher*, http://www.sagepub.com/chamblissintro/
study/materials/cq_researcher/cq_08Sharia.pdf (accessed May 22, 2014).

Sturcke, James. 2008, February 28. Sharia Law in Canada, Almost. *Guardian*, http://
www.theguardian.com/news/blog/2008/feb/08/Sharialawincanada
almost (accessed May 22, 2014).

Taylor, Pamela. 2010, August 7. Malaysia Appoints First Female Sharia Judges,
http://newsweek.washingtonpost.com/onfaith/modernmuslim/2010/08/
malaysia_appoints_first_female_Sharia_judges.html (accessed May 22, 2014).

Think Africa Press. 2013, December 10. Tunisia: Protecting Bin-Ali's Feminist Legacy, http://thinkafricapress.com/tunisia/future-state-feminism (accessed
May 22, 2014).

UNESCO. 2006, June 14. Women, Law and Judicial Decision-Making in the Middle
East and North Africa: Toward Gender Justice. Seminar, Amman, http://
www.unesco.org/new/fileadmin/MULTIMEDIA/HQ/SHS/pdf/ender
_justice.pdf

Vikør, K. S. 2005. *Between God and the Sultan: A History of Islamic Law.* London: Hurst.

Weiss, Bernard. 1998. *The Spirit of Islamic Law.* Athens: University of Georgia Press.

Zafar and Associates. n.d. Family Law in Pakistan, http://www.zallp.com/family
.html (accessed May 22, 2014).

CHAPTER 17

Lebanese Women's Nonviolence: Action and Discourse

Rita Stephan[1] and Nicole Khoury

Lebanese women have consistently opposed violence, struggled to reduce it, and engaged in alleviating its negative effects. Like women elsewhere, since the 19th century they have drawn on both maternalist and egalitarian frames in their mobilizations (Kutz-Flamenbaum, 2011; Costain, 2000). Their special, traumatic experience of violence, due to Lebanon's 15-year civil war and the 15 subsequent years of Syrian occupation, has given them an even stronger stake in nonviolence. They have combined the nonviolent struggle for gender equality, racial justice, and peace in formats that developed outside traditional political channels, that is, outside of the lobbying, electioneering, and legislating that define the normal political sphere (Stephan and Chenoweth, 2008). However, unlike traditional nonviolent activists who mobilize the street and conduct various interventions (such as strikes) to call for achieving demands against the will of the establishment (Stephan and Chenoweth, 2008), Lebanese women persuaded their opponents in the establishment and "won them over" by using insider actors and strategies (Chaney, 2007; Jordan and Maloney, 1997; Lovenduski, 2005; Grant, 2000; Grant, 2001), such as persuasive arguments and appeals to shared cultural and symbolic values (Taylor and Whittier, 1995; Ferree, 2004).

Throughout history, political conflicts have infringed on Lebanon's political sovereignty and weakened its political and legal institutions. The tumultuous modern history of Lebanon has left a strong imprint on Lebanese society. Lebanese today suffer from the consequences of the emigration of their able youth, a growing elderly population, disruption of family structure, and a society polarized over political division. Political instability has pushed women, who constitute the majority in Lebanese society, to reclaim some of their forgotten rights and fight against the frictions and decentralization that have threatened democracy and peace in Lebanon.

In this chapter, we approach Lebanese women's nonviolent activism from two angles: words and actions. We examine what women did to advance the nonviolence movement in Lebanon and how they framed their activism. By focusing on the initiative of such women as Rose Ghurayyib, Laure Moghaizel and Nora Jumblat as well as others, we highlight that the Lebanese nonviolent movement is both indigenous and global. Women responded to social and political problems that were both unique to Lebanon and global in their scope. War, emigration, and occupation are all universal problems. Nonviolent responses to these problems are also universal. However, Lebanese women contextualized both the struggle and the solution by Lebanon-izing the means by which they spread the nonviolent movement.

We rely on the documentation of the Lebanese women's movement found in *Al-Raida* journal from 1976 to 1985 and interviews with activists and their associates. We employ a qualitative methodological approach, through content analysis and interviews, to rhetorically analyze the ways in which the arguments for peace are positioned in relation to the immediate local context. Specifically, we use archival research to find documentation of women's peace movements during the Lebanese civil war in Lebanese American University's *Al-Raida* ("Pioneer") quarterly journal. In addition to archival research, we conducted interviews with Lebanese activists involved in the nonviolence movement during the civil war and in the 2005 nonviolent protests in Lebanon. To supplement the information from the archival research and the interviews, we incorporated content from newspapers and Internet articles that relate to the more recent 2005 demonstrations when interviews were not available.

To draw a complete picture of the Lebanese women's movement, we begin by illustrating the impact of the political conflict in Lebanon. We specifically discuss the era of civil war and occupation. Then we trace the emergence of the Lebanese women's nonviolent movement through the writings and actions of activists. The call for nonviolence was first sounded by Rose Ghurayyib and others in their *Al-Raida* articles. Through their exchange with the activists in the international community, scholars wanted a Lebanese-style nonviolent activism. Inspired by their call and her own activism, Laure Moghaizel led a country-wide response to the war and engaged women and the youth to demand an end to the fighting. Fifteen years after the end of the war and the burden of the Syrian occupation, Lebanese women again rose to demand freedom and dignity, nonviolently. In the darkness of war, Lebanese women found the light of nonviolence, and here's where it all started.

CIVIL WAR AND THE POSTWAR LANDSCAPE

The historical context of Lebanon's civil war is an important issue that needs to be considered in order to understand the significance of Lebanese women's activism. This section will present a short overview of the series of events that led to the Lebanese civil war. Although we present some of the events that have shaped the civil war context in Lebanon, we would like to emphasize that there has been no unified narrative of the Lebanese civil war, and what is presented here is an incomplete picture of the complexities of the local context. The short and incomplete history that we offer here attempts to demonstrate that the events that led to the civil war divided the country along rigid sectarian lines that shaped the discourse on women's nonviolent activism. Between 1975 and 1990, Lebanon witnessed a bloody civil war that divided Beirut, and the rest of the country, into a Christian east and a Muslim west. The civil war destroyed Lebanon's social and economic structures, and forced many of Lebanon's most productive citizens to flee the country. The civil war era started in 1975 after the Palestinian refugee population reached 300,000 and established its quasi government within the Lebanese state.[2] Tensions grew between the Palestinians and the Christians, inviting the intervention of the Syrian army on behalf of the Christians. In 1978, Israel invaded Lebanon in response to Palestinians' attacks within Israel, and it took over Beirut in 1982. As some Lebanese leaders allied themselves with the Israelis, the war proliferated into many fronts and included foreign powers such as France, the United States, Saudi Arabia, and even Iran. Many view the civil war era as a dark mark in Lebanon's long history of coexistence and civility. The civil war claimed 100,000 lives, left another 100,000 disabled, but most important, about 900,000 people (up to one-fifth of the prewar resident population) were displaced from their homes. Perhaps a quarter of a million emigrated permanently. Cities became segregated into religious pockets and families were separated. Trust and hope were lost and strong reactionary movements emerged. Powerful militia groups like Amal and Hezbollah emerged as revolutionary clusters of the Shiite poor, once again threatening the security and stability of the country.

The postwar era, otherwise known as the Second Republic, witnessed the return of confessional democracy, but not without the undesirable partners Amal and Hezbollah. The Taef Accord, engineered in the city of Taef in Saudi Arabia in 1989, reshuffled the power cards between Christians and Muslims, giving equal representation to both religions at every level of governance.[3] The accord specifically declares the president to be a Maronite Christian, the prime minister a Sunni Muslim, the parliament speaker a Shiite. All militia were integrated within the unified Lebanese army with the exception of Hezbollah, which continued to fight Israel beyond the latter's withdrawal from south Lebanon in 2000. According to the accord, the Syrian army was to remain in Lebanon temporarily to shepherd the re-institutionalization of the Lebanese state. Syria overstayed its welcome and was ushered out of Lebanon only in 2005, when 1 million peaceful Lebanese demonstrators demanded its departure in the largest nonviolent demonstration in Lebanese history, known as the Cedar Revolution of March 14, 2005. Shortly after, in 2006, Israel invaded again in response to Hezbollah's abduction of two Israeli soldiers.[4]

The political instability caused by the war with Israel; the continuous frictions between internal powers with external loyalties to Syria, Iran, or the United States; and the decentralization of the consensual democratic system are closely intertwined with the power struggle between the different sects and the autonomy of the state. Women's organizations emerged in this era as the only nonsectarian, nonaligned, and neutral agents that gained great reputation on the ground for focusing their energy on relieving the humanitarian needs of the war victims. They launched many projects that provided social welfare services, especially to women left behind by male family members who fought and died in the war or fled the country. The war only underlined the urgent need to create a national policy to integrate female citizens into public life.

THE CALL FOR A PEACE MOVEMENT:[5] ROSE GHURAYYIB

As the women's movement became more vocal and integrated into public life, their public writing and calls for peace were published and distributed widely. One of the most prominent voices of the Lebanese nonviolence movement was Rose Ghurayyib's, the editor of *Al-Raida*. *Al-Raida*, a Lebanese feminist journal, was initially published in English and in Arabic to reach a larger audience. The Institute for Women's Studies in the Arab World (IWSAW), established in 1973 at the Lebanese American University in Beirut, Lebanon (formerly Beirut University College), began publication of the journal in 1975. IWSAW is part of a consortium with nine other Asian universities, established by Christian missionaries in Iran, Korea, Japan, India, and Pakistan.[6] The Ford Foundation contributed the initial funding for the institute, which reflects both the discourse in which *Al-Raida* was established and the local and international audience of the journal. The journal continues publishing today on various women's issues in the Middle East, and has recently developed into a peer-reviewed academic journal.

Rose Ghurayyib initially wrote most of the articles for *Al-Raida*, translating articles from Arabic and French newspapers and magazines, as well as past publications of Arab women's fictional and literary work. Rose's editorials are of particular interest to our discussion because they reflect the discourse on the nonviolent movement in Lebanon by locating their concerns within a global peace movement. The Lebanese women's non-violent movement was initially influenced by the international women's campaigns for peace. By locating the Lebanese nonviolence movement within the larger global nonviolence movement in the early 1980s, Rose's arguments for nonviolence encouraged local activists to incorporate international calls for peace, while simultaneously urging international peace movements to call global attention to the deteriorating situation in Lebanon. For example, Rose responded to the Women's International League for Peace and Freedom's (WILPF) peace campaign issued to Stop the Arms Race (STAR). Launched in the United States on March 8, 1982, the STAR campaign took the form of special cards designed to collect signatures of women pacifists and a star button for each signature collected. WILPF delivered a message to former president Ronald Reagan demanding that no "Cruise and Pershing II missiles be deployed in Europe." This initiative, shared at the United Nations Disarmament Conference in 1982 (Stop the Arms Race, 1982, p. 8), inspired Lebanese women to call for action in their own local contexts. The initial approach was to request that international movements extend their framework to include Lebanon and the Middle East, requesting an integration of international movements to apply to local contexts.

While we strongly support the STAR international campaign for peace, we urge that the call be extended to Eastern Europe, to Soviet Russia and to other countries in the Middle and Far East, in Africa and in Latin America.

Our world is so interdependent and its problems so interrelated that it is useless to limit peace efforts to one part of the world while other parts are in an actual or potential state of war. The hot spots of the world in the Middle East and in Latin America need immediate consideration and help. (Stop the Arms Race, 1982, p. 8)

The call for understanding the interdependent and interrelated problems of the world echoes a transnational and global understanding of the women's movement, particularly in response to the systematic structures of violence and war. Thus, calls for the extension of international movements to the Middle East are directed at an international audience that initially established the institute as part of the Asian Women's Institute. Thus, it is not uncommon to find articles that speak to an international audience and reports of international conferences and movements published in *Al-Raida*.

Rose's editorial for the thematic issue on peace, published at the end of 1982, reiterates the introduction of the WILPF movement and the STAR movement, in addition to the Asian Women's Role in Peace and Development conference (Ghurayyib and Stephen, 1983, p. 1). Furthermore, the editorial references the June 13, 1982, protest in New York in which around 500,000 people marched from the United Nations to Central Park.[7] Rose suggests that for a successful peace movement to take place, "[it] should be global and simultaneous; otherwise it would result in an imbalance of power and favor aggressiveness among those who support it only by word but not by deed" (Ghurayyib, 1982c, p. 1). She concludes that the women's movement in the past 150 years has been active in promoting peace, "but the women's movement cannot be of real help unless it becomes global . . . only through reaching a universal dimension, may a project or movement be said to have achieved real power" (Ghurayyib, 1982c, p. 1). Referencing Robin Morgan's anthology of feminist literature *Sisterhood Is Powerful* and her follow-up anthology *Sisterhood Is Global,*[8] she illustrates that the peace movement indeed needed to take into consideration systems of oppression on a global scale.

In addition to defining peace movements, Rose challenges definitions of violence in Lebanon. In particular, she challenges definitions of terrorism. For example, in the article "Should We Lose Faith in Man?" Rose (1983a) defuses terrorists' claim that their actions are justified as a form of retaliation for past injustices. She argues that such actions lead to chaos: "When terrorism takes the form of blind aggression against the innocent, nothing can justify it. It is then a reversion to wild and irresponsible behavior, resulting in wholesale destruction, despotic rule and general extermination" (p. 2). Instead, Rose[9] makes a plea for the "civilized man" not to succumb to such forms of incivility: "We believe in civilized man because the gap between him and those who are still at the primitive stage or behind their time, is so wide that it would seem unthinkable for the former to revert to the low condition into which the latter may sink" (1982a, p. 2). Her discussions of civility and incivility reflect the events that occurred in Lebanon during 1982. The year marks the invasion of Lebanon by the Israeli Defense Forces (IDF), the Sabra and Shatila massacres that resulted in the death of 3,500 innocent civilians, the subsequent occupation of south Lebanon by the IDF, and the assassination of Lebanese president Bachir Gemayel. Rose's reference to terrorist acts suggests recognition of the devastating effects and results of the civil war during this period. Consequently, the article's call for peace and civility is an attempt to provide readers with a workable method for active participation in the peace process, which seemed a large undertaking at the time.

Stressing the role of women, as well as men, in peace building, Rose's article "What Can Women Do for Peace?" builds on the Socialist International Women bulletin, whose authors recommended the following measures for instilling peace: developing cooperative structures, designing educational curricula based on equality for schools, omitting violence from television programs, providing facts and information on wars, and establishing an egalitarian relationship between the sexes (Ghurayyib, 1982b, p. 3). Her article brings the recommendations home to the Lebanese war. It portrays the "cult of manliness" as the result of larger systematic oppressive structures that valorizes violence:

In Lebanon, the horrors endured by the population during the 8-year-war should have created by now a general attitude of abhorrence to war, particularly because it evolved into terrorism in its varied atrocious forms: assassinations, kidnappings, sniping, wholesale massacres, the use of booby-trapped cars and other explosive weapons, destruction, and the burning and plundering of property.

Here as elsewhere we have to fight the destructive cult of tough manliness[10] which persists in the traditional hero-worship of the "abadaye,"[11] the tough, aggressive, pugnacious fellow.

More destructive still has been the influence of terrorist political systems and parties which persuade people, through bribery and luring promises, to take terrorism and guerrilla warfare as a profession. To these parties, destruction and assassination become the shortest way to world power and domination. Their adherents may forget that the violence they practice may also result in their own destruction. (Ghurayyib, 1982b, p. 3)

This article aims to awaken women's awareness of the risks of war and shows that the protest movement is not just an issue for women. It calls upon everyone to participate, not least of all men, with their heritage of military traditions and thinking (p. 3). The inclusion of men and women in the discourse on peace reveals the necessity for collaboration across systems of gender, class, race, and national cohesion for the purpose of implementing a peace process. The rather direct message to include men in the process illustrates the acknowledgment of the root causes of gender oppression.

The article positions Lebanese women's activism within the larger, global systematic oppression that fosters violence, including power struggles in political contexts, exploitation of men and women for national concerns, and the division of religious sects. This awareness of the global structures that oppress women is echoed in other contexts such as Cheryl Johnson-Odim's argument about women in the Global South: "The point is that factors other than gender figure integrally in the oppression of Third World Women and that, even regarding patriarchy, many Third World women labor under indigenous inequitable gender relationships exacerbated by Western patriarchy, racism, and exploitation" (Johnson-Odim, 1991, p. 327).

As a forum of intellectual discussion, gender identity became contested and transformed within the framework of war and violence in *Al-Raida*. Instead of being articulated as a category of analysis, presenting issues of family planning, women in development, and women in Islamic laws, gender identity became rearticulated within a comprehensive and inclusive theory on feminism, to use Johnson-Odim's terms. *Al-Raida* witnessed the rise of arguments for the inclusion of men as victims of violence and terrorism, defining terrorism as the result of the dissolution of civility, and collaborating to end the violence that has claimed countless lives in Lebanon.

As a result of the call for action, public conferences on peace building were held in Beirut. The Role of Women resolutions of the Save Lebanon campaign held by the National Conference of the Lebanese Women's Council on April 23, 1983, place an emphasis on launching peace building activities, ending the war, creating a unified Personal Status code, expelling all foreign troops from Lebanon, and increasing the number of women in governmental and nongovernmental organizations, among other recommendations (Ghurayyib and Stephen, 1983, p. 9).

The reaction of women to the results of the conference was one of disappointment: "Many women who had hoped to come out with definite answers and a clear plan of action were disappointed to find out that the final recommendations were more of a reiteration of old demands for the improvement of women's status in Lebanon" (Ghurayyib and Stephen, 1983, p. 9). However, the women at the conference did also declare that such conferences were integral to the opening of dialogue between women's organizations, which had been nonexistent throughout the past eight years of the Lebanese war. That the conversation on peace building was an ongoing process reflects the continuing efforts of women in constantly rethinking and reiterating similar problems. This realization that the issues they were dealing with were similar to ones discussed at earlier times helped women rethink their strategies for public arguments. The calls to action were futile at ending the civil war. Thus, the public arguments eventually became more personal with an emotional appeal, as described in the next section.

Since its debut publication in 1976, a year after the onset of the Lebanese civil war, *Al-Raida* increasingly published public arguments, testimonies, and narratives against the civil war. As a result of the prolonged violence in Lebanon, the pioneering journal argued for the importance of peace building activities and for the participation of women in such activities to oppose the civil war. In particular, *Al-Raida* helped initiate, provide information about, and document the peace movement in Lebanon.

LAUNCHING THE NONVIOLENT MOVEMENT: LAURE MOGHAIZEL

Women's activism during the civil war helped establish an image of women as peace builders, nonviolent and committed in their efforts to establish civil egalitarianism. This section will further explore the nonviolence movement throughout the war and in a postwar context. Women's participation in the war was "neither in its decision-making process nor in its efforts to achieve reconciliation" (Stephan, 1984, p. 2). Instead, they provided relief efforts, attempted to "hold together the collapsing structures of Lebanese society," volunteered with social welfare organizations, protested the violation of human rights, attempted to "appease the fighters by paying visits to refugee camps and military headquarters and putting flowers in the nozzles of guns," participated in national and international conferences on the problems facing Lebanon, organized demonstrations and sit-ins, and "stormed into the local TV station[12] to interrupt the news in order to have their demands broadcast" (Stephan, 1984, pp. 2–3). Their activism helped establish the Lebanese women's nonviolence movement as a powerful means of challenging the dominant discourse.

In 1984, a prominent Christian female lawyer, Laure Moghaizel, insisted, "Peace can be only achieved through the joint struggle of men and women" (Chkeir, 2002, p. 88). She urged women to stop being silent witnesses and to intervene not only by caring for the wounded, but also by asserting their rights to stop the bloodshed. With this call, the nonviolent movement in Lebanon was recognized as an important component of a peace "constituency." By implication, in order to exert their power, women had to gain it in the public sphere. Thus, Moghaizel was calling for women to enter contentious politics and make their voices heard.

The nonviolent movement mobilized Lebanese men and women to participate in protests, sign petitions, and join forums, and in the process provided women's agency with legitimate organizational structures. The movement, under the slogan "No to War, Yes to Life," collected 62,533 signatures petitioning against the war, and set up a blood donation drive advocating "one blood, one nation, and one destiny." Moghaizel joined efforts with Lebanese Monsignor Gregoire Haddad, founder of the Secularist Movement (Tayyar al-Almani) in 1980 (Ellis, 2002, p. 9), which was committed to advance gender equality, civil society, and human rights. They both worked with the French priest Christian Dolorme, known for his interfaith dialogue and his commitment to Gandhism and human rights. Their combined efforts to raise Lebanese public awareness of nonviolence principles concentrated on setting up monthly teach-ins to distinguish nonviolent resistance from pacifism.

In 1987, the movement held a march that lasted five days, during which the demonstrators made a 195-kilometer circuit around the Lebanese regions, where they received great public support. Among the protesters were victims of the war: 12 Lebanese who had lost their sight, 40 who were confined to a wheelchair, and 20 more who had become disabled. To symbolize peace, the protesters dressed in white, released pigeons, carried the Lebanese flag, and distributed white carnations. A year later, on July 28, 1988, Moghaizel organized a vigil at the checkpoint between East and West Beirut. This vigil, which lasted from the evening until the next morning, was attended by representatives of 40 nongovernmental organizations, who exhibited the signatures they had collected in earlier years (Stephan, 2010).

The movement transformed into the Lebanese Association for Human Rights in 1985 under the leadership of Laure and Joseph Moghaizel. Believing in democracy, equality, and secularism, the association called upon the Lebanese government to grant all people the right to "life, liberty and security without discrimination" and to guarantee people's freedom of religion and expression. The association also focused on raising public awareness of the relationship between human rights and peace. Considering people's right to life as a basic human right, Moghaizel defended the association's emphasis that "building the humanity of Lebanese is the hope to rebuilding Lebanon" (Chkeir, 2002, p. 153).

The association's goal was to combat violation of human rights and advocate on behalf of the Lebanese war victims. Its key achievements were to urge the Lebanese government to adopt the Universal Declaration of Human Rights and to advance women's rights in a number of legal reforms. As a key force in several initiatives aimed at ending the civil war, Moghaizel was convinced that "peace can be only achieved through the joint struggle of men and women" (Moghaizel, 1969). The war only underlined the urgency of creating a national policy to engage female citizens in public life. This policy, according to Laure, constituted a starting point for women to practice their citizenship rights and responsibilities and to join the state and other civil organizations in rescuing the country from the disaster of violence (Stephan, 2010).

The Lebanese Association for Human Rights also adopted gender justice as one of its goals. It successfully campaigned to eliminate legal punishments for the sale or use of contraception in 1983. They also petitioned the state to institute 64 as the age for retirement for both men and women (previously women were forced into retirement at 55 and men at 60). Additional reforms that Laure and Joseph helped introduce through the association included granting women the right to be witnesses in real estate contracts, in 1993; the right for women to practice commerce without being obliged to obtain the consent of their husbands, in 1994; the right for women who work in the diplomatic field to maintain their Lebanese citizenship and jobs upon marrying foreign men, also in 1994; and the right for women to obtain life insurance, in 1995. Laure and Joseph struggled to eliminate honor crimes, which remain a serious social problem that plagues the Middle East and other Muslim states. In remembrance of their work, in 1999 the Lebanese government adopted a partial reform of the honor crime law that created a sentencing structure for those convicted, instead of granting them total acquittal (Stephan, 2010).

The image of women as nonviolent and prone to civil egalitarianism has shaped women's rights activism in Lebanese society and politics, just as it did in the United States (Costain, 2000). Through their commitment to nonviolence, Stephan and Chenoweth (2008) posit that activists gain domestic and international legitimacy—the goal toward which Lebanese activists have worked since the successes of the 1980s (Schulze, 1998). Lebanese activists kept striving to build their capacity after the end of the civil war, through fortifying the women's movement and its organizations, in the context of a greater international concern with gender equality issues. Although the war officially ended with the signing of the Taef Accord in 1990, Lebanon fell under the protection of the Syrian regime, which was effectively a military occupation, until 2005.

TRIUMPH OF NONVIOLENCE: THE CEDAR REVOLUTION[13]

The Lebanese women's nonviolence movement was particularly active during the Lebanese civil war from 1975 to 1990, and continued to challenge the dominant discourse in a postwar Lebanon, as evidenced by Laure's activism. Having established the initial call for peace and the emergence of the Lebanese women's nonviolent movement, this chapter will now consider the largest political protest in Lebanon, now known as the Cedar Revolution. As a result of the stagnant political context, and the challenges to public participation in such a fragmented society, the women's movement made relatively little progress between 1990 and 2005 (Stephan, 2012). This is how things stood in March 2005, when the Cedar Revolution emerged as a result of the assassination of the former prime minister Rafiq Hariri. During this period of revolt, Lebanese civilians successfully employed nonviolent methods (including boycotts, strikes, protests, and organized noncooperation) to "challenge entrenched power and exact political concessions" (Stephan and Chenowith, 2008, p. 8). Observers noted the significant role played by Lebanese women in these events, which energized political activism among women where it had, perhaps, grown tired. This section will explore women's involvement in the Cedar Revolution by drawing from interviews with participants and organizers in an attempt to demonstrate that the Lebanese women's nonviolence movement became an essential means for women's political participation.

On February 14, 2005, a massive car bomb exploded in Beirut, taking the life of former prime minister Rafiq Hariri and several other people. This tragedy left the entire country in shock and in a general state of insecurity and political instability. Immediately after the explosion, individuals gathered at the scene of the assassination—which later became known as "ground zero." The scene, as described by Mrs. Nora Jumblat, became the epicenter of ensuing protests:

On Tuesday night, the 15th of February, [my driver and I] went down [to Martyrs Square, the site of Rafiq Hariri's assassination,] and I saw a few people standing there with candles, just about ten to fifteen people and I went down. They said you want to put a candle here, and I said yeah of course. I said who are you? And they said you want to sign this petition? And the petition said they're asking for an international investigation of the Hariri [assassination]. And I said who are you? They said we're nobody, we're just citizens and we think. Can you help us? . . . They were ten or fifteen and there was nobody, nobody, in town; it was a ghost town. So I said yes of course, how can I help you? They said if you can bring the press and we can do something around it. (Jumblat, 2006)

At first, people gathered to light candles and pray for the souls of the victims. They also came to search for the missing, whom the government had failed to find. A petition was circulated demanding an honest investigation that would uncover the identity and motives of the assassins. The petition further demanded that these individuals be brought to justice. "On impulse they asked passersby to sign a petition calling on the pro-Syrian Lebanese government to resign; after four days, they were wrestling with a scroll of signatures some 400 meters long" (Macleod, 2005). Asma-Maria Andraos, who, along with several dozen friends, initiated the petition, states that no one had an overarching political plan in mind. Rather, they simply viewed the petition as a way of expressing anger over both the crime and the deteriorating conditions in the country.

Those spontaneous expressions of anger became a burgeoning protest movement (Stephan, 2012). In less than a week, the protest had drawn people from all walks of life, eventually gaining the sponsorship of professional syndicates, political parties, government officials, artists, and intellectuals. Thousands of people gathered every night and the government grew weary of them. On February 28, 2005, the Minister of Interior branded the demonstrations unlawful, and a military judge imposed a ban on assembly starting at 5:00 a.m. (Shaea, 2005a, p. 10). This declaration set the stage for the largest collective show of civil disobedience in Lebanese history, as thousands of people from all over Lebanon crowded into the streets. By 6:00 p.m. that same day, due to popular pressure exerted by the crowd, the pro-Syrian prime minister Omar Karami resigned. Five days later, Syrian president Assad announced plans to withdraw his forces from Lebanon.

On March 14, 2005, to commemorate the one-month anniversary of the assassination of Prime Minister Rafiq Hariri, over 1 million Lebanese men, women, and children rallied in central Beirut chanting "Freedom, Sovereignty, Independence." They came from every Lebanese region and from all faiths, partly in response to the March 8 rally. Their message was twofold: the majority wants Syrian troops out of Lebanon, and pressure must be continually exerted on the establishment to step away from the politically dishonorable situation in Lebanon. It was the largest demonstration in Lebanon's history. Not only did this protest receive approval from a number of international political leaders, but significant media coverage ensured that it was viewed around the world. Multiple political parties were involved in organizing the demonstration and Hariri's Future group (political party, TV, and newspaper) took an active role in orchestrating the various events that day.

The demonstrators demanded an international investigation of the circumstances surrounding the murder of Rafiq Hariri, the arrest of the chief security officers in the Lebanese government, and the total withdrawal of Syrian forces from Lebanese soil. Women were heavily represented, both as leaders and as participants in this demonstration. Bahiya Hariri, a member of parliament from Sidon and sister of the slain former prime minister, addressed the crowd saying, "Your family and all the Lebanese will keep your history alive. We came to vow before you that we will not let anyone hurt our Lebanon, the Lebanon you wanted, and we will proceed with the path you drew for us" (Shaea, 2005b, p. 7). In the crowd was Maya, a 38-year-old Shiite Muslim archaeologist, who considered the demonstration a good first step. "There may be many more [steps] to take. Maybe these won't be taken in the streets like today, but we must continue" (Shaea, 2005b, p. 7).

During all the events following Hariri's assassination, women's organizations were united in expressing their anger and demanding the establishment of an investigative commission. When Mother's Day arrived in Lebanon on March 21, 2005, a young woman, Leila Saad, issued a call to all Lebanese mothers to pray at 12:55 p.m. (the time of the assassination) wherever they were:

Lebanon needs our prayers . . . Lebanon is like a sick child in desperate need of care. We must act like we do when our children get sick. We must come together and pray intensely for the health of our country. (Des Mamans, 2005)

Various women's associations and civil society organizations echoed Saad's call in a show of solidarity (Haddad, 2005b). Hundreds of mothers, sisters, wives, and daughters arrived from regions throughout Lebanon, some dressed in black, others in white, carrying candles and demanding the truth.

"This is a sad day for all mothers in Lebanon," said a woman who came from the city of Akkar in northern Lebanon, "we did not have the desire to celebrate our holiday while all of Lebanon is mourning. The best Mother's Day gift we could receive is to know the truth about the circumstances of the attack. This is the only thing that would bring true pleasure to our hearts. We all wish to uncover the truth quickly in order to be able to celebrate our holiday next year in peace." (Haddad, 2005b, p. 4)

Subsequently, on March 19, 23, and 27, a number of bombs exploded in Beirut's Christian suburbs, killing 5 and injuring 20. People knew that these explosions were set off to terrify and divide them. Women's associations called upon all women to overcome their fears, assemble in the streets, and carry the following messages: "No to Fear and Yes to National Unity," "Enough Terrorism, Our People Are Fearless," and "Stop State Terrorism." They called this particular protest movement "the quake of love" (Shaea, 2005b, p. 7). Thousands of women, dressed in white just as in the movement in 1985, responded to the call and filled the Martyrs Square. While some associations provided buses to transport their members, most participants organized themselves in small groups of friends and colleagues. They were all motivated by the same desire: to show that women also have a powerful message. They chanted:

Every mother, every child, and every heartbeat asks the same question:
    Where is the Truth?
    We want love, we want peace, and we want truth and freedom. (Shaea, 2005b, p. 7)

This demonstration brought together a cross-section of social classes: wives of dignitaries, female parliamentary members, little girls dressed in white, old veiled women with their backs bent with age, progressive modern young professionals, and housewives who refused to play a secondary role in the struggle for independence. Member of Parliament (MP) Nayla Moawad addressed the crowds, asserting:

We have come to say enough to the attacks and the explosions. They do not scare us. We demand the truth, free elections, and a free and independent international commission of investigation. Each new explosion adds a page to their file which is already full of security violations. This file will be examined by the international investigation commission. (Haddad, 2005a, p. 5)

A committee headed by MP Bahia Hariri and Mrs. Nora Jumblat organized Lebanon's National Unity Festival in downtown Beirut on April 11, 2005. This spectacular marathon was packed with families from all Lebanese regions who came to show their support (Dempsey and Taan, 2005). One young participant named Mirna, age 22, viewed her participation in the marathon as a duty "which every true patriot should feel." She said, "As I ran, I truly felt that I'm doing this for Lebanon. We should show everyone that we are united regardless of what happens" (Hatoum, 2005). Similarly, a six-year-old named Jennifer, also at the marathon, was happy to be doing something positive for Lebanon. Her father claimed, "I want my daughter to grow up loving everything, and appreciating life and freedom, and [to] be open to others' opinions rather than [having to] teach her to stand against other Lebanese citizens whenever they disagree on something" (Hatoum, 2005, p. 1).

Nora Jumblat's name has been associated indissolubly with this revolution from the beginning to the very end. Mrs. Jumblat, a Syrian-born Sunni and an art history graduate of Paris's l'École des Beaux Arts, is married to one of Lebanon's most prominent Druze leaders, Walid Jumblat. For almost three months, Mrs. Jumblat managed a large part of the protest's logistics and organized various aspects of the revolution. When the first demonstrations headed to the streets, she made sure that banners, Lebanese flags, and signs were distributed from her office. Mrs. Jumblat coordinated with the newspaper Annahar to hide all the protest materials in the paper's trucks: "They came in here and all the students came . . . and all the parties . . . to take all the banners and everything. That was the beginning of everything. Of course different parties started doing their own things [later]" (Jumblat, 2006). After coordinating a number of the demonstrations from her office, the army and the pro-Syrian government discovered Mrs. Jumblat's activities. At that point, she and other organizers moved the distribution center to a new location.

Nora Jumblat became the natural mediator between demonstrators in the street and members of the elite class. As social movement scholars have noted, ordinary citizens engaging in social movements normally lack direct access to power and resources. Thus, including sympathetic members of the élite as allies increases a movement's chance for access and success; this holds true even if those individuals' political influence is minimal at the onset of the social movement (Rucht, 1996).

The candlelight vigil for Hariri's funeral at ground zero suggests that the revolution was representative of a collective loss in many ways. Women's participation in traditional funeral processions shaped the roles women played in the demonstrations. First, the public vigil indicates a distinctly feminine influence through the abundant use of flowers and candles as a tool of opposition. Second, the body and its adornment served as an instrument of protest as well. In the crowds, one observed a

rich diversity of dress codes, including traditional horsemen with Arab headdresses, clerics in their distinctive robes and turbans, and young girls with bare midriffs and pierced navels. . . . Those who were not carrying flags had them smeared on their faces or tattooed and inscribed on visible parts of their bodies. (Khalaf, 2005, p. 1)

The following is Anisa al-Amin Merei's eloquent description of the significant contributions women made to this revolution:

They turned their country into a flag, an anthem, a candle and a flower.
Does the country need more than love? This is an emerging language that the youth created and the women dedicated: mothers, friends, lovers and sisters. This language became a flag and a national anthem of a country that has been historically suppressed. They are guarding this nation for a beautiful tomorrow for their men by protecting them from war, submissiveness and helplessness. (Merei, 2005, p. 20)

By openly protesting in the streets and by contributing to key aspects of planning the nonviolent resistance against the Syrian occupation,

Lebanese women added a feminist dimension to the liberation of Lebanon. They wore banners on their heads and carried Lebanese flags to show solidarity. Women participated with men in a competition of patriotism and nationalism. In addition to leading demonstrations, women filled the streets in protest and held their own events. Women became in March 2005 liberators and nonviolent resistors.

CONCLUSION

In this chapter, we have provided readers with a historical overview of Lebanese women's nonviolent activism. Throughout the years, Lebanese women have been cognizant of the results of violence on their lives, the lives of their families, and the lives of their communities, and on the destruction it has caused in their country. They have been careful to construct alternative methods of protest, alternative means of political representations, and alternative possibilities for the future of their country. They have publicly advocated for peace, held conferences, shared their personal war narratives, written literature about the war, challenged the law, participated in national movements, and in the process constructed an image of women as peace builders, prone to civil egalitarianism.

We also have examined the ways in which women participated in developing and defining a nonviolence movement in Lebanon during the civil war, how they articulated public arguments for their call to peace building as an active participation in the political process, and how they defined their role as women in the larger national movements. We have been careful to allow the women's voices from our interviews and the documentation in *Al-Raida* to speak for themselves. We are aware that further research and analysis are needed in order to reveal a more thorough rereading of women's historical participation in Lebanon. Further interviews and archival research are needed to engage in deeper discussions on how women constructed their citizenship in relation to the state and how they envisioned the role of the state in the larger Middle East, as well as the relationship between the international women's movements and the local Lebanese women's movements, especially in the post–Arab Spring era.

As this condensed history shows, the struggle for an independent Lebanon that maintains basic human rights despite its confessional system is intertwined with the development of Lebanese women's rights activism, which coordinates with other social movements to pressure for peace, democracy, and equality. Imbued with the spirit of democracy, Lebanese activist Mona Modad asked after the Cedar Revolution: "Will this wonderful phenomenon finally prove that Lebanon is ready to embrace democracy and accept women as equal citizens?" (Modad, 2005). This question still remains to be answered. Having lived through 15 years of civil war, women's rights activists realize that they will never achieve their goal unless they can end violent practices in the political, social, religious, and patriarchal structures that not only oppress them, but also divide community against community, and have motivated, time and time again, the flight to a clientelist system for maintaining oneself in the midst of a state of total insecurity (Abiyaghi and Catusse, 2001). Lebanese activist and professor Fehmieh Charafeddine argues, "Achieving equality between the sexes is a true thermometer of the presence of equality in a society and of the wide public participation, and both constitute the actual foundation of democratic processes" (Charafeddine, 2004, p. 7). This convergent path has been a characterizing feature of the women's rights movement in most of the Arab world. While we are unable to determine whether a true democratic process will ever take hold in Lebanon, we are confident that the women in Lebanon will continue to promote peace building, gender equality, and civil egalitarianism in myriad ways.

NOTES

1. The views expressed in this chapter are those of the author and do not represent the views of, and should not be attributed to, the U.S. Department of State.

2. Initially the Palestinian leadership, the Palestinian Liberation Organization (PLO), was stationed in Amman, Jordan. However, in 1970 King Hussein of Jordan crushed the PLO's increasing power in the kingdom, killing tens of thousands of Palestinians, an event known in history as Black September. Upon this brotherly violence, the PLO moved its headquarter to Beirut. Upon the Israeli invasion of Lebanon, the PLO leadership moved to Tunis, where it remained until the Oslo Accords in 1994 and the establishment of the Palestinian Authority as a semi-autonomous state in the West Bank and Gaza Strip.

3. It reads: "Until the Chamber of Deputies passes an election law free of sectarian restriction, the parliamentary seats shall be divided according to the following bases: a. Equally between Christians and Muslims. b. Proportionately between the denominations of each sect. c. Proportionately between the districts."

4. According to a World Bank Economic and Social Impact Assessment (ESIA), the 2006 war caused $2.4 billion in direct damage to the Lebanese infrastructure and up to $800 million in indirect losses (Reform Program for the Energy Sector, 2007).

5. We used the term "peace" instead of "nonviolent" in this section in order to maintain the voices of the women who participated in this movement and defined it as such. We argue that this term is synonymous with the term "nonviolent," since the discourse on nonviolence had not included social movements in the Middle East at that time. Thus, while we use the term "peace movement" as a proper noun to refer to the specific women's movement in Lebanon, we argue that this movement bears all the characteristics of a movement that espouses nonviolence as an aim and methodology.

6. The nine universities comprised the Asian Women's Institute and participating colleges were divided into three main areas: Area A consisted of Beirut

University College in Beirut, Lebanon; Damavand in Tehran, Iran; and Kinnaird College, in Lahore, Pakistan. Area B consisted of Isabella Thorburn in Lucknow, India; St. Christopher's in Madras, India; and Women's Christian College in Madras, India. Area C consisted of Ewha Women's University, Seoul Women's College, and Tokyo Women's Christian College.

7. The Cold War provided two "rallying points in the peace movement" in the two peace demonstrations, STAR and the antinuclear demonstration in New York in 1982, as a result of the "concern over President Ronald Regan's loose rhetoric about nuclear war and the buildup in military spending" (Hastedt, 2004, p. 387).

8. Ghurayyib contributed an article on the Lebanese feminist movement titled "The Harem Window" to Morgan's anthology in 1984. In her piece, she presents three fields that Lebanese women have contributed to: journalism, literary, and artistic. She argues the patriarchal system that has been exploiting women, like her sisters around the world, has been one of the main problems for women's development.

9. Although the author remains anonymous, it is indicated on the last page of the journal that Ghurayyib is the "author of unsigned articles."

10. Again, Ghurayyib's definition of masculinity as a socially constructed concept is illustrated.

11. Tough guy or hero.

12. While the article mentions in a footnote that this did occur between July 7 and July 10, 1983, no further information is provided.

13. For a more thorough analysis of the Cedar Revolution, consult Stephan (2012).

BIBLIOGRAPHY

Abiyaghi, Marie Noelle, and Myriam Catusse. 2001. Non à L'etat Holding, Oui à L'etat Providence: Logiques et Contraintes des Mobilisations Sociales Dans le Liban de L'après-guerre. *Tiers Monde* 206: 67–93.

Chaney, Paul. 2007. Strategic Women, Elite Advocacy and Insider Strategies: The Women's Movement and Constitutional Reform in Wales. *Research in Social Movements, Conflicts and Change*, 27: 155–185.

Charafeddine, F. 2004. Musharakat Al-maraa al Lubnania fi al Hayat al Siyasiya: al Waqe' wa al Afaq. In *al-Musharaka al-Siyasiya lil Maraa al-Arabiya*, edited by A. T. al-Bakoush. Tunis, Tunisia: Arab Center for Human Rights.

Chkeir, I. C. 2002. *Nisaa fi Imraa: al sirat Laure Moghaizel*. Beirut, Lebanon: Annahar.

Costain, Anne N. 2000. Women's Movements and Nonviolence. *PS: Political Science and Politics* 33: 175–180.

Dempsey, Michael, and Hania Taan. 2005, April 11. Lebanon Kicks off National Unity Festival: Thousands Take to Streets to Participate in Celebrations. *Daily Star*.

Des Mamans du Liban se Recueillent sur la Sépulture, Place de Martyrs. 2005, March 22. *L'Orient Le Jour*.

Ellis, Kail. 2002. Lebanon's Challenge: Reclaiming Memory and Independence. In *Lebanon's Second Republic: Prospects for the Twenty-first Century*. Gainesville: University Press of Florida, pp. 1–13.

Ferree, M. M. 2004. Soft Repression: Ridicule, Stigma, and Silencing in Gender-Based Movements. *Research in Social Movements, Conflicts and Change* 25: 85–101.

Ghazal, Rym. 2005, October 14. Asma Andraos Honored as "Hero of Change." *Daily Star*.

Ghurayyib, Rose. 1982a. Should We Lose Faith in Man? *Al-Raida* 5 (22): 2.

Ghurayyib, Rose. 1982b. What Can Women Do for Peace? *Al-Raida* 5 (22): 3.

Ghurayyib, Rose. 1982c. World Campaign for Peace (Editorial). *Al-Raida* 5 (22): 1.

Ghurayyib, Rose, and Wafa' Stephan. 1983. National Conference of the Lebanese Women's Council 23-4-1983. *Al-Raida* 6 (25): 9.

Grant, W. 2000. *Pressure Groups and British Politics*. London: Macmillan.

Haddad, Scarlett. 2005a, March 29. Manifestation—Lorsque Les Femmes Veulent Faire Entendre Leur Voix, Place des Martyrs: Par Milliers, Elles Ont Réclamé la Vérité de Défié la Peur et l'Angoisse. *L'Orient Le Jour*: 5.

Haddad, Scarlett. 2005b, March 22. Les Femmes dans la Rue pour Défier les Poseurs de Bombes. *L'Orient Le Jour*: 4.

Hastedt, Glenn P. 2004. *Encyclopedia of American Foreign Policy*. Facts on File, p. 387.

Hatoum, Leila. 2005, April 11. Tens of Thousands Mark Civil War's Beginning with "Unity Run": Young, Old, Christian and Muslim Run for Lebanon. *Daily Star*: 1.

Johnson-Odim, Cheryl. 1991. Common Themes, Different Contexts: Third World Women and Feminism. In *Third World Women and the Politics of Feminism*, edited by Chandra Talpade Mohanty, Ann Russo, and Lourdes Torres. Bloomington: Indiana University Press, pp. 314–327.

Jordan, G., and W. Maloney. 1997. *The Protest Business? Mobilizing Campaign Groups*. Manchester: Manchester University Press.

Jumblat, Nora (Director, Beiteddine Festival). 2006, July 10. Interview in Beirut, Lebanon.

Khalaf, Samir. 2005, March 29. Lebanon's Youths Are Now Writing Their Own Future. *Daily Star*: 1.

Kutz-Flamenbaum, R. V. 2011. Recruiting or Retaining? Frame Reception in the Women's Peace Movement. *Research in Social Movements, Conflicts and Change*, 32: 191–218.

Lovenduski, J. 2005. *Feminizing Politics*. Cambridge: Polity.

Macleod, Scott. 2005, November 2. Days of Cedar. *Time*.

Merei, Anisa al-Amin. 2005, March 30. A Shiite Progressive Woman. *Annahar*: 20.

Modad, Mona. 2005, March 13. Is it Time for Women's Participation in Social and National Politics? *Annahar*.

Moghaizel, Laure. 1969. Interview published in *L'Orient Le Jour*, October 22.

Reform Program for the Energy Sector. 2007, May 3. *Rebuild Lebanon*, www. Rebuildlebanon.org

Rucht, Dieter. 1996. Campaigns, Skirmishes, and Battles: Anti-Nuclear Movements in the USA, France, and Western Germany. *Industrial Crisis Quarterly* 4: 193–222.

Schulze, Kirsten. 1998. Communal Violence, Civil War and Foreign Occupation: Women in Lebanon. In *Women, Ethnicity and Nationalism: The Politics of Transition*, edited by Rick Willford and Robert E. Miller. London: Routledge, pp. 130–146.

Shaea, Manal. 2005a, March 1. The Sky Is Their Cover and the Flag Is Their Weapon, Along with the White Flowers Which They Offered to the Soldiers, Demonstrators in the Freedom Square Awaited a New Dawn: We Will Not Leave Unless the Syrians Apologize and the State Shows Remorse for Their Crime. *Annahar*: 10.

Shaea, Manal. 2005b, March 29. Thousands of Women Delivered One Message: Our Unity Is Greater than All Their Explosions. *Annahar*: 7.

Stephan, Maria, and Erica Chenowith. 2008. Why Civil Resistance Works: The Strategic Logic of Nonviolent Conflict. *International Security* 33: 7–44.

Stephan, Rita. 2010. Couple's Activism for Women's Rights in Lebanon: The Legacy of Laure Moghaizel. *Women Studies International Forum* 33: 533–541.

Stephan, Rita. 2012. Women's Rights Movement in Lebanon. In *Mapping Arab Women Movements*, edited by Nawar Al-Hassan Golley and Pernille Arenfeldt. Cairo: American University of Cairo Press.

Stephan, Wafa'. 1984. Women and War in Lebanon (Editorial). *Al-Raida* 7 (30): 2 (print).

Stop the Arms Race (STAR). 1982. *Al-Raida* 5 (21): 8.

Taylor, V., and N. Whittier. 1995. Analytical Approaches to Social Movement Culture: The Culture of the Women's Movement. In *Social Movements and Culture*, edited by H. Johnston and B. Klandermans. Minneapolis, MN: University of Minnesota Press, pp. 163–187.

CHAPTER 18

The Syrian Revolution as Lived and Led by Women Activists

Rajaa Altalli and Anne-Marie Codur

During the wave of social and political uprisings known as the "Arab Spring"[1] of 2011, women were able to seize the opportunity to open a political and social space that had been closed to them previously, and as a result, they played a particularly important role in the revolutionary phases in all the countries involved (Tunisia, Egypt, Yemen, Bahrain, and Syria). Everywhere, women were prominently featured at the forefront of mass demonstrations, and as bloggers, citizen journalists, and digital activists, mobilizing their social networks through Facebook, Twitter, Youtube, and other modern media.

In this chapter, we explore the experience of the Syrian women who have had leadership roles in the Syrian uprising, based on the findings of a survey covering the period March 2011–June 2012.[2]

WOMEN IN CIVIL RESISTANCE

The role of women in civil resistance movements has long gone under documented if not ignored by historians and other social scientists. More recently however, feminist scholarship has been increasingly shedding light on the remarkable record of women's involvement in struggles for rights, freedom, and social justice, throughout times and places. Pam McAllister (1999, p. 21) even suggests that "most of what we commonly call 'women's history' is actually the history of women's role in the development of nonviolent action."

As social scientists are unearthing this historical record of women's key contributions to the development of the methods and practices of nonviolent action, they are also paying closer attention to what women bring to current struggles, all over the world.[3]

In the context of societies where sociocultural norms keep women at the margins of the public and political spheres, women activists face a double challenge, as political activists engaged in a struggle of defiance vis-à-vis the power structures of repressive regimes, and as women going beyond established norms and defying those norms as well.

THE WOMEN OF THE ARAB AWAKENING

When the Arab uprisings started in 2011 the sociocultural context in most Arab countries was generally not conducive to the political empowerment of women. In 2002, the Arab Human Development Report, published by UNDP, observed,

The utilization of Arab women's capabilities through political and economic participation remains the lowest in the world in quantitative terms, as evidenced by the very low share of women in parliaments, cabinets, and the work force, and in the trend toward the feminization of unemployment.

This report argued that the deficit in women's empowerment was not simply a problem of justice and equity, but a major cause of the Arab world's lagging economically: a "society as a whole suffers when a huge proportion of its productive potential is stifled" (UNDP, 2002, p. 3). However, there were major differences among Arab countries in that regard, with Tunisia, which had been a leader in passing equal rights in family law as early as 1956 (Charrad, 2001), on one side of the spectrum and on the other side countries such as Yemen, where the sharia is still strictly applied, making women legal minors and a woman equal to half a man in the court system (where the testimony of a man equals that of two women). Discriminating laws against women are numerous in several Arab countries, notably unequal systems of family law. Women have gained the right to vote in all Arab countries except Saudi Arabia, which announced in 2011 that it would pass that right for the next elections in 2015 (Saudi women are still waiting to exercise that right as this chapter is being written, at the end of 2014). However, since almost all Arab countries have been under nondemocratic regimes over the past 40 years or more, this right to vote has been meaningless, at least until 2011, the year of the Arab awakening.

Where regimes have quickly fallen, opening the way to phases of transition, the roles of women have followed diverging paths, from a "gender-conscious" approach in Tunisia (where women were granted a quota for the elections) to a more conservative, "women-averse" path in Egypt, where there have been systematic attempts by the authorities (whether under military rule or under the short-lived Morsi government) to minimize women's role and marginalize them and to roll back gains women had made in advancing their rights during the revolution.

Our research aims at examining the role of women activists in Syria, which presents a very different case of a much longer revolutionary phase, where the contest between the regime and the opposition has grown into a full-fledged civil war.

THE CASE OF SYRIA

When we conducted the interviews of 20 Syrian women activists, in May and June of 2012, the situation in Syria had already turned toward a predominance of the armed struggle over the unarmed, nonviolent civilian struggle. As the intensity of armed confrontations increased throughout 2012 and 2013, it became more challenging for the civilian movements that had shaped the first phase of the revolution to continue and sustain their impact, and in many cases they disappeared altogether. Women played an essential role in these civilian movements, in ways that arguably might offer them stronger leverage in advocating for women's rights in the future rebuilding of their country, once the Syrian society emerges from the chaos of civil war.

There has been so far very little in-depth coverage about the role of women activists during the civilian-led part of the Syrian revolution.

Our research seeks to shed light on the involvement of women during that phase, the strategies they developed, the challenges they faced, the success they had, and the opportunities that arose for them to design innovative strategies and tactics of resistance.

THE SURVEY

We developed a questionnaire designed to analyze the profile of 20 Syrian women activists and their activities during the period between March 2011 and June 2012, exploring the following questions: Were Syrian women activists at an advantage or at a disadvantage compared to male activists? Were there cases where they were able to accomplish things that men could not have done? How different were their styles and practices as leaders, strategists, and organizers of the revolution, alongside male activists?

The questionnaire included four sections[4]:

1. Personal background of the interviewee: her family roots, religious/ ethnic background, education, marital status and profession, as well as her history of political/social activism, in her family and in her life, before the revolution started

2. Personal involvement in the revolution: a detailed account of the type of activities the interviewee took part in from March 2011 to June 2012
3. Personal analysis of the movement: what worked, what didn't work, and observations on the role of women in the revolution
4. Vision of the future, aspirations and goals

We asked our network of contacts among male and female activists in Syria to identify some of the most active women in the revolution, at the local level and throughout Syria, in order to establish a sample that would reflect the wide ethnic and religious diversity of the Syrian population as well as its geographical dispersion.

Because of the way these activists have been identified, based on their visibility and recognition inside the movement as leaders, organizers, and coordinators of various groups, we acknowledge that this sample may not be representative of all female activists. This sample includes women who have shown constant and sustained involvement in the revolution for long periods of time, in most cases since the beginning of the revolution (and even before March 15, 2011). Women activists who have had lower levels of involvement are therefore not represented in this survey. We tried to mitigate this effect by asking the interviewees questions about their observations of other women activists (including women not in positions of leadership).

Of the 20 Syrian women activists surveyed, 16 lived in Syria at the time of the interviews and 4 were outside the country (they had already left Syria for safety reasons by May 2012 but had been key activists during the first year of the revolution).

PROFILE OF THE INTERVIEWEES[5]

In terms of ethno-religious background—a criterion of particular importance considering the internal divisions among communities in Syria—our sample group offered a fair representation of the country's demographic profile: 14 are Muslim Sunni (among whom 2 are Kurds), 2 are Christians, 2 are Druze, 1 is Ismaili, and 1 is Muslim Shiite. However, our sample regrettably did not include any Alawite activists. Although a very large majority of Alawites have supported the regime, there have been some notable exceptions, in particular among celebrities, such as the famous actress Fadwa Sulaiman.[6]

As for other socioeconomic, cultural, and educational indicators, our sample is not representative of the female Syrian population. Between 20 and 45 years old, only 6 of them were married at the time of the interview, whereas typically the average Syrian woman is married at age 21.[7] They are also much more educated than the average Syrian woman and reflect high rates of employment. All these indicators point to a profile of high levels of personal and professional empowerment.[8]

REASONS FOR THEIR INVOLVEMENT

Family History

Many of these women are the daughters and sisters of men who fought for freedom in the previous generation or more recently. Out of the 20 activists, 14 come from families that have been politically active, and of those 14 women, 10 had at least one of their close relatives detained—their father, grandfather, brother, or cousin—and in a few cases, some of their family members have been killed by the regime (in the 1980s). As expressed by B. from Homs, "I have been raised up on hating the regime."

Two of the six married interviewees mentioned their husband as their main role model and source of inspiration to get involved in the revolution, and in both cases the husband had been in jail either before or during the revolution.

Those who were not from a politically active family joined the revolution out of sheer outrage over living in a country where a handful of people have captured all the wealth and held an iron fist over the rest of the population.

Other Influences

All of these women shared that they have been politically influenced not only by the history of Syria, but also by the Palestinian uprisings and Israeli repression, and by the war in Iraq. A few mentioned also the movement in Lebanon (the "Cedar revolution") as another important eye opener in recent years. The Arab uprisings of Tunisia, Egypt, and Libya in early 2011 had a catalyzing effect on all of them. As expressed by an activist from Banias,

I wished for the best when Hafez Assad died but unfortunately Assad the son appears to be much worse. . . . I used to hate Syria, all I wanted to do was travel abroad . . . but I saw the Tunisian Revolution. . . . I got afraid at first that they may kill us and that massacres happen. But, when the revolution started, I said to myself that this is the day. We will be free and Syria will be more beautiful . . . we will live just like the people wish to live . . . hand in hand, we will build Syria and become the most democratic country in the world.

THE TIMELINE

Most of the respondents became involved in the first days of the revolution, in March 2011. A few of them had been active even before the revolution started, organizing demonstrations in solidarity with the Tunisian, Egyptian, and Libyan people in January and February 2011.

All their testimonies recount the same course of events:

1. In the first phase of expansion of the revolution, leading to climactic massive demonstrations, they were all intensely engaged in the struggle, taking on different roles, leading demonstrations by chanting or singing, coming up with slogans, organizing committees to recruit more women and youths, and communicating through blogs, videos, and photos (using social media);

2. When the regime launched the first wave of brutal repression in their neighborhoods and towns, their role shifted to respond to the needs of the population, providing relief, comfort, and support to the families of the victims. It seems that all activists, female and male, had to significantly change their priorities in that second phase and adapt to the circumstances; however it is difficult for us to infer if the change affected more women's activities than men's. Were the women drawn to relief and humanitarian tasks and activities more than men on the basis that they are considered as more experienced caregivers? From the women's testimonies, it seems indeed that in many cases their previous activities related to the struggle receded significantly, except for those who were involved in the communication/media aspect of the revolution, who continued covering events through blogs and Youtube videos.

The timing of this second phase differed according to geographic locations. One of the first cities to be hit by brutal retaliation from the regime was Lattakia, the bastion of the Alawites. The demonstrations, led by Muslim Sunnis, seem to have quickly become unacceptable to the regime, which repressed them bloodily as early as April 17, 2011, killing 70 people in one day. Homs followed a few weeks later, in May 2011; Idlib in May/June; and Hama in August 2011. The regime did not have the resources to hit the resistance everywhere at the same time. In the case of major cities such as Homs and Damascus (including Damascus suburbs), the repression focused on one neighborhood at a time. The military strategy used by the regime consisted of hitting a place very hard for a few days—including shelling—to wreak havoc with the resistance, and then moving on to another place.

The "threshold" of what the regime has "tolerated" in terms of civil unrest in the first year of the revolution has been very different from place to place. The regime has chosen not to repress the Kurds harshly, in all likelihood so as not to provoke a possible violent insurrection demanding secession, which could be easily fueled through the border by the Iraqi part of Kurdistan. Therefore, the Kurds have had more leeway to organize their civil resistance to the regime and the Kurdish interviewees have not had to face the harsh repression many of the other interviewees faced in other regions. The Kurdish resistance was able to continue to organize in a relatively safe environment up to 2012.

As for the two main cities of Syria, Damascus and Aleppo, they seemed to have been immune to the harshest forms of repression during the first year of the revolution, due to the fact that they represent the nerve center of the regime, hosting all the major administrations and businesses, and are home to the regime's elite. This has implied the use of more military restraint on the part of the army when dealing with civil resistance in those sensitive cities—at least in the central neighborhoods, since such restraint has never been applied in the suburbs. However, by June 2012, the opposition had strengthened its position inside Damascus and Aleppo to such an extent that the regime started using its most brutal methods of repression even in those two critical cities, at the core of the system.

Several suburbs of Damascus, in which many of our interviewees lived and led the resistance at the time of the interviews, have been shelled and heavily repressed since the earliest times of the revolution. Each neighborhood where our interviewees lived has been hit by successive waves of repression from March 2011 to June 2012. There has been no clear patterns in the timing of that repression, but there were periods of several weeks in a row when each of these neighborhoods was released from the security grip. During those times of respite, the civil resistance was able to re-emerge to a certain extent.

MAIN ROLES AND ACTIVITIES OF WOMEN ACTIVISTS

During the first phase of expansion of the revolution all of the interviewed activists were actively involved in demonstrations—in recruiting others to join the demonstrations, in designing and carrying banners and signs, and in leading demonstrations through chanting and singing.

B. from Homs related this variety of activities: "I have participated in the revolution in all possible forms, demonstrations, sit-ins, strikes, documentation, taking photos, video shooting, uploading videos and sending them to TV channels."

We have observed two broad categories of work/activities:

1. Activities that require a lot of organization and coordination among several activists.
2. Activities that can be conducted in isolation, by oneself. This category includes some of the professional activities such as media/communication and human rights law practice. We will qualify this category as "stand-alone" activities.

Fourteen of the interviewees have been involved mostly in the first type of activities and six of them have focused on stand-alone activities. Although most of our interviewees have had some kind of a role and presence in social media, only four of them have focused their activism mainly if not exclusively on that function—as citizen journalists covering the events and reporting on the human rights violations. We will analyze in another section the special challenges that they faced in that role.

Most of the 14 who have been involved in planning and implementing activities that involved large groups of activists had important leadership roles inside those groups. For the purpose of analyzing the role of women in these groups and committees, we make a distinction between

1. Groups and committees that are composed of male and female activists, and
2. Groups that are exclusively composed of women activists.

Women Activists in a Male-Dominated Activist World

In our sample, seven women have been involved in committees that included both male and female activists. Although we don't know the proportion of women in these committees, as a possible point of comparison in that regard we can observe that the higher level of coordination of the revolution at the national level, represented by the Syrian National Council, in exile, included only about 10 percent women (although there had been a vote allowing for a quota of 30 percent). In local committees of the revolution, the proportion of women might in some cases have been higher, but still very far from parity. We can say that these women activists were therefore working in an environment that was mostly "male driven" and male led. However, when it came to the relief work, women have been taking prominent positions.

The organization of humanitarian relief, after neighborhoods had been shelled, usually emerged from the local revolution committee. Testimonies from the interviewees seemed to indicate that women had important roles in this relief effort.

In Lattakia, this relief work was led by a woman, S., who described her responsibilities in detail: coordinating 10 people, acting as liaison with the donors (inside and outside of Syria) and fund-raising for the relief effort. The activities in that committee, as in other cases of relief work described by other activists, included (1) during the height of the crisis itself, organizing the logistics of field hospitals, the collecting of blood, and other activities; and (2) in the aftermath of the bloody repression wave, organizing to meet the longer-term needs of people whose houses had been demolished and whose livelihoods had been destroyed.

Most of the women activists we have interviewed had participated in one phase or the other—maybe not all at the leadership level like S. from

Lattakia, but in some capacity. They showed a quick adaptation to situations of crisis and long-term involvement in relief efforts with the families who had suffered the losses.

All Female Activist Groups

When looking at the role of women in civil resistance, everywhere in the world we can observe the emergence of all-female activist groups, from the Mothers of Plaza de Mayo in Argentina, to the Women of Liberia Mass Action for Peace, in Liberia.[9] Especially in patriarchal societies that do not offer women space for political expression, the formation of all-female groups and organizations is sometimes the only way for women to get involved—in an environment that feels "safer" for them in social terms, as they interact exclusively with women.

Seven interviewees in our sample were involved in such female activist groups, working in their cities and neighbourhoods by drawing on the social network of their family and friends. They developed their own campaigns locally and a wide variety of tactics to advance their campaigns. Though such groups may not have emerged everywhere in Syria, where they have, they seem to have shown great levels of cohesion, trust, unity, and efficiency.

Here are two illustrative examples, one in a town in the province of Hama, the "Revolutionary Women of Salamieh," and one in a suburb of Damascus, "Daryya's Free Women Group."

THE REVOLUTIONARY WOMEN OF SALAMIEH

In the province of Hama, a group of women have organized in the small town of Salamieh. This region is inhabited mostly by Ismailis, a minority group practicing a heterodox version of Islam that has historically caused them to be discriminated against inside of Syria as "heretics." Because of their strong sense of solidarity as an oppressed minority, the Ismailis have always had strong community institutions. Salamieh had an Ismaili local council even before the start of the revolution. One of the female members of that council created the group Revolutionary Women of Salamieh, which focused on mobilizing the women and girls of that town in a context where families were particularly conservative and where women's involvement in the revolution would not be socially acceptable. As members of an exclusively female group, they have been able to network, recruit, and develop tactics such as chants, slogans, and statements. While conducting actions in the streets, they covered their faces so as not to be recognized by the spies and cameras of the regime, and also in order for them to occupy the public space in a way that hid their identities, since in this conservative environment it is considered shameful for women to shout in the streets.

DARYYA'S FREE WOMEN GROUP

In Daryya, a suburb of Damascus, a group of 10 women organized during the first months of the revolution and developed their own actions. Called "Daryya's Free Women Group," they have been nicknamed the "spray women" as they have been spray painting messages across the walls of their neighborhood and town, a less risky activity—although they have been very much involved in demonstrations as well, designing their own banners and slogans, and chanting and singing.

The messages they diffused were meant to unify all the residents of the town around a single objective. They reminded them to stay focused on that goal, and to remain nonviolent; one of their messages was "remember that we went out first for the rule of law." Their ideas would leave a permanent trace in town, one of the simplest being those powerful words "the revolution passed through here." The group released a statement declaring their strict commitment to nonviolent discipline. They were also able to organize various activities aiming at creating unity in the opposition, such as meetings including religious leaders, engineers, and doctors, and sit-ins asking for the release of detainees. Other actions were aimed at fraternizing with the police, to avoid alienating them and to show them that they, too, were victims of the regime. For example, they asked the policemen to protect them against the thugs of Al-Shabiha[10] (who came from out of town). They have also been able to convince mothers in Daryya to keep their children at home for months and to boycott the schools, whose teachers were all civil servants paid by the regime. They organized various cultural activities, including training children to perform plays that they co-wrote, telling stories about their resistance in Daryya. Finally, they also developed the online tools to present themselves and publicize their actions.

In short, this group was particularly well organized and efficient in designing a broad variety of tactics that all served the purpose of building internal cohesion in the community, facing the brutality of external threats from the regime and its militias.

THE CHALLENGES OF BEING A WOMAN IN THE REVOLUTION

Many of the activists expressed that being a woman activist in a sociocultural context that hinders women's empowerment poses many challenges. Some have been harassed, bullied, and intimidated, told that their place was not in the streets. J. from the Damascus suburbs said that religious leaders accused the women (Muslim Sunni) of being atheists if they participated in demonstrations. Once, a group of male demonstrators who didn't want women to be present started shouting that they wanted to overthrow women before overthrowing the regime.

In many cases, women fought back against the bullies. S. from the Damascus suburbs, recalled an anecdote when she faced one of these male demonstrators being aggressive toward women:

I called him by my finger so he came quickly thinking I needed some help, and I told him: Look, I went to the demonstrations and I have been hit, detained and shot at, only to get my freedom and my dignity back. Therefore I ask you to leave now before I start a powerful revolution against you and against whoever undermines women and considers them incapable creatures that they can control.

The bully retreated after that public scolding. This is but one anecdote of many about women who had to hold their ground against various attempts at intimidation. There were also reports of cases of jealousy within groups, as some male activists were resentful to see women leading some of the efforts. These women have shown tremendous courage and determination in facing these internal obstacles.

Such cases of hostility were observed at all levels, including in the leadership of the revolution at the national level. C, a member of the Syrian National Council for five months, reported that she encountered hostile reactions from several conservative male members of the council who systematically opposed the actions she proposed.

The interviews also revealed that social pressure and constraints were particularly strict for young unmarried women. Families often deemed it unacceptable for them to go out by themselves and get involved in groups and actions (especially if those actions included male activists). Many of these young women activists were therefore conducting their actions among groups of female relatives (sisters) and friends, so as not to be "alone" in the streets.

These constraints explain why it is easier for women and girls to join groups that are exclusively composed of female activists.

Our sample group was mostly composed of unmarried women. At the time of the interviews, among the 8 activists under age 30, only one was married, and among the 12 activists above 30 years old, 4 were single (never married) and 2 had been married but were then either divorced or separated from their husbands. This marital status profile probably contributed to give these women a higher degree of freedom to join the revolution.

Among the 6 interviewees who were married, having the support of their husband was in most cases a condition sine qua non of their ability to be involved in the revolution. However, in one case, M. had to face the fact that her husband was at first absolutely opposed to her engagement, to the point of telling her, "it's me or the revolution," to which she answered, "in that case, it's the revolution." He changed his mind and decided to be supportive of his wife's choice and actions. In two cases, husbands were very involved activists (one of them being in jail) and provided the main motivation to their wives' involvement. In the three other cases, husbands were to a certain degree supportive of their wives' action, but possibly to a lesser extent than their wives. The husbands were involved at least financially, providing a support system and helping with the logistics, but were not necessarily involved in the organization and implementation of actions.

The main concern of women activists in being arrested was, of course, being subjected to sexual abuse in jail. Cases of rape used as a weapon of war have been broadly reported. The young women victims of such acts tend to be hidden by their families, sometimes sent abroad and quickly married to men from the family, who accept to "hide the shame." However, some of the victims have decided to speak up. C. from the Damascus suburbs has documented the stories of women who had been raped during the first year of the revolution. Several human rights organizations inside and outside of Syria have been documenting cases of rape in Syria since the conflict started.[11]

THE OPPORTUNITIES OF BEING A WOMAN IN THE REVOLUTION

In the first year of the revolution, women were not repressed in the same manner as men. The data provided by members of the opposition[12] show that among all the people killed by the regime between March 2011 and June 2012, 7 percent were women. However, this figure includes people who were killed in the shelling of cities—a death toll that does not discriminate between men and women. The percentage of women among activists targeted by snipers and executed by the regime would be much lower. To estimate the order of magnitude, if we consider the data of detainees, we observe that of the 26,000 detainees in June 2012, only 360 were women, which represented about 1.5 percent.

Thus, it is clear that women were at an advantage in terms of being targeted for repression, because in the conservative Syrian society, the arrest of women is considered particularly unacceptable and would backfire in the face of the regime if it were conducted at a larger scale. The security forces were more reticent to arrest women and to use violence against them. In addition, whenever women were detained, it was generally for a shorter time than for men. Women were also less frequently searched than men, and therefore able to smuggle leaflets, flyers, and medicine to war-torn zones, moving between neighborhoods that were separated by checkpoints.

Because women have this advantage, our interviewees have mentioned that in many cases, they were able to rescue male activists and prevent them from being arrested, by surrounding and overwhelming the police force. An activist from Banias shared with us that: "men think we are weak creatures who should be protected by the men when in fact we protect them! . . . I rescued men from the hands of security people . . . many women did and the security people didn't utter a word!"

S. from Dara'a recalled:

Once we were in a demonstration, the security forces and Al-Shabiha attacked us, arrested many young men and detained them in a bus. The women attacked the bus with stones and their bare hands until they set the detainees free. There was a security officer sitting in the bus with no uniform. So one of the women who got into the bus asked him to get down because she thought he was a detainee. When he told her who he was, she slapped him, spit on him and got off the bus after releasing all the detainees.

In the beginning of the revolution, in Albaida, a small village near Banias, the women stood up en masse against the forces of the regime. The security forces had gathered all the men on the central square, tied their hands behind their backs, put them on the ground, hit them and stepped on them, after which they detained them.

On April 13, 2011, the women of Banias came in support of the women of Albaida to ask about their men. They organized a blockade of the main highway between Lattakia and Damascus.

One of the activists from Banias explained: "We spent the whole day. I saw much suffering: mothers carrying their son's photos and crying. There were elder women who walked for hours to reach that place. We were about 2000. We stayed till sunset." Eventually the security forces gave in and released the men. This show of courage gained the women of Banias the admiration of a colonel in the Security forces, who stated in typically patriarchal language, "there are no women in Banias, only men."

The remarkable result of this action led by Banias women is reminiscent of several other historical cases where the mobilization of women has been critical in obtaining the release of their husbands, including, in the worst-case scenarios, facing the most brutal forms of regime—such as the German wives of Jewish men, facing the Gestapo for days in Berlin, in the winter of 1943, and being able to pressure and embarrass the Nazi authorities enough that they would release their husbands.[13]

The women of Syria, when mobilized, were able to design actions that forced the regime to face a huge dilemma: either massively repress them (which would backfire much more than repressing men) or give in to their demands.

The courage of women often gained the admiration of male activists. M., a middle-aged woman from Idlib, by her courage and determination, was nicknamed "sister of men" among the male activists of her town, which in the Arab patriarchal culture means that she is a strong woman, as courageous as a man. Women activists have a keen sense that they are in fact often more courageous than men. J. from Hasakeh exclaimed,

"Where were you men when I, a woman, was facing bullets and you were just sitting silent?" Older women can in general get away with speaking their minds to the security forces without risking much retaliation. S. from Dara'a reported that an older woman was asked by an arrogant officer, in front of the ruins of the city: "Hajja.[14] Do you still want freedom in Dara'a?" The old woman answered, "No, we got our freedom, now we want to overthrow the regime."

Because women do not seem as threatening to police forces, they also can play a mediating role between the resistance and the authorities, sometimes even facilitating the defection of security forces. J. and other women activists in the Damascus suburbs were trying to prevent the male activists from storming and burning the police department. J. and the wives of the detainees went to the police to ask for help to get their protection from the thugs of Al-Shabiha who were attacking the women. They were able to convert the police to their cause and, by doing this, to reestablish trust between the community and the police, and to avoid antagonizing them.

OVERCOMING THE FEAR OF DEATH

Many of our interviewees expressed that the situation in May and June 2012 was especially trying for them, and that they occasionally felt despair. But to be fair to them, they also expressed how determined they were to continue the struggle. Their determination and courage in face of fear of death can be illustrated by this testimony by O. from Damascus:

The bullets were passing above my head and I was able to escape and hide in a farm for 30 minutes while the bullets fell like rain. I felt I was weak and I was afraid and that their bullets would kill me just because I dared to dream. I was wounded that day in my hand and in my leg as people were pushing each other. My camera with which I was filming, got broken. The next day, I decided to be stronger than their bullets and stronger than my fear, I went to Kafrsouseh and I participated in the funeral of the five victims and I filmed the funeral with my cell phone. I challenged their bullets and my fear. I succeeded.

Their greatest victory was to conquer their fears. An activist from Banias proudly claimed, "Fear has gone. The regime's bullets have killed nothing but fear in Syrian's hearts." The same sentiment is powerfully expressed by S. from the Damascus suburbs: "The Syrian people have burned their ship . . . there is no way back . . . the Syrian regime is dead, it's only kept alive by force."

KEEPING A NONVIOLENT DISCIPLINE?

The purely nonviolent involvement of the first months of the struggle had given way for a few of our interviewees to active support to the Free

Syrian Army by the beginning of 2012—financially and logistically at least, since very few if any would consider joining its ranks as soldiers. However, several of our interviewees still expressed their determination in keeping a nonviolent discipline. As mentioned above, Daryya's Free Women Group was still, in June 2012, focused on its nonviolent mission and spraying messages on the walls of Daryya to call for nonviolent discipline.

The emergence of armed resistance has brought more challenges and contradictions among these women. Many expressed their fears that the violent confrontations, unfolding since the spring of 2012, were creating larger divisions in Syrian society that could sow the seeds of ethnic and religious conflicts for years to come.

BEYOND THE ETHNO-RELIGIOUS DIVIDE: DIVISION OR UNITY?

Many activists expressed their determination to keep the ties of unity among communities and fight the forces of division. O. from Damascus, even refused to answer our question concerning her religious background: "I don't talk about religion. I am Syrian, that's all."

"Syria is for all, we will remain one till we win," expressed a Muslim Sunni, S from Dara'a, and a Kurdish activist from Hasakeh added, "Bullets don't differentiate between us."

R. from Suwaida (in the Druze province) said, "We need to build a democracy in a country which is inclusive for all its people and components without exception—a civic democratic state which respects the rights of all its citizens—this should be our compass and we should not forget that."

An activist from Banias, a Muslim Sunni in a town known for being conservative Muslim, said, "I wish that people take into consideration that the first Christian martyr in Syria was in Banias—his name was Hatem Hanna. We have gathered around his mother and we chanted: 'We are all Hatem.' These are unforgettable moments."

S. from Dara'a, talks about the amazing solidarity from other communities. When Dara'a was shelled on April 24, 2011, people helped each other regardless of their religious identity: "Our Christian brothers opened their churches to the wounded."

The desire for a pluralistic democracy is expressed over and over again among these women's testimonies—even if blended with the dream of autonomy for Kurdistan -in the case of one of the Kurdish interviewees.

In June 2012, all our interviewees expressed their hopes that the regime would fall quickly, and they were worried about the transition phase and the risk that religious forces might take over. "We do not want to topple a political dictatorship to have a religious dictatorship," said S. from Qamshli, in the Kurdish province.

To put their convictions in action, many of these activists were taking part in activities with women of other faiths and other communities.
C., a Christian activist, has demonstrated alongside conservative Muslim women in several suburbs of Damascus. N. from Suwaida (Druze
province) has been working closely with other women from different
communities—Alawites, conservative Sunni, Christians—in organizing
demonstrations in Midan, a neighborhood of Damascus. N. is also working with another group of women, making handicrafts and selling them
inside and outside of Syria to raise funds and support their activities. All
of these groups are multiethnic and multiconfessional.

To summarize the impact of these efforts by Syrian activist women in
bringing unity to a divided society, here is what M. from Damascus said:
"Women who were able to get unified and sit together, in spite of all their
different backgrounds, are able to do anything. The Syrian women are
extraordinary."

ORGANIZING IN A LEADERLESS AND HORIZONTAL WAY

In the groups where women activists worked exclusively among other
female activists, they described a way of working together that was nonhierarchical and horizontal, and where decisions were discussed and made
collectively.

According to an activist of the group Revolutionary Women of Salamieh,
"There is no leader. As a group, we discuss the ideas and suggest them to the
other girls." J. of the Damascus suburbs described the same horizontal structure in her group: "We don't have a leader. We all decide together for any project. It's me who supervises the implementation of the project and the work as
a whole." Interestingly, even when they obviously had a leadership role, these
women often mentioned that there was no leader—or at least they didn't consider themselves as leaders, maybe because the idea they have of a "leader"
belongs to the traditional, patriarchal, pyramidal "top-down" structure.

The reluctance on their part to be seen as leaders also involved obvious
security reasons, and the fear of being recognized and arrested. But their
conception of a "leader" in a traditional sense might not fit with the vision
they have of themselves. A "leader" in the Arab world might be more a
figurehead type who talks well, an orator of a sort who might speak more
than act. These female activists, who all displayed several key leadership
qualities, even though they might not see themselves as leaders, shared
with us that "I don't like to talk much. I like to act. Action yields more
power of conviction than words" (J. from the Damascus suburbs).

WORKING RELATIONSHIPS WITH MALE ACTIVISTS

Most of the interviewees also interacted with male activists in several
components of their work. According to S. from Dara'a, "Women are

pushing men forward" in the demonstrations, and it was through their powerful and inspired chanting and singing that the women played an important role in energizing the crowd of demonstrators (men in the majority). When it came to working together, in committees where women worked alongside male activists, we can observe how S. from Lattakia, for example, led the relief committee for the city, having both men and women under her responsibility. Her leadership style is such that her team worked closely together through an inclusive decision-making process that allowed members to easily reach agreement. In many ways, these inclusive committees, if only they had been able to continue developing and spreading in the months and years that followed, could have provided incubators for democratic governance in civil society and for the future institutions of Syria.

COMMUNICATION: THE WOMEN'S CHALLENGE TO COVER THEIR OWN NEWS

One area where women activists had a particularly challenging task in getting their voices heard is in the media—where they felt the need to organize to get their own stories out.

One day in June 2012, in one of the suburbs of Damascus, there was a female demonstration that included almost 500 women activists. It was neglected in the media and did not even appear on a Facebook page because priority was given to another demonstration that happened the same day and was dominated in attendance by men. Why such discrepancy in the news coverage?

It has been observed (independently from our survey) that most informers of international media are male activists. And, as is often the case when male journalists cover the news, there is an underrepresentation of women's activities (this has been observed all over the world and in many different historical and social contexts). There seems to be a gulf between what the women bloggers and citizen journalists are doing in terms of documenting their reality on the ground and the exposure they get on the Internet and in international news outlets—where their actions are almost invisible.

As mentioned earlier, almost all the activists we interviewed have been involved in documenting their actions at some level. However, among the 20 activists, only 4 have almost exclusively devoted their time and effort to the documentation of the revolution in their city.

From the testimonies of these 4 bloggers and citizen journalists, it appears that most of their efforts consisted in making sure that the historical memory of these events would not be lost. They recorded absolutely everything they could in a systematic way. B. from Homs has been relentlessly covering the revolution in her martyred city day by day. In August

2011, she started to search systematically for the martyrs' stories, to put a face on the number of deaths, "to know who they were, what were their thoughts, their dreams, their sufferings, their life story, so that they are not just statistics, but real people." She described her mission as that of a historian whose only wish is that future generations never forget. Her work will be essential in the eventual legal pursuits for the crimes committed, or at least for the truth and reconciliation process, in the reconstruction phase that will follow the civil war.

However, this is only one approach to the use of the media. Besides documentation and recording of history, there are many other ways to use the media in a movement, notably as a means of mobilization used to galvanize the people, to publicize events, and to gather support. However, in order to do this efficiently, those apprentice citizen journalists would need to better understand how they could use the online tools to make their videos go viral. When we interviewed them their presence on the net was unnoticeable, gathering no more than a few hundred "likes." They needed help and training to get to the next level. Daryya's Free Women Group launched in the beginning of June 2012 a new Web site in order to be more effective in their communication strategy. The women understood that if they didn't cover their own news, nobody else would.

It is worth noting that one of our citizen journalists from Banias had prepared a thorough documentary on the events in her town, which was shown on Orient TV in May 2012, a rare case where a woman-produced documentary was shown on an international TV channel (broadcast from Dubai and reaching a broad audience in the Arab world).

A famous example of a successful media campaign through a video that went viral and inspired the beginning of a movement was the "Stop the killing" campaign.[15] A young woman, Rima Dali, started her isolated action on April 10, 2012, the day when the cease-fire negotiated through Kofi Annan's initiative was supposed to go into effect. Rima poured white paint on her red dress in front of the parliament, holding up a sign that read, "Stop the killing. We want a homeland for all Syrians." Her action was carried on Youtube and followed by viewers online. A few days later, four young women sprawled like corpses on the floor of Damascino Mall while upper-class shoppers tripped over them. They too filmed their action, which was also shared on Youtube. From then on, several other women started in their neighborhoods and cities similar actions, holding signs saying simply "Stop the killing" while other activists around them, male and female, would clap and chant. We don't have an estimation of how many activists participated in "Stop the killing" actions. Among our 20 interviewees, 2 reported being involved in one of these actions. These isolated acts sparked a whole movement, as in the following weeks many women activists throughout Syria adopted the slogan "Stop the killing."

CONCLUSION: VISION OF THE FUTURE

Finally we asked the activists to share with us their dreams and vision of the future, to tell us what they would want (as of May/June 2012) if they were granted a wish. They all wished that the bloodshed would stop as soon as possible, and that the transition would lead them to a democratic, pluralistic regime: "We will suffer, there will be huge obstacles, but Syria will be the way we want it to be," insisted R. from Suwaida.

B. from Homs shared with us, "We will be free and Syria will be more beautiful . . . we will live just like people wish to live."

A few of them expressed wishes that the revolution would allow for a transformation of society to bring equality for women, and liberation: "I hope the Revolution succeeds in liberating women. Without women's liberation we will never have a peaceful society and we will not be able to develop," said S. from Damascus.

In facing a double challenge against the repression of a brutal regime, aiming at more openness and democratic structures on the one hand, and facing the limitations of constraining social norms on the other, women activists have been able to carve out for themselves a relatively safe space for their activism, especially in organizing all-female activism groups. They have been able to claim victories through such groups (as modest as they may be) and to keep their spirits up, hoping to contribute to the changes they wish to see in society. Despite the obstacles, in terms of their social acceptability and their visibility (and the challenges of their presence in the media), they have been building strong foundations for the future.

They have shown tremendous resilience in their struggle and were determined to continue the fight no matter how big the sacrifices: "It doesn't matter how many Syrian people will be in prison, the Syrian regime will not be able to imprison the words of freedom. Even if they arrest 23 million people, the words will be free," said M. from Damascus.

Despite the destruction and the high death toll, despite the risk of ethnoreligious civil war that was already looming in June 2012, the women activists we have interviewed were determined to continue their struggle for the unity of Syria in the respect for differences and the coexistence of minorities. Their accomplishments showed that the strengthening and broadening of networks of such groups of women activists throughout Syria could have paved the way to the deep structural changes that the Syrian society needed to set off on a successful path toward a pluralistic democracy. But as we are writing these lines, at the end of 2014, more than two years after these interviews were recorded, Syria is being torn apart by a devastating civil war. Between March 2011 and March 2014, the terrible bloodbath unleashed by the Assad regime has claimed the lives of more than 146,000 Syrians, according to an estimate of the Syrian Observatory for Human Rights.[16]

However, the voices of these brave women must remind us that one day, when Syria emerges from chaos, these women will be there, strong and determined as ever, and continuing their struggle to rebuild their country on new foundations, respectful of democratic and pluralistic values, and inclusive of all.

ACKNOWLEDGMENTS

The authors want to express their gratitude to Jack DuVall and to the International Center on Nonviolent Conflict for providing funding and support for this research. They are also grateful to Mary E. King for offering her invaluable advice and comments on an earlier draft of this chapter. Some of the findings of this work were used in an article published in openDemocracy, http://www.opendemocracy.net/civilresistance/nada-alwadi/voices-of-syrian-women-in-civil-resistance.

NOTES

1. The authors prefer not to use the term "Arab Spring" commonly used in the media, which wrongly seems to imply that after a short revolutionary episode, things are supposed to quickly turn for the better. We use instead the term "Arab Awakening," describing the beginning of a long process of social transformations, which will unfold for many more years and decades.

2. Our survey is based on interviews of 20 Syrian women activists conducted via Skype between May and June 2012 (3 of them answered the questionnaires in writing).

3. See Chapter 24 in Volume 2.

4. See the detailed questionnaire in Appendix 2

5. To protect the identity of all those who have been interviewed, no full names will be included in this study.

6. We make an exception in disclosing her name because of her fame—which she used on behalf of the revolution. We approached her for an interview but she declined the invitation.

7. Source: http://genderindex.org/country/syrian-arab-republic

8. A detailed description of the socioeconomic, cultural, and educational backgrounds of the interviewees is presented in Appendix 1.

9. See their story in the documentary *Pray the Devil Back to Hell* (2008), directed by Gini Reticker and produced by Abigail Disney.

10. Al-Shabiha are groups of armed militias in support of the Ba'ath party and the Assad government.

11. According to the Syrian Network for Human Rights (SNHR), the number of rapes of women had reached 6,000 in 2013. Source: http://www.euromedrights.org/eng/wp-content/uploads/2013/11/Doc-report-VAW-Syria.pdf

12. See the Web site http://syrianshuhada.com/default.asp?a=st&st=1

13. See this remarkable story of unarmed resistance against Hitler in Nathan Stoltzfus's *Resistance of the Heart: Intermarriage and the Rosenstrasse Protest in Nazi Germany* (1996).

14. "Hajja" is a respectful term for an older woman ("Haj" for a man) meaning that the older person has done the pilgrimage to Mecca.

15. We did not have the opportunity to interview the initiator of this action, Rima Dali.

16. The United Nations's last estimate dates back to July 2013, with a figure of at least 100,000, but the UN declared in January 2014 that it would stop updating the death toll as conditions on the ground made it impossible to make accurate estimates. It is believed that a third of the casualties are civilians. Reuters, March 13, 2014, http://www.reuters.com/article/2014/03/13/us-syria-crisis-toll-idUSBREA2C1ZR20140313.

BIBLIOGRAPHY

Charrad, Mounira. 2001. *States and Women's Rights: The Making of Postcolonial Tunisia, Algeria, and Morocco.* Berkeley, CA: University of California Press.

Euro-Mediterranean Human Rights Network. 2013, November. Violence against Women: Bleeding Wound in the Syrian Conflict. Available at http://www.euromedrights.org/eng/wp-content/uploads/2013/11/Doc-report-VAW-Syria.pdf

McAllister, Pam. 1999. You Can't Kill the Spirit. In *Nonviolent Social Movements: A Geographic Perspective*, edited by Stephen Zunes, Sarah Beth Asher, and Lester Kurtz. New York: John Wiley & Sons.

United Nations Development Program (UNDP). 2002. *Arab Human Development Report 2002.* New York: Oxford University Press, p. 23.

APPENDIX 1

Detailed Description of the Socioeconomic and Educational Backgrounds of the 20 Interviewees

Interviewees' ages ranged between 20 and 45 years old, 7 of them being in their early twenties. Fourteen of these 20 women were single (12 never married, 1 separated from her husband, and 1 divorced) and 6 were married (all 6 having children—either one, two, or three). Their profile in terms of marital status indicated that they are not representative of the Syrian female population, for whom the average age at first marriage was 21 years old in 2005.

Of the eight women activists under 30 years old, only one was married. The high proportion of single women among these 20- to 29-year-olds is characteristic of the demographics of highly educated women, who statistically tend to marry later—as observed in all societies. Indeed, our sample is composed of 19 college-educated women (including 6 with master's degrees), while 1 of the older women of the sample has only secondary education.

Half of the interviewed women belong to the middle class (and 2 to the upper class); 7 of them come from a modest background, being the first generation in their family to reach college.

Throughout the interviews, many noted that most of the other female activists were also well educated. One of the women groups in the Hama region, The Revolutionary Women of Salamieh, was almost entirely composed of engineers, teachers, and other highly qualified professionals. This socioeconomic composition of the sample raises a new set of questions:

1. Is our sample skewed toward including almost exclusively educated women because we have chosen these women based on their leading roles in the revolution?

   or

2. Is there in general an over-representation of educated women among women activists in Syria?

An interesting corollary would have been to ask how levels of education compare between female and male activists. However, our questionnaire does not allow us to give a definite answer to these questions, which would require a more systematic comparison with male activists.

In that regard, we can compare the six married women activists of our sample with their husbands. Three of them have husbands whose level of education matches theirs (college-educated men); as it happens, those three men were particularly active in the revolution, and two of them were detained at the time of the interviews. The other three married women have husbands whose degree of education is lower than theirs (either primary or secondary), and they indicated that their husbands were somewhat involved (as protestors in demonstrations, for instance) but at a level of involvement seemingly lower than their own. They shared that they had an influence in convincing their husbands to join the revolution.

As for their professional activity, 7 were students at the time of the survey, and the other 13 women were all employed and economically independent at the beginning of the revolution: 5 as educators/teachers (one of whom has established her own private school), 4 in the field of human rights (two human rights lawyers, one NGO leader, one journalist), 2 in the sector of health (one midwife, one pharmacist), 1 in the arts (scenarist) and 1 in business (tailor and business owner).

The proportion of professionally active women in our sample is 13/20, that is, 65 percent. This high rate is not representative of the Syrian female population, whose rate of employment is much lower, as in many other Arab countries. World Bank data indicate that 13 percent of women above 15 years old are employed in Syria (http://data.worldbank .org/indicator/SL.TLF.CACT.FE.ZS[0])—this figure is to be compared with 58 percent in the United States and 50 percent for most European countries.

APPENDIX 2

The Questionnaire

Your background

Describe your upbringing:

1. Tell me about your family, your roots, your hometown, your religious background.
2. What is your educational background?
3. a. Are you married?
   b. Is your husband from the same socioeconomic and religious background as you?
   c. Do you have children?
4. What is your age bracket (20–30; 30–40; 40–50; 50–60; 60+)?
5. What is your professional activity?
6. When you were growing up, were there politically active family members around you?
7. Who or what would you say influenced you most in shaping your ideas about society and politics—as a child, or as an adult?
8. Do you have role models?
9. a. Are there any events or episodes in the history of your country, prior to March 2011, that have particularly marked you?
   b. In the history of the broader Arab world?
   c. In the history of the world?

Your involvement with the Syrian Revolution since March 2011

10. Before the start of the revolution, were you active in civil society and how (NGO, association, informal and formal political involvement)?
11. When did you start getting involved and what was your first action?
12. a. What was your principal motivation for getting involved?
    b. Was there a pivotal moment?
13. Who was influential in your decision of getting involved (family, friends, others)?
14. The narration

Please narrate your experience in the last 12 months, if you can week by week, or at least month by month, with the main events you have been involved with as an active participant or as a witness and supporter.

15. Today, we are in May 2012; what is your assessment of the situation?
16. a. Suppose that things continue for one year or more to be in a stalled/ frustrating/tragic stage. What do you think can be done to shake things up?
    b. What would you, personally, do differently?

Examining your role, and the role of women in general, in the Syrian revolution

17. Tell us about the actions you were involved with.
    a. Who was leading?
    b. Who was following?
    c. What was your role (top/leading, design the activity, organize it, or other role)?
    d. How did you get to a position of leadership?
18. a. In your own family, did you feel supported for your involvement?
    b. If you are married, what was your husband's reaction to your involvement?
    c. Is your husband also involved and, if yes, in what capacity?
19. What are the major challenges you faced in your action over the past 12 months? Please give specific anecdotes illustrating a point.
20. Do you feel most of these challenges were shared equally by men and women, or are there specific challenges for women?
21. Did you encounter obstacles because you are a woman? Of what sort?
22. a. Did you encounter hostility from other men and women in the opposition?
    b. How can you explain this hostility (purely disagreement on ideas/ strategies/tactics or was there also prejudice because you are a woman)?
23. Did you experience moments when you wish you could have done something (initiative, different strategy, different tactic, different kind of organization, etc.) but were prevented from doing so? What obstacles did you face?
24. a. As a woman, did you feel that there were things/activities/initiatives that you could do and that men could not do?
    b. Did you experience moments when other women were able to achieve things that men could not have done? Which actions, strategies, tactics, and in what context?
25. a. What was your most successful action?
    b. How do you explain its success?

26. What would it take to do it more and even more successfully?

IMAGINE: Visions of the future

27. Think out of the box and imagine your future and the maximum impact you can have as a woman and as a leader.
28. Even if the current situation continues, what could you do, and what could other women do to find an innovative way to move forward?
29. If you could do it again, what would you change?
30. If you could be granted any wish, what would you wish for right now?

CHAPTER 19

Women and the Egyptian Revolution: A Dream Deferred?

Althea M. Middleton-Detzner, Jillian M. Slutzker,
Samuel F. Chapple-Sokol, and Sana A. Mahmood

INTRODUCTION

The events that took place in Egypt between January 25 and February 11, 2011, arrested the world's attention. All eyes were on Tahrir Square, at the center of Cairo, witnessing the power of nonviolent civil resistance to overthrow one of the most entrenched dictators in the world. The message was unified, "Mubarak Out," and the tactics were myriad: demonstrations, marches, acts of civil disobedience, political satire, creative messaging, labor strikes, and more. In just 18 days of action, these protests led to the announcement by Vice President Omar Suleiman that President Hosni Mubarak would step down, ushering in an era of excitement and uncertainty. What has occurred since that historic day has been uncharted territory for Egyptians, who had been under Mubarak's rule for more than 30 years.

The success of the movement, and its unprecedented brevity, were due to many factors, including a dedication to nonviolent action, unity of vision, and the inclusion and participation of a large cross-section of society. This final aspect, the wide range of participants, was key: nonviolent civil resistance movements need all the bodies they can get, and therefore, extensive inclusion is vital. In Egypt, women became involved in all aspects of the movement—from background planning to front-of-the-line protesting—providing the necessary people power to fuel the overthrow of Mubarak. The ways in which men and women participated in the protests reflected gendered dynamics of Egyptian society, from the nationalist rhetoric that fueled the protests, to the online and physical spaces in which they operated, to the nonviolent strategic tactics they employed.

In the aftermath of the revolutions, though, we have observed a reversion to an atmosphere of repression, in which activist women are shouted down and shut out of positions of power. What did women actually achieve through their participation, and how can they attain their goals of expanded political and public inclusion? While he answer is still unclear, in order to be more involved in post-Mubarak Egypt, women must continue to speak up and speak out to ensure that their voices are not silenced by men.

WOMEN, NONVIOLENT ACTION, AND THE CYCLE OF MARGINALIZATION

Nonviolent action, or civil resistance, is a civilian-based method of waging asymmetric conflict. It has been used in struggles for human rights, democracy, self-rule, social justice, anticorruption, and the overthrow of dictatorships in countries all over the world and throughout history. Using "nonviolent weapons" such as boycotts, strikes, protests, petitions, and sit-ins, nonviolent movements often apply traditional military strategic thinking, tactical diversity and sequencing, and creativity to build pressure against their opponents and force them to make concessions or acquiesce. Nonviolent movements that succeed in achieving their objectives tend to involve the effective application of three principles: unity, planning, and nonviolent discipline (Chenoweth, 2008). Without these components, it may be difficult for a movement to understand its opponents, develop strategies that weaken its opponents' pillars of support, and recruit participants to join the struggle.

Women's participation is essential to any successful nonviolent movement. Because civil resistance relies quite literally on "people power," women's active and authentic participation will be an essential strategic element. Without mass mobilization, both men's and women's know-how, and networks working together to undermine the opponent, nonviolent movements will fail to shake powerful regimes. Revolutionary leaders, consequently, rely on and seek out the participation of women, who account for half of the population and often play critical roles both as supporters and key players in revolutions (Henderson and Jeydel, 2007).

In some cases women are able to use specific tactics unavailable to men because of their particular roles in society: as mothers, daughters, and sisters, and symbolically as "gatekeepers" of peace and as the embodiment of the nation. "Women, in many societies, are not seen as a threat. They are often viewed as complacent, apolitical, and solely concerned with their children and home. These assumptions allow them a certain cover, and even provide them with hidden venues in which they can organize" (Henderson and Jeydel, 2007, p. 73).

During the height of military dictatorship in Argentina, mothers of "the disappeared"—political activists and intellectuals abducted, arrested, and often killed by the regime—came together for weekly marches in the Plaza de Mayo seeking to be reunited with their missing children. Organized through religious and social groups, the Mothers of the Plaza de Mayo showed up every week wearing white scarves embroidered with the names of their children, employing their respected societal role as protective mothers strategically. Despite the extreme level of repression in Argentina at the time, mothers, and later grandmothers, were able to march in public without being attacked by police and security forces. In Liberia women across religious groups united to fight for peace, issuing petitions and protests outside of formal peace talks. The women threatened to disrobe in front of negotiators, which is culturally considered extremely shameful, if they failed to come to a peace agreement. In Serbia, after careful calculation of an anticipated response by the Serbian forces under Milosevic, the student-led nonviolent movement OTPOR placed women carrying roses at the front lines of their protests to protect protestors from arrest or abuse by the police and security forces.

In addition to employing a variety of methods that play on traditional and perceived women's roles in society, women's movements throughout history and across the globe have been largely nonviolent and thus have contributed greatly to the canon of nonviolent action. Because women have historically been excluded from formal political structures, they have a tendency to utilize nontraditional forms of political organizing and action, including shrouding political dissent under the notion of "social justice" in order to create space to voice their demands and address their concerns. Some women's movements have utilized the rhetoric of democracy and human rights strategically: to increase the participation of popular masses who may not otherwise support a movement perceived to be dedicated solely to women's issues. The assumption is that ultimately democratic gains will result in women's rights. But many feminists are critical of this approach and argue that women's movements ought to put their issues at the forefront of their activism rather than sidelining their own interests for the sake of more palatable goals.

In Egypt, women were not mobilized around women's issues but rather fought side by side with men as citizens to oust Mubarak and "were instrumental not just in protests but in much of the nitty-gritty organisation that turned Tahrir Square from a moment into a movement" (Rice et al, 2010). All too often the contributions of women to national democratic movements rarely translate into an equal share in the core decision-making of transitional regimes (Rice et al., 2010). Carla Power (2011) writes, "Women are good for revolutions, but historically revolutions haven't been so good for women," alluding to the marginalization women often face after a revolution succeeds and power changes hands. Capitalizing on the participation of women, "revolutionary leaders arc adepl at promising rewards for women in return for their support," explain Henderson and Jeydel (2007, p. 73), "but they are much less successful in (and committed to) working to ensure that these benefits actually materialize under the new order."

In the post-revolution transition period, issues such as women's rights, equal political representation, and family law are relegated to the feminine sphere and therefore subordinated to more important (i.e., masculine) causes, such as national self-determination or democratic governance, for which the revolution fought (Henderson and Jeydel, 2007). What results is a cycle of post-revolution marginalization in which women are mobilized to join revolutionary causes, galvanized by rhetoric of increased rights and political participation both as women and as citizens, and subsequently pushed out of the new political space that was presumably created on their behalf.

Although the motivations and mobilization of Egyptian women in the January 25 movement were not explicitly shaped by expectations of increased women's rights under a new regime, the movement's focus on democratization and freedom implied that women, especially those taking part in the protests, should enjoy the fruits of the new democratic system as equal citizens of Egypt. Unfortunately, despite Egypt's remarkable success in its nonviolent overthrow of Mubarak, the course of the Egyptian revolution and its aftermath are proving to align all too closely with the expected cycle of post-revolution marginalization of women. As the dust settles in Egypt, women find themselves excluded from power and decision making in the transitional period and even targeted as women for their participation in the movement during the 18 days.

REVOLUTIONARY REVERBERATIONS: EGYPT'S GEOPOLITICAL IMPLICATIONS

The Egyptian case was not the first such successful overthrow of an autocratic leader in the wave of nonviolent pro-democracy movements sweeping the Middle East and North Africa (MENA), which scholars are now calling the "Arab Spring." However, by virtue of Egypt's geopolitical importance and the revolution's profound influence on other regional youth and democracy movements, the Egyptian case carries unique implications for regional politics, the field of nonviolent civil resistance, and the future of women's political space in Arab societies.

With 83 million people, or 22 percent of the overall population of the Middle East region, Egypt is the most populous Arab country and is geopolitically situated at the center of the region, influencing the regional cultural, economic, and political climate (Central Intelligence Agency, 2009). As incumbent president for 30 years, Mubarak's regime represented the prototypical entrenched Arab dictatorship: any opposition was marginalized or persecuted, and the space for political decision making was tightly secured in the hands of elites and Mubarak's inner circle (Singerman, 2004). Additionally, Mubarak enjoyed the strong support of the United States. Having received over $60 billion in military and economic aid since the Israel-Egypt peace treaty at Camp David in 1978, Mubarak's Egypt was "the linchpin of Pax Americana" in the region (America's Lieutenant, 2010). Thus, beyond domestic political implications, the unlikely nonviolent overthrow of Mubarak, a superpowers-backed ruler, entails a recalculation of American foreign policy and a critical evaluation of America's support for autocratic regimes versus popular democracy movements. In the midst of the protests, Egyptian journalist Mona Eltahawy (2011) explained,

Mubarak is our Berlin Wall. When Tunisia had its revolution and toppled Ben Ali, everyone thought, "Beautiful little Tunisia, you're so brave. But it's never going to happen anywhere else." Now it's happening in the traditional leader of the Arab world. . . . Every Arab leader is watching right now in terror, and every Arab citizen is elated and cheering Egypt on, because they know the significance of this.

Egypt's revolution achieved the virtually unimaginable—deposing one of the region's most durable dictators in a matter of days through nonviolent strategic action. Even before the Tunisian revolution there had been numerous cases of civil society groups in the MENA region successfully using nonviolent strategies to secure social and political gains. However, the barrage of media coverage and international attention garnered by the Egyptian case gave nonviolent strategic action a new place of prominence in international politics and the Arab world. Egypt's success has since inspired other movements throughout the region as "the governed have discovered that they can, if necessary, take back their consent to be governed and thereby compel regime change" (Freeman, 2011). As a result of Egypt's revolution, nonviolent strategic action has emerged as a key tool for Arab civil society.

Nonviolent strategic action, and particularly its gendered uses in the Egyptian revolution, also has significant implications for women as political players in a region in which women are typically marginalized politically and face significant socioeconomic inequalities. A 2010 Freedom House report finds that progress on women's rights and empowerment in MENA has been "stymied by the lack of democratic institutions, an independent judiciary, and freedoms of association and assembly" (Kelly, 2010). The Egyptian revolution not only created a political opening for citizens and a possibility to reshape new democratic institutions, but also reacquainted Egyptian women, on a mass scale, with a strategic tool—nonviolent action—by which to potentially seek and secure rights and equality in the coming period of democratic transition to power. Whether these tools and skills will translate into improved conditions for women in a new MENA, however, remains to be seen.

WOMEN'S MOVEMENTS IN EGYPT: A BRIEF HISTORY

As women have a long history of activism in Egypt, their involvement in the January 25movement was hardly unprecedented. Elite women had established a political culture in Egypt by the late 19th century, and were actively involved in the struggle for Egyptian independence. During the 1919 national revolution, women participated in letter writing campaigns, petitions, strikes, marches, and demonstrations against the British (Nadje, 2000). Women's demands in these protests were nationalist, not specifically feminist, in nature. However, Egyptian women's rights movements emerged as part of, or perhaps in reaction to, the nation building process that followed (Baron, 2007).

Huda Sha'arawi and the Egyptian Feminist Union led the first phase of feminist activism in Egypt (Baron, 2007). During the postcolonial period, the women's movement was elitist and largely welfare oriented (Nadje, 2000). The second phase, during the 1940s and 1950s, was headed by Doria Shafik and the Bint El Nil (Daughters of the Nile) group; it revolved around political rights, equal pay, education and literacy campaigns, and health and social service programs (Nadje, 2000).

Women also played an active role in the 1952 independence movement; however, nationalist priorities soon overtook the political sphere, and women's groups and issues were relegated to the periphery. Some have described the appropriation of women's issues by the state that ensued as "state feminism" (Nadje, 2000). The 1956 constitution declared all Egyptians equal under the law, regardless of gender, origin, or ideology, and the state granted women the right to vote and to run for political office. However, discriminatory Personal Status laws were maintained (Nadje, 2000). Under President Anwar Sadat, due largely to the insistence of his wife, Jehan Sadat, the Personal Status Law of 1979 granted women legal rights in marriage, polygamy, divorce, and child custody (Nadje, 2000). Nonetheless, the state did not have a comprehensive program to guarantee women's rights, nor did women have any autonomous representative groups of their own.

Independent women's activism did not officially resurface until 1985, when President Mubarak amended the Personal Status Law, taking away many of the rights women had gained in the past (Nadje, 2000). The late 1980s and 1990s saw the emergence of a number of nongovernmental organizations (NGOs) devoted to women's issues, leading to the "NGOization of the movement" (Tadros, 2008). The women's movement splintered during this period, as differences among the groups were underlined.

For example, prominent women's rights activist Nawal al-Sa'dawi transformed the dialogue on women by taking on the sensitive issues of women's reproductive rights and sexual violence against women, facing opposition from women and men alike.

Women still face major economic, political, and religious obstacles to advancement in Egypt. These include limited employment opportunities, few positions in parliament, and the reinforcement of traditional gender roles due to a rise in religious conservatism. While they continue to engage in activism, participating in such forms of protest as strikes and sit-ins, women have been noticeably less active in explicitly feminist causes. The marginalization of feminist activism may be linked to the emergence of state feminism with semigovernmental institutions such as the National Council for Women (NCW), established in 2000 by Suzanne Mubarak, the wife of the former president. NCW has co-opted female activists, claiming to act as a representative voice for Egyptian women (Tadros, 2008), though it faces significant opposition from women's groups who view it as a tool of the state and have called for its immediate disbanding (Coalition of Women's NGOs in Egypt, 2011). However, the different forms of women's activism have yet to come together in a unified movement, which will be essential to the realization of women's goals in Egypt moving forward.

GENDERING NATIONALISM

The history of Egyptian feminism is rooted in the identity of the state itself, which at its core is "imagined as a woman" (Baron, 2007). The word for Egypt in Arabic, *Misr*, is gendered female, and the nation is commonly referred to as Umm al-Duniya, or "Mother of the World." Historically, the nation was linked to the concepts of fertility, morality, and honor, all of which were associated with the female domain, as women were charged with the biological and cultural reproduction of the nation (Baron, 2007). There seems to be an inherent contradiction in the centrality of women in the imagery of the nation during nationalist movements and the exclusion of women from the political sphere once nationalist objectives have been achieved.

According to Beth Baron, women were also used as "subjects and symbols around which to rally male support" (Nadje, 2000). She said, "By depicting the nation as a woman, nationalists hoped to stimulate love for the nation and draw male youth to the cause. . . . The man was the actor, the speaker, the lover; the woman was acted upon, the listener, the beloved" (Nadje, 2000). Twenty-six-year-old Asmaa Mahfouz, called the "bravest girl in Egypt" (Beenish, 2011), played on this sentiment in the video call she made to fellow Egyptians, which many say sparked the revolution. Her language was explicitly gendered as she called upon the masculinity, honor, and dignity of Egyptian men by urging them to come to Tahrir

Square to play the role of both protestor and protector of the women and girls in the demonstrations. She said, "If you have any honor and dignity as a man, come and protect me and other girls in the protest" (Meet Asmaa Mahfouz, 2011). Yet while Mahfouz's speech portrays women as the weaker sex, vulnerable in the face of all-male security forces and in need of protection, she simultaneously exploits this gender stereotype to catalyze the movement.

Nationalists also employed familial metaphors in their rhetoric for political purposes. The nation was portrayed as "one family," with young men as its "sons" and young women as its "daughters" (Baron, 2007). This rhetoric was intended to engender among citizens of the nation the same sense of loyalty and kinship felt among members of a family. The notion of family honor, which hinges on the conduct of its women, was equated with national honor. The rape of Egyptian village women by British soldiers in 1919 was described as the rape of the nation. As British occupation was considered an insult to national honor, it was incumbent upon Egyptians to struggle to protect "faith, honour, and the homeland" (Baron, 2007).

During the January 25 revolution, President Hosni Mubarak used familial rhetoric to inspire loyalty and obedience among the citizens of Egypt. In his final presidential speech to the nation on February 10, 2011, he began, "I am addressing all of you from the heart, a speech from the father to his sons and daughters" (Hosni Mubarak's Speech, 2011). His rhetoric throughout the 18 days was one of a stern father reprimanding his children, threatening to punish those who committed wrongdoing.

WOMEN'S PRE-REVOLUTION STATUS IN EGYPT

Women in Egypt are considered to be nurturers, mothers, and upholders of national and familial honor and morality. In private life this role is respected and encouraged. In public, though, women's lives are fraught with discrimination and harassment. Women are underrepresented in the political sphere and discriminated against in the law. Although Egypt became a signatory in 1981 to the United Nations (UN) Convention on the Elimination of All Forms of Discrimination Against Women (CEDAW), which ensures women equal access to and enjoyment of political, economic, social, cultural, and civil rights, its enactment has not been actualized. Instead, women face significant challenges in all of these spheres and struggle to maintain what limited rights they have.

In 2010, the World Economic Forum Gender Gap Report placed Egypt at 125 out of 136 countries in terms of the gap between women and men. This ranking, based on economic participation and opportunity, educational attainment, health and survival, and political empowerment, places Egypt only above such repressive regimes as Saudi Arabia, Pakistan, and

Yemen (World Economic Forum, 2010). Out of the four categories, Egypt ranks in the top 50 percent of countries only in the realm of health and survival, though it is reported elsewhere that up to 80 percent of women are forced to undergo female genital mutilation. In the other three departments Egypt fell in the bottom 20 percent of countries, based on factors such as number of women in the labor force, education of women, and women in political positions (World Economic Forum, 2010). In 2005, only 4 out of 782 members of parliament were female, and women headed a mere 3 out of 31 government ministries (McKellogg, 2011). Egyptian family law is also egregiously biased against women. As Egyptian writer and women's rights activist Nawal al-Sa'dawi says, "the family code in Egypt is one of the worst family codes in the Arab world. . . . The husband is having absolute control over the family" (Socolovsky, 2011).

Sexual harassment is a near-constant occurrence in the lives of Egyptian women; a 2008 study by the Egyptian Center for Women's Rights reported that 83 percent of women had been harassed, and 63 percent of men reported harassing women. More than half of male respondents blamed women for provoking the harassment, an indicator of the mindset of many of the harassers. This problem is structural and endemic: some cite men's sexual frustrations due to the vicious cycle of their inability to get married and afford a marriage ceremony until they acquire a job, while the weak job market pushes the age of marriage further and further back (Krajeski, 2011a). Many unemployed men may feel emasculated given these pressures and, as a result, may assert their masculinity by threatening and harassing women sexually. It was against this backdrop that Egyptian women took to the streets in late January with the hope of shrugging off the status quo and gaining equality in society by way of bringing democracy to Egypt.

THE 18 DAYS: GENDERING REVOLUTION

The 18 days of protests were supported by a broad cross-section of Egyptian society—men and women, young and old, Muslim and Christian, veiled and unveiled. Whole families came out to participate, as women brought their children to the square and young people brought their parents to introduce them to a different future for Egypt. Although precise numbers are not known, estimates put women's participation in the protests at up to 50 percent of the total (Krajeski, 2011b), a remarkable number considering the historical harassment, abuse, and discrimination that women face both in society at large and more specifically in large, crowded public spaces like Tahrir Square. Women participated for many reasons: some felt empowered socially and politically in rising up against Mubarak's patriarchy; others heeded the call of female leaders to join in; others saw it as a movement to create a better future for women in Egypt.

One woman framed the revolution in terms of motherhood and hope for the next generation: "If I wasn't pregnant, I would've just stayed home. I went out because of my baby. I owe this to him" (Rakhan, 2011).

Primarily spurred to action by the unifying goal of ousting Mubarak, Egyptian women, like their male counterparts, poured into Tahrir Square as citizens of Egypt with largely gender-neutral demands rather than as women with specifically gendered interests. Among other measures, the movement's list of demands included first and foremost the resignation of Mubarak as well as the repeal of Egypt's emergency law, which had been in place since 1981; a release of political prisoners; free press; the right to trade unions and a minimum wage; and a proper investigation of crimes propagated by state security forces against protesters in the movement (Demands of the Egyptian Revolution, 2011). The demands did not specifically speak to issues of equal rights for women or women's involvement in the political process; however, this omission did not deter women from joining the protests and making these national demands.

As Henderson and Jeydel (2007) found in an analysis of women in revolutionary movements, "while women may not have been motivated by concerns of gender equality, the ways in which they participate are rarely gender neutral." Women entered Tahrir Square as citizens sharing the commonly held grievances of government repression and demanding democratic political change on behalf of all Egyptian citizens. However, their preparation leading up to the protests, their very presence in the public political protest space, as well as many of the tactics utilized by female protesters during the 18 days specifically reflected gendered dynamics.

In the lead-up to January 25 several blogs and Web sites appeared targeting women protesters, advising them on safety measures to protect themselves from potential abuse at the hands of all-male state security forces and government-hired thugs, who, in previous demonstrations, had explicitly targeted females through physical and sexual assault (Michel, 2011). Women were advised to wear two layers of clothing, avoid zippers, carry cans of Mace, and wear two headscarves tied in a secure manner to prevent having them torn off. Through these preventive measures, Egyptian journalist Mona Eltahawy explains, "these young women were saying, 'we will not be scared away. We are standing up for our rights to be active and equal members of Egyptian society'" (Michel, 2011). Although their motivation for participation then was gender neutral, their method of engagement necessarily reflected gender dynamics and gendered expectations about Egyptian society and public space.

Once in the square, women participated on the frontlines of the protests, along with men, both utilizing tactics common to all protesters, such as leading chanting and carrying banners as well as taking on specifically gendered roles and tactics. Women served as volunteer guards at the entrances to Tahrir Square, conducting body checks on other women to ensure the safety of the protest space, a role that would have been culturally unsuitable for Egyptian men (Mekay, 2011). In the massive tent city that sprung up in the square during the 18 days, women took on key organizational roles—setting up makeshift kitchens and distributing food, water, blankets and medical supplies (Saoub, 2011). Additionally, by using specifically gendered tactics such as distributing flowers to security forces and hugging and kissing soldiers, women, particularly older women, were able to call upon their identities as mothers, which "has a significant cultural and political currency" and strategically juxtaposes the feminine concept of motherhood and affection against the masculine concept of armed security forces (Henderson and Jeydel, 2007).

By participating as mothers and reaching out to soldiers and police forces rather than viewing them as the enemy, women conveyed a message of inclusion and acceptance to the young men in Mubarak's forces. Women sought to shift the loyalty of the soldiers from Mubarak to the movement and offer them an avenue to join the people. A popular chant of the movement was, "The people and the army are one hand." Gendered tactics were certainly not the only tactics available to female protesters, and the involvement of women ultimately was the participation of women as Egyptian citizens; however, by utilizing gendered tactics women were able to contribute to the movement a tactical element uniquely available to them as women.

One of the ways that women were able to organize and participate in the January 25 movement was through use of Internet-based social media networks. The Internet provides a platform for people to come together and share information, crucial elements for political activism and organizing that may be unavailable offline due to political repression, government censorship, or geographical distance. Online communication and information sharing is often touted as democratic, gender-neutral space where everyone's socioeconomic, cultural, and gendered statuses exist on a level playing field. In fact, while there are many ways in which women gain access to new forms of power through their access to the Internet, many if not most of the problems that women face in public offline spaces and communities exist in online spaces and communities as well, including barriers to Internet access, oppression, and harassment online (Morahan-Martin, 2000).

However the Internet *is* revolutionizing political activism and *does* provide a space in which individuals can explore various new identities before carrying those ideas out into public, offline spaces (Morahan-Martin, 2000). Egyptian blogger and human rights activist Dalia Ziada has led campaigns online and offline. She has used online spaces as a means to bring together youth from different religious groups to talk about tolerance and to air footage of local and national political debates:

"When you debate with someone online, they never care who you are, they never care if you are a man or a woman, if you are an upper-class family or a poor family, they just care about your point of view and really focus on what you say," Ziada said. "It is mind-to-mind talking." (Egyptian Cyberactivist, 2011)

In the Egyptian revolution, the Internet provided a safe space for women to publicly voice their political opinions. Much of the initial call to action took place online by computer-literate and social-media-savvy Egyptian youth, including many young women. This online activism provided a low-risk entry point to action and segued into their participation in the physical space of the square. When the Egyptian government shut off the Internet, just three days into the public street protests, rather than inducing the anticipated result of stifling the movement, this action instead brought individuals closer together and forced the movement onto the streets. These online strategies facilitated women's ability to participate in the public political space, once considered male-only.

A motivating factor for women to come to Tahrir Square was the reported safety felt by women. Before January 25 the streets of Cairo were a fearful place for women. Public spaces, especially in Egypt, are male dominated, preventing women from feeling comfortable in public. As Koskela writes,

With violence—and with a threat of violence . . . city streets are kept as male-dominated, heterosexual spaces. The gendered exclusions, which produce space as a masculine arena, mean—in women's daily lives—that many women spend their lives under "a virtual curfew." (Koskela, 1999, p. 113)

Many women in Tahrir, though, cited the fact that the front lines of the protests, and the square in general, were largely free from sexual harassment during the 18 days of protests. In place of the old cultural norms allowing impunity for men to harass women, a new moré was settling into the square: gender equality. As Egyptian writer Ahdaf Souief (2011) said,

This movement does not see gender as an issue. Women are citizens, just like men are. And a lot of girls, a lot of young women will tell you that, for the first time in years, they feel that they are not objectified as sexual objects in this space. This is the first time in a very long time that young women have been in the streets without any danger of harassment.

Souief went on to say that men in the square "channeled their machismo in the right direction." Women and men stood next to each other under a unified message and without gender. While Asmaa Mahfouz had framed the role of men as protecting women in the square, in fact, traditional protector/protected roles shifted. Some described the square as being "Utopian," and others called the protestors "family."

SHATTERING "UTOPIA": NEW EGYPT, OLD PATTERNS

The harassment-free and gender-equal nature of the square was shattered on February 11, hours after Vice President Suleiman announced Mubarak's resignation. Whereas before, the various entrances to the square were closely guarded, with self-appointed sentinels checking all entrants for identification and weapons, after the announcement the space was opened up to the world. Mona Eltahawy described people who flooded into the square as "tourists with cameras" and claimed that the brutal acts of sexual violence that occurred that day were by the hands not of the celebrating protestors but of new arrivals to the square. These acts represent the re-gendering of the square: as the checkpoints opened up, the streets once again became heterosexual spaces, and with that, the threat of violence reappeared.

In the midst of the rejoicing crowds, women such as 24-year-old Mariam Nekiwi became victims of sexual assault just hours after Mubarak stepped down:

First someone grabbed her groin, she said. Other hands groped the rest of her body, pinching hard and yanking at her clothes. She was shoved one way and then the other. The frenzy was so sudden, the crush so stifling, that she could barely see. She shouted, and then screamed. The reaction was swift. "People started yelling at me to be quiet," recalled Nekiwi. "They said: 'Don't tarnish the revolution. Don't make a scene.' They said: 'We are men. We're sorry. Just go now.'" (Drogin, 2011)

The "utopian" environment that so many women had acclaimed during the demonstrations seemed to have vanished as quickly as it had appeared. On March 8, 2011, International Women's Day, a mob of men descended upon women demonstrating for political representation and equal rights in Tahrir Square. They harassed and groped female demonstrators, chasing them and telling them to go home; they scrawled the words "Not now" across women's posters. One man justified these actions, explaining, "It is about all Egypt now. We have to stand together. No one group should act alone. We have other goals first. Later they can talk about what they want" (Johnson, 2011). Meanwhile, labor strikes and protests calling for better working conditions and wages continued daily after the fall of the Mubarak regime; yet these protests had not been thwarted in the interest of national priorities.

Women were again being pushed out of the public space and back to the private sphere, and their demands were being sidelined. Amnesty International reported that several women detained on International Women's Day were subjected to harassment, torture, and forced virginity tests in front of members of the military who took photographs (Egyptian Women Protesters, 2011). Women found not to be virgins were accused of prostitution.

In the post-Mubarak period, women have been blatantly absent from the constitutional process. The 10-member committee tasked with drafting amendments to the constitution, dubbed the "Council of Wise Men" (Who Holds Power in Egypt?, 2011), did not include a single woman, despite the central role women played in the revolution. In response to this exclusion, women's rights activists engaged in another form of nonviolent action, organizing a petition drive challenging the criteria for selecting and form- ing the panel (Petition, 2011); 63 groups signed on.

Women's groups were further incensed when the constitutional commit- tee introduced Article 75, a proposed amendment to the constitution that reads, "Egypt's President is born to two Egyptian parents . . . and cannot be married to a non-Egyptian woman." The wording of this amendment implies that the head of state will be a man, effectively excluding women from Egypt's presidency (McKellogg, 2011). A coalition of 117 women's groups called for a rewording of the constitutional amendment (Power, 2011). Soon thereafter, women achieved a victory when the last word of the proposed amendment was removed, as the constitutional committee suc- cumbed to pressure and opened the presidency to both men and women (Texts of Constitutional Articles in Question, 2011). Buthayna Kemal, an activist and talk show host, announced her candidacy for president in the following days.

As the initial euphoria has abated and the reality of rebuilding the gov- ernment has set in, women are facing the prospect of continued exclu- sion from the political process. The new Egypt is threatening to be just another example of the cycle of marginalization that has affected woman all over the world and throughout history. This does not have to be the case, though. If women continue to be active and make their voices heard in the political sphere, the road forward may indeed be more inclusive.

THE ROLE OF WOMEN MOVING FORWARD: PROMISES AND PERILS

While revolutions are remembered in history for their key moments—the storming of presidential palaces, the announcements of resignation, or the final surrender of state security forces—it is essential to keep in mind that revolutions are processes of continued negotiation and reformation that carry on well after power has officially changed hands and the revolu- tionaries have cleared the streets. Revolutions entail competing visions of how a better society should be formed (Henderson and Jeydel, 2007). Although thus far women have been marginalized from the political space and told that their vision of Egypt's future has no place in the transitional regime, their revolution is far from over. "Things have not changed, they are changing," said Mozn Hassan, the executive director of the women's rights research organization Nazra for Feminist Studies. "Revolution is not about 18 days in Tahrir Square and then turning it into a carnival and loving the army. We have simply won the first phase" (Otterman, 2011).

In the subsequent phases of revolution, women's success in securing political access and increased rights may depend on their continued use of strategic nonviolent action. Women's involvement in nearly all aspects of the revolution has laid the tactical groundwork for a sustained push for equal involvement in the political space, as well as for increased women's rights more broadly in Egyptian society. "There's also a new level of confidence and self-awareness among women as a result of their integral role in the revolution," said Hoda Badran, chair of the Alliance for Arab Women (Khan, 2011).

While Egyptian women's groups have a long history of using civil resistance to push for increased rights, the 18 days provided an opportunity for women beyond the current NGO community to capitalize on the moment. The momentum from this movement may have a lasting effect on how Egyptian women as a group perceive their role and potential influence in the political process. "Women are bolder now, and more outspoken," said journalist Mona Eltahawy. "They recognize that the personal and political exist side by side" (Sarhaadi Nelson, 2011). Women's issues, typically demoted to the private sphere and pushed aside to make way for other causes, have been and can continue to be reframed as national issues moving forward, calling upon the themes that propelled the January 25 movement: equality and justice for all Egyptians.

Nonviolent strategic action is not exclusively reserved for national movements aimed at toppling dictators; they can also be a viable tactic for securing gains for women in the transitional period. Since Mubarak's resignation, women's groups have coalesced around the goal of securing an increased role in the new Egypt. On March 14, the Coalition of Egyptian Feminist Organizations issued an open letter to the prime minister demanding "the participation of all forces in the rebuilding of our country, with women on the heart of these forces." It also called for more specific measures, such as the disbanding of the National Council for Women and the purification of the police corps from those involved in crimes against protesters during the revolution and in the aftermath (Egypt: Coalition of Egyptian Feminist Organizations, 2011). On April 10, a group of 16 women's organizations formed the Women's Organizations Coalition, demanding equal political space for both the women and men who took part in the revolution (Hesham, 2011).

Still, in light of the familiar cycle of post-revolution marginalization of women, further action may be needed as women move forward in post-Mubarak Egypt. Nawal al-Sa'dawi says the solution may lie in the same type of action that succeeded in the 18 days. Just as diverse groups united to call for Mubarak's overthrow, she proposes that women's groups unite as well. "Women should be in the street in millions. If women make a march with all their demands, this is the pressure." Arguably this technique was attempted and failed on March 8. The extensive work put into the 18 days, though, shows us that successful nonviolent strategic action requires time, endurance, and planning and that it may regrettably at times provoke a violent reaction by those defending the status quo. Perhaps with unity, planning, and nonviolent discipline, Egyptian women will be able to escape the cycle of post-revolution marginalization and carve out a new space for women in a new Egypt.

BIBLIOGRAPHY

America's Lieutenant. 2010, July 25. *Economist*, http://www.economist.com/node/16564218 (accessed April 17, 2011).

Baron, Beth, 2007. *Egypt as a Woman: Nationalism, Gender, and Politics*. Berkeley: University of California Press.

Beenish, Ahmed, Egyptian Riot Grrls: Finding the Feminine Face of Fury. 2011, February 4. *Pulse*, http://pulsemedia.org/2011/02/04/egyptian-riot-grrls-finding-the-feminine-face-of-fury/ (accessed February 4, 2011).

Central Intelligence Agency. 2009. Egypt. In *The World Factbook*, https://www.cia.gov/library/publications/the-world-factbook/geos/eg.html (accessed April 17, 2011).

Coalition of Women's NGOs in Egypt: National Council of Women Doesn't Represent Egyptian Women. Call for Rapid Dissolution. 2011, February 24. *Nazra for Feminist Studies*, http://www.en.nazra.org/18-coalition-of-womenvs-ngos-in-egypt-national.html

Demands of the Egyptian Revolution, The. 2011, February 10. *Code Pink*, http://www.codepink4peace.org/article.php?id=5695 (accessed February 10, 2011).

Drogin, Bob. 2011, February 23. Egypt's Women Face Growing Sexual Harassment. *Los Angeles Times*, http://articles.latimes.com/2011/feb/23/world/la-fg-egypt-women-abuse-20110223

Egypt: Coalition of Egyptian Feminist Organizations Open Letter to Prime Minister. 2011, March 14. *Women Living Under Muslim Laws*, http://www.wluml.org/node/7020 (accessed March 14, 2011).

Egyptian Cyberactivist Focuses on Women and Minorities. 2011, March 29. *Smart Grid*, http://smart-grid.tmcnet.com/news/2011/03/29/5410637.htm (accessed March 29, 2011).

Egyptian Women Protesters Forced to Take "Virginity Tests." 2011, March 23. *Amnesty International*, http://www.amnesty.org/en/news-and-updates/egyptian-women-protesters-forced-take-%E2%80%98virginity-tests%E2%80%99-2011-03-23

Eltahawy, Mona. 2011, February 1."Mubarak Is Our Berlin Wall": Egyptian Columnist Mona Eltahawy on How the Youth Drove the Uprising in Cairo and Implications for Democracy in the Region. *Democracy Now*.

Freeman, Chas. 2011, April 6. The Arab Reawakening and Its Strategic Implications. *Carnegie Endowment for International Peace*, http://www

.carnegieendowment.org/publications/index.cfm?fa=view&id=43471#
(accessed April 17, 2011).

Henderson, Sarah L., and Alana S. Jeydel. 2007. *Participation and Protest: Women and Politics in a Global World.* New York: Oxford University Press.

Hesham, Heba. 2011, April 10. Egyptian Women Organizations Coalition Announced Today. *Bikyamasr,* http://bikyamasr.com/wordpress/?p =32225&utm_source=twitterfeed&utm_medium=twitter

Hosni Mubarak's Speech to the Egyptian People: "I Will Not . . . Accept to Hear Foreign Dictations." 2011, February 10. http://www.washington post.com/wp-dyn/content/article/2011/02/10/AR2011021005290 .html

Johnson, Glen. 2011, March 9. The Other Side of Tahrir Square. *New York Times,* Opinion, http://www.nytimes.com/2011/03/10/opinion/10iht-edjohnson10.html?_r=1

Kelly, Sanja. 2010. Hard-Won Progress and a Long Road Ahead: Women's Rights in the Middle East and North Africa. *Freedom House,* http://freedomhouse .org/template.cfm?page=384&key=270&parent=23&report=86 (accessed April 17, 2011).

Khan, Sheema. 2011, April 7. Egypt's Revolution Is Leaving Women Behind.*Globe and Mail,* http://www.theglobeandmail.com/news/opinions/opinion/ egypts-revolution-is-leaving-women-behind/article1973918/ (accessed April 10, 2011).

Koskela, Hille. 1999, January 1. "Gendered Exclusions": Women's Fear of Violence and Changing Relations to Space. *Geografiska Annaler. Series B, Human Geography* 81 (2): 111–124.

Krajeski, Jenna. 2011a, February 14. Love and Revolution. *New Yorker,* http://www. newyorker.com/online/blogs/newsdesk/2011/02/love-and-revolution. html#ixzz1E5BC6pSZ

Krajeski, Jenna. 2011b, January 27. Women Are a Substantial Part of Egyptian Protests. *Slate,* http://www.doublex.com/blog/xxfactor/women-are-substantial-part-egyptian-protests

McKellogg, Julieann. 2011, April 1. Egyptian Women Search for Place in New Government. *Voice of America,* http://www.voanews.com/english/ news/middle-east/Egyptian-Women-Search-for-Place-in-New-Government-119063689.html

Meet Asmaa Mahfouz and the vlog that Helped Spark the Revolution. 2011. You-Tube, http://www.youtube.com/watch?v=SgjIgMdsEuk&feature=yout ube_gdata_player

Mekay, Emad. 2011, February 11. Arab Women Lead the Charge. *IPS,* http://www .ipsnews.net/news.asp?idnews=54439 (accessed February 11, 2011).

Michel, Martin. 2011, February 4. Women Play Vital Role in Egypt Uprising. *National Public Radio,* http://www.npr.org/2011/02/04/133497422/ Women-Play-Vital-Role-In-Egypts-Uprising (accessed February 4, 2011).

Morahan-Martin, Janet. 2000. Women and the Internet: Promise and Perils. *Cyberpsychology, Behavior, and Social Networking* 3 (5): 683.

Nadje, Al-Ali. 2000. *Secularism, Gender and the State in the Middle East: The Egyptian Women's Movement.* Cambridge: Cambridge University Press.

Otterman, Sharon. 2011, March 5. Women Fight to Maintain Their Role in the Building of a New Egypt. *New York Times,* http://www.nytimes .com/2011/03/06/world/middleeast/06cairo.html?ref=sharonotterman

Petition: Egypt Constitutional Committee Starts Working While Neglecting and Excluding Female Legal Experts. 2011, February 17. Egyptian Center for Women's Rights, http://www.wunrn.com/news/2011/02_11/02_14/ 021411_egypt2.htm

Power, Carla. 2011, March 24. Silent No More: The Women of the Arab Revolutions. *Time,* http://www.time.com/time/world/article/0,8599,2059435,00.html

Rakhan, Marwa. 2011, February 2. Egyptian Women Show Courage Participating in Mubarak Protests. *Huffington Post,* http://www.huffingtonpost .com/2011/02/02/egypt-women-protests_n_817822.html

Rice, Xan, Katherine Marsh, Tom Finn, Harriet Sherwood, Angelique Chrisafis, and Robert Booth. 2010, April 22. Women Have Emerged as Key Players in the Arab Spring. *Guardian, UK,* http://www.guardian.co.uk/world/2011/ apr/22/women-arab-spring?CMP=twt_fd (accessed April 22, 2010)

Saoub, Esther. 2011, February 10. The Unseen Factor: Egypt's Women Protesters. *DW-World,* http://www.dw-world.de/dw/article/0,,14834006,00.html (accessed February 10, 2011).

Sarhaadi Nelson, Soraya. 2011, April 19. Women Press for a Voice in The New Egypt. *NPR,* http://www.npr.org/2011/04/19/135523441/women-press-for-a -voice-in-the-new-egypt (accessed April 19, 2011).

Singerman, Diane. 2004, July 20. Women and Strategies for Change: An Egyptian Model. *Arab Reform Bulletin* 2 (7).

Socolovsky, Jerome. 2011, February 8. Egypt Protests Level Playing Field for Women. *Voice of America,* http://www.voanews.com/english/ news/middle-east/Egypt-Protest-Leveling-the-Playing-Field-for -Women-115591364.html

Soueif, Ahdaf. 2011, February 10. People Have Found Their Voice. *Democracy Now,* http://www.democracynow.org/blog/2011/2/10/people_have_found_ their_voice_acclaimed_egyptian_writer_ahdaf_soueif_on_the_egyptian_ uprising

Stephan, Maria, and Erica Chenoweth. 2008. Why Civil Resistance Works: The Strategic Logic of Nonviolent Conflict. *International Security* 33 (1): 7–44.

Tadros, Mariz. 2008, February 13. Egyptian Women Activists without a Movement. *Carnegie Endowment for International Peace—Arab Reform Bulletin,* http:// www.carnegieendowment.org/arb/?fa=show&article=20685&zoom_ highlight=Egyptian+Women

Texts of Constitutional Articles in Question. *Al-Ahram,* http://weekly.ahram.org .eg/2011/1039/eg22.htm

Who Holds Power in Egypt? 2011, February 6. *Al Jazeera English,* http://english .aljazeera.net/indepth/spotlight/anger-in-egypt/2011/02/20112665 73647420.html

World Economic Forum. 2010. Global Gender Gap Report 2010, http://www .weforum.org/reports/global-gender-gap-report-2010

CHAPTER 20

The Egyptian Revolution Empowers Women

Mariam M. Kurtz

Eighteen days of widespread protests in Cairo's Tahrir Square: thousands of women were seen alongside men bringing democratic reform to Egypt. Egyptian women transcended their traditional roles and found themselves outside, working in public doing similar jobs as men. They were leading chants, cooking, distributing blankets, donating medical supplies and food, securing the square, and doing the body searches at the entrance. Asma Mahfouz, Nawara Negm, Isra Abdel Fattah, and Gigi Ibrahim were among many other women activists who rallied people to Tahrir Square (Winegar, 2012). Others were active in the social media, getting their messages out to demonstrators. It was the awakening of the Egyptian women.

On January 28, Jessica Wineger was in Cairo. It was the "Friday of rage," the first Friday after the Egyptian revolution began. People called for a mass demonstration after the prayers. Women were in Tahrir Square regardless of their religion or class. Wineger observed women taking on different roles in the revolution; she saw women taking care of children because the schools were closed, and managing the household budget because the banks were closed. Many young women were in Tahrir Square.

Egyptian women found their voice through the revolution. For the first time women spoke out in the media about sexual assaults. Egyptian women started fighting in a new way for women's rights. For example, Mona Seif is working on raising awareness about the issue through peaceful protests and social media activism. Bothayna Kamel is the first female to have the courage to run for office as a presidential candidate, although, unfortunately, she could not gather the required number of signatures. Heba Morayef, Egypt's director of Human Rights Watch, has documented and spoken out about the human rights violations under the post-revolution regimes, the Supreme Council of the Armed Forces (SCAF), and Morsi's Islamist rule.

There are women founders of nongovernmental organizations (NGOs) fighting sexual harassment, such as Azza Kamel of Fouada Watch Women Rights; and Soraya Bahgat, founder of the anti–sexual harassment organization Tahrir Bodyguard. Samira Ibrahim had the courage to speak out about her ordeal and filed a lawsuit against the military, resulting in a court ruling that the tests she endured would never be performed again.

After the revolution, many women have joined political parties, and some are helping to train other women to campaign publicly and to rise within their parties. Hala Shukralla, a Christian, is the first female to head a major political party, the Dostour Party. In March 1, 2014, she was quoted by the *Observer*: "Our parties have always been a one-man show—both in the way that it's been ruled by one personality, and that it's usually been men who've been in the position" (Kingsley, 2014).

Women's active involvement in revolution changed the perception of women in this patriarchal culture, and women redefined their status and their role in the society. Egyptian women became more outspoken and actively involved in the struggle for women's rights and gender equality in Egypt. During the post–Egyptian revolution period, for example, 50 marches for women's rights took place in 2012. During the elections, at the polling stations, women's lines were longer than the men's. The referendum held in December 2012 on Egypt's constitution saw attempts to prevent women from voting by blocking them from entering in the voting stations (Mabrouk, 2014).

Shahira Amin, former deputy head of Nile TV, who resigned her position because of biased coverage by the state television, which did not allow news reporting from Tahrir Square, said in an interview,[1]

The revolution has empowered and emboldened our women, just as they, the women, empowered the revolution. The change is irreversible. There is no going back to the old ways. Egyptian women will no longer tolerate repression or oppression. They have found their voices and the fear barrier has been broken. . . . I remember how shocked people were when hearing the women speak about the sexual assault incidents that took place in Tahrir on the anniversary of the revolution. In the past, the "normal" reaction would have been to blame the victim, to say well, they should not have been there; they may have been dressed immodestly, etc. But this did not happen. Many admitted that these were brave women for daring to speak out and to join NGOs that would help other women and girls defend themselves against harassment.

The fear is gone. They've broken a lot of taboos. They're fighting for their rights and with Morsi. He had a constitution that tried to link women's rights with sharia law. We camped out on the streets. And they had to take that article out of the constitution, because of the pressure that the women kept on.

. . . So the women were there in Tahrir, and we thought that this would be a whole women's revolution afterwards. But then, very quickly, after the revolution, we found women being attacked on Women's Day, on the 8th of March. Mubarak fell on the 11th of February. On the 8th of March, when women went to Tahrir to celebrate International Women's Day, they were chased by a mob of men and told to go home where they belong. That was the first big shock. . . .

And then, when the SCAF, the Supreme Council of the Armed Forces, formed a committee to plan how things will go from then on, they had a committee of wise men, and there was not a single woman on that committee. . . . The parliament, our first democratically elected parliament after Mubarak fell, had only 2 percent women's representation. Even though the women's lines, the women that went out to vote, were far longer than the men's line. The women didn't vote for the women because of the patriarchal system. Women just don't trust women. And they don't see them fit for politics.

It's the culture, it's the media, and it's the stereotype, that there's some jobs that's made for women, others are not. But then, we had our first woman presidential candidate, and that was a breakthrough. She didn't get enough votes so she could eventually be in the race, because she had to gather a certain number of signatures. She didn't make it. Again, for the same reason. But Bothaina Kamel, actually, opened the door for other women. I think it was a real milestone, the fact that she did run.

VIOLENCE AGAINST WOMEN PROTESTERS

Gender-based violence exploded in Egypt after the 18-day revolution, even during the protests in Cairo's iconic Tahrir Square, where female protesters were targeted by the security and armed forces. Women were detained by the military and forced to undergo viginity tests, and some were sexually assaulted. Since the 2011 uprising against Hosni Mubaraka and then Mohamed Morsi, there were 156 cases of sexual assault, many of them in Tahrir Square that had never been reported, simply because people did not want to spoil the integrity of the movement and some were not willing to step forward for their own personal reasons. Those who reported the incidents to the legal institutions nonetheless failed to bring the attackers to justice.

According to an Amnesty International report of March 9, 2011, when army officers violently cleared Tahrir Square of protesters, they took at least 18 women into military detention. Seventeen of those women were detained for four days. Some of them told Amnesty International that during that time the male soldiers beat them, gave them electric shocks, and subjected them to strip searches. They were then forced to undergo "virginity tests" and were threatened with prostitution charges. Before they were released, the women were brought before a military court and received one-year, suspended sentences for a variety of allegedly false charges.

Twenty-five-year-old Samira Ibrahim was among the17 female activists who were arrested during protests in Tahrir Square. She filed a case against the military doctor Ahmed Adel, who forced her and other women to strip and have their hymens checked. The military physician was acquitted, however.

Shahira Amin broke the silence by reporting the virginity test story on CNN. As she recalls,

And two months later, in May, I broke the story on the virginity test, because I got the first admission from a senior general that they had done it. They had been denying it. The military had said they didn't do those tests until this military general with Amnesty released the report saying that rights violations were worse after the revolution than under Mubarak. So, I interviewed somebody from Amnesty and he told me about the virginity tests. Then I interviewed Samira, the girl who spoke out.

And I thought, okay, I can't run this story without going to the military and asking them. And I told the general, you're being accused of conducting the test. And he told me, we did it. It's self-defense, so that they wouldn't say we raped them. This wasn't rape. It's a kind of rape, a kind of sexual assault. So, we broke the story on CNN and eight local websites said I was being tried in a military court. Those were rumors to intimidate me; it wasn't true, because it wasn't me who said it—it was the general. So I got away with that. I just kept thinking, it could have been my daughter.[2]

Amnesty International reports that some women filed complaints against Egypt's Supreme Council of the Armed Forces (SCAF) for violence targeting women at public demonstrations, including the protests in December 2011 in front of the Cabinet building on Qasr El Einy Street, where protesters were demanding an end to military rule and which left at least 17 people dead (Amnesty International, 2012).

A video circulating on the Internet showed the military police dragging, beating, and stamping on two women, one of whose clothes had been torn off. A 49-year-old, Azza Hilal, was one of the women in the video. She was repeatedly beaten with sticks on the head, arms, and back, causing her to bleed heavily and lose consciousness. Following the assault, she was hospitalized for three weeks and still suffers from memory problems. An X-ray later showed her skull was fractured (Amnesty International, 2012).

Mirette Mabrouk reported in the *Midan Masr* that the increase in sexual assault against women, especially in Tahrir Square, is aimed at preventing the women from participating in politics. These attacks were perpetuated by mobs and appeared to be well organized, using tactics of separating women, ranging in age from teenager to pensioner, from their companions. Then the women would be stripped and assaulted.

From the Nour party, Salafi preacher Ahmed Abdallah, also known as Abu Islam, stated on television that women who went to Tahrir were essentially there to blow off a little sexual steam, and thus raping them "was not a red line" (Mabrouk, 2014). Also, the party view women as teachers and nurses, but not qualified for leadership positions over men (Shehata, 2011).

According to Amnesty International, sexual assaults are being used to stereotype and marginalize protesting women in order to discourage them for getting involved. Opponents are discrediting the protestors by using a stigma in the culture that is attached to victims of gender-based violence for the purpose of preventing and discouraging Egyptian women and girls from participating in public demonstrations (Amnesty International, 2012).

Women were in for a surprise when the first elections were held after the revolution. The National Democratic Party had guaranteed 64 seats for women in the parliament, but it was a trick designed simply to get more party members. The quota was canceled and women were guaranteed only 1 seat instead of 64. Women's groups and even the state-run National Council for Human Rights objected, but with no result. The women candidates were placed at the bottom of the party lists and had very little chance of getting elected (Mabrouk, 2014).

Most of the other parties followed similar tactics, some of them even more restrictive. Mahmoud Amer, the Salafi leader, for example, insisted that female candidates had to cover their face, with only their eyes visible, and not speak to men unless absolutely necessary. In the end, with their options severely limited, women only won 2 percent of Egypt's parliamentary seats, compared to 24 percent in Tunisia (Mabrouk, 2014).

Egyptian women's role in removing Mubarak from power is a reminder of the strength and courage of Egyptian women and their long history of revolution despite the patriarchal structure and culture keeping them in the private sphere. Society had perceived it as normal that women were weak and needed men, who were strong, to protect them. Activist Abdallah Hendawy reflected,

I think it's more into the societal issue as to how we perceive women, but I think the revolution has changed this society to a large extent. In the very beginning one of the things that the pro-Mubarak people used to use during the revolution was like, so all those women on the street, what are they doing? They must be prostitutes. They must be like street children. They must be like not educated. Well, in fact, when people start to realize the women are actually well-educated, well-respected, and famous names in the streets fighting against repression.[3]

NOTES

1. Personal interview, April 3, 2014.
2. Personal interview, April 3, 2014.
3. Personal interview, April 3, 2014.

BIBLIOGRAPHY

Adel, Deena. 2012, March 19. Samira Ibrahim, "Virginity Test" Victim, Fights
    Egypt's Military Rule. *Daily Beast*, http://www.thedailybeast.com/
    articles/2012/03/19/samira-ibrahim-virginity-test-victim-fights-egypt-s-
    military-rule.html
Amnesty International. 2012 Egypt: A Year after "Virginity Tests," Women Victims
    of Army Violence Still Seek Justice, http://www.amnesty.org/en/news/
    egypt-year-after-virginity-tests-women-victims-army-violence-still-seek-
    justice-2012-03-09
Amnesty International. 2013. *Egypt: Gender-Based Violence against Women around
    Tahrir Square*. London: Amnesty International, http://www.amnestyusa.
    org/sites/default/files/mde120092013en.pdf.
Armbrust, Walter. 2014. The Ambivalence of Martyrs and the Counter-
    Revolution—Cultural Anthropology, http://culanth.org/fieldsights/213-
    the-ambivalence-of-martyrs-and-the-counter-revolution (accessed April 7,
    2014).
Burleigh, Nina. 2013. Gang Rape, the Dark Side of Egypt's Protests, http://www
    .cnn.com/2013/07/03/opinion/burleigh-rapes-tahrir-square/
Kingsley, Patrick. 2013. 80 Sexual Assaults in One Day—The Other Story of Tahrir
    Square: Egypt's Women Increasingly at Risk of Rape and Sexual Assault
    as Rights Groups Warn of a Step up in Attacks, http://www.theguardian
    .com/world/2013/jul/05/egypt-women-rape-sexual-assault-tahrir-
    square
Kingsley, Patrick. 2014, March 1. First Woman to Head a Political Party
    in Egypt Says It Proves the Revolution Has Changed Attitudes.
    Observer, http://www.theguardian.com/world/2014/mar/02/
    egypt-christian-woman-leads-dostour-party
Mabrouk, Mirette F. 2014, April 6. The Case for Women's Rights in Post-
    Uprising Egypt. *Midan Masr*, http://www.midanmasr.com/en/article
    .aspx?ArticleID=301
Shehata, Said. 2011, November 25. Profiles of Egypt's Political Parties. *BBC News*,
    http://www.bbc.com/news/world-middle-east-15899539
Trew, Bel. 2013. Egypt's Sexual Assault Epidemic: Women at Egypt's Pro-
    tests Often Must Fight More Than the Political Cause That Brought
    Them into the Streets, http://www.aljazeera.com/indepth/features/
    2013/08/201381494941573782.html
United Nations News Centre. n.d. Egypt: UN Concerned about Rising Vio-
    lence against Female Protesters, http://www.un.org/apps/news/story
    .asp?NewsID=44046#.Uz8PPq1dV7E
Winegar, Jessica. 2012. The Privilege of Revolution. *American Ethnologist* 39
    (1): 67–70.

CHAPTER 21

Women in Combat: The Quest for Full Inclusion

Meredith Kleykamp and Molly Clever

INTRODUCTION

Despite a trend of increasing women's integration in the armed forces across most Western nations, it is clear that women still have a long way to go to reach full formal and social integration into all areas of the military profession. Although past examples demonstrate women's service in combat, in many countries today women remain excluded from service in combat roles requiring them to engage in offensive actions that put them into close, direct contact with the enemy. Even when women are allowed to serve in these roles, their numbers are limited by a lack of interest in serving in the male-dominated combat occupations, or by the demanding physical requirements of those jobs. Contemporary experiences of multinational forces in in Iraq and Afghanistan have highlighted that although women may be officially excluded from serving in combat occupational roles, many are now exposed to combat owing to the changing nature of warfare. Women are serving in combat, they are experiencing combat, they are being injured and killed, even when they are not able to be assigned to military jobs in the combat arms areas such as infantry, armor, special operations, and others with the primary responsibility to "close with and kill the enemy." It is this tension, perhaps hypocrisy—that women are in combat although not allowed to serve in combat roles—that, in part, led to the plan for official integration of U.S. forces by 2016. Now the U.S. military is grappling with how to implement this new mandate, or how to justify the continued exclusion of women from those roles, as the United Kingdom did in 2010. This process has already played out in other nations, and their experience may have lessons to provide. In this chapter we provide an overview of research on women's roles in the military, and the specific experiences of women in combat across several nations. We then turn to a more detailed case study of the process of women's inclusion in military roles in the United States.

WOMEN'S INCLUSION IN COMBAT, HISTORICALLY AND CROSS-NATIONALLY

Cross-nationally and historically, the extent of women's inclusion in military roles and experiences has been structured by four major sets of variables: *armed forces* variables such as the function of the force, the organizational structure, accession policies, and so on; *social structure* variables to reflect the demographics of the nation, women's participation in the labor force, levels of segregation in society, and other economic and family structural measures; *cultural* variables that reflect the norms and values around military, gender, family power and force, equality, and any other cultural issues specific to the nation; and *political* variables that reflect forces driving both international and domestic relations, such as civil-military relations, egalitarian laws and policy mandates, and the national security situation (Sandhoff et al., 2010; Iskra et al., 2002; Segal, 1995).

Segal's model (and those extending it) remains the primary theoretical perspective used to understand women's roles in the military across time and place. It provides one way to examine variation in women's participation in military services and can be applied to specific cases to better understand which factors exert relatively more or less influence in women's combat roles. But, as Carreiras (2006) points out, the model is less useful that it may seem in that it provides limited attention to how to actually measure women's participation in military roles. It offers the metrics of women's degree of representation (meaning the numbers of women serving) and the nature of their activities (i.e., what occupational roles they fill). The model is best used to understand the expansion and the contraction of women's opportunities in the military, including the expansion to full participation in combat roles.

The Segal model is complemented by several other studies that engage with the formal and social dimensions of women's integration into the military generally, and combat roles specifically. These perspectives go beyond an emphasis on policies limiting or extending women's ability to serve and address their actual experiences in serving or their full social inclusion in those roles. For example, Winslow and Dunn (2002) define integration as having two components: a legal component based on equal opportunity, and a social component based on the full acceptance of women as equals. While women may be granted full formal access to all military roles, the masculine culture of the military and the combat arms forces may prohibit their full social inclusion. Similarly, Harries-Jenkins (2004) describes four stages related to women's participation in the military and combat roles: total exclusion, partial exclusion, qualified inclusion, and full inclusion. Thus, women's full inclusion in the armed forces amounts to their full membership in the community and their ability to serve in all roles, including combat roles that require them to "close with and kill the enemy." He connects this developmental process to the process of movement from institution to occupation as described in Moskos (1977), and suggests the military organization will have to move to an explicit focus on diversity to enable women's full inclusion in all aspects of military professional life.

Segal's model (1995) and its variants are more theoretically detailed and allow for predictions and explanations for the variability of women's inclusion in the military, but the Winslow and Dunn (2002) and Harries-Jenkins (2004) frameworks emphasize that formal policies opening opportunity to women are not enough to ensure women's equal integration into combat roles or the involvement of large numbers of women in combat. Thus, it is useful to think about using multiple theoretical frameworks to understand the nature of women's integration into combat roles and combat experiences. Just as broad changes to the military environment and structural, cultural, and political forces lead to changes in policies for women's equal participation in different military occupations, once opportunities are extended, further cultural and structural changes may be required to establish women's full inclusion in these roles.

A strongly culturally embedded link between masculinity and combat serves as a major impediment to women's full inclusion. Dunivin (1994) describes this ethos as the combat masculine-warrior (CMW) culture, in which the practices of combat (e.g., killing and dying) are defined in exclusively masculine terms. Women who do serve in combat roles are viewed as having the appropriate masculine characteristics (e.g., physical strength and mental fortitude); they have "proven" their belonging in a masculine culture. Women's service in combat can therefore serve to reinforce the gendered boundaries that surround combat service rather than eroding them. Opening combat positions to women does not necessarily change the gendered nature of the organization; women who choose to serve in the combat arms and who are competent to do so are seen as aberrant to femininity; thus, the gender order is unchanged, as women who serve in combat are the exceptions to, not evidence against, the rule (Macdonald in Carreiras, 2006). However, the increased presence of women in the combat ranks can challenge traditional notions of both women's roles and combat as the province of masculine men when legal and social inclusion becomes culturally normative (Segal and Segal in Winslow and Dunn, 2002; Herbert, 1992).

HISTORICAL CASES: BRITAIN, GERMANY, AND RUSSIA

Women have served in combat roles in the past, but until the 1970s and 1980s, their service in this capacity was limited to brief periods of wartime need. Upon conclusion of a conflict that necessitated their participation in combat roles, women's services were no longer needed or desired, and they were again excluded from these positions at war's end. For example, during World War II, women were used in combat roles in Britain and Germany, and most extensively by the Soviets. British women trained and served in anti-aircraft batteries alongside men, but were expressly forbidden to fire anti-aircraft weapons, as a nod to public opinion, which did not approve of women serving in combat (Campbell, 1993). Women were kept noncombatants by limiting their actions to aiming and loading, but not firing, the weapons. The enemy, however, did not limit their targets to men, and several women serving in these batteries were killed while on duty (Campbell, 1993). Further, because of this division of combat labor, when a unit came under attack, men might be given awards for bravery, while a woman serving alongside them could not receive such an honor, since she was not technically in combat (DeGroot, 2001).

In Nazi Germany, women were strongly discouraged from participation in the war effort. Only under desperate times did the Nazis allow German women to be involved, like British women, in defensive anti-aircraft activities. German women served as spotters and searchlight operators, but they too were not allowed to fire a weapon. In fact, in November 1944 Hitler ordered that no women be trained to use weapons (Campbell, 1993). *Flintenweiber* ("gun women") was the derisive term used by Germans to refer to women who took up arms. The term was a direct reference to the Soviet women who fought in the infantry, and who were seen as unnatural and as "vermin," subject to execution upon capture (Campbell, 1993). While women were allowed to take on combat roles, it was only out of military necessity, and their presence in the ranks laid bare the tensions between the need for (wo)manpower and the cultural aversion to women working or serving outside of gender-typical norms.

Soviet women served in both World War I and II in combat roles. In World War I, the Women's Battalion of Death was formed in 1917, in part to embarrass Russian male soldiers who were deserting or derelict in their military duty. These women formed all-female combat battalions after the Revolution and served as equals to the men: they shaved their heads, received equal pay, and were promised veterans' benefits (Stockdale, 2004). When they arrived to fight at the front, they experienced mixed reactions. While some reports contend they were seen as competent and equals in fighting, other reports suggest most male Russian soldiers jeered them, recognizing they were sent to shame them into continued military service (Stockdale, 2004). In typical fashion, upon the conclusion of the war, women returned to their traditional roles.

Once again, in World War II, the Soviets faced the need to use women in all military capacities. Women volunteered and served as tankers, snipers, fighter pilots, and anti-aircraft gunners as well as in the support roles where women more typically served in the military. It is estimated that 8 percent of all Soviet combatants were women (Griesse and Stites, 1982). Women who served were not allowed to continue a military career when the war ended.

In this and previous historical cases, women served during times of critical need for personnel, but upon conclusion of the conflict, when their services were no longer demanded, their opportunities to serve were curtailed (Segal, 1995). Thus, in the past, women's limited involvement in combat operations has fluctuated primarily with changing military needs, which led to a partial and only temporary expansion of opportunity to serve in combat positions rather than any restructuring of the gendered nature of the armed forces or the gender order in society.

CONTEMPORARY CASES

Except for a relatively small (but growing) set of nations that have removed all legal barriers to women's full integration into their forces, the greatest barrier to women serving in combat in most nations remains the legal restriction of their assignment to combat roles. Recent experiences of women serving with U.S. and U.K. forces in Iraq and Afghanistan highlight that women assigned to non-combat specialties have found themselves at the front lines, and engaging in direct combat. Their presence at the front lines has been beneficial to intelligence gathering in a highly gender-segregated and stratified society. Having women attached if not assigned to combat units has complemented and improved operational effectiveness, because women added value to the mission by facilitating intelligence gathering in a society where male and female spheres of life rarely intersect.

The continued exclusion of women from combat roles has rested on a circular logic from which women could not escape. Combat assignment is seen as too important to allow women, who presumably do not meet the physical and mental requirements, to serve in those roles because they might put a whole unit at risk. And yet there is no mechanism for women to demonstrate their competence and ability to serve in these roles, because no "test" is seen as sufficient to replicate the true experience of combat. Thus, women have been excluded because there was no evidence to counter the assumption that they are not physically able to serve, and yet no test could be devised that would provide valid evidence of their competence. The recent experience of U.S. women soldiers and Marines who found themselves exposed to ground combat or attached to combat units has served as the "test" demonstrating that women can succeed in these positions. We discuss the U.S. case in greater detail in the latter half of the chapter.

In other nations, the opening of combat positions in the military to women has come because of the expansion of equal rights laws. Women's integration into combat roles specifically has been directed by laws enforcing gender equality or human rights (Winslow and Dunn, 2002; Pinch et al., 2004). Canada serves as the first major example where national equity laws (the Canadian Human Rights Act in 1978 and the Canadian Charter of Rights and Freedoms in 1982) mandated that the Canadian Forces could exclude women from combat or other roles only on the basis of bona fide occupational requirements. Thus, women could be excluded, but only on the demonstrable basis that they could not perform the tasks required of the job. After years of legal battles, concluding in 1985, nearly 75 percent of positions were opened to women. In 1989, the Canadian Human Rights Tribunal mandated the removal of all legal restrictions on women's occupational assignments, with the exception of the submarine forces (Carreiras, 2006). In 2001, all remaining restrictions, in particular service on submarines, were lifted. There are no remaining legal restrictions on women's occupational assignments in the Canadian Forces (CF).

While Canadian women are now allowed to serve in infantry, submarine, or other combat positions, few women have volunteered or are qualified to do so. The highly physical nature of most combat jobs demands tremendous strength, upper-body strength in particular, which severely limits the number of women who qualify for these positions. Eliminating legal barriers to women's ability to serve in combat roles does not guarantee widespread participation in those roles. One women serving in the CF infantry casually estimated the male-to-female ratio she observed to be about 1,000:1 (King, 2013). Although in reality about 3–4 percent of the combat occupations are held by women, in the most masculine area of the military—the infantry—most women in these positions will likely find themselves working in a nearly all-male environment. Herein lies much of the current and coming tension around women's full integration into the military and combat in particular: if the number of women who will qualify to serve in these roles is truly as low as 1 in 100, can they ever be fully socially integrated into the combat arms?

In other nations, laws have also opened the ground combat occupations to women. Norway stands as a leader in integrating women into all occupational roles, including combat arms. In 1984 Norway opened all positions to women who could qualify and meet the requirements for the job, and was the first NATO country to do so. While Norway eliminated legal restrictions on women's service, the legal opportunity to serve has not led to a gender-balanced military. Women represent less than 10 percent of the force, and only 1.5 percent of officers are women (Gustavsen, 2013).

Thus, in Norway, equality concerns center on how to increase equality of outcomes rather than equality of opportunity.

Other nations that allow women in some or all close combat roles include Australia, Denmark, Finland, France, Germany, Israel, the Netherlands, New Zealand, Poland, Romania, Spain, and Sweden (Fitzsimmons, 2013; Rogers et al., 2010).

Israel is often touted as having a gender-neutral military force because it conscripts both men and women. However, its inclusion of women is more limited than its conscription policy suggests. Israeli women can serve in some combat arms branches, but their actual positions have mostly been limited to serving as trainers for the men in these branches. Some opportunities to serve in close combat roles were opened when women were authorized to serve as border patrols, in the Caracal units beginning in 2000. These units have experienced ground fighting, notably the incident in September 2012 in which female soldiers engaged with terrorist infiltrating the border with Egypt. One female soldier shot and killed one of the terrorists, while another, who called in the initial report, was found hiding in nearby bushes. However, these units, although part of the infantry, do not engage in offensive attack missions. Although Israel Defense Forces (IDF) policies appear gender-neutral, feminist scholars such as Sasson-Levy (2003) suggest that the nature of women's service in the IDF is driven by and reinforces traditional gender norms in Israeli society, leading to a decided lack of social integration in the IDF, alongside continuing formal or structural exclusionary policies. Yagil Levy has argued that the rise of the religious sector in the ranks of the IDF is leading to a theocratization of the IDF at the expense of women's inclusion (Levy, 2014).

Although our review only briefly touches on the range of experiences of women's inclusion in combat and combat roles, we turn to an extended analysis of the U.S. case and the recent policy mandate to open all military positions to women by 2016. According to the analysis by Carreiras (2006), which measured women's integration in the military across eight dimensions, the United States lagged only Canada in terms of its inclusion of women, while maintaining a policy of exclusion from close combat occupations such as infantry and armor, which comprise a large fraction of the positions in the Army and Marine Corps. Repeal of these restrictions will likely make the United States the most gender-inclusive military among NATO and other peer nations.

AN EXTENDED CASE: THE UNITED STATES

Women in the Draft Era Force

For much of U.S. history, women's military participation was legally restricted to nursing and administrative support roles during wartime, and never exceeded 2 percent of the total force (Segal, 1995). Despite official restrictions, women have a long history of active participation in U.S. combat operations. During the Civil War, hundreds of women cross-dressed as men and fought for the Union or Confederate forces, although some were more successful than others in their efforts to pass as men (Blanton, 2004). In the early 20th century, women's military participation was driven by both enabling factors—cultural and political trends such as women's suffrage, transforming citizenship status, and labor force participation—and driving factors—manpower needs during both world wars that necessitated women's inclusion in the military in clerical, transportation, and other support functions (Meyer, 1996; Sandhoff et al., 2010). Women were not considered uniformed personnel, however, until the Women's Army Corps (WAC) was given official military status in 1943, and they were not fully integrated into the armed services until the Women's Armed Services Integration Act of 1948, which formally barred women from combat service and capped women's enlistment at 2 percent (Burelli, 1996).

The All-Volunteer Force

By the 1960s, the mass mobilization model that had characterized U.S. military organization since its foundation had become untenable. Technological advancements, the dynamics of Cold War conflicts within a bipolar superpower system, and the social upheaval accompanying the Vietnam War all coalesced to undermine the credibility and sustainability of a conscription-based force (Clever and Segal, 2012). The 1970 Gates Commission Report established the blueprint for the all-volunteer force (AVF) that would be implemented in 1973. The AVF was premised on a free-market model of military organization in which wages and benefits competitive with the civilian labor market would attract sufficient high-quality personnel to maintain an effective force. The Gates Commission report predicted that the demographic characteristics of military personnel would not be drastically altered with the implementation of the AVF, and on the whole, the report failed to consider the possibility of women's service beyond the small number of women in administrative, nursing, and other support roles that had existed in the draft era.

Despite the expectation that they would not play a significant role in the AVF, women's military participation steadily rose from 2 percent in the 1970s to approximately 15 percent by the early 2000s. The transition to an AVF altered the relationship between state and citizen in important ways that created an opening for women's increased participation in the military. Military service became oriented toward labor market dynamics and the composition of its members became more reflective of the civilian labor market. Women's increasing labor force participation as well as broader social pressures to end gender-based employment discrimination in civilian society had, by the 1990s, put pressure on the military leadership to revisit women's military participation policies.

1994 Ground Combat Exclusion Policy

Despite the dramatic organizational transformation that accompanied the transition to an AVF, military culture continued to be characterized by a CMW cultural paradigm (Dunivin, 1994). The CMW paradigm defined military service in terms of combat practices; thus, the exclusion of women from those activities associated with combat practices (e.g., the acts of killing and dying in war) legally and culturally entrenched the perception that women were not "real" soldiers. Although the CMW paradigm continued to guide the cultural ethos of the military, by the 1980s the AVF was not in practice an exclusively combat-oriented organization. Rather, military missions had expanded to include peacekeeping and disaster relief, and technological advancements required that an increasing proportion of the military force work in noncombat occupational specialties. In addition, broader societal transformations that brought increasing numbers of women into the labor force directly challenged the CMW paradigm in general and women's exclusion from combat in particular. The incompatibility between the CMW paradigm within military service and the organizational and societal context surrounding military service led to a series of debates about women's military roles in the 1970s and 1980s. Although they are still officially barred from serving in combat roles, policy changes opened an increasing number of occupations in which women could come into harm's way. Most notably, noncombat aviation duty was opened to women in the Army in 1974 and the Air Force in 1977. The 1988 Department of Defense (DoD) Risk Rule established a service-wide standard for women's service, barring women from service in noncombat units or missions in which the risk of combat exposure, hostile fire, or capture was equal to or greater than that associated with the combat units they were assigned to support. Thus, women were permitted to serve in support of combat units if their risk in doing so was relatively less than those serving in the combat unit. As a result, the Risk Rule opened more than 30,000 positions to women that had been previously closed (Burelli, 2013; Manning, 2005; U.S. General Accounting Office, 1988).

The Persian Gulf War (1990–1991) provided further impetus to revisit women's military roles. Over 40,000 women deployed to the Persian Gulf during the conflict, during which 15 women were killed and 2 were taken as prisoners of war (U.S. General Accounting Office, 1998). In 1994, Secretary of Defense Les Aspin rescinded the Risk Rule, arguing that because everyone in a theater of war is potentially at risk, the rule was no longer appropriate and would be replaced with a direct ground combat assignment rule in which women could not be assigned to units below the brigade level, whose primary mission is to engage in direct ground combat (Manning, 2005). These included assignments in infantry, armor, field artillery, and special operations, excluding women from approximately 105,000 military occupations. An additional 115,000 occupations were closed to women because they were co-located with ground combat units or would require women to live on ships or submarines, where the cost to retrofit the living arrangements was considered prohibitive. None of the 220,000 occupations closed to women after the 1994 ground combat exclusion policy went into effect were closed on the basis of job-related physical requirements; rather, the DoD's rationale for women's exclusion from these occupations was based on (1) an adequate number of men available to serve in these positions so that women's service was not operationally necessary, (2) a lack of public or congressional support for women's combat service, and (3) a lack of support among servicewomen for involuntary assignment to combat units (U.S. General Accounting Office, 1988).

A sequence of sexual harassment and assault incidents in the early 1990s were also linked to the 1994 policy changes related to women's service. Accusations of widespread sexual harassment involving retired and active naval officers at a 1991 conference of the Tailhook Association in Las Vegas led to a congressional investigation that accused Navy leadership of failing to properly investigate accusations and pursue charges in an effort to avoid public embarrassment. Subsequent reports of widespread sexual harassment of female cadets at each of the service academies, as well as accusations by servicewomen that the reporting of sexual harassment and assaults often led to retaliation against the victims sparked further debate about the masculine culture of the military and a culture of inequality that perpetuated various forms of discrimination against servicewomen (Burelli, 1996).

The War on Terror

As was the case in 1994, transforming operational dynamics and an ongoing sexual assault crisis prompted policy makers to revisit women's combat exclusion in the 2000s. The dynamics of conflict in Iraq and Afghanistan made the provisions of the 1994 ground combat exclusion policy obsolete. The use of roadside bombs transformed highways into the front lines of the war, turning conventionally noncombat roles such as truck driver into one of the most dangerous occupations in the theater. Insurgents using handheld rocket-propelled grenade launchers shot at military helicopters without distinction between those on combat and those on transport missions. In the wars in Iraq and Afghanistan, 155 women were killed and 965 injured (DMDC, 2013). In addition to the increasingly blurred boundaries between combat and noncombat roles, the operational needs of these conflicts necessitated that women be directly involved in combat units. In both wars, female linguists, intelligence specialists, and military police were needed to speak with and search Muslim women who traditionally avoid contact with men outside of their families. These operational needs created a messy patchwork of rules and policies that allowed women to be attached to, but not assigned to, forward deployed units in which they were needed.

In addition to changing operational needs, the problem of gender inequality as manifested in an ongoing sexual assault crisis prompted leaders to revisit the combat exclusion policy. Rates of reported military sexual trauma (MST) were as high or higher than reported sexual trauma among women in the civilian population, a fact that is striking because overall reported crime in the military is far lower than in civilian society (Turchick and Wilson, 2010). Although some evidence suggests that women with combat experiences are more likely to report sexual harassment or assault, others argue that the high prevalence of MST is itself a consequence of women's systematic exclusion from combat roles (LeardMann et al., 2013; Hunter, 2007). Elements of military culture contribute to the high rates of MST, including a general acceptance of violence and sexually violent language, training that encourages the objectification of others, and a strong emphasis on group cohesion and de-individuation that promotes an insular culture and the belief that those outside of the military cannot understand military culture (Mazur, 2007). The power differential between men and women in positions of leadership may also contribute to high levels of MST, leading Mazur to argue that different assumptions about men and women in leadership "is the single greatest impediment to solving issues of sexual misconduct in the military" (Hunter, 2007). Chairman of the Joint Chiefs of Staff General Martin Dempsey likewise suggested that the high rates of sexual assault in the military could be in part attributed to a culture of inequality between men and women:

We've had this ongoing issue with sexual harassment, sexual assault. I believe it's because we've had separate classes of military personnel, at some level. Now, you know, it's far more complicated than that, but when you have one part of the population that is designated as warriors and another part that's designated as something else, I think that disparity begins to establish a psychology that in some cases led to that environment. I have to believe, the more we can treat people equally, the more they will treat each other equally. (Steinhauer, 2013)

Reducing inequality between service members, however, requires a substantial transformation in military culture. Reforming military culture, especially at the highest levels of leadership, has been especially difficult because combat service is a major factor contributing to promotion. Thus, the combat exclusion policy has served as a barrier to women's representation in the highest echelons of leadership.

Full Legal Gender Integration

It was in this context that Secretary of Defense Leon Panetta announced in January 2013 plans to rescind the female combat exclusion policy, setting a deadline in 2014 for each service to develop a plan for the full integration of women into all military roles, including developing "gender-neutral" standards for each occupation, or to petition for an exemption from the policy. The policy states that gender cannot be used as the basis for exclusion from any military occupation, and that for occupations that require specific physical requirements for the fulfillment of duties, evaluation of those standards must be "applied on a gender neutral basis" (Burelli, 2013). Clearly defining what is meant by "gender-neutral physical standards" has presented challenges, however, as similar terms in the past have been interpreted to mean that men and women must exhibit an equality of energy exertion rather than an equality of actual performance. Although DoD leadership maintains that standards will not be lowered to allow for women's integration, it remains to be seen precisely how gender neutrality will be implemented in the standards for each combat-oriented occupation.

As with previous efforts to open more military positions, the announcement of women's combat integration in 2013 was met with fierce debate and opposition. Opposition centered largely on perceptions of women's inability to meet the physical and mental requirements of combat roles, the threat to unit cohesion and fighting effectiveness that women's integration would present, and the opposition of many servicewomen to being involuntarily assigned to combat roles (Burelli, 2013). In particular, opponents argue that the push for combat integration is driven by political motivations to increase diversity in the military and not by operational needs. Retired Army lieutenant colonel Robert Maginnis has been a vocal opponent to women's combat integration, arguing that it is inevitable that standards will need to be lowered in order for the integration policy to succeed, that the lowering of standards will degrade combat effectiveness and harm recruitment and retention efforts, that women serving in combat will suffer disproportionate physical and mental harm, and that sexual assault among military women will increase as a result of greater integration (Maginnis, 2013). Proponents of the policy change are quick to point out that nearly identical arguments have been used in opposition to the integration of African Americans and homosexuals; in particular, previous studies of cohesion have found that social cohesion based on racial, ethnic, religious, or sexuality characteristics become less relevant when task cohesion, based on professional competence, is prioritized in training (King, 2013). Thus, cohesion and effectiveness are actually undermined when women are as a matter of policy excluded from particular roles or held to a different standard than men; "Since cohesion in a professional military relies primarily on competence, successful female integration relies on gender-blind selection processes and the establishment and enforcement of a professional ethos in which women are judged on the basis of their performance, not their gender" (King, 2013, p. 9). Thus, the success of women's combat integration is likely to depend on the extent to which performance standards can be made—and, more important—be perceived to be gender neutral.

Implementation of Combat Integration

The January 24, 2013, announcement of full combat integration issued by the Joint Chiefs of Staff mandated that full integration be implemented by January 1, 2016; that each branch submit a plan for implementation by May 15, 2013; and that any requests for exceptions to full integration must be approved by both the Chairman of the Joint Chiefs of Staff and the Secretary of Defense (Department of Defense, 2013). Given the different operational priorities and organization of the branches of service, each service branch faces unique challenges to full integration.

Prior to the 2013 integration order, 99 percent of occupations and positions in the Air Force were open to women (Manning, 2005, p. 13). Only seven occupational specialties were closed to women: combat rescue officer, enlisted para-rescue, enlisted combat controller, special operations weather (officer and enlisted), and special tactics (officer and enlisted). The Air Force implementation plan includes opening all of these occupations to women by November 30, 2015, after reviewing, validating, and implementing gender-neutral physical and cognitive standards relevant to each position (Secretary of the Air Force, n.d.).

In addition to the challenge of assessing modifying the physical and cognitive standards of combat roles, the Navy and Marines also face the logistical challenge of integrating women into ships and submarines, where berthing arrangements and privacy considerations have previously precluded their service. Of the six positions and two occupations closed to women as of January 2013, four of these positions and one occupation were closed to women on the basis that the cost of retrofitting to accommodate berthing and privacy arrangements on the ships and submarines associated with these duties would be prohibitive. The remaining two positions (small combat craft and Marine Corps ground combat) as well as the Navy SEALs were closed to women on the basis of combat assignment. The Navy implementation plan includes opening positions for women on Virginia class submarines in January 2013 and on small combat craft beginning in July 2013; decisions on how and when to integrate other submarine classes will be made by March 2015 on the basis of an evaluation of the integration on the Virginia class submarines. Because women already serve on nearly all surface warships, decisions about their integration into those ships on which they do not currently serve (FFGs, MCMs, and PCs) will be held until June 2014. These ships are scheduled to be largely decommissioned over the next decade, and the newly commissioned ships set to replace them will be built with the necessary berthing accommodations to support a gender-integrated force (Secretary of the Navy, n.d.).

The Marine Corps, as the most combat-oriented branch of service, has had the highest proportion of its positions (38 percent) and occupations (8 percent) closed to women compared with the other services. The first phase of the Marine implementation plan involves reviewing and validating the physical standards of all occupational specialties, including those that are currently open to women. The Marine Corps began integrating a small number of women into combat battalions in the summer of 2012, and began conducting physical performance testing among 400 male and 400 female Marine volunteers in the summer and fall of 2013 in order to assess and analyze the integration process. Further positions will be opened and assessed during 2014, and, contingent upon the assessment of these tests, the Marine Corps will determine specific plans and a timeline for full integration in 2015 (Secretary of the Navy, n.d.).

Much like the Marine Corps, the Army implementation plan includes a staggered integration with a study period to review and assess occupational standards and possible integration challenges. Beginning in 2012, the Army assigned women leaders to maneuver battalion headquarters in nine brigade combat teams (BCTs), with the goals of assessing the impact of integration on these units, establishing standards for equal opportunity and sexual harassment training programs, and ensuring that female leaders were in place to serve as mentors when these BCTs were opened more fully to female enlisted. Beginning in July 2013, the Army opened 76 enlisted and 19 warrant officer previously closed occupational specialties to women, as well as 35 officer areas of concentration. Data collected from the integration processes of these occupational specialties will be used to inform how to evaluate the gender-neutral standards and specific integration procedures for the remaining closed occupations will be implemented; the Army plans to make these decisions for the engineer branch in July 2014, for field artillery occupations in March 2015, for infantry and armor occupations and for the ranger course in July 2015. At each stage, the TRADOC analysis center will be working with academics, retired military leaders, and other analysis agencies to conduct interviews, focus groups, and data analysis to study the institutional and cultural factors associated with integration (Secretary of the Army, n.d.).

The common challenge faced across the services is the review and validation of occupationally specific physical standards. Because there is currently no cross-service definition of gender-neutral standards, each service may interpret how to implement these standards differently. Gender norming, in which gender neutrality is interpreted as an equality of effort whereby men and women have separate standards for measures such as push-ups or running time, has been used across the services in physical assessments. The practice of gender norming, however, is associated with men framing women as incompetent in physically demanding roles and is used to construct and reinforce gender difference while asserting male superiority (Cohn, 2000). Particularly for the Army and the Marine Corps, the current implementation plans do not make clear whether gender-normed standards will be used, or whether the same occupational standards will be used to assess each individual. Across the services, however, each implementation plan indicates that review and assessment is needed to ensure that the physical and mental standards required for each occupation meet its actual needs and demands.

SUMMARY

Although the United States already stands as one of the most gender-integrated militaries in the world by one metric (Carreiras, 2006), it currently continues to exclude women's formal participation in combat. With the potential changes to the ground combat exclusion, the U.S. military is poised to eliminate the impediments to women's full formal integration in the armed forces. It remains to be seen how the elimination of formal barriers to inclusion will alter their full social integration over time. The incorporation of women into combat roles in low numbers has not changed the masculine orientation of the combat arms in other nations, and is not likely to alter that culture in the United States. Women who wish to serve in these roles are likely to continue to face questions about their competence and tests of their ability in this arena.

BIBLIOGRAPHY

Blanton, DeAnne. 2004. Women Soldiers of the Civil War. *Prologue* 36 (1): 62–63.

Burelli, Daniel. 2013. Women in Combat: Issues for Congress. Congressional Research Service (CRS) Issue Brief 2013, https://www.fas.org/sgp/crs/natsec/R42075.pdf

Burelli, David F. 1996. Women in the Armed Forces. Congressional Research Service (CRS) Issue Brief, http://www.fas.org/man/crs/92-008.htm

Campbell, D'Ann. 1993. Women in Combat: The World War II Experience in the United States, Great Britain, Germany, and the Soviet Union. *Journal of Military History* 57 (2): 301–323.

Carreiras, Helena. 2006. *Gender and the Military: Women in the Armed Forces of Western Democracies.* New York: Routledge.

Cawkill, Paul, Alison Rogers, Sarah Knight, and Laura Spear. 2010. *Women in Ground Close Combat Roles: The Experiences of Other Nations and a Review of the Academic Literature.* Ministry of Defence, https://www.gov.uk/government/uploads/system/uploads/attachment_data/file/27406/women_combat_experiences_literature.pdf (accessed March 4, 2014).

Clever, Molly, and David R. Segal. 2012. After Conscription: The United States and the All-Volunteer Force. *Sicherheit und Frieden [Security & Peace]* 30 (1): 9–18.

Cohn, Carol. 2000. How Can She Claim Equal Rights When She Doesn't Have to Do as Many Push-Ups as I Do? The Framing of Men's Opposition to Women in the Military. *Men and Masculinities* 3 (2): 131–151.

DeGroot, Gerard J. 2001. A Few Good Women: Gender Stereotypes, the Military and Peacekeeping. *International Peacekeeping* 8 (2): 23–38.

Department of Defense. 2013, January 24. Memorandum of the Joint Chiefs of Staff. Available at http://www.defense.gov/news/WISRJointMemo.pdf

DMDC (Defense Manpower Data Center). 2013. Conflict Casualties. U.S. Department of Defense. Available at https://www.dmdc.osd.mil/dcas/pages/casualties.xhtml

Dunivin, Karen O. 1994. Military Culture: Change and Continuity. *Armed Forces & Society* 20 (1): 531–57.

Fitzsimmons, Angela. 2013. Significant change, Everything Remains the Same: Putting the Combat Exclusion into an International Context. *Critical Studies on Security* 1 (2): 251–252.

Griesse, Anne Eliot, and Richard Stites. 1982. Russia: Revolution and War. In *Female Soldiers: Combatants or Noncombatants? Historical and Contemporary Perspectives*, by Nancy Loring Goldman. Contributions in Women's Studies. Westport, CT: Greenwood, pp. 61–84.

Gustavsen, Elin. 2013. Equal Treatment or Equal Opportunity? Male Attitudes toward Women in the Norwegian and US Armed Forces. *Acta Sociologica* 56 (4): 361–374.

Harries-Jenkins, Gwyn. 2004. Institution to Occupation to Diversity: Gender in the Military Today. In *Challenge and Change in the Military: Gender and Diversity Issues*. Canadian Forces Leadership Institute, Canadian Defence Academy, pp. 26–51.

Hunter, Mic. 2007. *Honor Betrayed: Sexual Abuse in America's Military*. Fort Lee, NJ: Barricade Books.

Iskra, Darlene, Stephen Trainor, Marcia Leithauser, and Mady Wechsler Segal. 2002. Women's Participation in Armed Forces Cross-Nationally: Expanding Segal's Model. *Current Sociology* 50 (5): 771–797.

King, Anthony. 2013. "Women in Combat." *The RUSI Journal* 158(1):4-11.

LeardMann, Cynthia A., Amanda Pietrucha, Kathryn M. Magruder, Besa Smith, Maureen Murdoch, Isabel G. Jacobson, Margaret A. K. Ryan, Gary Gackstetter, and Tyler C. Smith. 2013. Combat Deployment Is Associated with Sexual Harassment or Sexual Assault in a Large, Female Military Cohort. *Women's Health Issues* 23 (4): e215–e223.

Levy, Yagil. 2014. The Theocratization of the Israeli Military. *Armed Forces & Society* 40 (2): 269–294.

Maginnis, Robert L. 2013. *Deadly Consequences: How Cowards Are Pushing Women into Combat*. Washington, DC: Regnery Publishing.

Manning, Lori. 2005. *Women in the Military: Where They Stand*. 5th ed. Washington, DC: WREI.

Mazur, Daniel H. 2007. Military Values in Law. *Duke Journal of Gender Law and Policy* 14: 977–1008.

Meyer, Leisa D. 1996. *Creating GI Jane: Sexuality and Power in the Women's Army Corps During World War II*. New York: Columbia University Press.

Moskos, Charles C. 1977. From Institution to Occupation: Trends in Military Organization. *Armed Forces & Society* 4 (1): 41–50.

Pinch, Frank Conrad, Allister T. MacIntyre, Phyllis Browne, and Alan C. Okros. 2004. *Challenge and Change in the Military: Gender and Diversity Issues*. Canadian Forces Leadership Institute, Canadian Defence Academy.

Sandhoff, Michelle, Mady Wechsler Segal, and David R. Segal. 2010. Gender Issues in the Transformation to an All-Volunteer Force. *The New Citizen Armies: Israel's Armed Forces in Comparative Perspective*: 111. https://www.deomi .org/EOEEOResources/documents/Gender_Issues-Sandhoff_Segal.pdf

Sasson-Levy, Orna. 2003. Feminism and Military Gender Practices: Israeli Women Soldiers in "Masculine" Roles. *Sociological Inquiry* 73 (3): 440–465.

Secretary of the Air Force to the Secretary of Defense. n.d. Air Force Implementation Plan for Integrating Women into Career Fields Engaged in Direct Ground Combat. Available at http://www.defense.gov/news/Air_ ForceWISRImplementationPlan.pdf

Secretary of the Army to the Secretary of Defense. n.d. Plan for Integration of Female Leaders and Soldiers Based on the Elimination of the 1994 Direct Ground Combat Definition and Assignment Rule. Available at http:// www.defense.gov/news/armywisrimplementationplan.pdf

Secretary of the Navy to the Secretary of Defense. n.d. Department of the Navy Women in the Service Review Implementation Plan. Available at http:// www.defense.gov/news/navywisrimplementationplan.pdf

Segal, David R., and Mady Wechsler Segal. 1983. Change in Military Organization. *Annual Review of Sociology*, pp. 151–170, http://www.jstor.org/ stable/2946061

Segal, Mady Wechsler. 1995. Women's Military Roles Cross-Nationally: Past, Present, and Future. *Gender & Society* 9 (6): 757–775.

Steinhauer, Jennifer. 2013, June 17. Elite Units in U.S. Military to Admit Women, *New York Times*. Available at www.nytimes.com.

Stockdale, Melissa K. 2004. "My Death for the Motherland Is Happiness": Women, Patriotism, and Soldiering in Russia's Great War, 1914–1917. *American Historical Review* 109 (1): 78–116.

Turchick, Jessica A., and Susan M. Wilson. 2010. Sexual Assault in the U.S. Military: A Review of the Literature and Recommendations for the Future. *Aggression and Violent Behavior* 15 (4): 267–277.

U.S. General Accounting Office. 1988. *Women in the Military: Impact of Proposed Legislation to Open More Combat Support Positions and Units to Women*. GAO/ NSIAD-88-197BR.

U.S. General Accounting Office. 1998. *Gender Issues: Information on DoD's Assignment Policy and Direct Ground Combat Definition*. GAO/NSIAD-99-77, http://www.gao.gov/archive/1999/ns99007.pdf

Winslow, Donna, and Jason Dunn. 2002. Women in the Canadian Forces: Between Legal and Social Integration. *Current Sociology* 50 (5): 641–667.

CHAPTER 22

Spousal PTSD: Eradicating the Cycle of Violence

Jonathan Edmunds

In the age of media-monitored warfare, families of combat fighters have never been more engaged in the processes of war, and a key aspect of their experience has been coping with posttraumatic stress disorder (PTSD), "a mental health condition that is triggered by a terrifying event" (Mayo Clinic, n.d.). While combat veterans suffering from PTSD have received a great deal of attention, their spouses have not. Their largely untold story is the focus of this inquiry into the impact of posttraumatic stress on the spouses and family members of a combatant, especially the wives of soldiers. In addition to exploring the scant research on this topic, I draw upon my own personal experience and interviews I conducted with spouses of veterans.

While a spouse or family member is deployed to a combat zone, those who remain at home may be living through a prolonged event of terror, even though they are far removed from the actual fighting. Members may experience anxiety, a constant state of fear, while anticipating their loved one's death; have upsetting dreams; or feel emotionally numb with a tendency to avoid the realistic aspects of war. These feelings can be intensified by the abundant amount of information about the conflict that a spouse is provided through various media systems. Access to this information further connects members to the war and violence that their loved one may be facing.

War encapsulates various aspects of violence and has the propensity to affect not only individuals directly involved, but the people who are indirectly involved, specifically spouses and family members. Indeed, it might be said that combatant spouses and other family members are experiencing something like PTSD as well.

Spouses and family members deal with both psychological and physical violence. Not only do they suffer while the absent loved ones are at war, they are sometimes subjected further to violence once their absent ones return home. Coming from a situation in which they were trained and immersed in violence, veterans sometimes resort to violence in dealing with personal conflicts. Witnessing violence can result in perceived violence. War thus affects individuals both directly and indirectly. With a concentrated effort and an open mind, violence against family members or spouses of combat operators can be reduced if not eliminated as an outcome of war.

RESEARCH

In recent years, a number of studies have examined patients who suffer from various forms of PTSD, providing crucial information about points of origin, symptoms, and prescribed remedies. Numerous studies and interviews of U.S. military personnel and those affected by war both directly and indirectly provide insight into the struggles of those dealing with PTSD and how it has affected their lives.

Often the research is oriented toward identifying the violence done to women (wives) as a result of the husband's PTSD. The focus is on the symptoms of the husband's trauma and how to get the wife to curtail her actions and mold her behavior to meet his needs. A wife's support is indeed pivotal for the re-acclimation of a military husband. However, failure to recognize that the wife has needs as well, and to study and document those needs, constitutes a type of structural violence committed against spouses of combat operators.

Jennifer L. Price and Susan P. Stevens, of the U.S. Department of Veteran Affairs National Center for PTSD, contend in their *Partners of Veterans with PTSD: Research Findings* (2009) that "in addition to more general relationship problems, families of Veterans with PTSD have more family violence, more physical and verbal aggression, and more instances of violence against a partner."

Violence against families with members having PTSD who returned from war are more likely to perpetrate violence than families whose members were not in the war and do not have PTSD. This is further proven by Nelson and Wright's (1996; cf. Price and Stevens, 1995) study, *Understanding and Treating Post-Traumatic Stress Disorder Symptoms in Female Partners of Veterans with PTSD*, who argue that

partners of PTSD-diagnosed Veterans often describe difficulty coping with their partner's PTSD symptoms, describe stress because of difficulty coping with their partner's PTSD symptoms, describe stress because their needs are unmet, and describe experiences of physical and emotional violence.

The violence that a loved one was subjected to while deployed to a combat zone can cause indirect trauma to a spouse. Having physical violence committed against a spouse by a loved one who has returned from a war zone not only perpetuates the violence of war but also keeps the trauma current for the spouse, even though the violence might be a derivative of the combat operator's own PTSD.

Emily Ozer and Daniel Weiss (2004) note,

According to generally accepted criteria, diagnosis of PTSD requires exposure to a traumatic event that causes feelings of extreme fear, horror, or helplessness. Traumatic events are defined as experiences that involve death, serious injury, or threat of death.

This observation, similar to the Mayo Clinic's information, proves that anyone can have PTSD (169). For spouses of combat operators the perceived threat of death that comes from the media, movies, and the realities of war, is enough to be a traumatic event, even though they have not been diagnosed with the disorder.

This difficulty, coupled with a loved one's multiple deployments to combat zones, witnessing the return of a wounded warrior, and learning of new threats and potential causes of war can keep spouses in a constant state of fear for their loved ones and in turn for themselves. These events, which are common during war, can easily result in PTSD in spouses or others who have a loved one in a combat zone. Deep care for another means that the traumas that the combat operator are exposed to have a profound impact on the spouse who is waiting at home. Ozer and Weiss (2004) observe,

The two most influential cognitively oriented formulations of trauma response and recovery highlight either the importance of beliefs and linked emotions about the self and the world or the network of associations linking thinking about or reminders of a traumatic event to cognitive, emotional, physiological, and behavioral responses. In the former formulation, a traumatic event is conceptualized as shattering the previously held assumption that though the world is not always safe, the lack of safety affects other people only. (p. 170)

In this case the combat operator is the link between the spouse and the world that was previously undiscovered.

With that undiscovered world comes danger, death, and other consequences of war, including peace. Rachel Dekel et al. (2005) support this theory of violence perpetuated through a spouse, contending, "Clinical observations and empirical studies have indicated that the consequences of traumatic events are not limited to the victim, often affecting significant others in the victim's environment" (p. 24). Their study also supports the idea of a spouse being negatively affected by a combat veteran with PTSD: "The

literature has shown that wives and families of war veterans with posttraumatic stress disorder (PTSD) were also affected negatively" (p. 24).

NEW DIRECTIONS

Research is trending toward examining the effects combat has on
spouses, as a consequence of living with a veteran who has PTSD. Studies are being conducted and programs are being developed to prepare
spouses better, informing families as well as combat operators about some
of the struggles of returning home as well as maintaining healthy relationships during a deployment. Programs also venture into instruction on
what to expect while a loved one is deployed to a combat zone as well as
what support groups or networks are available to help deal with some of
the harder parts of having a loved one deployed. Other programs help
families to understand what combat operators are going through and how
the war affects the spouse as the soldier.

Ameesha Felton (2013) reports on some of these programs and organizations, such as Spouse Experience:

In honor of Military Spouse Appreciation Day on May 10, 2013, the Marine Corps
Family Team Building program aboard Marine Corps Base Quantico hosted Mili-
tary.com's Spouse Experience. The hope was to demonstrate the base's appreciation for military spouses and help them tackle issues that are relevant to their lives.

These are some of the organizations involved in supporting military
spouses; they are oriented toward addressing issues relevant to the lives
of military spouses, who must often deal with deployments and PTSD.

Although these programs are growing, we need more research to investigate the inner workings of relationships between combat operators and
their spouses or other loved ones. The goal should be to determine what
factors lead to PTSD in the spouses as well as what actions spouses take
to maintain strength and continuity in their family dynamics even as they
are being altered by each member's interaction with war, both directly and
indirectly. The lack of research into the strength and endurance of spouses
is supported by Rachel Dekel et al. (2005). They claim

Most of the existing research on spouses of traumatized veterans has examined
various manifestations of distress, yet this domain lacks a reference to the strength
and resilience of these women. . . . In addition, most of the research on PTSD
couples has used a quantitative approach, whereas qualitative methods are more
appropriate for research in these fields, which have yet to develop solid theoretical
frameworks. (p. 25)

They highlight the necessity for qualitative research on PTSD couples in
order to gain an in-depth knowledge of the experience of spouses, which

has been largely neglected. The military as well as corporations that deal with combat should support the continued research and development of programs to minimize and eliminate the residual effects of war.

My own investigation of the direct and indirect effects of combat on combat operators and their spouses through interviews with both groups confirmed these conclusions.

One spouse, whose loved one was deployed to Iraq and spent several days under the detention of Iraqis, emphasized the fear she experienced on a number of levels:

I felt a constant fear for his safety but was worried about what he would do once I found out he was detained. I was at the airport waiting, frantically checking flights and nothing. I was so scared of what happened to him, then I found out he was detained and I was so scared of what he would do to the people who detained him, that it would keep him from coming home to me. . . . How were we supposed to deal with that when he got home and how was I supposed to deal with that before he got home?

The spouse went on to talk about how therapy and time helped resolve some of these issues but that she definitely went through a trauma that she still struggles to understand. Moreover, she began to fear not only for her spouse but also for herself, creating very complex emotional reactions to their situation. She added,

I went from fearing him not coming home because I knew if he had to do things he would and protecting his mission and team were priority, to fearing what he would do to me, but even with that fear I couldn't keep myself from unleashing my anger and sometimes hatred towards him.

Her spouse commented on how hard it was for him coming back from war. He said he could not imagine how she dealt with it all but that it hurts him to know, as he put it, that

there wasn't much information available on how to deal with things as far as her pain and aggression, specifically for a women like her. A lot of the things we looked into were couples counseling and wounded warrior programs, but the majority of those programs are based off of rank, and for women who are strictly spouses of younger enlisted. Not many programs were equipped to deal with women who are forward thinking, independent and not easily satisfied.

When asked about possible PTSD in spouses of combat operators as well as if there is a need for more research, he replied,

There is definitely plenty of cases of PTSD in the spouses of operators. Research needs to investigate the effects of war on spouses as the biggest problem is that it is unexpected. Warriors know they will have challenges. I don't think they or anyone else realizes that some of those challenges would be dealing with PTSD from their spouses, who was at home, trauma.

Although the problem of PTSD among combatants is widely known, there is currently no adequate psychological preparation for the parallel effect on noncombatant spouses. If PTSD and other effects of violence are to be minimized and changed, research must focus on the spouses and other members who are also affected by war. PTSD has to be recognized as a condition that can affect both the combat operator and the spouse. Spouses have to be included in the overall consciousness of war and its effects.

In a comparison of PTSD measures, four commonly used stress disorder measures—Keane et al.'s (1984) Minnesota Multiphasic Personality Inventory (MMPI) PTSD Scale, Robins and Helzer's (1985) Diagnostic Interview Schedule (DIS)PTSD module, Kean et al.'s (1988) Mississippi Scale for Combat-related PTSD, and Watson et al.'s (1991) PTSD Interview (PTSD-I)—were used to identify overlaps in the different instruments' successes in measuring PTSD. These trials involved male Vietnam veterans who had and had not been in combat. The tests are an accumulation of questions asking the subject to identify and rate traumatic experiences as well as gauge experiences on a Likert scale. The trial was a success in that it found that

substantial agreement between the four measures provides evidence that they measure the same construct, presumably PTSD. The comparative convergent validities of the four varied with the uses to which they were put. When employed just to identify the presence or absence of PTSD, their overall concordance rates and average intecorrelations were nearly identical.

These methods used only male subjects and an ethnic mix that was "typical to the Midwestern region." If applied to female dependents this study would be able to expose not only PTSD results that are similar between both Veteran's and dependents, but also trigger areas that are identified among the majority of participants. Identifying the triggers for PTSD will help toward not only the prevention of but also the coping with this manageable affliction. Dependents are subjected to limited courses and learning experiences. If the military better educates families, the results of traumatic experiences will change and so will the cycle of violence. The military offers information on how wives can deal with their husbands' PTSD. Now they need to offer information on how wives can deal with their own PTSD. Some dependents will have PTSD. Knowledge will lead to bettter PTSD manageability and the cycle of violence will end. Servicemen are told that some of them will have PTSD; they are even told what they might feel. Women deserve the same information so they will be more equipped to handle their PTSD. Servicemen in turn should be aware of the trauma their wives face. They should be equipped to manage their wives' and their own PTSD. An implementation of this technique could lead to a shortening of the effects of war as well as an outlet to the cycle of violence.

Servicemen go to combat and experience trauma. Wives remain home and experience trauma. Servicemen return with PTSD; wives are waiting with PTSD. They recognize that they both need help and proactively address their traumas. Future violence is prevented as routines of violence are avoided and a proactive cycle of understanding is established.

Upon witnessing her veteran fiancé's PTSD, via physical destruction and verbal abuse, a woman I interviewed resorted to cutting herself in order to obtain a release and avoid the current situation. The serviceman saw this later and had feelings of defilement, relived his hatred for the enemy, causing him to be full of hate and resentment toward himself. This also has affected his future wife and created a distance between them. The woman felt humiliated, believing she could not be understood and she could not understand him. She is failing as a woman to provide him comfort because she is suffering, and knowing that he was going to be different did not suffice as an antidote to a disease that is a derivative of exposure to death and war.

CYCLES OF VIOLENCE

Spouses experience trauma from their loved ones' involvement in war, which in many cases continues once the loved one returns from war with PTSD (MacNair, 2002). Although Jones's (2012) "Intimate Partner Violence in Military Couples" finds inadequate research exists on the issue, she reports that

Intimate partner violence is found to be more common in military couples than its civilian counterparts. Yet, violence in intimate relationships, especially violence against women in intimate relationships, with military men is swept under the rug, with the victims having to keep the violence a secret or face the severe consequences of disclosing to a health practitioner or military police. As a result, many victims are not treated for injuries and the violence goes unevaluated by the Case Review Committee, and abusers go without consequence (Stamm, in Jones 2012, p. 156).

Moreover, Marshall et al. (2005, p. 862) in their study of intimate partner violence (IPV) by veterans found, "For veterans, posttraumatic stress disorder also is an important correlate that largely accounts for the relationship between combat exposure and IPV perpetration." They report that one study of Vietnam veterans found that 58 percent had perpetrated IPV since their discharge from the service (2005, p. 866; see Hiley-Young, Blake et al., 1995).

Combat operators with PTSD deal with feelings of guilt, violence, and depression. Their spouses deal with fear, anger, and depression. As a combat operator prepares for another deployment to war, the spouse can have repressed feelings resurface such as reliving the feelings of terror and fear that are part of PTSD. Deployments every six months or yearly create a cycle of violence that disrupts normalcy, family continuity, and separation from or healing of the conditions that cause PTSD.

Even if deployments are no longer an option for combat operators, a cycle of violence may still be perpetuated. They may be using different tools to deal with their stress and PTSD but that have a minimal impact on the fears and anxieties that caused a spouse's PTSD. Treatment of one person can improve the relationship between an operator and spouse but not necessarily fix both individuals' problems. A cycle of violence as a result of exposure to war can continue even if it is just the spouse who is dealing with PTSD. This cycle will continue; research on PTSD in spouses needs to be undertaken. They should become a larger part of the PTSD research and treatment consciousness.

One combat operator I interviewed observed,

It took what seemed like a long time for me to get myself back together. I never really considered her having PTSD but once I came to grips with mine, I realized she was suffering more. She had anger, fear and even rage. It caused us problems even after I got back to being a normal person as she would randomly become enraged and the mere mention of me going on another deployment caused her to be angry or extremely upset, even if I am just expressing my feelings or hypothetical thoughts. Sometimes I don't react well to this.

In other words, a cycle of violence is perpetuated by the combat operator; it can also be sustained by the spouse, as the symptoms and consequences of PTSD are real regardless of which one exhibits them.

Several spouses I interviewed agreed with this observation, one of them noting,

Thinking about him going back just makes me upset. What is he going to do? Why does he want to go? What happens to me and the kids if he dies? Sometimes I find myself treating him like shit for no reason. I think I am upset with him but don't know why. The anger I feel doesn't compare to some of the things he did when he got back.

The consequences of the spouse's experience are obviously complex and significant. Further research could lead to better treatment for both parties, as well as a better defense against potential cycles of violence. Another spousal interviewee admitted,

I did not realize until much later that I had some problems that I needed to deal with if we, (spouse and combat operator), were going to make it and get better. I was angry and hurt and that took its toll until I was able to deal with it.

Just as standards and practices are still being developed to diagnose PTSD, it should not be assumed that all spouses have PTSD as a result of their trauma; with further research, medical professionals will be more apt to assess their needs. This is especially true within the organizations of the military, as research could arm organizations with more tools and information to help people deal better with life as a spouse of a combat operator. If they were identified as having PTSD or at least suffering from trauma, then the cycle of violence could potentially be overcome and its effects mitigated.

The Veteran's Affairs National Center for PTSD states,

After a trauma or life-threatening event, it is common to have reactions such as upsetting memories of the event, increased jumpiness, or trouble sleeping. If these reactions do not go away or if they get worse, you may have Post-traumatic Stress Disorder (PTSD).

Effects of a spouse's deployment may be intensified by media coverage of the conflict, lack of contact, death, and fear of the unknown. During these traumas a person may be heading toward PTSD but still be emotionally intact until the spouse arrives home. Seeing the loved one, who has PTSD, may be a trigger for the spouse's PTSD as they realize the loved one is not the same person and violence is the cause of the transformation. This realization may act as a trigger because the spouse's reality is "shattered," which Ozer and Weiss (2004, p. 170) classify as a root cause of PTSD. Seeing their loved one harmed by the consequences of war makes all of their fears and anxieties materialize. They realize the war is real, and the pain and all of their fears can return with an overwhelming effect that can disrupt sleep and cause anxiety, anger, and depression.

A woman whose fiancé is a combat operator stated,

Having him home was better than not having him home, but only because it was better than him being dead. He was not the same and it made me realize that all the horrible things were true. I had no control over anything and being a controlling person by nature, made his return home even worse. It made everything real and it made me go from intense fear to intense anxiety as I didn't know how to act around him and what would set him off.

A woman's fear can materialize when her spouse returns from combat as a different person.

Additionally, a loss of control can materialize with the arrival of the spouse. A woman assumes primary if not complete control of the house and the responsibilities of the family in the absence of her partner. This is enhanced with women who have children. Women create routines and a comforting environment that helps maintain them while their spouses are deployed. Upon arriving home the spouse has to either adjust to the routines and rules of the house or change them. Changes to the rules and routine can add to the stress of women as their home is no longer a sanctuary but rather the place where their spouse's PTSD is most prevalent. The home is where the cycle of violence is perpetrated. A woman whose husband returned home from combat commented,

I was in complete control of everything and when he comes home it changes. When he left I had to get used to taking care of the kids, the house, the bills, rodents, everything. I felt alone but got used to it. When he comes home from deployments it could all change. I never know what to do. He is good about helping out so it makes a difference and we talk a lot, which helps us stay connected. However, I know plenty of women whose husbands don't help out and don't like the way the woman has kept the house. In spousal training they tell combat operators that if their wives changes the furniture arrangement it's okay, leave it alone. That is the extent of the training for spouses and wives. Better training could help bridge the gap between spouses, especially if it didn't just focus on the serviceman, as wives are the support structure when their husbands are away and our needs need to be addressed or at least not forgotten.

Integrated training could benefit both spouses as they can learn to cope with the deployments as individuals and as partners. A woman's needs and trauma have to be identified and respected in order to disrupt the cycle of violence. By doing so combat operators will be more aware of how their PTSD affects their wives and also how their wives' stresses or PTSD affects them. Women will also be able to adjust more easily to the return of their spouses as they will become more self-aware and able to identify their feelings. With added self-awareness steps can be taken to avoid triggers and work through them instead of living in the cycle of violence that war and PTSD create in relationships.

Women whose spouses died in combat or who anticipated their husbands dying are vulnerable to the conditions of PTSD as their triggers are the anticipation of and the news of their husband's death. This results in the women's world being "shattered" when their spouse returns home with PTSD or dead. Some women actually experience grief-like symptoms when their husbands deploy. This is an act of preservation, an attempt to come to terms with the possible results of their spouse being in combat. Carr et al. (n.d.) found that

spouses of the men serving in World War II experienced grief-like symptoms (or "anticipatory grief") before their spouses actually died. Military wives tended to emotionally detach in anticipation of their spouses' deaths, and thus did not appear to be highly grief-stricken upon the actual death. . . . Individuals who anticipate their spouse's death will use the forewarning period to make peace with their partner, to disengage from the relationship, and to prepare psychologically and practically for the transition to widowhood.

Servicemen returning home can act as a trigger for women while secretly having to cope with feelings of distance and separation. This also contributes to the sense of numbness that is common in sufferers of PTSD. One interviewee observed,

I would see the media and just try to think it wasn't him being killed or bombed. I would wait till I heard from him and just told myself that I would. When I didn't hear from him it was the worst. I thought about the possibilities of him in combat. He told me he was good at his job but when I didn't hear from him I was afraid and just tried to get away from that feeling. When he came home and had PTSD I didn't know what to do and at times I couldn't feel anything for him because I was thinking about what I felt when he was gone. I was angry. Sometimes I was preparing myself for him to not come home but then he did with PTSD and I didn't know what to do or how to feel. It was the worst.

Some women have had success with their spouses and been able to make it through PTSD. Education, awareness, and a support system are common solutions used by couples who were able to end or disrupt the cycle of violence. One spouse observed,

Exercise, therapy, stability helped him a lot. He had to get it out of him. Things didn't get to be better than ever until his therapy helped him be able to address my feelings and my traumas. Knowing he cared made the difference because I felt trust in him again and I was able to realize that there were feelings and tendencies I had that were still causing us problems.

Identification and having available resources are key for women to start dealing with PTSD in their spouse, their relationships, and themselves. A focus on women by men and the military in addition to self-awareness can help end the effects of PTSD in relationships by making it more manageable. A wife of a former Marine and combat veteran supported the idea of resources that focused more on the wife and integrated their struggles into pre-deployment training. "I think it could aid spouses who have to work through deployments and life after," she said.

The military zeroes in on the servicemen who are serving and fails to incorporate or acknowledge the struggle of wives who remain at home. Being at home, as a wife and mother, was more difficult than my deployments because I had so many different responsibilities and I had to worry about my daughter and the life of my husband. These struggles being recognized and addressed will absolutely contribute to better relations between wives and their husbands.

CHANGES

Better understanding of the effects of war not only will help to mitigate the war itself but more importantly will work to ensure that the war is better contained. Combat operators return home and are not able to escape the war as the effects of PTSD plague their daily lives. Spouses with a loved one with PTSD must still try to deal with their own PTSD and traumas. War is a plague and will continue to affect both combat operator and spouse until symptoms of trauma are realized and dealt with collectively. Research into the effects of war and PTSD on spouses will serve to reduce the violence against spouses and combat operators alike as the cycle of violence will cease to be perpetuated as identification, treatment, and information become more effective. Combat operators and spouses have the potential to recover from war faster, which means that additional deployments will be executed by more effective forces and also life after deployments will be better for combat operators and their spouses. Research and techniques developed to deal with PTSD in spouses can also be used to create new measures of peace in communities exposed to war, as more information and coping techniques become available to deal with PTSD in noncombatants, and as they recognize and understand the traumas they may be experiencing as spouses of combatants. Understanding the different people of a population is a key to peace, and as most combat operators have a spouse or are a loved one, the population that could be better understood is significant.

HOME

I write about PTSD found in spouses or family members affected because it is a personal issue for me. I have come home and dealt with the effects of war myself: detachment, anger, remorse, and an insufferable need to serve until the job is done. I felt as if many of my feelings arose because I felt guilty that my job was not complete. Others were off fighting the "War on Terrorism" and I was in the luxuries of home complaining about my anxiety and the morbidity of life. I felt as if I wandered without a purpose all the while neglecting, hurting, and distancing myself from the one I loved.

My family members were not concerned about those issues or, as far as I could tell, even affected by my involvement with war. I base this on the zero contact I received over years of deployments, a lack of conversation about my job or well-being, and overall a disinterest in anything that didn't involve their immediate circle. One family member actually commented to me, "Well, I am sitting here struggling while you went off on vacation in Iraq." I will not trivialize or undermine their feelings, but I can objectively state, and others agree, that my family is not concerned with the elements or residual effects of war.

As I went through the roller coaster of acclimating to life back in the United States I started to think about my spouse. When she spoke of the pain and fear she felt during my absence, it always evoked deep emotions in her. Since my return I have been committed to continuous reflection of myself, others, and the emotions of all. I have realized that although I had significant hardships during and after the war, my spouse did as well. Sometimes during an outbreak of violent emotion I would wonder how she could continue to pursue me on issues even though she would have already admitted to being afraid of me. She would often challenge me and speak to me as few had before—and no one who was so utterly incapable of defending herself if I became physically aggressive. No matter how many times I thought about this or even mentioned it to her she would continue to pursue. She was hurt and PTSD was a label that I never would have considered. As much as I hurt or questioned myself, her pain was significantly worse. My commitments and feelings of loyalty and honor are painful for her as they re-invigorate old feelings of fear and death. I will always push forward and pursue, but one thing that was completely outside of my depth was the ability and knowledge to soothe her pains. Caring for another on an emotional level was never a part of my family dynamic, but caring for a spouse who was subjected to significant trauma and possibly had PTSD was completely outside of my reach.

Additional research into spousal PTSD could have various impacts on life, but most important it would give wives and combat operators tools not only to help heal their spouses but also to heal themselves through the improvement of their relationships. And as long as they seek to heal themselves, the cycle of violence can be ended; at least certain aspects of residual violence as a product of war could be diminished. I believe that new research can change the way that PTSD and the war affect people.

Some people might no longer feel the need to return to war, as they would be able to find comfort at home with their spouse and in a relationship that is no longer plagued by PTSD.

CONCLUSION

PTSD as a condition spurred by a trauma or series of traumas and can result in anxiety, anger, fear, terror, and avoidance, which can be found in combat operators but also in their spouses or other family members. PTSD research is primarily focused on combat operators, with minimal focus, in comparison, on spouses and family members. Additional research is especially needed to identify the strength of spouses as well as how they remain resilient. Comparing spouses with and without PTSD or trauma-related problems could increase the effectiveness of PTSD treatments as well as work to end the cycle of violence that is often perpetuated during and after war. Organizational and medical professionals would be able to use this research to treat spouses more efficiently and equip them with the tools and information needed to face the plagues of war. These changes would further the understanding of dealing with violence as a result of war and thus perpetuate peace for those affected by violence, perhaps even precipitating cycles of peace instead of violence.

Information regarding spouses' PTSD and trauma suffered by indirect and direct exposure to war would help peace movements and governments deal with different people who have experienced trauma. Being in tune with their needs as spouses or family members can help with their healing as well as aid in the establishment and sustainability of peace in combat-affected areas.

The establishment of peace through understanding trauma and providing effective treatments to the spouses of wars could lead to peace now and later as the fourth-generation war is fought by people who are not yet born. An established cycle of peace, or at least a relationship that is initiated from understanding will work in favor of future peace instead of future violence, which is often the result of war, even if it is the fourth generation as the cycle of violence will continue to be perpetuated until root causes, such as PTSD in spouses, are addressed and healed.

BIBLIOGRAPHY

Blake, D. D., F. W. Weathers, L. M. Nagy, D. G. Kaloupek, F. D. Gusman, D. S. Charney, and T. M. Keane. 1995. The Development of a Clinician-Administered PTSD Scale. *Journal of Traumatic Stress* 8: 75–90; doi: 10.1002/jts.249008010.

Carr, Deborah, James S. House, Randolph Nesse, and Camille Wortman. n.d. Forewarning of Spouse's Death and Psychological Adjustment to Widowhood among Older Adults, http://www.psc.isr.umich.edu/pubs/pdf/rr00-462.pdf

Dekel, R., H. Goldblatt, M. Keidar, Z. Solomon, and M. Polliack. 2005, January. Being a Wife of a Veteran with Posttraumatic Stress Disorder. *Family Relations* 54 (1): 24–36.

Felton, Ameesha. 2013, May 7. "Spouse Experience" Honors Military Spouses, Offers Marriage Advice. *News Article Display*, marines.mil (web, November 12, 2013.

Grossman, David, and Bruce Siddle. 2008. Psychological Effects of Combat: Psychological Characteristics of Aggression. In *Encyclopedia of Violence, Peace and Conflict*, edited by Lester R. Kurtz. Amsterdam: Elsevier, pp. 1796–1805.

Hiley-Young, Bruce, Dudley David Blake, Francis R. Abueg, Vitali Rozynko, and Fred D. Gusman. 1995. Warzone Violence in Vietnam: An Examination of Premilitary, Military, and Postmilitary Factors in PTSD in-Patients. *Journal of Traumatic Stress* 8 (1): 125–141.

Jones, Alysha D. 2012. Intimate Partner Violence in Military Couples: A Review of the Literature. *Aggression and Violent Behavior* 17 (2): 147–157.

Keane, T. M., P. F. Malloy, and J. A. Fairbank. 1984. Empirical Development of an MMPI Subscale for the Assessment of Combat-Related Posttraumatic Stress Disorder. *Journal of Consulting and Clinical Psychology* 52: 888–891.

Keane, T. M., J. M. Caddell, and K. L. Taylor. 1988. Mississippi Scale for Combat-Related Posttraumatic Stress Disorder: Three Studies in Reliability and Validity. *Journal of Consulting and Clinical Psychology* 56: 85–90.

Kurtz, Lester. Fighting Violence: A Sociological Toolkit. Available online at https://drive.google.com/file/d/0B9ydHnuCkyP8Yk9hdHlGaU5iaFE/edit?usp=sharing

MacDermid Wadsworth, S. M., and Southwell, K. 2011, November. Military Families: Extreme Work and Extreme "Work-Family." *Annals of the American Academy of Political and Social Science* 638 (Work, Family, and Workplace Flexibility): 163–183.

MacDermid Wadsworth, S. M. 2010, June. Family and Resilience in the Context of War and Terrorism. *Journal of Marriage and Family* 72 (3): 537–556.

MacNair, Rachel. 2002. *Perpetration-Induced Traumatic Stress: The Psychological Consequences of Killing*. Westport, CT: Praeger.

Marshall, Amy D., Jillian Panuzio, and Casey T. Taft. 2005. Intimate Partner Violence among Military Veterans and Active Duty Servicemen. *Clinical Psychology Review* 25 (7): 862–876, doi:10.1016/j.cpr.2005.05.009, http://www.sciencedirect.com/science/article/pii/S0272735805000619

Mayo Clinic. n.d. Post-traumatic Stress Disorder (PTSD). Retrieved from http://www.mayoclinic.com

Nelson, B. S., and D. W. Wright. 1996. Understanding and Treating Post-Traumatic Stress Disorder Symptoms in Female Partners of Veterans with PTSD. *Journal of Marital and Family Therapy* 22: 455–467.

Ozer, Emily J., and Daniel S. Weiss. 2004. Who Develops Posttraumatic Stress Disorder? *Current Directions in Psychological Science* 13 (4): 169–172.

Population Studies Center, University of Michigan. 2014, January 3. PTSD: National Center for PTSD. *PTSD Basics*, by U.S. Department of Veterans Affairs (web, March 26, 2014).

Price, Jennifer L., and Susan P. Stevens. 2009, May 9. PTSD: National Center for PTSD. *Partners of Veterans with PTSD: Research Findings*. U.S. Department of Veterans Affairs (web, November 12, 2013).

Robins, Lee N., and John E. Helzer. 1985. *Diagnostic Interview Schedule (DIS), Version III-A*. St. Louis, MO: Department of Psychiatry, Washington University School of Medicine.

Watson, C. G., M. P. Juba, V. Manifold, T. Kucala, and P. E. Anderson. 1991, March. The PTSD Interview: Rationale, Description, Reliability, and Concurrent Validity of a DSM-III-Based Technique. *Journal of Clinical Psychology* 47 (2): 179–88.